$29.60

To Karl

his students

from

Ilse Graham

Nov. 7, '77.

WALTER DE GRUYTER, INC.
3 Westchester Plaza
ELMSFORD, N.Y. 10523
(914) 592-5890

Ilse Graham

Heinrich von Kleist   Word into Flesh:
A Poet's Quest for the Symbol

Ilse Graham

Heinrich von Kleist
Word into Flesh:
A Poet's Quest for the Symbol

Walter de Gruyter · Berlin · New York
1977

Library of Congress Cataloging in Publication Data

Graham, Ilse, 1914—
   Heinrich von Kleist.

   Bibliography: p.
   Includes index.
   1. Kleist, Heinrich von, 1777—1811 - - Criticism and
interpretation.
   PT2379.Z5G7   838'.6'09   77—9541
   ISBN 3-11-007165-7

CIP-Kurztitelaufnahme der Deutschen Bibliothek

Graham, Ilse
Heinrich von Kleist: word into flesh, a poet's quest for the
symbol. — Berlin, New York: de Gruyter, 1977.
   ISBN 3-11-007165-7

Satz und Druck: Walter de Gruyter & Co., Berlin
Umschlaggestaltung: Rudolf Hübler, Berlin
Bindearbeiten: Lüderitz & Bauer, Berlin
Printed in Germany

For
Sydney Evans
Dean of King's College London
who taught me to walk surely in the dark

Introduction

During the thirty years or so that I have been preoccupied with the figure of Kleist, wondering in what shape my thoughts could possibly be cast, I scarcely once stopped to ask myself whether yet another study of this much discussed poet was needed. Now, with the bicentenary of his birth around the corner, the completed book before me and my knowledge of the vast secondary literature refreshed, I am bound to face the question I have shelved for so long.

If I feel hopeful that my study will gain acceptance here and abroad, it is for two related reasons which I shall seek to sketch in outline. Underlying both is my belief in the viability of insights which have been so long in the making. In the first place, a critical position which began by being bafflingly complex, during the course of time has attained an ever greater simplicity of design. From a whole battery of keys which I previously had to operate I have forged for myself something of a master key which, without undue difficulty or oversimplification, seems to enable me to unlock a good many critical doors. I do not claim to offer a grand solution to the phenomenon Kleist that is novel in the sense that it bears no resemblance to those offered in the past. Such a claim would be suspect in the extreme and, without any special acknowledgements, my footnotes will make it abundantly clear how much I have learned from my fellow scholars, past and present, in the field. What I do believe is that my solution is more economical as well as cogent and, in this sense, neater than some proffered previously.

This process of scaling down has, moreover, been accompanied by a gradual change of attitude which may be regarded as salutary. When the figure of Kleist first burst upon my imagination, I responded to it with an untried enthusiasm which I now recognise as having been a relic of youth. In the process of hammering out, late in a career largely given over to Schiller and Goethe, a genuinely critical position, I emerged greatly sobered without any lessening of that disinterested enchantment which is the precondition of all creative criticism. As I see it, this is as it should be. Kleist was indubitably a very damaged person and this impairment, so plainly perceptible – as I shall try to show – in his letters, has left an indelible mark upon his *œuvre* in its entirety. Nevertheless what his detractor Goethe once wrote remains in force with respect to my own critical response to him: 'Unless one speaks of a man's writings, as indeed of his actions, with a kind of loving identification, a certain partisan enthusiasm, so little is left that it isn't worth writing about.' Thus Goethe to Schiller. I trust that enough 'loving identification' and 'partisan enthusiasm' have survived the test of a sustained critical encounter to entitle me to speak of this great and bruised artist fruitfully, as an ambassador of two worlds: as a native of his own Mark Brandenburg, able to

understand and interpret the hard-headed literalness as well as the slow illuminations of that race, and yet as one who has become gratefully attuned, over
what is virtually a life-time, to the more temperate spiritual climate of my second
home.

It is just possible that this slow process of gestation and the metamorphoses it
brought in its train have left their mark on my critical procedure. The present
study deals with its subject in much the same manner in which Kleist himself dealt
with the principal figure of his last and maturest play, Prinz Friedrich von Homburg. It divests its hero of all his alleged virtues and dismantles him in order to lay
bare the true foundations of his being and to illuminate his own peculiar greatness.
As the prince turns out to be a strictly 'unheroic' hero measured against the
yardstick of the conventional Prussian code, so his creator emerges as a strictly
'unpoetic' poet measured against the canon of traditional aesthetics, but one whose
relevance to us in this day and age may well be bound up with that very fact.

The view of Kleist taken in more recent times in Germany has been one which
is likely to obscure, rather than to clarify, the essential modernity of a writer
whose deep concern with the dilemma of scientific knowledge and near-despair
over the possibility of transcendence could make him a recognised master of many
sharply contemporary themes. Since Gerhard Fricke's seminal study Gefühl und
Schicksal bei Heinrich von Kleist (Feeling and Destiny in the Work of Heinrich von
Kleist) Kleist has been seen as a pre-eminently metaphysical poet and as one in
whose work pure feeling is raised to the power of a religion. In spite of some
critical reservations voiced here and there, these assumptions continue to be
generally accepted by specialists and their public. In my view, a systematic
analysis of them is overdue, not least because they obscure the potential
significance of Kleist for the modern European and American reader who may not
necessarily be tuned in to characteristically German modes of thought.

As I see Kleist, the inborn tendency of the poet towards concretion possessed
him to a fault. Propelled by an insuperable psychological mechanism on which I
shall expatiate in due course, he would make into and treat as a material substance
things which are of their nature unsubstantial. The notion of the immortal soul,
for instance, in his mind would become compounded with the tangible virtue of a
hoard or treasure defying the threat of extinction. Similarly, he would mentally
materialise animate beings, converting them into things and treating of them as
though they were lifeless objects. Thus he would define the heart as 'that quaint
property which only needs to be taken away to bear interest'. Often, these twin
tendencies towards hypostasization and reification would run fluid into one
another, each reinforcing its companion. Thus, Penthesilea experiences the
Absolute of Love hypostasized in the person of Achilles and in turn reifies
Achilles whom she envisages as the sun of the physical universe.

This hankering after the palpable and the concrete was to receive its philosophical ratification through the poet's vehement revulsion from the Transcen-

Author's Note

Quotations from Kleist's works are cited according to the Hanser edition in two volumes, *Heinrich von Kleist. Sämtliche Werke und Briefe,* ed. H. Sembdner, 2nd edition, Munich 1961. I am grateful to the editors of the *Modern Language Quarterly* for allowing me to reprint, with slight modifications, my article 'The Broken Pitcher: Hero of Kleist's Comedy' which appeared in Vol. XVI, 1955, of that journal; also to the editor of *Heinrich von Kleist,* ed. W. Müller-Seidel, *Wege der Forschung* CXLVII, Darmstadt 1967, where this essay was reprinted in German translation.

My gratitude is due to Anne Shotts who typed my manuscript with her usual competence and good humour; most of all however to my friend Mary Gilbert who followed my work with a keenness and joyful anticipation which were − and continue to be − a constant source of encouragement.

Christmas Eve, 1975

dental Idealism of Kant. To one as wedded to the real as was Kleist that thinker's two-pronged move to erode its immediacy from either end was bound to be felt as a profound threat. He could not tolerate the alleged phenomenality of objects so forcibly impinging on his own senses any more than he could brook Kant's insistence on the inaccessible remoteness of things as they might be in themselves, in some mental reserve beyond the boundaries of time and space. To one possessed of Kleist's emphatic need for the incontestably real, all ultimate realities were converted into things and all things, in turn, were registered as being close at hand and overwhelmingly 'there'.

Thus we find this ingrained realist stormily wooing, in the shape of sense-objects that are palpable, quantifiable and capable of empirical verification, an Absolute which the more temperate mind of a Kant or a Goethe would revere from afar or as it becomes manifest in and through the veil of phenomena. It is this paradoxical twist in Kleist's mind, his − dare I say it? − fetishistic attachment to objects charged with numinosity which may be presumed to have given rise to the characterisation of him as a 'metaphysical realist', a formulation coined by Fricke, echoed by Korff and most recently reiterated by Blöcker.

This description is apt in so far as it expresses the sheer *intensity* of this poet's assault upon the material world, the rugged facts of reality. It fails in that it does not take into account the deterioration of *quality* in the mode of apprehension which is bound to set in when the Absolute is sought out in an object directly given to the senses. Once it is hypostasized and entrapped in material shape, the intangible mystery of the divine or a loved person, like any other object of the physical world, is placed on the rack of impartial scrutiny, interrogated, handled, manhandled, even literally incorporated. Any reader who is familiar with Kleist and questions this account is advised to call to mind Amphitryon's cross-examination of his wife, the methods adopted in Kleist's comedy to tease that elusive quality, Eve's integrity, out of the jigsaw puzzle of circumstantial evidence, or indeed Penthesilea's prising open of the shell that contains the mystery of Achilles' loving.

Thus I would dismiss the fashionable cliché of Kleist's being a 'metaphysical realist' as being inadequate and positively misleading on at least two counts. However intense in terms of force of assault, a quest which is directed towards the Absolute hypostasized into a material object almost by definition is not *meta*-physical but grossly and atavistically *physical*, as is evidenced by Penthesilea's mode of 'having' Achilles by an act of physical incorporation. Furthermore, such a quest cannot reasonably be maintained to be of a religious nature, or indeed be regarded as being one that is born of pure feeling and sustained by it. Directed as it is to an object of the senses, it degenerates into *a wholly misplaced act of the empirical intelligence,* an act, moreover, in which the cognitive functions are hopelessly and tragically confounded and which lapses into intellectually ever more primitive modes. Religious certainty at best turns into theoretical probability and at worst degenerates into blind reliance on the testimony of the senses, winged intuition gets bogged down in the labyrinth of conflicting facts, spontaneous *élan* fractures as it comes up against the walls of sheer physicality in which the Absolute is ensconced. In the end, the assault on the materialised Absolute — be it the Absolute of Faith as it is revealed in the religious encounter or the Absolute of Trust as it is experienced in human relationships — glances off an object that is so wholly incommensurate with it, and the seeker is thrown back onto the bleak awareness of a cognitive equipment which has so dismally failed him. Kleist's writings abound with unbridled invectives against the five senses and, in particular, against the noblest of them all, the human eye.

This is the story of the poet as I shall try to recount it in chapter upon chapter, as it is the story of his creations; a tale endlessly retold. Both, creator and creation, equally and continually expend their religious energies upon objects directly given to the senses, an incongruity I seek to pinpoint by calling such fetishistic objects '"articles" of faith', the word 'articles' being understood in its literal meaning as 'items' or 'things'. Both equally and perpetually find themselves nonplussed in front of an insuperable stumbling-block: the absurdity of the immaterial locked up in a material substance, of the supersensible hidden in the sensible, of the invisible concealed in the visible. This is the paradox that is enshrined in the sacramental doctrine of the incarnation, of the Word become Flesh in the divine hypostasis, that is to say, the 'absurd' union of the divine nature with the human nature of Christ in one person. This paradoxical aspect of Christianity it is which was to be explored, not many decades after Kleist's death, by the single-minded ingenuity of Sören Kierkegaard. The affinity between Kleist's position and Kierkegaard's existentialism has often enough been stressed. This observation is correct as long as the term 'absurd', nowadays so often bandied at Kleist in a profane and, indeed, nihilistic sense — 'Kleist committed suicide because life to him seemed utterly absurd', a recent newspaper notice read — is restored to him, as it ought to be, in Tertullian's meaning in which it was to become one of the mainstays of Kierkegaard's theology, and so long as we remember that the affinity between the two men is pre-eminently by way of a *formal* analogy. Because of the peculiar *form* or *structure* of their experiencing — an 'incarnation' of the spiritual and unsubstantial in the depth of physicality felt to be paradoxical and absurd — Kleist and his figures hover on the verge of a potentially Christian credo, forever falling short of its actual acceptance; and, indeed, a transcendence in faith of the paradox at the heart of their consciousness would constitute an all but superhuman feat for minds so riveted on the realm of material things. However, by the paradoxical pointing of his plots as much as through the sensibilities of his figures Kleist is forever putting out feelers in the direction of *the* incarnational doctrine *par excellence*; and it is at those rare moments when he is able reverently and humbly to endure the pure awareness of paradox at the heart of things without clamouring to transcend its absurdity — and he does so through the figures of, say, Die Marquise von O., Alkmene, Don Fernando and the Prince — that his writing scales its steepest and serenest heights.

In the opening chapter of this study which treats of the essay *On the Puppet-show* I seek to isolate the model of man's spiritual quest − better described in cognitive than in religious terms, as I have indicated − which informs Kleist's *œuvre* in its entirety. This I believe to have found in the biblical story of the Fall as recorded in Genesis 3, references to which reverberate not merely through the famed essay but throughout his poetic *opus*. It is the model of Adam and Eve reaching out, in a primordial metaphysical bid, for the knowledge of good and evil and instead − eating apples and knowing themselves and one another in their nakedness.

A later chapter, given over to Kleist's early letters, endeavours to lay bare the psychological roots of this obdurately regressive model of cognitive experience. Through what is a largely stylistic analysis I demonstrate in the biographical sphere the self-same hypostasization of what is unsubstantial and reification of what is animate which has found its precipitate in the metaphysical obtuseness evinced by his poetic figures and the cognitive *impasse* experienced by them all. Such a drive towards atavistic forms of regression was bound to result in the poet's catastrophic misreading and vehement repudiation of Kant's Transcendental Idealism with its bifocal vision, that is to say, its careful distinction between the phenomenal and the noumenal spheres and the underlying differentiation between sense-knowledge, on the one hand, and the radically different − that is to say, practical − mode of knowing that appertains to the moral and religious domains, on the other.

Thus I show Kleist's *œuvre* to be dominated by a deeply regressive model of the act of knowing − I use the term in the wide spectrum of meaning it has in the Bible − which, in the face of any supersensible reality, turns into a grotesque parody of what it might be − namely an empirically ungrounded act of trust or faith. Nevertheless, the poet and his figures are not beholden to this primitive formula at all times. Every so often they feel their way towards a mode of apprehending the Absolute that is deeply ingrained in the European mystical tradition. If for the longest stretch of the way their mental mould is profoundly unmetaphysical, now and then, at the end of it, they take a leap into this inaccessible territory, suddenly, momentarily and, as it were, by a blinding flash of illumination. To try and see with the naked eye where there is nothing to be seen by the naked eye leads both to a mistaken seeing and an oversight − two nuances of meaning that are ever present in that crucial Kleistean term 'Versehen'. As against this, acceptance of the inability thus to see may itself be a source of light. In Kleist's world, salvation is found, if at all, in a renewed, higher form of blindness which transcends physical perception in that it apprehends the invisible numinous realm by the disclosure of a new, religious organ of cognition. Time and again, Kleist articulates, in terms of different levels of vision, the basic stumbling-block of the realist who believes what he sees: and it is at these points that he comes closest to a specifically Christian statement and, indeed, solution of his besetting problem.

Such an organ of religious knowledge is vouchsafed to some of Kleist's figures, sometimes — as in the instance of Käthchen von Heilbronn — from the outset and as an inalienable grace, more often at the end, but never without the most excruciating tribulations. Amongst such figures are the lovers and the grandfather in *Die Familie Schroffenstein* — significantly the old man is blind — Alkmene, die Marquise von O., Trota and, of course, the Prinz von Homburg as through his bandaged eyes he gleans an immortality no 'article of faith', not even an apple straight from the Garden of Eden, could vouchsafe.

As I read Kleist, his mind is stationed on the bottom or on the top rungs of the cognitive ladder, never in its middle ranges. Beast or God, he either atavistically assaults a reality shot through with the supersensible with the blunt tool of an ultimately perceptual analysis or, relinquishing the empirically knowable altogether, takes a leap into the mystical intuition of the Numinous apprehended with the eyes of the spirit in a state of illuminated blindness. In pinpointing both these characteristically Kleistean extremes and showing them to be his proper home ground, I go well beyond any critical position maintained hitherto.

Having opened up such vistas, I broach the fundamental question this study sets out to ask and to answer. How can one who 'mis-takes' the hypostasized, concrete phenomenon for 'the thing-in-itself', the Absolute, rise to the power of the poetic symbol, the artist's master tool which relies both upon a differentiation between the phenomenal and the noumenal spheres and upon a confidence in the ultimately 'analogous' status of what is given to the senses? At this juncture of my argument I shall have demonstrated this poet's myopic embroilment with the all too real peered at from too nearby and mistaken as the Absolute. I shall have shown this congenital short-sightedness turn by turn, through close textual studies and stylistic analyses, as well as by a detailed examination of his aesthetic as in fact practised — a very different thing indeed from the credo he consciously adhered to. As a result of all this stripping down I find I have a picture of stressful greatness and a power of assault deriving, precisely, from unspirituality and dogged immanence. It is above all the unresonant opacity of Kleist's metaphors, their being such and no other — one thinks of Michael Kohlhaas' blacks or even the irreducibly Prussian mould of his last, and maturest, play — and some lightness miraculously snatched from the dead weight of matter which fascinates us by its authenticity now, two hundred years later, as we face a world that has become all but impermeable. For such is our mental scene that it seems more amenable to being articulated through the windowless visions of a Kleist or the cryptic (because parodistic) parables of a Kafka than by the translucent symbols of an earlier age such as that of Goethe, which still had confidence in some ultimate meaning shining through the phenomena here and now.

I have paid limited attention to questions of chronology which, in any case, remain highly controversial. My ground-plan has been dictated, rather, by the internal logic of the interrelated themes I pursue in their various phases and aspects. It is this coherent intellectual structure, intended to illuminate individual works whilst at the same time placing them into an embracing context that I seek to put before my readers. The exploration in depth of my theme, or themes, has sometimes involved a repeated treatment of the same work from different angles in the diverse stages of my argument. Thus *Penthesilea* and *Prinz Friedrich von Homburg* have been the subject of more than one analysis, according to the intellectual frame in which I moved at the time. Conversely, it was on occasion found advisable to embed the detailed treatment of a given work exemplifying paradigmatically, as it were, a crucial phase or feature of Kleist's poetic imagination within a survey which makes the finality of his statement in the work under discussion plainly visible. Such seeming repetitions or digressions will, I trust, be revealed as necessary and even instructive to anyone alert to the design of my argument.

To facilitate the non-specialist's acquaintance with a German writer of the first rank whose work is virtually unobtainable in translation, I have translated into English all quotations from German texts in addition to quoting the German original. But quotations of no more than one or two lines to which no particular stylistic interest attaches are given in English only. Where the object has been to let the poetry speak for itself I have given priority to rhythm, imagery and other expressive devices over exactitude of word order or, indeed, punctuation. Where, on the other hand, I have endeavoured to render special syntactic or other idiosyncrasies I have sacrificed ease and elegance of expression in order to demonstrate my point.

I hope that my English-speaking readers will bear with me in what may be a faltering execution of a difficult task. The translations I offer − as, indeed, my study in its entirety − are governed by the desire to secure an adequate hearing for a great if puzzling − and puzzled − author, one who is above all quintessentially modern. If I have succeeded in this task, I shall be well satisfied. For it is my firm conviction that if we neglect a deepened understanding of this figure it will be to our own irreparable loss.

Blatten, Christmas Eve 1975.

I Paradise lost

And she took the fruit thereof, and did eat,
and gave to her husband who did eat.
And the eyes of them both were opened.
Genesis 3.

Die Forderungen von oben herein zerstören jenen unschul-
digen produktiven Zustand . . .
Goethe to Schiller

1 Concerning the Theology of Puppets: 'Über das Marionettentheater'

Almost exactly halfway through the essay *Über das Marionettentheater*, the conversation between the speaker and Herr C., leading dancer at the opera which sees their chance meeting, seems to have reached an impasse. The dancer, asked about the reasons for his lively interest in the local puppet-show which he has been seen watching several times, has explained his preoccupation with this seemingly rudimentary form of entertainment. He has put forward his thesis that theoretically a puppet could be constructed the grace of whose movements would transcend by far anything he, or any other dancer, could hope to achieve; and has given his listener some rough idea of the extraordinarily simple mechanics employed to produce effects suggesting a high degree of complexity[1]. The prime virtue of the puppet over its human prototypes, he has suggested, lies in the total absence of any affectation in its movements[2]. This stems from the fact that the puppet-master, through the strings attached to them, controls them at their true centres of gravity, the extremities following mechanically, like dead pendula. To illustrate this point the dancer describes the girations of some of his colleagues at the opera, notably those of the young Mr. F. in his role of Paris, as he passes the coveted apple to Venus, thereby singling her out as the loveliest of the three goddesses vying for his favour. 'Die Seele sitzt ihm gar (es ist ein Schrecken, es zu sehen!) im Ellenbogen'[a], he exclaims. Obviously he has touched on something central here, perhaps too central for him readily to communicate; for we are told that he abruptly terminates his discourse, adding: 'Solche Mißgriffe . . . sind unvermeidlich, seitdem wir vom Baum der Erkenntnis gegessen haben. Doch das Paradies ist verriegelt und der Cherub hinter uns; wir müssen die Reise um die Welt machen und sehen, ob es vielleicht von hinten irgendwo wieder offen ist.'[b] He breaks off and his companion laughs, uncomprehending and a trifle uneasy; yet he encourages his eccentric artist-friend to speak on, feeling that he has a good deal more to say.

The dancer does so and continues to extol the excellence of the wired dolls. Being in the hands of a master who pulls them and holds them up, he points out, they are exempt from gravity, a force to which even the finest human dancer is more or less subject. His partner now takes over from him and verbalises the

---

[a] 'His soul lodges — it is terrible to behold — in his elbow'

[b] 'Such mis-takes are inevitable, since we have eaten off the tree of knowledge. But Paradise is bolted and the cherub stands behind us. We must journey around the world and see whether perchance there is not an entry somewhere at the back.'

thesis which is implicit in these observations — namely, that the mechanically animated wooden doll possesses more grace than that miracle of nature's organising power, the human body. It is the same thesis the dancer had voiced before and illustrated by his reference to Greek myth; but whilst then his companion had laughed in evident embarrassment, mocking his partner in thought without voicing his doubts, he now takes courage and flatly dismisses the dancer's paradoxes as so many extravaganzas. However, far from being impressed by his scepticism, Herr C. proceeds to cap his argumentation by the most outlandish claim made so far. It is quite unthinkable, he replies, that any human being could anywhere near equal the grace of the mechanical *Gliedermann* — 'jointed man'. Only a God might conceivably prove a match for its excellence: 'und hier sei der Punkt, wo die beiden Enden der ringförmigen Welt ineinander griffen.'[a] At such far-flung claims his companion is speechless. However, with the same agitated preoccupation he had shown when he had touched on that particular topic earlier on in the conversation — this time he seeks refuge in taking snuff — the dancer reverts to the subject at the back of his mind and replies that evidently his acquaintance has not read Genesis 3 with sufficient attention. Another pause, marked by a new paragraph; clearly, this cryptic allusion has not been altogether lost on the speaker. For he himself now takes it up and carries the conversation forward by an extremely telling and relevant anecdote: the anecdote of the youth who, 'gleichsam vor meinen Augen, seine Unschuld verloren und das Paradies derselben, trotz aller ersinnlichen Bemühungen, nachher niemals wieder gefunden.'[b] Incomprehensibly and visibly, he had lost his natural grace the moment he had become conscious of it by seeing his mirrored reflection. The young man who had shown the perfection of Greek youth at its most consummate while he had no knowledge of possessing it — he had unwittingly imitated the pose of the famous *Dornauszieher* — had lost his grace day by day the moment he had seen himself until, before a year was out, he had become positively plain. Smiling approval, the dancer tops this story by another, even stranger one, the anecdote of the fencing bear who parried his every stroke — like many members of his profession, Herr C. is an acknowledged master in the art of fencing — and seemed to see straight through the complicated strategy of his quick-witted peer.

   The speaker receives this story enthusiastically and the conversation, from this point onwards, moves swiftly. The dancer formulates his thesis in a final and culminating paradox, saying that in the realm of organic nature grace and reflection are present in inverse proportions: the less reflection, the more grace, and vice versa. Except that somewhere in infinity the two meet again: 'so findet sich auch, wenn die Erkenntnis gleichsam durch ein Unendliches gegangen ist, die

---

[a] 'and this is the point where the two ends of the ring-like world interlace.'

[b] 'the anecdote of the youth who had lost his innocence before my eyes, as it were, and, for all his conceivable efforts, had never retrieved the paradise of it.'

Grazie wieder ein'[a]; such that grace is at its maximal in the human in whom consciousness is nil or infinite, 'd. h. in dem Gliedermann oder dem Gott.'[b] And now this paradoxical equation – and indeed the extraordinary claims as to the inverse ratio of reflection and grace that had led up to it – are enthusiastically acclaimed by the speaker to whom, but a little while before, they had caused such uncomprehending embarrassment. Now it is he himself who reverts to the topic his dancer friend had so urgently and reticently touched on twice before, and brings the conversation to its effective close. And interestingly enough, as he ventures into the hidden territory of the dancer's thought, he evinces the same air of distractedness which had accompanied Herr C.'s most daring formulations. ' . . . ein wenig zerstreut' – 'a trifle absent-mindedly' – he concludes: 'Mithin müßten wir wieder von dem Baum der Erkenntnis essen, um in den Stand der Unschuld zurückzufallen?'[c] The dancer nods assent, adding that this event does indeed constitute the final chapter of the history of the world; and on this unresolved chord the conversation ends.

To anyone familiar with the inner world of Kleist's figures and the mental gestures through which they make themselves known the strange abstraction evinced here, first by the dancer and then by the speaker, by itself suggests the centrality of the topic which calls forth this reaction. One need only think of the state of near-stupor in which Achilles and Penthesilea inform their flabbergasted followers of their intention to pursue their quest of one another, or of Prince Friedrich von Homburg's famous 'gleichviel' – 'never mind' – to be convinced of this. 'Für Kleist ist die Sprache eine Vielfalt von Mißverständnissen'[d], Max Kommerell sensitively observed more than thirty years ago[3]; and critics since then have been at pains to stress the effort and the difficulty experienced by Kleist's characters in the act of significant communication. They do not take communication for granted, and neither did their creator, Kleist himself. One glance at the telling essay *Über die allmähliche Verfertigung der Gedanken beim Reden* – *On the Gradual Fashioning of Thought in the Process of Conversing* – tells us so. For here speech – and the dialogue situation – are not presented as a benign medium which carries nascent thought to its destination, as a river will carry a ship on the tide. Speech and dialogue are, rather, envisaged as a system of vices in which the speaker is caught, out of which he must prise his way back into the freedom of the completed utterance. Communication is generated by the resistance to pressure and inseparable from both. And the depth of the communication is measurable by the strength of the recoil which accompanies it.

---

[a] 'such that, when consciousness has, as it were, traversed an infinity, it is once again joined by grace.'

[b] 'that is to say, in the puppet or in the god.'

[c] ' . . . thus we would once again have to eat off the tree of knowledge to relapse into the estate of innocence?'

[d] 'For Kleist language is a maze of misunderstandings.'

Thus the abruptness with which the dancer first throws out the allusion to the opening book of the Bible, the snuff he takes at its second mention, and the *Zerstreutheit* – absent-mindedness – with which the speaker of the essay finally takes up the reference once again to conclude the argument propounded in it – all these gestures equally testify to the centrality of the topic which evokes them. These abstracted gestures speak of a deep inner preoccupation. Thus we have every reason to pay the greatest attention to a subject broached repeatedly, and with every characteristic sign of inner urgency: the first book of Genesis which forms the opening chapter of the history of the world. We must pay heed not only because the references to this record are juxtaposed to a nicety to the 'last chapter of the history of the world' the enigmatic allusion to which lingers in the mind long after the speaker has recorded the last words of the conversation. But also, and principally, because the protagonist of that essay, the dancer, himself tells his partner – and us – that we must do so; for: 'wer diese erste Periode aller menschlichen Bildung nicht kennt, mit dem könne man nicht füglich über die folgenden, um wieviel weniger über die letzte sprechen.'[a] If then we wish to follow the dancer and his acquaintance in the silent musings in which the concluding words of the essay terminate and move with them into the vast territories of thought at the frontiers of which the spoken word ceases; if, in short, we are to comprehend anything of the cosmic perspectives which these concluding words open up before our eyes, we must needs begin at the beginning. We must take thought on the first chapter of the history of the world as related in Genesis 3 and on the reverberations of this chronicle throughout our essay, in what it communicates through its words as much as through its final silence.

It is neither within the purview of this enquiry nor indeed within my competence to essay a learned exegesis of this crucial biblical passage here. All I intend – and need – to do is to read it without any fixed assumptions as to its meaning or regard for customary ways of approaching it, through the sensibility of Kleist as it were, training eye and ear to pick up any echoes that have remained resonant in Kleist's essay and, indeed, in his work in its entirety. We shall have our work cut out doing just this. For I venture upon the proposition that Genesis 3 is nothing less than the fountain-head of Kleist's poetic world in its entirety, and that the intricate criss-cross of strains combining to furnish its symphonic weave can be traced back to that tonic chord above all. To indicate something of this dependence, first for the *Marionettentheater* and then for Kleist's work at large, is the purpose of these opening remarks. In doing so, the intellectual skeleton of this study as a whole will gradually become discernible.

Genesis 3 records the Fall and the expulsion of Adam and Eve from Paradise. For a moment, however, we must go beyond this culminating event in the first chapter of humanity back, to the beginning of the beginning. For here we come

---

[a] 'for one not familiar with this first phase of all human development would be unfit to be a partner in a conversation about the ensuing ones, and most especially the last one.'

upon a somewhat puzzling duplication. A first summary account of organic creation, including that of man and woman, is already given in Genesis 1. This done, the account of the creation of animals, of 'every beast of the field and every bird of the air', is once again recapitulated in Genesis 2. But this time it is told under the aspect of the Lord's concern for man. It is in the recognition that 'it is not good that the man should be alone' and in order to give him 'a helper fit for him' that the Lord creates first, beasts and birds, and finally, woman. The whole of living creation is thus once more reviewed, and re-enacted, from the viewpoint of God's concern for man, and especially from his awareness of man's need to be related. It is worthy of note that the Lord who has acclaimed every phase of the creation as good — 'And God said that it was good' — should specifically single out 'the man's' solitary estate as being 'not good'; worthy of note because in this singular criticism the value attached to relatedness as inseparable from human existence becomes manifest. We shall have more to say about this in connection with Kleist's poetic work. And it is of equal importance to note — again in relation to Kleist — by what means the Lord enables 'the man' to enter into relationships with the living things about him. These spring into being in and through the act of naming. The Lord once again creates beasts and birds from the ground 'and brought them all to the man to see what he would call them; and whatever the man called every living creature, that was its name.' 'But for the man there was not found a helper fit for him.' Finally woman, made of man's rib 'while in a deep sleep', is brought to him: and here a new awakening unmistakably coalesces with the recognition of closeness, the act of naming and indeed the name. Adam says:

> This at last is bone of my bones
> And flesh of my flesh;
> She shall be called Woman,
> Because she was taken out of Man.

It is at this point that Adam for the first time speaks and refers to himself by the personal pronoun 'my'. (The use of the personal pronoun in the first person singular, we may add in parenthesis, will wait until after the first couple have eaten off the tree of knowledge; a point, as we shall see, of some significance for Kleist.) It is through the act of relating to something not himself yet akin to him that 'the man' comes to have a sense of identity enabling him to refer to himself; that is to say, his nascent sense of identity is contingent upon being related to something other than himself.

Modern philosophers and, for that matter, psychologists would not, I think, wish to quarrel with this account of man's first mental steps as a triad involving the experience of being related, the awakening of a sense of identity and the act of naming. We know that the very young child is not psychologically separate from the mother and that it gradually establishes a sense of its abiding existence *within* the relationship with the mother[4]. He must learn that the mother continues through her absences and that he himself continues through them, too. This he does by learning to pick out abiding patterns and associations from the flux of sensations which assail him: for instance the coupling of his sense of gratification with the presence of the mother, be it her breast or the bottle she offers him. From the welter of undifferentiated and fragmentary sensa – rage, hunger, satiety etc. – gradually a continuing sense of self and a continuing image of non-self – breast, bottle, mother – will emerge; and the naming of the relevant cluster of sensations which signal for instance the bottle is an extremely important aid in the process of being able to envisage its continuing existence during the periods of its actual withdrawal, as well as towards making the nascent conception of the feeding-situation as such independent of this particular constellation here and now. It can be 'held' and deliberately used outside the situation in which it first arose[5]. This weaning of the named concept from its original context is a process that parallels, aids and in turn is aided by the weaning of the child itself from the primordial undifferentiatedness of the nursing-situation in which its identity is as yet indistinct from that of the mother. And this capacity to 'hold' in phantasy the conception of a given object and the associated situation and to attach it to different objects and different situations in turn constitutes the rudiments of our symbol-making faculty which is at the root of all our specifically human mental activities[6].

It will be seen that a considerable amount of abstraction is involved in all three of these interconnected developmental processes: establishment of self, relation to 'other' and the naming of what is so separated out from its sense-environment. From the kaleidoscopic flux of sensa accompanying the feeding-situation – the temperature of the bottle, the efficacy of the teat, accidents of positioning and light etc. – the child must select and abstract the permanent elements which regularly recur in, and are essential to, a situation of 'this kind'. By this process he gradually learns to recognise the typical in the transient and the general in the particular – e.g. the mother, and finally the conception of mother, in the breast that is offered to and withdrawn from him, or 'cowness' in this particular dappled patch on the green grass – and this development towards conceptualism and indeed the manipulation of objects as symbols rather than signs which is operative even on the level of perception, is aided by, and in turn aids, the employment of general and denotative terms.

It will be seen that the Lord, in causing the cavalcade of created life, and finally his own kind, to pass before 'the man's' sight, is giving 'the man' precisely that perceptual education – *Bildung* is the term Kleist characteristically uses – which enables him to recognise himself, and himself as one of a kind related to him yet not part of him, to have a sense of his own abiding existence as well as that of the patterned flux which passes before his eyes, to break it down into recurrent and meaningful elements and to 'hold' these by naming them. He has in fact led Adam through his mental infancy to the point where he experiences the 'other' as separate yet akin – this is the double condition of relatedness – and is able to form and 'hold' significant patterns of mental experience through the use of language.

Genesis 3 must, I think, be viewed as the culmination of this rudimentary cognitive development. Adam and – by implication – Eve have reached the level of perceptual experience, recognising and naming their environment and knowing themselves to be part of it yet apart from it. They have enjoyed the Garden of Eden in that simple and sensuous fashion which befits their state of mental development. Barring alone the forbidden tree of knowledge of good and evil, they have been allowed the freedom of the Garden, the enjoyment – to eye and palate – of its trees all of which were 'pleasant to the eye and good for food'. Thus they have lived a life firmly rooted in the senses, in a simple rhythm of sensory pleasures, appetites and gratifications. They have most certainly seen these trees and enjoyed seeing and tasting them in a straightforward physical manner.

Now, however, another kind of experience is held out in God's absence by the 'subtle' serpent. 'Eat from the tree of knowledge', he whispers, 'and your eyes will be opened and you will be like God, knowing good and evil'.

Clearly the promise 'your eyes will be opened' means something other than simple sensory perception. That they have sampled, and the Lord has exercised that faculty, not only by letting the procession of animals pass before Adam's eyes, but by presenting to the perception of the couple a Garden every tree of which was 'pleasant to the eye'. The serpent holds out another promise: the promise of a mental experience of an altogether higher order. Once they have eaten from the tree, their 'eyes will be opened' in a special manner: they will 'see', and thus know, an order of reality which is strictly invisible. Unlike greenness or 'cowness', good and evil are not only general, but abstract terms, not being derived by a process of selection and generalisation from this particular patch of green or this particular cow, but denoting a quality itself abstract and eluding perceptual experience. We cannot see, hear, smell, touch or taste the good, nor any manifestation of it.

In fact, the serpent has played the hoax of all times on the unsuspecting couple. He has led Eve – and by implication, Adam – into regions remote from those in which their senses had pastured. He has led them into the recondite territory of abstract concepts, invisible guards of an invisible noumenal realm. That they have no mental tools to reach out for this new order of reality is plain from the description which precedes the actual tasting of the forbidden fruit: 'So when the woman saw that the tree was good for food, and that it was a delight to the eyes, and that the tree was to be desired to make one wise, she took its fruit and ate.' Significantly the order of experiences is now reversed. The more primitive – gustatory – expectation is placed first; it is in this context of a highly undifferentiated sensory experience that the visual element appears, significantly now also in intensified form. The trees had been 'pleasant to the sight'. The tree of knowledge which is now being pointed out is 'a delight to the eyes'. This intensification betokens an increasingly sensuous experience; and being also, and in the first place, 'good for food' and, besides, 'to be desired' to make one wise – a condition as yet unknown and capable only at this moment of being

envisaged vaguely, along the familiar lines of physical appetite — its appeal proves
to be irresistible. And now disaster ensues. The Fall — that first *Mißgriff* —
'mis-take' — as Kleist so graphically has it — occurs before our very eyes. The
initial perceptual experience — one involving considerable differentiation as we
have observed — the act of seeing the tree, progressively deteriorates, becoming
ever more primitively sensual. Seeing becomes desiring, desiring touching and
touching eating. True, Adam's and Eve's eyes *are* opened as the serpent has said
they would be. But what do those eyes perceive? The spiritual vision of good and
evil, in the sense in which God saw his handiwork 'and saw that it was good'?
That is to say, an order of being which is abstract and eludes physical perception
— the order of values? No. In straining to see what no pair of eyes can see, Adam
and Eve become aware of themselves in the very act of seeing. Their uncomprehending gaze rebounds as though reflected back by the opacity of a mirror and,
turned in upon itself, the organ of perception perceives itself in its pitiful
physicality[7]. And they feel exposed and naked in the merciless glare of such
self-consciousness. Whatever else the primitive act of eating means, it is a lapse
into the deepest regression in the face of a confrontation with a spiritual reality
they have no means of comprehending. And this shamed self-consciousness *per se*
is an evil condition in that it is destructive, once and for all, of that innocent
sensuousness in which they had been close to their Maker. Now they long to be
invisible and they hide themselves from each other and from the sight of the Lord
walking 'in the cool of the day'. But they cannot hide themselves from themselves.
Nothing can shelter them from the reflected glare of their own startled consciousness. Their pristine spontaneity is ravaged. Before ever the Lord pronounces
judgment, they have fallen from the state of grace and suffered expulsion from
Paradise.

    Howevermuch else is hidden in these momentous paragraphs of this momentous
chapter in the history of human kind, this is the way — perhaps a not particularly
mature or profound way — in which I submit that Kleist read them. To Kleist, the
events chronicled in Genesis 3 are a cypher for the pernicious onset of self-
awareness in the face of a complex situation disturbing the primordial simplicity
and innocence of a wholly instinctual response to reality. The dispenser of this
venom is the serpent who invites the couple to 'eat' off the tree of knowledge and
thus teaches them what it is like to have open eyes and yet to be bereft of vision.

    Adam and Eve before the Fall, taking their first steps in unself-conscious grace,
unquestioning in their concord with themselves and at the hand of their Maker,
prime mover of their simple impulses: this is the theological reality behind the
symbol of the puppet-show[8]. For the puppet, too, in all its movements executed at
any one time, totally 'de-pends' on the one single impulse transmitted to it by the
hand of the puppet-master, the harmonious and apparently free play of its
constituent parts notwithstanding. Indeed, the name Kleist gives to this construct
— he calls it *der Gliedermann*, 'the jointed man', — on closer inspection turns out
to be a startling misnomer[9]. For this *Gliedermann* paradoxically turns out to be

the most undifferentiated – the German word would be *ungegliederte* – model of the human psyche for the reason, precisely, that its semblance of complexity, and indeed autonomy, is misleading: *one* movement animates its parts automatically and homogeneously; and even this movement obeys an impulse which has an external if congenial source.

The longer one ponders Kleist's seminal essay, the more inescapable does the impression become that the puppet-show, for him, was a perfect model of that undisrupted and felicitous concord, before the Fall, between the Lord and the creatures made in his image, that is to say, at the time when the impulses implanted and directed by him represented their sole animating force. Once however their consciousness of themselves is awakened by a situation disturbing this primordial harmony, the divinely directed puppets begin to move of their own accord, that is to say, knowingly and, in that sense, freely; and the idyllic bond tying them to their Maker is rent. It is at this point in the history of human kind – when, significantly, Adam and Eve cease merely to re-act, and act in the absence of their Master – that the analogy with the puppet-show ceases to hold good. Instinctuality innocently geared to and unfailingly directed by a divine agency gives way to that capriciousness, complexity and unsureness of motivation which is the besetting curse of self-consciousness; and the inner and external reality to which human consciousness awakens, inevitably becomes what it has remained ever since: 'die Welt noch, die gebrechliche, auf die nur fern die Götter niederschaun'[a]. (*Penthesilea*, 24).

It would be difficult to find more eloquent comments on Genesis 3, and on the ravages of self-consciousness, than two passages contained in two letters from Kleist's hand: one in a letter to his step-sister Ulrike, written at the very moment when the 'Kant-crisis' burst on him with its full force; the other in a letter to his friend Rühle von Lilienstern which accompanied the MS of the almost contemporaneous comedy *Der Zerbrochene Krug*. In the first of these documents we still find him groping for the cause of his *malaise*. He dislikes people, he writes; but quickly adds that he is well aware that the cause of this may lie in himself rather than in others, much as a warped mirror flaws the objects it reflects by its own faultiness. The mirror of his being, he suspects, may well be 'schief und schmutzig' – 'warped and sullied'. And he goes on to say: '– Ach, es gibt eine traurige Klarheit, mit welcher die Natur viele Menschen, die an dem Dinge nur die Oberfläche sehen, zu ihrem Glücke verschont hat, . . . sie zeigt mir alles, was mich umgibt, und mich selbst in seiner ganzen armseligen Blöße, und dem Herzen ekelt zuletzt vor dieser Nacktheit – – Dazu kommt bei mir eine unerklärliche Verlegenheit, die unüberwindlich ist, weil sie wahrscheinlich eine ganz physische Ursache hat.'[b][10] The built-in mirror, it will be seen, is suspected of being 'schief

---

[a] 'the fragile world/ On which the gods gaze down but from afar.'

[b] 'Alas, there is a melancholy kind of lucidity Nature has spared the many fortunate ones that only perceive the surface of things . . . to me she shows everything around me, and

und schmutzig', not so much because of *what* it reflects, but, first and foremost, because *it is a mirror*; because it *reflects* himself and what is around him with a merciless sharpness, taking the bloom off things, stripping him down, and leaving him with a nauseating sense of being naked, exposed. Is this not a thinly disguised account of Adam and Eve once they have eaten off the tree of knowledge? 'And the eyes of them both were opened; and they knew that they were naked; and they sewed fig leaves together, and made themselves aprons.'

In the other letter Kleist reflects on the torments which paradoxically beset that lightest and most near-divine of human manifestations, the making of art. 'Warum ist es denn so schwer?', he asks; and answers his *cri de cœur* thus: 'Jede erste Bewegung, alles Unwillkürliche, ist schön, und schief und verschroben Alles, sobald es sich selbst begreift. O der Verstand! der unglückselige Verstand!'[a][11]

'. . . schief und verschroben Alles, sobald es sich selbst begreift . . .'[b]: eloquent lament at the balefulness of Adam and Eve's estate when they had reached out to grasp – *begreifen* – absolute truth and had grasped – *ergriffen* – an apple instead, and the measure of their abysmal inadequacy besides; grovelling in toil and dust for the length of their days, abjectly subject to gravity; at the youth's expulsion from the paradise of innocence – Kleist's own words – the moment he had grown aware of – and tried to grasp – his own ineffable grace; and indeed at the tortuous girations of Herr F. 'whose soul (it is terrible to behold!) lodges in his elbow'. Lament and horror indeed: for the arbitrary emancipation of the dancer's extremities from an ideal centre of gravity controlled and transcended by a divine impulse which annuls gravity and ensues in a kind of airborne grace, for Kleist is the direct, and grotesque, reflection of man's disastrous alienation from divine Grace at the dawn of consciousness. The Fall, for Kleist, is neither more nor less than the death of spontaneity felt as closeness to God – the two are inseparably linked and virtually interchangeable – a morally neutral event issuing in a kind of adolescent gawkiness experienced on a cosmic scale. We may infer that this is what Genesis 3 meant for the poet, both from the evidence of the essay *Über das Marionettentheater* and from the cumulative evidence of his writings taken in their entirety. As for the former, a closer look at the anecdote of the youth who by one inadvertent glance in the mirror lost *das Paradies der Unschuld* before the speaker's eyes, as it were, will help illuminate this point; and it is to this story that we must now turn.

Reflecting on the dancer's allusion to the chapter of Genesis we have been discussing, the speaker has taken it up and uses it in order to introduce an

---

my own self, in all their shabby bareness, and at long last the soul is revulsed by such nakedness – – Superadded to that, I suffer from some inexplicable self-consciousness which, stemming in all probability from a plain physical cause, is unsurmountable.'

[a] 'Why then is it so hard? Every initial move, all that is involuntary, is beautiful; and all becomes askew and tortuous as soon as it becomes aware of itself. Alas and alack for reflection! wretched reflection!'

[b] 'All becomes askew and tortuous as soon as it becomes aware of itself . . .'

illustration of his own. 'Ich sagte', he reports, 'daß ich gar wohl wüßte, welche Unordnungen in der natürlichen Grazie des Menschen das Bewußtsein anrichtet. Ein junger Mann von meiner Bekanntschaft hätte durch eine bloße Bemerkung, gleichsam vor meinen Augen, seine Unschuld verloren und das Paradies derselben, trotz aller ersinnlichen Bemühungen, nachher niemals wieder gefunden.'[a] A number of points are noteworthy here. First, it is significant that the author should choose the epithet 'ersinnlich' instead of the more familiar 'erdenklich'. *Ersinnlich* renders with much greater exactitude the misbegotten reliance on the senses in a situation which bedevils perception and the percipient. Second, the word 'Bemerkung' strikes us by its ambiguity. True, the speaker may have in mind his own malicious remark which helps to confound the young man's unconscious grace. But equally it refers to the 'Entdeckung' the lad had made in the first place — namely that his pose was the reflected image of the one in which the Greek artist had exhibited the melting loveliness of adolescence. In that case, the 'Bemerkung' which wreaks such damage is an observation — a perceptual act like the seeing of the tree of knowledge. And this is paralleled by the speaker's comment that the youth lost his grace 'gleichsam vor meinen Augen' — 'as it were, before my eyes'. Third — and most important — the speaker in this introductory reflection, which serves to join Genesis 3 to the illustration he is about to relate, charges the advent of *Bewußtsein* as being the exclusive cause of man's fall. The mere estate of self-consciousness, without any moral connotation whatever, is held responsible for the ensuing loss of natural grace; and to this corresponds the definition of the state preceding his lapse from grace: it is the *Paradies der Unschuld*; by which, clearly, Kleist means the paradise of unself-conscious spontaneity, again without any added moral overtones.

The illustration the speaker then proceeds to give confirms the significance of these pointers. The young man is no Dr. Faustus. He does not court any extra-human knowledge by extra-human means. He is merely possessed of 'eine wunderbare Anmut' — 'a marvellous grace' — that is to say, of no more than that evanescent physico-spiritual charm which is the glory of adolescence — and, incidentally, of ancient Greek statuary — in which future complexity lies momentarily and harmoniously dormant, as leaves are latent in the bud. All he does is to glimpse this delicate aura, with the result that it escapes his scrutinising gaze and he merely perceives himself trying to perceive what the naked eye can neither see nor 'take in'. Here again, as in the introductory remarks preceding the story of the youth, as, indeed, in Genesis 3, to the understanding of which the speaker wishes to make a contribution, good and evil are immanent in the event of seeing oneself seeing, and seeing nothing but the reflected organ of perception,

---

[a] "'I said", he reports, "that I knew very well indeed what disorders self-consciousness has wrought in the natural grace of human beings. A young man of my acquaintance had by a mere observation lost his innocence, before my eyes, as it were, and, for all his conceivable efforts, never retrieved the paradise of it."'

because the reality one is trying thus to decipher is not amenable to physical perception. Being refractory to sense-perception, good and evil themselves do not at any point enter as *objects* of apperception; it is not *what* is perceived but *the act of seeing itself* which becomes evil. In the confrontation with more ineffable ranges of reality – good and evil, or as in the case here an evanescent spiritual-physical harmony – the naked eye is brought up short against its insufficiency and boggles. As Adam and Eve see themselves unavailingly trying to see (and in fact wishing themselves invisible), so does the youth. The innocence of paradise, i.e. the spontaneity of unconsciousness, has irretrievably gone. His reflection has destroyed his grace[12]. And as Adam and Eve's organ of perception is turned inward upon itself and becomes as it were its own exclusive and unrewarding object, so with the youth. Hour by hour, and day by day, he watches and scrutinises himself in the mirror which shows him watching and scrutinising himself, until the phenomenon he had unwittingly glimpsed – his grace – is totally lost from sight, and all he experiences is an atomisation of his own perception.

The youth seeing himself reflected in the mirror: this is a transparent symbol of that destructive reflection which in the coda of the essay is named as the arch-enemy of grace and, indeed, innocence. 'Wir sehen', so the dancer sums up the argument, 'daß in dem Maße, als in der organischen Welt die Reflexion dunkler und schwächer wird, die Grazie darin immer strahlender und herrschender her-vortritt.'[a] It is reflective self-awareness *per se*, not any given content of that awareness, that for Kleist is original sin, the venom injected by the serpent. Such *rising* reflective consciousness, paradoxically, leads to a *fall* from grace which is marked by a continual process of regression within that faculty of perception which had caught sight of itself inadvertently, in a cognitive encounter to which it had proven itself unequal: from sight to touch and thence, in extreme cases, to the most rudimentary 'taking in' of the object by an act of eating. In work upon work – dramatic or epic as the case may be – we shall come upon the symbol of falling or stumbling set at the beginning of an Odyssey of spiritual emancipation which, paradoxically, is a journey leading through the deepest regression[13]. And we shall have no trouble in relating these individual lapses back to the Fall of the first Adam as Kleist read this epoch-making lapse. We shall do well to remember God's pronouncement on both the serpent and the first human couple as we encounter the painful eclipse of all spiritual vision and the cleaving to the dust of literalness which besets those characters that have fallen from the grace of un-reflecting spontaneity. They are earthbound well and proper, and the imagery of poison – the poison of self-consciousness injected into the first couple by the 'subtle' serpent – as well as the nostalgic imagery of flying recalling a grace as yet unfettered by the law of gravity, will continually remind us of their fallen estate

---

[a] 'We see that in the measure in which reflection in the organic realm grows dimmer and feebler, grace becomes manifest in it more radiantly and powerfully.'

and its biblical ancestry[14]. In this connection we shall also be aware of the winged figure of the Cherub who guards the gates of Eden and himself participates in the ineffable grace which was the price of self-reflectiveness; a figure to which, in the essay alone with which we are concerned, significant allusion is made twice[15].

To understand the genesis of this regressive process, however, we must still make allusion to the story with which the dancer caps the one just related by his companion: the anecdote of the bear who, with unerring sureness of aim, parried and indeed forestalled every sally of an acknowledged master in the art of fencing and beat him at his own game.

The bear is clearly not capable of reflection. In that sense he is the epitome, in the organic realm of nature, of that grace which we are told manifests itself more radiantly in the measure in which reflection recedes, becoming ever more dim and feeble. Not indeed does he possess self-consciousness, the root of all evil. Unlike the youth whose awakening to himself is ushered in by the reflection of himself he catches in the mirror, the bear does not see himself fencing; he has no mental image of himself. In fact, his every action and reaction is what we would call a reflex-action, determined and executed without the intervention of the higher centres of the nervous system. His sallies – it is impressed upon us twice within a few lines – are performed with the highest degree of economy. All he does is to execute 'eine ganz kurze Bewegung' – 'a quite short movement'. In this, he is comparable to the *Gliedermann* whose extremities are mechanical appendages directly controlled from the puppet's centre of gravity like dead pendula obeying the law of gravity. The bear's short reflex-movements express the messages from his nerve centre with a similarly automatic immediacy. Thus he is the analogue, in the organic sphere, of the puppet, and as close to the unerring poise of the God as is the *Gliedermann*. Conversely, he is the exact opposite of the dancer's colleague, the young Herr F., whose mental leverage is so long and whose arm is so alienated from his centre and so perverse in its arbitrariness that his very soul seems to have come to reside in his elbow.

Not only does the compactness of this beast make for the quality we would least associate with him – a perfect poise: the unreflecting, and unreflected, immediacy of his responses – reflex-actions all of them – also lends him an extraordinary power of perception. He is not engaged in a quixotic and involuntarily comic fight with his own reflected image; his perception is geared to his opponent and his objective. Looking the dancer straight in the eye – again this is impressed on us twice – he confronts him squarely, measures him 'Aug in Auge, als ob er meine Seele darin lesen könnte' – 'eye in eye, as though he could read my very soul in it' – piercing all appearances and attempts at dissimulation and scoring an effortless all-out victory.

In the sequence of the narrative with which we are concerned, the anecdote of the bear is placed last, well after the allusion to the dancer's colleague whose infelicitous 'Mißgriff' – he is, significantly, passing an apple – gives rise to the first mention of Genesis 3, and after the story of the bashful Northern Narcissus.

He stands at the nadir, and therewith at the apex, of development in the organic realm. It is he who forms one of those 'Enden der ringförmigen Welt' — 'ends of the ring-shaped world' — as does the *Gliedermann* on the inorganic level — which, at some point in infinity, coalesces with the flawless grace of the God at the other extreme and completes the circle of evolution.

And, sure enough, we discover something of the bear's penetrating perception, and the longing for an immediacy of vision to match his, in some of the most highly differentiated and enigmatic figures from Kleist's pen: in Graf vom Strahl, the Count F. in *Die Marquise von O.*, in Hermann and, of course, in Jupiter — demonic figures all of them, eluding ordinary standards of assessment, surrounded by an aura of the Numinous, God-like and diabolical, soul-melting and barbaric in one. They also seek to 'know' the other directly, with an immediacy of vision that penetrates the husks of the phenomenal as unerringly as does the bear's gaze. Where the Adams and Eves of Kleist's imagination fail in that they mistake the invisible order of things for so many tangible objects to be seen, touched and even eaten, these more sophisticated figures hold the phenomenal in contempt and seek to gain immediate access to the hidden essence of the other, in a direct communion of souls. But as they enter the human arena in all its complexity their quest for immediacy of knowledge comes to grief, even as the rudimentary perceptual 'Mißgriff' of their simpler cousins is doomed to failure. Their extreme subjectivism falls as short of true knowledge of the other in the act of relatedness as does the more primitive tendency of their counterparts to treat the invisible as though it were a perceptual object, and to grasp that ineffable 'other' by thus reifying it. And indeed, as one would expect in an order of things where the most differentiated manifestations of human life circularly link up with its most rudimentary beginnings, these two aberrations — I propose to call them the subjective and objective fallacy respectively[16] — at some points coalesce and become all but indistinguishable from one another in point of undifferentiatedness. I shall have occasion to treat at length these two principal variants of human behaviour in the cognitive encounter which is — we have seen it in the discussion of Genesis 3 — inseparably interwoven with the encounter of the 'other' in relationship. Indeed, a large part of this book will be taken up with the tracing of these two basic modes of cognition — both equally surrogates of the true knowledge of relatedness — throughout Kleist's epic and dramatic work[17].

From the preceding pages it will have become apparent that Kleist's reading of Genesis 3 — as I see it — involved and confirmed him in a kind of cognitive dilemma of metaphysical dimensions. This found its precipitate in his encounter with Kant's philosophy. In dealing with this chapter in his life, it is important to remember that the ostensibly epistemological questions which assailed him — and the encounter with Kant has more often than not been tackled along epistemological lines — are in fact problems of the second order. They are offshoots from the more fundamental ontological problem of 'knowledge' as formulated in Genesis 3. It is essential to bear in mind the enormously wide range and looseness of the concept of knowledge in the biblical account, which ranges from the cognitive act of perception to the awakening of man to the consciousness of himself and, indeed, to the knowledge of man and woman in the sexual act. This breadth of meaning should not be left out of sight; indeed in the biblical record it is, as we have seen, doubly underscored by the fact that the more specifically cognitive events which culminate in the eating off the tree of knowledge are unswervingly geared to the encompassing issue of relationship − God's relationship to man and man's relationship to living creation and especially his kin, woman. This sweeping context should at no point be left out of sight, lest an account of Kleist's fatal and fructifying encounter with Kant be bogged down in academic niceties[18].

The artist's relation to 'the other' is bound up with the nature of his relation to his medium, for his medium is that 'other' in its most intimately personal form. Thus Kleist's epistemological position − again taking the word in its broadest sense − inevitably puts its stamp on his aesthetic. Here we shall have to be on our guard, however, to distinguish between Kleist's conscious stance − a very consistent one as it happens − and what he does unconsciously, *qua* poet. Careful exploration of this area will yield what is possibly the most reliable evidence as to what aspect of Kleist's art is anchored in his poetic vision, necessary and fruitful to it, and what residue there remains which we must regard as essentially pathological[19]. And from there again we must press on and ask − as I shall do in the concluding chapter of this book − whether the poet himself was the victim or the master of the primitive model of cognition he puts before us in the essay on the puppet-show.

Finally we shall have to enquire what form the redemption from the cognitive *débâcle* of the Fall can possibly take. In the concluding paragraph of the essay *Über das Marionettentheater* the speaker absent-mindedly muses: 'Mithin müßten wir wieder von dem Baum der Erkenntnis essen, um in den Stand der Unschuld zurückzufallen?'[a] To which the dancer assents, adding, 'das ist das letzte Kapitel von der Geschichte der Welt'[b]. These are cryptic words indeed, and none more so than the strange *zurückfallen*. What is the dancer's meaning? Does the term he chooses − a term of regression if any − and does the remedy he suggests imply resignation, or even cynical disillusionment? Is he envisaging − the image used earlier on in the essay of the *ringförmige Welt* might almost suggest something of the kind − a circular evolutionary movement, such that the end of human development coalesces with its undistinguished beginnings? Are we to redress, in a uniquely vicious circle, the regression which began when Adam and Eve, by a Gargantuan *Mißgriff* − mis-take − reached out for the knowledge of ultimate realities and ended up eating apples and perceiving their naked selves, by retracing

---

[a] 'Thus we would once again have to eat off the tree of knowledge to relapse into the estate of innocence?'

[b] 'that is the last chapter of the history of the world.'

our steps and returning to the primordial innocence of the first couple contentedly walking amongst trees which were pleasant to the sight and good for food? Or to the simplicity of the bear who neither reflects nor sees his reflected image but whose being is narrowly bounded by automatic reflexes? Or indeed to the grace of the *Gliedermann*, most undifferentiated of human models in that its *Glieder* are dead pendula mechanically following the simple movements prescribed by the puppet-master's wrist? The dancer's allusion that we might sneak into paradise by way of some backdoor would seem to lend substance to such an essentially regressive solution.

We cannot rule out this possibility. And does not the speaker state expressly that we must once again eat from the tree of knowledge? This stipulation makes the prognosis dimmer still. Is the end of man's painful awakening from his atavistic beginnings to be a new atavism, a renewed eating of what cannot be 'taken in' by eating because it belongs to an immaterial and supersensible order of things?

Kleist's essay gives us no answer one way or another to these questions. It dismisses us into silence. Yet the possibility suggests itself that the poet may be continuing to think in terms of the symbolism which at a close reading is found to be at the heart of his essay – the symbolism of perception, first voiced in Genesis 3, which enshrines the paradox of Western man's spiritual venture; a paradox voiced – through the self-same symbolism – in pre-Christian as well as Christian and non-Christian cultures, in Sophocles' *Oedipus* tragedies as much as in St. John and St. Paul, in Shakespeare's *Lear*, Milton's *Samson Agonistes*, in Schiller's tragedies as well as in a contemporary writer like Canetti, and in none more urgently and obsessively than in Kleist's *opus*. Could it be that here, at the end of the *Marionettentheater*, and through his dramas and short stories as a whole Kleist is inviting us to think the paradox of seeing and blindness through to the end? Inviting us to take the last step and to understand that, even as the initial 'opening of the eyes' in the Garden of Eden ushered in a peculiarly obdurate form of blindness, so that very blindness – which is our human condition – accepted truly and lived through may in turn usher in a higher form of vision?[20] Could it be that he envisages the possibility of our perceiving a spiritual tree of knowledge with new eyes of the spirit and tasting of its spiritual fruit with our physical eyes firmly shut? That, in fact, we complete a benign circle and redress our original transgression – which was a regression – by going back beyond it, by being subtler than the subtle serpent?

The *Marionettentheater* makes us ask these questions. It is to Kleist's poetic work as a whole – and especially to its verbal fabric – that we must look for a definitive answer.

2 First Stop on Earth: 'Der Zerbrochene Krug'

1.

'Erlaubt! Wie schön der Krug, gehört zur Sache! —'[a] (7) cries the plaintiff, Frau Marthe, as the village judge asks her to spare the court further details of her object of contention. And although the speaker is but a character in a play, and not a very bright one at that, we may assume that in defending the importance of her pitcher Frau Marthe is speaking on behalf of the dramatist. For the broken pitcher is nothing less than the titular hero of this drama and as such eminently worthy of attention. A strange hero, it is true: for it is a dumb thing of clay, unable to protest its significance; a congenital affliction which has earned it the contemptuous disregard of the characters in the play and the smiling forbearance of its critics. A mere trifle it has been called time and again; and one critic has built up an elaborate theory proving that it has no business to be in the drama at all[1]. Others have added insult to injury by arguing that its very insignificance is its *raison d'être*: for the discrepancy between its real nullity and the ado it causes is the mainspring of the comedy[2].

Clearly this is no way to treat a hero. And, indeed, the broken pitcher has avenged itself by taking the secret of the play into its silent grave. For what has become of this comedy of which the poet himself could say at the close of his life: 'Es kann auch, aber nur für einen sehr kritischen Freund, für eine Tinte meines Wesens gelten'?[b][3] Many think it delightful, some find it ponderous even in its playfulness. But most are agreed that, born of the poet's will to prove his comic vein, it remains a product of his skill rather than his genius and lacks something of that formidable integrity so characteristic of his masterpieces; a judgment which is reflected in the extensiveness of the objections advanced even by its most well-meaning critics[4].

Thus either Kleist overrated his play, or we have yet to find its organic centre. But in what direction is the would-be critical friend of the poet to turn for a clue? Kleist's letter to Fouqué continues thus: 'es ist nach dem Teniers gearbeitet, und würde nichts wert sein, käme es nicht von einem, der in der Regel lieber dem göttlichen Raphael nachstrebt.'[c] The epithet *göttlich* sums up the associations evoked by the mention of Raphael: a name epitomising a grace so perfect as to transcend, almost, the limits of physical nature, the very law of gravity. And

---

[a] 'Excuse! The beauty of my jug is to the point!'
[b] 'To a very astute friend it may well pass for an imprint of my being.'
[c] 'It is after the manner of Teniers and would be worthless if it did not come from one who as a rule prefers to emulate the divine Raphael.'

Teniers, the robust painter of the rustic world in which Kleist has set his comedy? Surely he denotes the very opposite. Yet some connection between these two poles there must be. Even in the portrait after the manner of the Dutchman some trace of the divine Italian must linger: for it is that which gives the likeness its worth. But wherein can the connection lie? What did Teniers mean to Kleist?

At this point the essay *Über das Marionettentheater* comes back to mind. Written in December 1810, a few months before the poet dispatched his comedy to Fouqué together with his judgment about it, the narrator recounts reminiscences of a puppet-show he purports to have seen during the winter of 1801, a month or two before *Der zerbrochene Krug* took shape in his mind. On being asked by the dancer whether he did not think those puppets extraordinarily graceful, he had replied that indeed 'Eine Gruppe von vier Bauern, die nach einem raschen Takt die Ronde tanzte, hätte von Tenier nicht hübscher gemalt werden können.'[a] So Teniers, too – and the comedy after the manner of Teniers – in the poet's mind is associated with a certain kind of grace; the grace, as we have seen, of the puppet, of the youth who unwittingly imitated a Greek statue, and of the bear who instinctively parried every stroke of his human masters; that is to say, the natural grace which precedes consciousness and is destroyed by its advent; the grace of innocence – so the narrator sums it up – in which we live as in paradise until we eat from the tree of knowledge, and to which we shall return when we have transcended the shortcomings of human consciousness. It is a far cry from the *Gliedermann* to the *Gott* and yet, the poet tells us, the two meet like intersecting lines converging in infinity. And a far cry it seems from the dumb earthiness of Frau Marthe's world – Teniers' world – to that 'last chapter of the history of the world', the chapter of paradise regained, to which the narrator of the essay makes such significant allusion.

Yet paradise and the loss of innocence must have played a large part in the conversations between the young Kleist and three writer-friends of his which resulted in Kleist's comedy. *Innocence perdue* was the theme suggested by Greuze's painting *La cruche cassée* and elaborated in Debucourt's painting, an engraving of which hung in Zschokke's room in Berne. This engraving it was which inspired the idea of a literary competition amongst the four young men. And paradise lost, *innocence perdue*, is indeed the theme of Zschokke's short story and Geßner's idyll[5]. Critics have told us that Kleist for his part dropped these thematic associations. But what about the nomenclature of his play: Adam and Eve? Again we are assured that these names, like the pitcher itself, are relics from an earlier conception and have no legitimate place in the play as we know it[6]. Small wonder that, with its titular hero and two principal personages thus lightly dismissed, the drama still refuses to yield up the secret of its life. The poet's own words, at any rate, encourage us to look for such a secret. True, we have garnered

---

[a] 'a group of four peasants dancing a reel to a lively jig could not have been more attractively painted by Tenier.'

no more than a few pieces of circumstantial evidence; and circumstantial evidence, a tricky enough instrument to wield in a court of law, is more unsuited still to extract the truth from poetry. To do so, we must examine the drama itself. We must interrogate its silent hero, the broken pitcher and, through the offices of its interpreter, Frau Marthe, seek to discover its real significance.

2.

Four times does the broken pitcher dominate the scene by proxy, as it were: in the preliminary squabble about the legal aspect of the breakage, in Frau Marthe's description of its beauty, in her account of its history, and finally and appropriately, in the concluding words of the play. All these are eminently funny passages. But wherein does their humour lie? In the case of her quibble with Veit this is not difficult to see. Clearly, it revolves round her play on the words *entscheiden* – adjudicate, *ersetzen* – replace, and *entschädigen* – indemnify. She reduces each of Veit's statements *ad absurdum*, by reducing the operative word to the concrete meaning of its stem-component. *Entscheiden* to her quite literally means to un-sever the jug, in the sense in which it has been severed; *ersetzen*, to put it back into place, in the sense in which it has been dislocated; *entschädigen*, to un-damage it, in the sense in which it has been damaged. By taking abstract, legal terms in this literal meaning, she proves Veit guilty of so many contradictions in terms. For what is done cannot be undone. But this is not the sense in which we do use these derivatives. Contrary to their stem-words, *scheiden* – sever, *setzen* – place, *schädigen* – damage, they express, not a modification of the object itself, but rather a relation between the people concerned with the object. And this is, of course, the sense in which Veit uses them. He proposes not to mend, place back or un-damage the jug but to make amends to its owner, to replace it to her, or otherwise to indemnify her.

The breakage of the jug has created a complex situation requiring an ability to distinguish between different levels of reality. On one plane, the broken jug is an isolated material fact. On another, it is an object of contention and a factor in a human issue. On this plane, it is a thing of legal, moral and emotional significance with an abiding reality altogether distinct from its physical existence. It is on this plane that the words Veit uses are meaningful. By denying their meaning and consistently regressing to the concrete sense of their stem-components, Frau Marthe reveals a curious limitation of her mind. She is unable, or so it seems, to distinguish between the material and the mental dimensions of an issue, between things and their significances; indeed she seems unable to conceive of any order of reality beyond the tangible and visible one of the material world.

The same mode of perception informs Frau Marthe's description of the jug in the seventh scene. The material properties of the jug itself, the representation on it, and the historical world which is represented – these are three distinct dimensions of her pitcher betokening so many orders of reality. And here again

Frau Marthe is incapable of differentiating between them, indeed of recognising any reality beyond the tangible one of the material object before her. Thus, in describing the picture on the jug and the historical events to which it refers, she falls into a hopeless confusion which is pinpointed in a number of ways: by her incessant use of adverbs of time and place such as *hier, grade hier, noch, jetzt,* etc., she reduces the historical time and place of the pictured events, as well as the timelessness of the picture itself, to the temporal and spatial dimension in which her jug has, or had, its being. Again, throughout her long description she does not once make reference to the fact that she is describing a pictorial representation. It is not the material properties of the figure of King Philipp, but his own august person which now 'liegt im Topf, bis auf den Hinterteil' — 'lies in the pot, up to his hinder part'. (7) Similarly, she does not inform us that the surrender of the Dutch provinces is depicted or shown on the jug: on Frau Marthe's jug the Dutch provinces in their massive entirety are, in fact, surrendered.

Were it not for the fact that the pitcher is broken, such verbal contradictions might conceivably pass for mere colloquialisms. But it is broken, and consequently Frau Marthe's mode of expression leads her to speak of the entire Dutch provinces as being surrendered, not on the jug, but 'hier grade auf dem Loch, wo jetzo nichts' — 'just here upon the hole where now there's nought'. (7) This is ludicrous. The complicated situation which has arisen necessitates a differentiation not absolutely requisite before. For once the jug is broken, the continuum between its material and its pictorial properties is hopelessly disrupted. They have ceased to be expressive of each other, and thus can no longer be expressed in terms of one another. By disregarding this cleavage between its sundered elements, Frau Marthe's description of the pitcher lapses from the merely naïve into the absurd[7].

And indeed, the poet has found a drastic device to underscore this incomprehension. For he has led her into a perpetual confusion of the laws appertaining to the material and the pictorial spheres of her shattered pitcher. The queens of France and Hungary, one of whom can still be seen to weep, now lament the loss of their earthenware legs; Philibert, the rascal who has permitted the emperor to take the brunt of Ruprecht's blow, by rights should fall, like his master; a nosy onlooker is still peering from his window: goodness knows what he now sees; the Bishop of Arras has altogether gone to the devil, only his shadow has remained behind. Now ordinarily the continued presence of that figure's painted shadow would prompt the recognition that it is merely his moulded likeness which has vanished. Not, however, in Frau Marthe's case. Not even the fact that what she describes is contrary to the laws of nature — a shadow without an owner — induces her to abandon her way of thinking and to recognise that she is confusing two distinct orders of reality.

In the earlier scene, Frau Marthe equates the legal and moral aspects of the breakage with the physical fact itself. The same inability to differentiate causes her in the present scene to identify the pictorial properties of the jug with its material ones. The immediate physical reality is, or so it seems, the only reality she can see.

For a third time in the play the pitcher commands the stage when, through the mouth of Frau Marthe, we learn its bizarre history. Its survival through all the hazards of fights, falls and fire, underlined by the increasingly dismal fate that overtakes its changing owners, is so outlandish as to be little short of the incredible; and gradually it becomes clear that she believes her jug to be endowed with supernatural properties. Yet how do we come by this knowledge?

So terse is Frau Marthe's account of the first incident that happened to her jug that we have hardly time to wonder how it escaped destruction. In the very act of killing its owner the *Wassergeuse* seizes it, drinks, and is off. Nor does Frau Marthe dwell on the miraculous nature of her second story, the story of the aged owner of the jug and the amazing rejuvenation it works on him. On the contrary, she goes out of her way to stress the gravedigger's exceptional sobriety:

> Der trank zu dreimal nur, der Nüchterne,
> Und stets vermischt mit Wasser aus dem Krug − [a] (7)

and thence, without so much as a hint of discrepancy, she proceeds to relate the results of his temperance: the gravedigger takes a young wife, becomes a father,

> Und als sie jetzt noch funfzehn Kinder zeugte,
> Trank er zum dritten Male, als sie starb. [b] (7)

These momentous events, especially the wife's death when we expect to hear of the end of her aged husband, are comical in themselves. Their surprisingness is enhanced by the manner of the telling: Frau Marthe relates them perfunctorily, in two subordinate clauses. But to say this is not fully to account for the superbly funny effect of these lines. Had Frau Marthe said, more correctly, 'Nachdem sie jetzt noch fünfzehn Kinder zeugte, trank er zum dritten Male, als sie starb',[c] their force would have been considerably weakened. The poet clinches his point by using the same tense for two temporal clauses relating successive events. By this token the happenings are telescoped and belittled, as it were. A suppressed miracle if ever there was one, the feat of Fürchtegott's old age!

But it is in her account of the two last and most extraordinary hazards of the jug that Frau Marthe reaches the nadir of matter-of-factness. To save the jug from the French, its next owner threw it out of the window and jumped after it. The jug remained whole while the owner broke his neck, 'der Ungeschickte' − 'the clumsy clod'. This disapprobation is the key to Frau Marthe's attitude. For it implies that for the tailor to have landed intact would have been no more than natural and fitting. Anybody should have been able to do what a mere jug could do:

> Und dieser irdne Krug, der Krug von Ton,
> Aufs Bein kam er zu stehen, und blieb ganz.[d]

---

[a] He merely drank three times, the sober mutt,/ And always thinned with water, from the jug −

[b] When she gave birth to fifteen children yet,/ He drank the third and last draught as she died.

[c] 'When she *had* given birth to fifteen children yet, he drank the third and last draught as she died',

[d] This earthen jug, this pitcher made of clay,/ It landed on its foot and stayed intact.

Thus she takes the miracle out of its survival. And indeed, the true nature of the event and her incomprehension of it are pointed up in yet another way. Frau Marthe protests that the story was told by the dead man himself! A paradox more glaring than the escape of her earthenware jug, and yet she is unaware of it.

It is in her last story, however, that the incongruity between event and evaluation culminates: the story of the jug's escape from fire. Three times do we hear of the great conflagration of 'Anno sechsundsechzig' — 'Anno sixty-six'. By such reiteration and by everyone's evident familiarity with the event its magnitude is impressed on us. We imagine a terrible disaster recorded in the pages of history. And what befell your jug in this catastrophe, Frau Marthe is asked; she replies:

> Was ihm geschehen?
> Nichts ist dem Krug, ich bitt euch sehr, Ihr Herren,
> Nichts Anno sechsundsechzig ihm geschehen.[a]

The reiterated negation and the monotonous repetitiveness of the phrase as a whole do their work: our expectations are deflated like a pricked balloon.

The source of the humour in Frau Marthe's stories is evident. As before, it arises from her inability to comprehend an order of reality beyond the palpable physical reality of the jug itself. This time it is the rationally incomprehensible nature of her jug that eludes her. Its supernatural properties, like its moral and aesthetic properties, are something over and above its material nature and distinct from it. Indeed, unlike the former, its supernatural properties are paradoxically opposed to its material nature. It is precisely that contradiction which marks her jug as an 'absurd' object of faith. Frau Marthe's faith is funny in that it is totally unconscious of this, its paradoxical dimension, and is based, not on the imperceptible spiritual nature of the jug, but directly upon its physical properties. Objectively speaking, it is more comical than her moral assessment and her aesthetic appreciation were, in that the failure to perceive a paradox is more flagrant than the failure to perceive a mere distinction. Thus the triad of scenes we have examined culminates in the history of the jug on which it concludes. For here it is that the limitations of Frau Marthe's mode of perception are most glaringly exposed[8].

Having thus defined Frau Marthe's mentality and its comic propensities, the critic faces an ugly prospect: at any moment he may be told that the joke is on him. He may be laughed at for invoking the abstract pomp of moral, aesthetic, and religious categories in order to explain so dumb a creature as Frau Marthe. Yet this is precisely what the poet has done, in the oblique fashion which is the poet's triumph and the critic's envy. For how else was Kleist to characterise Frau Marthe's obtuseness, but by showing her inability to recognise any form of spiritual reality beyond the sheer facticity of material things? And if he was to keep within the narrow confines of his comic character, what could he do but let

---

What happened to it?/ I beg your pardon, sirs, nought happened to the jug,/ Nought happened to it anno sixty-six.

this inarticulateness speak for itself, without pointer or comment, at the risk that it might not make itself understood? It was essential for the poet to perform this delicate operation successfully; for Frau Marthe's mental make-up is the key to her actual behaviour, and it is this, more than any other factor, that determines the outer action of the play besides helping to define its theme.

It has been remarked that Frau Marthe is inordinately concerned about her pitcher, whilst to the real issue, Eve's happiness and honour, she seems impervious. 'Er?' she exclaims, when the identity of the nocturnal intruder is revealed; and from that moment onward lapses into a virtually complete silence broken only to announce, at the end of the play, that she will go to Utrecht there to seek justice for her damaged jug. Clearly Eve's vindication has made no impression on her. Yet care for Eve's honour she does; but in what way is revealed by the form and imagery of her final invective:

> Und auf den Scheiterhaufen das Gesindel,
> Wenns deine Ehre weiß zu brennen gilt,
> Und diesen Krug hier wieder zu glasieren!a   (6)

The disparity between the two issues — the moral and the material — is ignored. Both are treated on the same footing, in a single sentence. Two object-clauses coupled by 'und' and sharing the same verb are made to cover the diverse aspects of the case. What is more, both the moral and the material are expressed in terms of the same imagery. And the image, significantly, is taken from the sphere of the material object!

Signs such as these indicate that Frau Marthe's reaction to the practical situation is consonant with her response in those reflective moments in which the essential shape of her mind has been revealed. Indeed, her practical predicament is very much like the intellectual impasse which resulted from her attempt to define the significance of her jug. Here, as there, is a complex situation. To assess it requires a capacity for differentiation. For in this human situation, as in the case of the shattered ornament, the habitual congruence between signs and their significances, feeling and fact, has been irrevocably disrupted. The physical facts of the situation no longer express its spiritual meaning. To be sure, Eve's innate rectitude signifies her innocence. As a matter of indisputable fact, however, a stranger has visited her room at night. *Ergo* Eve is guilty.

In this confusion, Frau Marthe obdurately clings to the only tangible reality — her broken jug. She still clings to it in uncomprehending apathy when the full facts have long since come to light. There is only one explanation for this obsession: it reflects that basic limitation of her mind, her inability to grasp anything beyond the immediate physical reality. At the level of reflection, this limitation is revealed in her exclusive concentration on the material properties of her jug and her incomprehension of its overriding spiritual significance. On the practical level, the

---

a On to the pyre with that riff-raff there,/ When what's at stake is to burn clean your honour/ And to glaze this pitcher once again!

self-same limitation finds symbolic expression in her obsession with an isolated piece of material evidence – her jug – and her inability to appraise its true meaning in the light of the total situation.

The facts of the night can be explained, it is true. But they cannot be explained away and undone any more than amends, replacement, or payment of damages for her jug will mend her jug, place it back on its shelf, and undo the damage it has suffered. What has happened has happened and in one sense remains an ugly breach of propriety, even though in another and deeper sense it testifies to Eve's loyalty and pluck. A paradoxical state of things indeed! No less paradoxical than Frau Marthe's jug, which is both a thing of clay and a source of incorruptible life. And as Frau Marthe is unable to perceive the material nature of her jug and yet to believe in its spiritual propensities, so too is she unable to perceive the sordid facts of the night and yet believe in Eve's innocence. For this essential obtuseness the poet could not have found a more appropriate expression than Frau Marthe's dumbfounded silence. It parallels, on the dramatic level, her deep inarticulateness about the jug of which she talks so much and says so little.

3.

Frau Marthe's imperviousness to all but the visible reality is also the shortcoming of the lovers. They, too, believe what they see and no more. With his own eyes Ruprecht has seen Eve in the garden at night with another man. How then is he to believe in her faithfulness?

> Sieh da! da ist die Eve noch! sag ich
> Und schicke freudig Euch, von wo die Ohren
> Mir Kundschaft brachten, meine Augen nach –
> – Und schelte sie, da sie mir wiederkommen,
> Für blind, und schicke auf der Stelle sie
> Zum zweitenmal, sich besser umzusehen . . .
> Und schicke sie zum drittenmal, und denke,
> Sie werden, weil sie ihre Pflicht getan,
> Unwillig los sich aus dem Kopf mir reißen,
> Und sich in einen andern Dienst begeben:
> Die Eve ists, am Latz erkenn ich sie,
> Und einer ists noch obenein.[a]   (7)

It has become a commonplace to say, since Schiller's *Ästhetische Briefe*, that of all the senses the most highly differentiated and most nearly spiritual is the sense of sight. The object we touch or taste is upon us; we are overcome by its sheer

---

[a] Look now! I tell myself, there's Eve as yet/ And happily despatch my eyes to whence/ My ears had come back with their news –/ – And scold my eyes when they return again/ For being blind, and send them off forthwith/ A second time to make a better search . . ./ And send them off a third time, thinking now/ That, having done their duty, they will sulk/ And sever their connection with my skull:/ It's Eve they see, I know her by her bib,/ And someone else there is besides herself.

physical proximity. But what we see leaves us free, by virtue of the physical distance between eye and object. Unlike the tentacle or the tongue, the eye remains at a distance from its object; it is only our looks that go out to it. And contrary also to the ear, the eye can be averted or shut: of all the senses it is the most active and free, and this innate spirituality has found expression in the twofold meaning of the word 'vision'. But in describing what passes in the garden, Ruprecht does not speak of sending out his 'looks' to the distant scene, but his eyes themselves. As though they were tentacles or hands, he brings his eyes close to their object to touch it and feel it in its tangible reality. And indeed, what they disclose to him is the outermost surface of things, to wit, Eve's bib and, later on, the coat-tails of his rival: material enough objects, and yet how immaterial in the last resort! And as Ruprecht makes his eyes perform the offices of material organs, so he thinks of them under the materialistic image of hired servants.

Later on, when he pursues his rival, he is blinded by a handful of sand. This, he admits to Walter, has prevented him from identifying the intruder, an admission of failure which Adam maliciously underscores by asking:

> Warum sperrtst du nicht die Augen auf? . . .
> Ruprecht: Die Augen auf! Ich hatt sie aufgesperrt.
> Der Satan warf sie mir voll Sand.[a]

To which Adam replies, in a muttered aside:

> Voll Sand, ja!
> Warum sperrtst du deine großen Augen auf![b]   (10)

The palpable reason for question and comment is, of course, Adam's triumph at having fooled Ruprecht and thus bringing Walter's inquiries to a stop. But his taunt has another function of which the speaker himself is unconscious. By drawing on the imagery of sight, his statement serves to further the development of the central theme of the play. Ruprecht's insistence on seeing, so the poet tells us through Adam's aside, is his undoing, as it is Frau Marthe's. His rigid reliance on his eyes, the way he uses them, and on the material reality they disclose to him, in actual fact makes him blind. Adam can fool him only because he will keep his big and stupid eyes wide open. Had he not tried to see in this confusion but entrusted himself to another sensibility, he would have been spared error and pain. As it is, he experiences both. On coming to from his fall, he sees the humiliation he has caused Eve, and thinks:

> . . . blind ist auch nicht übel.
> Ich hätte meine Augen hingegeben,
> Knippkügelchen, wer will, damit zu spielen.[c]   (7)

---

[a]   Then why did you not open your big eyes?/
Ruprecht: My eyes? They were agog −/ The very devil peppered them with sand.
[b] With sand, indeed!/ Why did you goggle with your stupid eyes!
[c] Blind is not so bad, either./ I would fain have plucked out my own eyes/ For whosoever fancies to play tiddlywinks.

These words do not only intimate suffering. They betray a dim awareness of its cause. The comparison of his eyes with counters, a more material image even than the one he had used before, by its open contemptuousness implies that Ruprecht has come to doubt the value of perception and of the material reality disclosed by it. And indeed, his final allusion to the incident shows that he has learned his lesson:

Heut streust du keinen Sand mir in die Augen[a]   (11)

he cries as Adam attempts his last deception. From his use of a general figure of speech with its accepted metaphorical significance we may infer that he has understood the deeper meaning of his accident[9].

It is Eve, however, who most clearly defines the nature of Ruprecht's failure and the response he should have made. Indignantly, she exclaims:

Und hättest du durchs Schlüsselloch mich mit
Dem Lebrecht aus dem Kruge trinken sehen,
Du hättest denken sollen: Ev ist brav,
Es wird sich alles ihr zum Ruhme lösen,
Und ists im Leben nicht, so ist es jenseits,
Und wenn wir auferstehn, ist auch ein Tag.[b]   (9)

By thus imaginatively accentuating the actual situation, Eve reveals its paradoxical nature. In all essentials, the predicament in which Ruprecht finds himself corresponds to that presented by Frau Marthe's broken jug. For here too, fact and feeling, sign and significance, stand radically opposed. Ruprecht, Eve tells us, should have disregarded what he saw − whatever that might have been − and believed in what he could not see − in Eve *in* her deed: an absolute act of faith in an ultimate spiritual reality of which he is as incapable as Frau Marthe. Instead he disregards what he cannot see and believes only in what he sees. This failure of faith, the degradation of spiritual vision to sight and of sight to touch is the central theme of the play. It is summed up in Ruprecht's reply to Eve:

Was ich mit Händen greife, glaub ich gern.[c]   (9)

A realist at heart, Kleist has explored this underlying theme by a variety of techniques corresponding to the variety of his poetic materials. In relation to Frau Marthe it is stated negatively, by the device of omission. Neither by image nor by concept does the poet designate the deficiency of her response: her imperviousness to all but the visible reality. He merely presents it, by showing her in a number of situations which call for spiritual perception. In leaving her deficiency thus unspoken he enacts it truly, for even to name a thing is to give it being, and Frau Marthe's lack is absolute. The silence he keeps about Frau Marthe − and for all

---

[a] Today you shan't throw sand into my eyes.
[b] And had you spied me through the keyhole/ Drinking with Lebrecht from the jug,/ You should have said: Eve is a good girl,/ All will come out all right and do her credit,/ If not in this life, in the next one then,/ The day will dawn when we shall rise again.
[c] What I may grasp with hands, I'd fain believe./

her loquacity his silence surrounds her throughout the play – in truth is a statement of his theme in its most radical form. As consciousness dawns in his characters, his theme begins to flower into words. It emerges, on the poetic plane, in the images of perception which permeate the texture of Ruprecht's speeches. It is finally evolved as a theme of discourse between Eve and Walter, the most conscious characters in the play by far.

At the beginning of the *Variant*, Eve is confronted with a seemingly insoluble dilemma: if she refuses to clear her honour, she will sacrifice Ruprecht's love; if she unmasks Adam, she will sacrifice Ruprecht's life. Whatever she does, their happiness is ruined. In this extremity she throws herself at Walter's feet, refusing to get up

> als bis Ihr Eure Züge,
> Die menschlichen, die Euch vom Antlitz strahlen,
> Wahr macht durch eine Tat der Menschlichkeit.[a]   (*Variant*, 12)

To this plea Walter responds thus:

> Mein liebenswertes Kind! Wenn du mir deine
> Unschuldigen bewährst, wie ich nicht zweifle,
> Bewähr ich auch dir meine menschlichen.[b]   (*ibid.*)

A pledge based, it seems, on mutual trust in one another's integrity. But Eve has promised more than she can keep. Forced to choose between the elusive goodness of Walter's face and Adam's documented lies, she puts her trust in the latter. Thrice she insists that she has with her own eyes seen the letter containing the fatal instructions: how can she disbelieve their testimony? It is only when Walter bids her see what she ought to have believed that she recognises the truth:

> Du hast mir deines Angesichtes Züge
> Bewährt, ich will die meinen dir bewähren,
> Müßt ich auf andre Art dir den Beweis
> Auch führen, als du mir . . .[c]   (*ibid.*)

he says, handing her a bag of gold in token of his honesty.

> Sieh her, das Antlitz hier des Spanierkönigs:
> Meinst du, daß dich der König wird betrügen?[d]   (*ibid.*)

At this Eve yields. The solid symbol of worth before her eyes accomplishes what the fleeting testimony of Walter's features could never have achieved. Eve believes

---

[a] Until you prove the promise of your face,/ Which, full of warmth, shines with humanity,/ By the performance of a human act.

[b] My lovely child! if you will prove/ The innocence of yours as you will doubtless do,/ So shall I the humanity of mine.

[c] To your own features you have proven true,/ And so I will to mine,/ For all that I must demonstrate my proof/ By different means from yours –

[d] Look now, behold the features of the Spanish king:/ Do you believe your Monarch is a fraud?

in a sign so palpable, so hallowed by time and convention. Overwhelmed, she replies:

> Ob Ihr mir Wahrheit gabt? O scharfgeprägte,
> Und Gottes leuchtend Antlitz drauf. O Jesus!
> Daß ich nicht solche Münze mehr erkenne![a]   (*ibid.*)

This is Eve's final speech. The last word to pass her lips is 'erkenne'. It bears out what incident and image suggest alike. Eve knows the current coin of truth when she sees it. But at no point does knowledge flower into sheer faith in a spiritual reality unsupported by outward facts and signs. Of her, no less than of Ruprecht and Frau Marthe, the crucial words of the play remain true:

> Was ich mit Händen greife, glaub ich gern.[b]   (9)

At the end this thematic continuity is formally confirmed. Eve's crisis of faith is followed by Frau Marthe's obstinate request that justice be done to her broken jug. A contrast, certainly, but also an ironic parallel, this return to the *corpus delicti*. For the jug is the all-embracing symbol of that obtuse adherence to the physical fact, the visibly real, which informs all characters alike and binds them together in one poetic vision.

And still we have not done with the broken pitcher. Like the true poetic symbol that it is, its meaning seems inexhaustible and its force pervades beginning, end, and middle of the play. Frau Marthe's pitcher is there all the time, if only we care to see it. For what is the confusing world in which Eve's rectitude comes to grief, but the image on the jug come to life? Netherlanders and Spaniards solemnly united – this is the world betokened by the jug: but the picture is shattered, and Frau Marthe can no longer comprehend it. As symbols often do in the poetry of Kleist, this symbolic world and the fissure that runs through its fabric in the end become real. The commonwealth of nations in which Eve lives is united only in memory. In actual truth, it is as rent as is the picture on the jug. Spaniards and Netherlanders are at war, and the latter have turned against each other in strife and exploitation. It is a confusing world. Old signs assume new and ominous significances. The conscription of the militia, in a secure order of things a familiar landmark of life, now betokens sinister designs. This is Adam's account of it, not true, of course, but interesting in the sense of disorientation it reflects, and doubly interesting for the light it throws on the connection between symbol and reality. Asked whether Ruprecht is likely to be sent further than Utrecht, Adam replies:

> Folgt er einmal der Trommel,
> Die Trommel folgt dem Fähndrich, der dem Hauptmann,
> Der Hauptmann folgt dem Obersten, der folgt
> Dem General, und der folgt den vereinten Staaten wieder,

---

[a] The truth you gave me? O, 'tis sharply minted,/ And bears God's shining face. O Jesus!/ Not to recognise such coin!
[b] What I may grasp with hands, I'd fain believe./

Und die vereinten Staaten, hols der Henker,
Die ziehen in Gedanken weit herum.
Die lassen trommeln, daß die Felle platzen.[a]   (*ibid.*)

This passage is remarkable for the impression of incongruity it creates. Its logical meaning pulls in one direction, its form and syntax in another. As we learn eventually, it is in fact the central government which orders the mobilisation of the country and causes the drum to beat. But this comes as a surprise. For by various linguistic means Kleist has created the impression that the drum signals away on its own, mobilising one by one the military forces that obey its call, until in the last sentence the real motive force is disclosed. Drum and despotic designs, machinery and mover, matter and mind, are dichotomously opposed and held together by the most tenuous of connections. Each pulls its own way and obeys its own law. The signal of the drum, like the signs imprinted on the broken jug, sends out its mechanical message, betokening nothing of ultimate significance[10]; the meaning of the whole has become intractable. Could a fragmented reality and its fractured image have been presented in a more like fashion?

The broken jug, then, does not merely reflect the failure of the characters to comprehend a complex world. In the last resort, it symbolises that world itself in which appearance and reality lie promiscuously mingled and in which instinct untutored by consciousness is bound to come to grief. The broken pot of earthenware betokens

die Welt noch, die gebrechliche,
Auf die nur fern die Götter niederschaun,[b]   (24)

as Kleist has it in *Penthesilea*. Only it is not a world about to be transcended by grace, as in the tragedy, but a world just begun. For the picture imprinted on the jug bears witness to an earlier world where the gods were near and the truth, to be believed, had only to be seen and plucked from trees: a shattered idyll, a paradise lost for ever.

We are back at the beginning: at the conversations of the four young poets about the thematic implications of Debucourt's etching — *innocence perdue*; at Kleist's own assessment of his comedy; and, lastly, at the comparison of the puppet-show with the plump poise of Teniers' peasants.

The comedy of Adam and Eve is indeed the comedy of the Fall, the theme of Geßner's and Zschokke's poetic efforts; but in the hands of a Kleist the conception has become immeasurably deepened. He portrays the fall from that archaic state of grace of which the bear, the puppet, and the poise of Teniers' stocky figures are mute mementos, as is the picture on Frau Marthe's jug; a

---

[a] Once he obeys the drum,/ So does the drum the ensign, he the captain,/ The captain the colonel, he/ The general, and he the Commonwealth of Nations,/ And the united states, the devil take them,/ They roam about in their imagination./ They beat the drums, until their skins go bust./

[b] the world as yet, the fragile world/ On which the gods gaze down but from afar,

paradise lost at the first dawning of human consciousness which heralds dissonance and pain.

In Kleist's comedy the gates of Paradise are shut. The Fall has taken place. Like his renowned ancestor, Adam yields to temptation and falls[11], and in his wake fall Eve, Ruprecht, and the pitcher — falls a whole world. But unlike the lovers the principal comic figures, Adam and Frau Marthe, do not emerge from the twilight of creation into the day of consciousness. It is true, Adam knows good and evil and knows that he has slipped. Yet he denies that knowledge in a concerted attempt to cling to the paradise of unalloyed creature bliss. But deny consciousness as he will, he cannot feign the grace of innocence: his misshapen foot, 'der ohnhin schwer den Weg der Sünde wandelt'[a] (1) in the end is his undoing. Thus, heedless of his humanity, yet heavily subject to the law of gravity, he remains a hybrid creature on the threshold of the human world. So, too, does his counterpart, Frau Marthe. Her primitive poise is shattered and she stands before the human scene in sullen incomprehension, an inert clod bereft of beauty and devoid of sense, like her jug.

Not until Eve breaks her silence in the *Variant* and gives voice to her inner conflict is the first chapter of the world truly ended. As she accepts the burden of consciousness, the journey around the world begins; she is well on the road to humanity. But from her painful gropings toward knowledge it is a far cry to the effortless beauty of a Raphael, to the unerring poise of an Alkmene, to the unconscious grace of a Prince; a farther cry perhaps even than from the spiritual inertia of Frau Marthe and Adam. For grace, says the dancer in *Über das Marionettentheater*, manifests itself most purely where consciousness is nil or infinite, 'd. h. in dem Gliedermann, oder in dem Gott'[b]. The gulf between the primordial dimness of the comic hero and the rapturous eclipse of consciousness vouchsafed to the tragic hero is infinite, and the Kleist of 1801 could not span it within the confines of one drama. To achieve that he required the technique he was to elaborate later, of presenting the two phases of human development in two separate but intersecting spheres, as in *Amphitryon*, or of presenting them in one person, on different levels of one consciousness, as in *Prinz Friedrich von Homburg*. The five acts of that drama, beginning as they do with the sleepwalking unconsciousness of its hero, and ending in his final swoon of fulfilment, do indeed span the history of the world, from its first to its final chapter.

It was presumably Kleist's passionate preoccupation with the transcendent grace epitomised by the name of Raphael which led him to venture beyond the dumbness of Frau Marthe's world — Teniers' world — and to pursue his theme into the *Variant*. We would not gladly miss its riches: the flowering of Eve's humanity and the deepening of theme it brings. But undoubtedly it endangers the poetic unity of this play. Eve is too conscious, too articulate, to be comic. For this

---

a 'which heav'ly treads the path of sin in any case'
b 'i. e. in the puppet or in the god'

reason the poet wisely keeps her silent during the main part of the drama. On the other hand she is not conscious and articulate enough to rise to the wounded beauty of an Amphitryon or Penthesilea, let alone to reach the ultimate grace at the other end of consciousness of those Kleistean figures that transcend tragedy: Alkmene, Käthchen, and the Prince. She stands midway in a development the beginning and end of which give rise to a pure genre. Thus the *Variant* which she dominates, for all its beauty, is a hybrid form. Kleist seems to have been aware of this fact: witness his uncertainty about the ending of the play which is reflected in its different versions. He evidently attempted to integrate the *Variant* with the main body of the comedy by returning from its heights to Frau Marthe's ludicrous obsession with her jug. This rounding off is formally required and thematically justified. Nevertheless, the regression from Eve's articulate humanity back to the twilight of Frau Marthe's world and its hero, a dumb and senseless clod of clay, comes as something of a shock; a very Kleistean shock indeed, as we shall see later on in this study.

Perhaps his faltering steps toward a new genre yet to be developed were as much in the poet's mind as the actual theme of his play, when he wrote to Rühle von Lilienstern in a letter accompanying his comedy: 'Es gibt nichts Göttlicheres, als sie [die Kunst]! Und nichts Leichteres zugleich; und doch, warum ist es so schwer? Jede erste Bewegung, alles Unwillkürliche, ist schön; und schief und verschroben alles, sobald es sich selbst begreift. O der Verstand! der unglückselige Verstand!' [a][12].

---

[a] There is nothing more divine than art! And nothing that at the same time is easier; and yet, why is it so hard? Every initial move, all that is involuntary, is beautiful; and all becomes askew and tortuous as soon as it becomes aware of itself. Alas and alack for reflection! wretched reflection!'

II Trouble ahead

Wie du dir selbst getreu bleibst, bist du's mir.
Schiller

There seems to be an unalterable contradiction between the
soul and its employments. How can a *soul* be a merchant?
What relation to an immortal being have the price of linseed,
the tare on tallow, or the brokerage on hemp? Can an undying
creature debit *petty expenses* and charge for *carriage paid*?
The soul ties its shoes; the mind washes its hands in a basin.
All is incongruous.

Walter Bagehot

3   A Curable Condition? 'Die Familie Schroffenstein'

1.

It has been very pertinently observed that few mortals riddled with such radical distrust as was Kleist have made such radical demands upon the trust of others[1]. This is certainly true of Kleist's early letters, especially those addressed to his unfortunate fiancée, Wilhelmine von Zenge; it is no less true of his fictional characters. We need but think of Eve in *Der zerbrochene Krug,* who unreasonably expects her lover to trust her '*in* her deed', that is to say, in the highly compromising and ambiguous situation in which he finds her placed; or of Penthesilea who hounds down Achilles in hot-cheeked pursuit assuming him to understand that all this battling is in the name of love; or of Toni in *Die Verlobung in St. Domingo,* who would have her lover interpret what appears to be a gesture of betrayal as one of ultimate good faith; or indeed of Alkmene and the Marquise von O., both of whom expect to be vindicated in their integrity in circumstances that would condemn them to all but a superhuman comprehension.

The problem of trust — and the adjacent problem of faith — makes its first appearance in Kleist's first play, *Die Familie Schroffenstein*; and already here it is partnered by another, like a fresh wound in the poet's mind after his perusal of Kant: this is the question of the pernicious subjectivity of human knowledge, of the inextricable intermingling of appearance and reality breeding distrust in its turn; another power of the original problem which was to remain with him throughout the span of his life.

In his first drama the young playwright certainly gave these two protagonists a good run; and despite some melodrama which made the author and his friends double up with merriment at a private reading, these twin themes interweave with a relentlessness which marks the play as the first fruit of a potential tragic genius. In this tragedy, trust comes to grief in a world riddled by false appearances, and deluded despair takes the final curtain. Parents who have inadvertently murdered their own children in a tantrum of distrust do not recognise their own flesh and blood in the disguises they have donned; and a grotesque figure, straight from *Macbeth,* pronounces the grisly finale: 'Wenn ihr euch totschlagt, ist es ein Versehn' (V, I) — 'if you kill one another, it is an oversight' — words discrediting the competence of human perception which from afar foreshadow Penthesilea's horrified questionings at the savaged body of Achilles or those of Gustav after he has killed the half-cast girl he loved but could not trust. In this drama as in so many later works, perception is branded as the fool in a world of appearances and declares its tragic bankruptcy[2].

It is well known that the young Kleist, profoundly shaken by his encounter with Kant, resorted to the image of coloured spectacles to convey something of the sense of delusoriness with which Kant's phenomenalistic account of sense-knowledge had saddled him. 'Wenn alle Menschen statt der Augen grüne Gläser hätten', he writes to his fiancée, 'so würden sie urteilen müssen, die Gegenstände, welche sie dadurch erblicken, *sind* grün – und nie würden sie entscheiden können, ob ihr Auge ihnen die Dinge zeigt, wie sie sind, oder ob es nicht etwas zu ihnen hinzutut, was nicht ihnen, sondern dem Auge gehört. So ist es mit dem Verstande. Wir können nicht entscheiden, ob das, was wir Wahrheit nennen, wahrhaft Wahrheit ist, oder ob es uns nur so scheint.'[a][3].

The appropriateness of this metaphor to elucidate Kant's account of sense-knowledge has come under heavy critical fire[4], though some reputable Kant scholars have not hesitated to use it themselves by way of an expository gambit, no doubt in complete ignorance of Kleist's personal *cri de cœur*[5]. But the aptness or inaptness of Kleist's illustration for the understanding of Kant need not detain us here. What is important is that this is how Kant impressed himself on him, and that he should have chosen this metaphor in preference to any other to convey the impact Kant's message had made on him. For – as I shall be showing in the following chapter – both the excessive reliance on, and the excessive distrust of, perception, and especially visual perception which is our prime organ of empirical knowledge, although accentuated by Kant, have an ancestry in Kleist's personal history that is considerably older than his acquaintance with that philosopher.

Let us take a good look at Kleist's metaphor and hold it against its model, Kant's epistemology. Through the image of the green glasses Kleist conveys the subjective character, or colouring, of our sense-knowledge, on Kant's reading of the matter. The green glasses are interpolated between the world of objects and ourselves in the same manner in which, according to Kant, the pure forms of our intuition and the pure forms of our understanding intervene between the sense-data which are given to us and our experience of them as objects. It is only with the aid of these cognitive instruments – Kleist's green glasses – that we construe the manifold of the senses into the familiar objects of our experience. These mental filters, according to Kant, are built into our very consciousness. They inevitably modify what we know. The alteration of the known by the knower is inherent in the act of experiencing. So far Kant.

But what about Kleist? The image he uses of the tinted glasses leaves it open whether the modification of the experienced universe is intrinsic or extrinsic. It is true the fact that we have the glasses *instead* of eyes argues for the former option.

---

[a] 'If all men had green spectacles instead of eyes, they would be bound to judge the objects they perceive through them to *be* green – and they could never decide whether their eyes show them things as they are in themselves, or whether they do not superadd something to them which does not pertain to the object, but to the eye. It is the same with the human understanding. We cannot make out whether what we call truth, is indeed the truth, or whether it but appears to us as the truth.'

On the other hand, glasses are an extraneous adjunct of the person; they are not built in, like eyes: and to that extent the force of Kleist's image — a poet's image we are entitled to scrutinise as to its precise meaning — remains ambiguous.

2.

As soon as we come to Kleist's drama, however, the situation seems clarified at a stroke. In *Die Familie Schroffenstein* we encounter a large body of perceptual imagery. Its fountain-head is to be found in Sylvester's solemn admonition to his wife, Gertrude:

> Das Mißtraun ist die schwarze Sucht der Seele,
> Und alles, auch das Schuldlos-Reine, zieht
> Fürs kranke Aug die Tracht der Hölle an.[a]   (I, 2)

Clearly, the flaw in our vision is envisaged as being inherent in the perceiving eye itself. The diseased eye is part of ourselves, whether we like it or not. We cannot exchange it like a pair of spectacles. Whatever it perceives, it tarnishes with the stain of falsehood; and at the root of this vitiating addiction there lurks distrust.

Yet a diseased eye can be cured. Distrust can be overcome; and the question arises whether the cognitive and human condition, however radically it is articulated in *Die Familie Schroffenstein*, is ultimately a curable condition.

We may describe Kleist's first play as depicting a heroic attempt to remedy the inherent defect of human vision, vitiated as it is by distrust, an attempt overtaken — but only just — by the forces of darkness. Certainly the young poet probes deeply and relentlessly into the disease with which his drama is concerned. The defect he isolates is not just the web of falsehood woven by insufficient knowledge built on superstition or hearsay — such as the ugly rumours surrounding the death of Rupert's little son, Peter, or the corresponding suspicion that Sylvester's youngest, Philip, was poisoned by his uncle, that same Rupert. Such cobwebs of the imagination, however dangerous, can be brushed aside by a resolute will to discover the truth, as is shown by Ottokar when he succeeds in unravelling the true circumstances of his young brother's death.

The true, and worst, defect of human vision is much harder to eradicate. We may approach its definition by saying that we are constrained to see with and through our eyes, but cannot turn our gaze onto the instruments with which we see. The five noblest characters in this play, the lovers, Agnes' father, Ottokar's mother, and their cousin Jeronimus, are all suffering from this impediment; and they fight a running battle to surmount this human failing, in themselves no less than in their respective partners. What is the true nature of the disease they so manfully fight? It is no more than that they see, and evaluate what they see, through the green glasses of their own conditioning: the conditioning of up-

---

[a] Distrust is the black addiction of the soul,/ And everything, even the innocent and pure,/ To the diseasèd eye puts on the garb of hell.

bringing, inbred values and loyalties and of the concrete human context in which they find themselves placed. What partakes of this conditioning to them seems the untinted truth; what falls outside it by reason of being unfamiliar looks askew, warped, tainted. In a letter to Wilhelmine von Zenge written at about the same time as his first drama, Kleist formulates the problem thus: 'Wenn Du den Nebel siehst, der andere Gegenstände verhüllt, aber nicht den, der Dich selbst umgibt, womit ist das zu vergleichen?'[a] (11 [and 12] January 1801). He could not have stated his own problem more graphically.

We may express this predicament through a less elegant metaphor. It is often said that different races are unaware of their own smell, and that only the members of another race smell to them. So it is here. The odour of what is familiar is not perceived; it is only 'the others', the strangers, that appear afflicted with it. In fact, Kleist has made extensive use of olfactory imagery to drive home this partial immunity and equally partial susceptibility of untutored perception: to Rupert, the cousins of Warwand stink; his herald Aldöbern accuses Sylvester of spreading a stench such that his own dogs will not eat out of his hand. The fair minded Jeronimus joins in the hymn of hatred, saying that

> . . . hier in deiner Nähe stinkt es, wie
> Bei Mördern.[b] (I, 2)

And the mad Johann leads the blind Sylvus to Ottokar's corpse, masqueraded in Agnes' clothes, protesting that it is she, for:

> Ich könnt es riechen, denn die Leiche stinkt schon.[c] (V, 1)

We shall meet this and similarly primitive perceptual imagery elsewhere; always its function is to mislead and to underscore, by its very regressiveness, the fatal flaw attaching to perception *per se,* even in its intellectually most high-ranking form of visual perception, as an instrument for the detection of complex orders of emotional and spiritual significance.

In our play, the five characters named are fooled by their very rectitude, a sense of truth that is not yet weaned from conditioning influences too intimately familiar to be perceived. In unquestioning blind loyalty to his father's cause, Ottokar repudiates Jeronimus' 'Gefühl des Rechts' − 'sense of right' − passionately insisting on the uniqueness of his own, and partial, instinct:

> Das Rechtsgefühl! − Als obs ein andres noch
> In einer andern Brust, als dieses, gäbe![d] (I, 1)

---

a 'If you see the mist that shrouds other objects, but not the mist which shrouds you, with what is this comparable?'

b . . . in your proximity there is a stench/ As though of murderers.

c I could smell it, for the corpse already stinks./

d The sense of what is right! − As though there were another/ In another breast, than mine!

In his turn, the fair minded Jeronimus, now swayed this way and now that by what comes to his knowledge, rudely rebuffs Sylvester's protestations of innocence, exclaiming:

> O du Quacksalber der Natur! Denkst du,
> Ich werde dein verfälschtes Herz auf Treu
> Und Glauben zweimal als ein echtes kaufen?[a]   (I, 2)

Quite similarly, Eustache, incredulous of Johann's alleged confession that he made an attempt on Agnes' life, protests:

> Nun über jedwedes Geständnis geht
> Mein innerstes Gefühl doch. −[b]   (III, 2)

'My innermost feeling': here is the yardstick which will assume unconditional validity in Kleist's later creations. Alkmene and Käthchen and Littegarde and the Marquise von O. rely on it, and rightly so; and so will Hermann and Michael Kohlhaas, if in a more problematic vein. In this early play, however, consciousness — the consciousness on which Sylvester places his reliance in the dire attack Jeronimus levels against his integrity — is still prized as the final arbiter of truth; and unconscious instinct — the same instinct which was to become the infallible guide of Kleist's later characters — here is mercilessly stripped of its pretensions and its delusoriness is laid bare[6]. Sylvester seeks to cure the 'diseased eye' of his wife, Gertrude, by demonstrating to her that the slur cast on others, when viewed from the inside as it were, turns out to be as preposterous as the identical suspicion cast by others upon her own familiar self. The cousins from Rossitz as little dreamed of poisoning Gertrude's youngest son as she herself dreamed of smothering their newborn to death. By the same tactics Jeronimus puts Eustache to rights: teaching her, as Sylvester had taught his wife, that the case of the other party is as much in need and deserving of interpretative empathy — that good faith which is required over and above all impartial scrutiny to appraise a human situation — as is one's own. Eustache in her turn, having learned her lesson, by the gentle mercy of her participation all but liberates her alienated husband from feeling blindly incarcerated in his own evilness, as a being *sui generis*.

3.

It is, however, in the young lovers that the poet has most fully shown the education — or shall we say, the enlightenment — of senses that are as yet unweaned from the promptings of blind instinct. This educational process takes place in two distinct stages: the one, before the lovers know one another's

---

[a] O you mountebank of Nature! Do you think/ That I shall purchase your adulterated heart/
[b] For one that's true, in good faith, twice?
My inmost feeling does outweigh/ All mere confessions. −

identity, the other following upon its disclosure. In the first phase, Ottokar
impetuously woos the unknown girl, reaching out for a full and direct communion
between their souls.

> Nun will ich heiter, offen, wahr
> Wie deine Seele mit dir reden. Komm!
> Es darf kein Schatten dich mehr decken, nicht
> Der mindeste, ganz klar will ich dich sehen.
> Dein Innres ists mir schon, die ungebornen
> Gedanken kann ich wie dein Gott erraten.[a]   (II, 1)

Later he will nostalgically look back upon this phase, saying:

> Deine Seele
> Lag offen vor mir, wie ein schönes Buch . . .   (III, 1)
> . . .
> Nun bist du
> Ein verschloßner Brief.[b]   (ibid.)

This is what, in the opening chapter of this book, I have called 'the subjective
fallacy': the belief that in the phenomenal world an unmediated, direct contact
between noumenal entities is conceivable. One thinks one hears Jupiter pleading
to commune with Alkmene, or Graf Wetter vom Strahl.

In a vacuum − the lovers know no more of one another than that they do not,
or so they think, belong to the warring branches of the Schroffenstein clan − such
perfect communion seems easy to achieve. They are God's own children, both of
them, with the same heritage of early impressions, the same untainted ideals and
beliefs, the same capacity for love. In fact, they are members of the human family.
What could possibly stand between them? Ottokar continues thus:

> Dein Zeichen nur, die freundliche Erfindung
> Mit einer Silbe das Unendliche
> Zu fassen, nur den Namen sage mir.[c]   (II, 1)

'What's in a name?' Here, as in every other work from Kleist's pen, it is more
than 'a sweet device to grasp the infinite within the confines of one syllable'[7].
Identity is the dread cypher for an infinity of impediments that remorselessly
build up walls too high to scale: the impediment of each person's phenomenal self
with its corona of race, culture or family, a conditioning to a personal context so
all-pervading that it is not even felt as such, which yet separates the self by an all
but unsurmountable barrier from the other who is similarly enveloped in a corona
of his own.

---

[a] Now I would freely, truly, happ'ly/ Converse with you as though I were your soul.
Come!/ Let no more shadow hide you, not/ The least, I would see all of you./ Your
inner self I know, and I can read/ Your unborn thoughts as though I were your God.

[b] Your soul lay/ Bared before me like a lovely book . . ./ . . ./ Now you are/ A letter
that is sealed.

[c] Only your sign − that sweet device/ To grasp the infinite within the confines of/ One
syllable − only your name betray.

This essential separateness of the individual, in his letter to his fiançée so succinctly expressed through the analogy of atmospheric pollution, Kleist has articulated in this, his first drama through the imagery of dress or garb. Dressed is how others see us, yet the dress is an accidental adjunct to the person; it is no more than appearance. Johannes, Ottokar's friend and confidant, saw Agnes in all the glory of her nakedness when he surprised her bathing in a stream. Even when she returned to him clothed, she was but *verhüllt* and bound up his wounds – he had been thrown by his horse – with a translucent veil. The veil which barely shrouds the true self: this is Agnes' symbol. Indeed when the lovers, alone in a hostile world, in total trust surrender to each other what they have and what they are, they will exchange clothes as a symbolic token of being transparent to one another.

Yet how impenetrable a weave is the 'habit' woven by the distrust and suspicion of the isolated self – the very suspicion the lovers will as yet have to face up to and shed before they are ready for their final communion. Sylvester finds the words for it in a solemn warning addressed to his wife to which I have already alluded, the fountain-head of this metaphoric pattern, too:

> Das Mißtraun ist die schwarze Sucht der Seele,
> Und alles, auch das Schuldlos-Reine, zieht
> Fürs kranke Aug die Tracht der Hölle an.
> Das Nichtsbedeutende, Gemeine, ganz
> Alltägliche, spitzfündig, wie zerstreute
> Zwirnfäden, wirds zu einem Bild verknüpft,
> Das uns mit gräßlichen Gestalten schreckt . . .[a]   (I, 2)

No sooner have the lovers circumnavigated the Scylla of trusting in a void than they come up against the Charybdis of having to preserve that trust in and through the fog of conditioning that surrounds them, isolating each from the other. In their second encounter, they know one another's identity, and that genial invention – the names they bear – has opened up a chasm threatening to engulf their love's infinity. They must now face 'the entirely common, the absolutely humdrum' – their background and those mutual suspicions each branch of the family has woven around the image of the other, and around their own souls, shrouding them from the truth. And now, almost without a transition, the subjective fallacy of desiring an unmediated rapport gives way to its obverse – the objective fallacy, which altogether transplants the intuitive knowledge of relatedness by the analytical intelligence placing its reliance on observable fact. Agnes who had so truly sensed the presence of the Numinous in the strange youth –

---

[a] Distrust is the black addiction of the soul,/ And everything, even the innocent and pure,/ To the diseasèd eye puts on the garb of hell./ The insignificant, the common, the humdrum,/ Like single threads is subtly laced into a weave/ That frightens us with terrifying shapes.

Sein Antlitz
Gleicht einem milden Morgenungewitter,
Sein Aug dem Wetterleuchten auf den Höhn,
Sein Haar den Wolken, welche Blitze bergen,
Sein Nahen ist ein Wehen aus der Ferne,
Sein Reden wie ein Strömen von den Bergen
Und sein Umarmen − [a]   (II, 1)

− Agnes now suspects Ottokar of wanting to take her life. And even when she has
recognised her error and calls herself his own 'in the most extravagant meaning
of the word', even when Ottokar confirms this pledge, saying

Wohl, das steht nun fest und gilt
Für eine Ewigkeit . . . [b]   (III, 1)

the deepest pitfalls of the lovers' alienation still lie ahead; and Ottokar is correct
when he concludes his statement by saying 'We shall need it'. For now each
suspects the other's father of a closely similar crime: Ottokar suspects Agnes'
father, Sylvester, of having engineered the murder of his young brother; Agnes in
turn suspects Ottokar's father, Rupert, of having prevailed upon the unbalanced
Johann to make an attempt on her life; and beneath the debris of this recent
suspicion there smoulders the older one relating to the nature of her own young
brother's death.

The lovers' confrontation is conducted with a relentless logic, and with an
acumen of verbal repartee which may well owe something of its brilliance to the
central dialogue in Lessing's *Minna von Barnhelm*. The young lovers are
encamped, each on its side. Each is equally identified with its own parent and its
own conditioning, refusing to believe of its own begetter what it readily credits
the other's with having perpetrated. The interpretative empathy which exonerates
what is familiar is withheld from the strangers who are scrutinised from without.
It is as though the eye were healthy in perceiving one set of facts and diseased
vis-à-vis another that is its precise replica. Agnes repudiates the charge that her
father has killed Ottokar's young brother with the same solemn vehemence with
which Ottokar had earlier on protested his own father's innocence and in much
the same strains in which, in the scene following, Ottokar's mother will protest
the innocence of Johann. For all that the alleged murderers of Ottokar's brother
Peter have confessed to having been hirelings of her parent, she dismisses such
evidence as ludicrous, arguing:

Mich überzeugt es nicht.
Denn etwas gibt es, das über alles Wähnen,
Und Wissen hoch erhaben − das Gefühl
Ist es der Seelengüte andrer. [c]   (III, 1)

---

[a] His face/ Is like a passing tempest in the morn,/ His eye sheet-lightning from the
mountain peaks,/ His hair like clouds that harbour thunderbolts,/ His coming is a
stirring from afar,/ His speech is like a streaming from the hills/ And his embrace −

[b] Good, that is for sure now, valid/ For an eternity −

[c] This is no proof to me./ For there is something which transcends by far/ All that we
think and know − the instinct/ For another's shining worth.

Strange: in every later play or story from Kleist's pen these words would have the unmistakable ring of the truth. This is not so here. There have been too many similarly highflown expostulations, and all have been shown up for the onesided distortions that they are and exploded. It is as though Kleist, in this early play, pledged as yet to the ideal of consciousness, were parodying the most sacred sentiments of his later creations. At any rate, if Agnes is 'not convinced', neither are we, nor indeed is Ottokar. For the youth retorts:

> Höchstens
> Gilt das für dich. Denn nicht du wirst verlangen,
> Daß ich mit deinen Augen sehen soll.
> . . .
>   Wirst nicht verlangen, daß
> Ich meinem Vater weniger, als du
> Dem deinen, traue.[a] (III, 1)

Each continues to take sides. A little later, Agnes frames her counter-accusation: Rupert has incited Johann, Ottokar's friend, to take her life. All evidence notwithstanding, Ottokar protests Johann's innocence, exactly as convincingly or unconvincingly as Agnes has done before him, saying:

> O Gott, das ist ein Irrtum — sieh, das weiß,
> Das weiß ich.[b] *(ibid.)*

And as he retorted before, so now she retorts in her turn, paying him back his own coin:

> Ei, das ist doch seltsam. Soll
> Ich nun mit deinen Augen sehn?
> . . .
>
> Soll *ich* nun deinem Vater mehr,
> Als du dem meinen traun?[c] *(ibid.)*

The stalemate is patent; and the workings in the young people's minds are made plain as much by what they say as by the long silences that punctuate their tentative probings into each other's predicament. Having led one another *ad absurdum*, each now makes the other perceive the exact parallel of his own case seen with the eye of familiarity and love, with that of the other tinted with the aura of strangeness and suspicion; and each teaches the other, if not to see with a borrowed pair of eyes, then at least to abstract from the blind spot he has for what is familiar in his *own* vision and to encompass the other's cause with respect and

---

[a] At most/ This goes for you. For you will not expect/ That I perceive through your eyes./ . . ./ Will not expect that/ I trust my own Father less,/ Than you do yours.
[b] O God, this is an error — that I know,/ I know it.
[c] Now, is that not strange? Am I/ Now to perceive through your eyes?/ . . ./ Am *I* to trust your father more,/ Than you do mine?

love for *his*[8]. The result is Ottokar's characteristically impetuous pipe-dream that the warring fathers see one another face to face as he and Agnes do:

> — Und schuldlos, wie sie sind, müßt ohne Rede
> Sogleich ein Aug das andere verstehn.[a]   *(ibid.)*

4.

As we know, things do not turn out that idyllically. Ottokar's father nurses his 'diseased eye' and prefers to cling to his evil vision of the other even at the cost of himself appearing, and becoming, more evil than he might be. Bad faith creates self-validating wicked fact. Similarly — the play is full of technically awkward yet formidably compelling parallelisms and reversals[9] — Agnes' mother insists on cleaving to untutored perception vitiated by prejudice and, in a characteristically Kleistean tantrum, abandons all faith in human nature, instead opting for a distrust that suspects poison in the very apple Ottokar might pluck for his beloved (and we may say that already here the apple — Adam's apple and Eve's — signifies that disastrous regression to a primitive perceptual mode in a complex spiritual situation demanding finer cognitive tools which it will continue to signify in this poet's creative imagination). Jeronimus, the fair minded, is literally torn to pieces, wedged as he is between the blindly warring parties, and even Sylvester's slow patience, taxed beyond its powers of endurance, gives way to a thunderous rage. By accident and design, the powers of evil prevail. Having only just learned to see truly, in an enlightened fashion, the lovers must now learn an altogether new kind of perception, the perception of unevidenced faith in total darkness:

> Es kommt, du weißt,
> Den Liebenden das Licht nur in der Nacht . . .[b]   (V, 1)

Ottokar says as, in a curiously chaste and voluptuous love-scene, he undresses Agnes so as to disguise her in his own clothes from his father's wrath. In the end the lovers are slain, each by his parent whose clouded vision sees the enemy even in his own, and last, child. This double murder which destroys the self in the other is the first of many orgies of Kleist's imagination in which the folly of physical perception in a situation demanding eyeless faith celebrates its dismal triumph. The bestiality of the end bears out the threat held out at the beginning, the threat that we move in a world which is as unnatural as are animals that talk:

> Doch nichts mehr von Natur.
> Ein hold ergötzend Märchen ists der Kindheit,
> Der Menschheit von den Dichtern, ihren Ammen,
> Erzählt. Vertrauen, Unschuld, Treue, Liebe,

---

[a] And guiltless as they are, one eye should without speech/ Fathom the other's meaning without fail.

[b] For lovers, as you know,/ The light shines only in the night . . .

Religion, der Götter Furcht sind wie
Die Tiere, welche reden — [a]   (I, 1)

as Rupert has it in the introductory scene of the drama. We must take this simile seriously. It is a dehumanised world through which this poet leads us, perhaps a prehuman one, the world of Penthesilea and Thusnelda and Nicolo, who may well be styled talking animals.

5.

And yet in the midst of this inferno there are the suffering figures of Jeronimus and Sylvester and Eustache, who have conquered the 'disease of their eye' and have learned to see with impartial gentleness. Most of all there are the lovers, who have refined their powers of empathic perception to the point where they see with one another's eyes, and who have in a treacherous world thrown even that tempered instrument to the winds and entrusted themselves to unseeing faith.

It is in such total surrender to one another that the young ones attain their true identity, even as it is in the dark cave in the middle of nowhere that they find their first true home: a merging, and emergence, of self and other which is foreshadowed in the solemn baptism Agnes receives at Ottokar's hands, and confirmed by their sacrificial change of clothes at the end. Relatedness, naming and true perception: this triad of developmental processes which is established in Genesis 3 we find here, in Kleist's first play. Such strengthening of the self through communion with the other we seldom meet in Kleist's world, a world filled with characters as profoundly unrelated to one another as they are undeveloped in their selfhood, for all the vehemence with which they protest it. This early supportive relation here is the prototype of the relationship to which Alkmene will win over Amphitryon, which Trota will establish with Littegarde, into which, at the end of a long and dark passage, Natalie will woo Prinz Friedrich von Homburg, those luminous figures whom no death can part. It is on the basis of having received their own self from the other, in the first instance, that these lovers can say, with Schiller's Thekla:

Wie du dir selbst getreu bleibst, bist du's mir. [b]

And indeed, as in Kleist's swansong, so it is already here: from the communion of lovers in total trust there flowers the faith of the individual. In faith a new organ of cognition is disclosed. This is what Ottokar says when, through his unfaltering trust in Agnes, he has been empowered to find the solution to his brother's death and with it, the assurance of benign powers at the helm of life.

---

[a] No more of nature now./ It is a pleasant tale/ Told by the nursemaids of men's infancy,/ The poets. Trust, loyalty and innocence and love,/ Religion and the fear of God, they are/ Like talking beasts —

[b] To thine own self be true, and so to mine.

Wiege
Mich, Hoffnung, einer Schaukel gleich, und gleich
Als spielt' geschloßnen Auges schwebend mir
Ein Windzug um die offne Brust, so wende
Mein Innerstes sich vor Entzücken. − ᵃ   (IV, 3)

The closed eyes, the floating sensation, the breeze, the transport: we shall meet
them all again in Kleist's last drama. Such were the synaesthetic images that came
to this poet when he gave utterance to the immediate knowledge of faith in his
first drama and his last, at the beginning of his career when he envisaged life as a
voyage and then again at the end when he speaks of himself and his companion in
death as 'zwei fröhliche Luftschiffer', dreaming of 'lauter himmlische Fluren und
Sonnen, in deren Schimmer wir, mit langen Flügeln an den Schultern, umherwandeln werden.'ᵇ

6.

In the last analysis, then, even such enlightened perception as is vouchsafed to us in
our saner moments does not avail. And not only because the labyrinthine
convolutions of life and relationships, too recondite to be decipherable by
perception, demand a plunge into unseeing and unreasoning trust, but also
because the challenge of death keeps us on a knife-edge between despair and
unsupported faith. We cannot conquer death with our seeing eyes.

This crisis of faith, the utter incomprehensibility of survival in the face of
physical corruption, Kleist has articulated in the second scene of his first play, in
the breath-taking conversation of Agnes − a mere child like Juliet, uninitiated as
yet into life and unconfirmed − with her blind grandfather.

Agnes confesses that she must weep at the thought of her dead brother even as
she must laugh when there is something laughable. Her response to death is as
automatic as any reflex-action. It is true that the priest says that Philip is happy
wherever 'he' is − in his grave? not in his grave? she cannot tell − but she cannot
believe the priest: by the unanswerable logic of cause and effect, when she sees his
grave she must think of his dead body:

Ich seh es, wo er ist, am Hügel. Denn
Woher, der Hügel?ᶜ   (I, 2)

After a pause, the grandfather − he is blind and cannot see what she sees − replies
that maybe the priest is right after all. He confidently believes in what he says:

− Agnes, der Pater hat doch recht. Ich glaubs
Mit Zuversicht.ᵈ   (ibid.)

ᵃ Cradle,/ O hope, me like a swing and e'en as though,/ Eyes firmly closed, a gentle
breeze caressed my barèd breast,/ Let my heart in my bosom turn for bliss. −
ᵇ 'two happy aeronauts dreaming of nothing but heavenly pastures and suns in whose
radiance we shall walk, with long pinions at our shoulders.'
ᶜ I see where he is from the mound. For whence/ The mound?
ᵈ Agnes, the Father speaks the truth. I believe't/ With every confidence.

At which Agnes retorts with a logic that betrays a young and as yet mechanistic mind:

> Mit Zuversicht? Das ist
> Doch seltsam. Ja, da möcht es freilich doch
> Wohl anders sein, wohl anders. Denn woher
> Die Zuversicht?[a]

In the end the paradox between the visible and the invisible worlds, between brute physical fact perceived with the senses and unseen significances that laugh the facts in the face, is absolute. To believe you have to close your eyes or, better still, be blind[10].

7.

Up to a point, the young poet with his *Lebensplan* who wrote *Die Familie Schroffenstein* believed in the education and enlightenment of senses that are a prey to the subjectivity of human vision. The lovers and the three just elders around them hold out, in some measure, a panacea for the diseased eye that the acquaintance with Kant had disclosed to him. *That* disease, in this early play, had not yet taken on the hideous form it was to assume later, when the imprisonment of the percipient in his own conditioning was to become so total as to make any relatedness at all a virtually impossible feat.

But beneath the tempered optimism of the young rationalist there lay *another*, older and tougher problem waiting to knock at the door of his consciousness, a problem to which he was born and which caught him unawares, even in this early play. It is the problem expressed in Tertullian's tenet *certum est quia impossibile*: the sheer absurdity of a faith in an invisible numinous reality paradoxically proclaimed in the teeth of physical impossibility. It is a paradox assuming many shapes, and around it Kleist's literal mind was restlessly to circle for the duration of his brief creative span. He envisaged it in the mysterious visitations suffered by Alkmene and the Marquise von O. – giddying modern metaphors for the perplexing plight of the Holy Virgin; he invoked it twice in *Die Verlobung in St. Domingo*, where an act of transcendent good faith wears the mask of the bitterest betrayal, Peter's betrayal of Christ; and he gave it final utterance in the Prinz von Homburg's unfaltering vision of his resurrected self as the ghostly leader of the elector's army and as the ghostly lover of his widowed bride.

For Kleist, a doubting Thomas if ever there was one, the absurdity of an empirically unsupported paradoxical faith represented a strain so severe as to be curable, in the last analysis, only by the crowning absurdity of an intoxicated death. Here, in this early work, Kleist broached the challenge of the absurd which was to break him and to make him with that same timorous humility with which his Agnes answers the grandfather's probing question as to whether she believes:

> Ich wills erst lernen, Vater.[b]   (I, 2)

---

[a] With confidence? That is/ Astonishing. Ah well, then things are different/ so it seems. quite different. For whence/ The confidence?

[b] I would fain learn it, Father.

4 A Young Man's Articles of Faith: Kleist's early Letters and the 'Kant-Crisis'

1.

It is usually maintained that the Kant-crisis burst upon Kleist suddenly and March 1801, the time at which he wrote the decisive letters to his fiancée Wilhelmine von Zenge and to his half-sister Ulrike, is cited as the precise date. This critical fiction is convenient enough, since in these letters Kleist gives unequivocal utterance to his sense of annihilation *vis-à-vis* the *Alles Zermalmenden*. Yet they must be seen as embedded in their context: not only does Kleist request a volume of Kant from Ulrike as early as August 14, 1800 and allude to his philosophy in September of that year, but also, for all his protestations of distress, he repeatedly mentions his plan to go to France there to spread the new gospel, at the time immediately following his *cri de cœur*. All this is well known. What it means, however, is that what we tend to envisage as an abrupt break had been simmering in the poet before it finally surfaced; and after a short acute phase it retreated to become one element of unrest amongst others, and one which Kleist himself, for a while at least, rated ambivalently and by no means only negatively.

If such facts argue for a measure of continuity of development beneath what appears as a sudden trauma, so do Kleist's early letters as a whole, and their imagery in particular. There is much in this imagery that prepares us for the outburst that is to follow, much even that helps us interpret it along lines that are somewhat deviant from traditional readings. If we approach these fateful documents carefully and genetically, we may see how deeply the crisis for which Kant acted as a catalyst in fact was embedded in the poet's own psyche, and may come to regard it and its repercussions as a break no less essentially Kleistean than the many others that were to follow it. Thus to interpret the encounter with Kant as a highlight in a continuous personal development, and to do so through close attention to the verbal fabric in terms of which it is related, is the purpose of this chapter.

In the crucial letter of this period, the one to Wilhelmine dated March 21, 1801, Kleist articulates his most sacred articles of faith, the belief, to date, in human perfectibility and in the immortality of the soul. He has rested all his hopes upon the expectation

> 'daß wir den Schatz von Wahrheiten, den wir hier sammelten, auch dort einst brauchen könnten. Aus diesen Gedanken bildete sich so nach und nach eine eigne Religion . . . *Bildung* schien mir als das einzige Ziel, das des Bestrebens, *Wahrheit* der einzige Reichtum, der des Besitzes würdig ist . . . Mir waren sie so heilig, daß ich diesen beiden Zwecken, Wahrheit zu sammeln, und Bildung mir zu erwerben, die *kostbarsten* Opfer brachte'[a].

Later in the letter, after having explained to Wilhelmine that, according to Kant, we cannot ever be sure that what we know is the truth, he continues: 'Ist das letzte, so *ist* die Wahrheit, die wir hier sammeln, nach dem Tode nicht mehr — und alles Bestreben, ein Eigentum sich zu erwerben, das uns auch in das Grab folgt, ist vergeblich —'[b].

This passage is stylistically remarkably homogeneous. It clearly stems from a deep-rooted conception consistently envisaged in terms of a unified metaphorical complex. The word *sammeln* — collect — used with relation to self-education and truth recurs three times, and its literal, economic connotation is reinforced not only by the twice repeated near-synonym *erwerben* — acquire — but also by the terms employed to denote the object of the exercise: *Schatz* — treasure, *Reichtum* — riches, and *Eigentum* — property — which have cost him dearly — *kostbare Opfer*.

Just how literal Kleist's animating conception is here may be shown by a comparison of his words with a passage from the Bible, that rich quarry of metaphorical thinking. In *Ecclesiastes* we read: 'Whatever thy hand findeth to do, do it with thy might; for there is no work, nor device, nor knowledge, nor wisdom, in the grave whither thou goest.' The writer, it is true, begins with an evocation of physical labour: 'Whatever thy *hand* findeth to do . . .'. But the fruits of such effort are envisaged in a series of formulations that are increasingly abstract: *work* — which is the total undertaking rather than the resultant artefact — *device, knowledge* and even *wisdom* — none of these are to be found in the grave 'whither thou goest'. The author's pessimism is great in that he envisages death as the uncaring leveller of the most incongruous goods, from man's handiwork to his wisdom. By comparison Kleist's words evince a different kind of poignancy which derives, precisely, from their stark primitiveness. He entirely fails to draw the distinctions which mark the biblical passage, perhaps even to perceive them. Abstract goods such as self-education and truth are envisaged and expressed with a physical concretion and literalness that makes their perishable nature less of a tragedy and more of a dismal certainty, a foregone conclusion.

One might argue that the economic metaphors Kleist uses to such annihilating effect were dictated by the devastation of the moment and prove no more than the susceptibility to the moment of an ultra-sensitive mind, the mind moreover of a poet[1]. Did Shakespeare not use financial imagery in one of the most finely tempered of his sonnets? That this, however, is not the explanation becomes clear from a perusal of the early letters in their entirety. For these abound with just such concreteness in the handling of abstract concepts; indeed, such is his consistency in treating abstract matters as though they were articles and articles,

---

[a] 'that we might use the treasure of truths which we had gathered here, one day, there, too. By and by a personal religion began to take shape from such notions . . . *Education* to me seemed the one goal worthy of our endeavour, *truth* the one riches worthy of being possessed . . . To me they were so sacred that I made the most *costly* sacrifices for the sake of those twin goals, to gather truth and to acquire education.'

[b] 'If the latter, then the truth we gather here no longer *is* after we die — and all our endeavour to acquire a property that follows us into our grave, is but vanity —'.

invariably, of the same material kind, that one may reasonably doubt that he was at all times aware of the figurative character of a statement which defines nothing less than his spiritual credo. Let me give some examples of this process of hypostasization.

In a long letter to Martini, Kleist attempts to outline his *Lebensplan* and, in order to do so, defines his conception of happiness, a very complex and controversial conception as he himself concedes. Nonetheless he asks: 'wo kann das Glück sich besser gründen, als da, wo auch die Werkzeuge des Genusses, unsere Sinne, liegen' and continues: 'Da ist es auch allein unser Eigentum . . .; kein Tyrann kann es uns rauben, kein Bösewicht es stören; wir tragen es mit uns in alle Weltteile umher.'[a] If one feels a slight shock at reading this passage, it is not so much because of the primitive eudaemonism or, indeed, sensualism it conveys, incongruent though such strains appear in the context of so much cerebrating elsewhere. It is rather because of the precise physical location of happiness in our senses, and the designation of our senses as 'die *Werkzeuge* des Genusses'. The grossness of this metaphor – it ominously adumbrates Thusnelda's use of the same word in her horrifying murder of Ventidius – colours its surroundings: the *Eigentum* – property – which is safe from attack and which we can carry about with us as we please, takes on the tinge of some conveniently sized physical object. This is the connotation which *Eigentum* – a highly emotive word which Kleist frequently uses – henceforth retains. To give one more example: he begs Wilhelmine to be industrious in the business of her self-education so that she may conquer his heart – 'denn Du weißt, daß es das seltsame Eigentum ist, welches man sich nur rauben lassen darf, wenn es Zinsen tragen soll.'[b] (To Wilhelmine von Zenge, March 22, 1801; also the letter to Wilhelmine of January 11 (and 12), 1801.)

Similarly, the plan of Kleist's life and the happiness which is central to that plan, are often designated by the term *Gegenstand*. Of those that muddle through life without any clear objective Kleist writes: 'Alle diese Leute schiffen ins hohe Meer und verlieren nach und nach die Küste mit ihren Gegenständen aus den Augen'[c] (to Martini, March 18 (and 19) 1799): a curiously vacuous word, especially when used in the plural, as here, expressive of nothing but the object-status of the abstract concept he is discussing. Analogously, in one of those tedious educational tracts Kleist was in the habit of writing to his long-suffering fiancée, he raises the question: which of the partners in a marriage loses most at the other's decease? The operative word in an argument concerned to assess the amount of happiness contributed by man and wife respectively, is, again,

---

a 'where indeed can happiness be more securely grounded than in that sphere in which the tools of enjoyment, our senses, are lodged'. 'There alone it is our property . . . no tyrant can rob us of it, no villain can disturb it; we carry it around with us to the four corners of the earth.'

b 'For you know it is that strange property of which one has only to permit oneself to be robbed for it to accumulate interest.'

c 'Such people embark on the high seas and gradually lose the coast and its objects out of sight'

Gegenstand. Five times does he reiterate it in statements of the type '. . . daß folglich das Glück des Weibes zwar ein wichtiger und unerlaßlicher, aber nicht der *einzige* Gegenstand des Mannes, das Glück des Mannes hingegen der *alleinige* Gegenstand der Frau ist . . .'ᵃ (May 30, 1800). One could not by any stretch of the imagination maintain that Kleist envisages his and poor Wilhelmine's happiness concretely, that is to say, in the lively fashion one might expect of a poet. On the contrary, it is as abstract as an algebraic equation and as plodding as a clumsy proof; but again the complex conception of marital happiness has, under his hands, become hypostasized, that is to say, has assumed the status of an object.

We have already noted the strong economic associations of Kleist's imagery, not only in the crucial Kantletter, but also in the strange definition proffered to his fiancée of the heart as 'that strange property of which one has to permit oneself to be robbed for it to accumulate interest'. There is undoubtedly a reality basis for such imagery: Kleist was poor and in constant financial trouble, and what with his highflown aims and the early decision to try his luck as a freelance writer, money assumed an exaggerated importance in his mind. In the early letter to Martini from which I have already quoted, he writes:

> 'Ein zufälliger Umstand schützt mich vor dem tiefsten Elende, vor Hunger und Blöße in Krankheiten. Ich habe ein kleines Vermögen, das mir in dieser Rücksicht – und weil es mir manchen Vorteil für meine Bildung verschaffen kann – sehr teuer ist, und das ich mir, aus diesem Grunde, möglichst zu erhalten strebe.'ᵇ

How lame and prosaic is this *teuer*, chosen to express what his capital means to him as a *human* being, how imprisoned it remains in the *material* sphere!

The generosity of his friend Brockes – who, as he writes to Ulrike, invested 200 Thaler on their joint mission to Würzburg (later, in a retrospective account of the trip to Wilhelmine the sum stated is 600 Thaler [January 31, 1801]) – accordingly rated high in Kleist's estimation of his friend's character, as did Ulrike's unfailing magnanimity in her stepbrother's affection. This is perfectly understandable. More remarkable is the completeness with which the practical and the emotional spheres merge, and the consequent wholesale transfer of images belonging to the former, to the latter. There seems to be no awareness of any incongruity nor, indeed, any accompanying sense that what has literal force in its own context takes on a metaphorical status when it becomes transferred to the emotional sphere. Summarising Brockes' helpfulness, Kleist writes to Wilhelmine: 'So teuer, Wilhelmine, ward unser Glück erkauft. Werden wir nicht auch etwas tun müssen, es zu verdienen?'ᶜ And, in the same letter: '– ja, Wilhelmine, sagte

---

ᵃ '. . . that consequently a woman's happiness, for all that it is an important and indispensable object of the man, is not his *sole* object, whilst conversely a man's happiness is the *exclusive* object of the woman . . .'

ᵇ 'A fortuitous circumstance protects me from the utmost wretchedness, from hunger and dire need in case of illness. I have a small capital which is very dear to me for this reason – and because it may be advantageous to me in my efforts to educate myself – and which on this account I seek to keep untouched as far as is ever possible.'

ᶜ 'Such was the price at which our happiness was purchased. Shall we not have to do something on our part to earn it?'

ich nicht, daß unser Glück teuer erkauft ward? Jetzt können wir es verdienen.'[a] (January 31, 1801). But it is not merely through their more or less direct association with factual concerns that abstract conceptions such as happiness or self-education are hypostasized and make their appearance in proprietory and monetary metaphors. Take the following instance from a letter to Ulrike in which he expresses his pleasure at being able to share his ideals with her, and being admired for them: 'Willst Du es doch eine Schwäche nennen,' he writes,

'so ist es höchstens die Schwäche eines Münzensammlers z. B. der zwar hauptsächlich für sich und zu seinem Vergnügen, zu seinem Nutzen sammelte, und daher auch nicht zürnt, wenn die meisten gleichgültig bei seiner sorgfältig geordneten Sammlung vorübergehen, aber eben deswegen um so viel lieber einmal einen Freund der Kunst in sein Kabinett führt. Denn meine Absichten und meine Entschlüsse sind solche Schaumünzen, die aus dem Gebrauche gekommen sind und nicht mehr gelten; daher zeige ich sie gern zuweilen einem Kenner der Kunst, damit er sie prüfe und mich überzeuge, ob, was ich so emsig und eifrig sammle und aufbewahre, auch wohl echte Stücke sind, oder nicht.'[b] (November 12, 1799).

What strikes the reader as incongruous here is not the emphatic fivefold reiteration of *sammeln* or its synonyms, nor the metaphor of the collector's coin, all of which form one coherent verbal pattern: it is the word *Kunst* which seems to have inexplicably strayed into a closed semantic system in which matters of the spirit have no part.

Again, there is the letter to Wilhelmine in which he exhorts her to observe the phenomena around her and to practise the art of seeing, and making, similes. She is to write them down at once: 'Denn *festhalten* müssen wir, was wir uns selbst *erworben* haben'[c]; and, clearly hinting at his *Ideenmagazin* − his file of ideas − he expatiates on his exhortation as follows:

'. . . wenn gar ein ganzer Tag ohne solche *moralische Revenüen* vergeht, und wenn gar ganze Wochen ohne solche Einkünfte verstreichen, − dann − dann − − Ja, mein liebes Minchen, ein Kapital müssen wir haben, und wenn es kein *Geld* ist, so muß es *Bildung* sein, denn mit dem Körper können wir wohl darben, aber mit dem *Geiste* müssen wir es niemals, niemals − und wovon sollen wir leben, wenn wir nicht bei Zeiten sammeln?'[d] (November 16 and 18, 1800).

----

a '− aye, Wilhelmine, did I not say that our happiness was purchased dearly? Now we may earn it.'

b 'If you insist on calling it a foible, it is at the most the foible of, say, a coin-collector who, it is true, for the most part collects for himself, for his own pleasure or his own use, and for that reason does not take offence if most people indifferently pass by his carefully arranged collection, but who is all the more delighted, for that very reason, to show his cabinet to the occasional connoisseur of his art. For my aims and resolutions are such collector's pieces which are out of currency and represent no market value; hence I like now and then to show them to one who is an expert in the art, for him to test them and convince me whether, what I so assiduously and eagerly collect and keep, are genuine pieces or not.'

c 'For we must *hold fast* to what we have ourselves *acquired*'

d '. . . when as much as a whole day passes by without such *moral revenues*, when even whole weeks go by without such earnings, − then − then − − To be sure, my dear

As with his artistic and intellectual aspirations — *Bildung* — so with his emotional expectations and dreams of fulfilment — *Glück*. Brockes and he, so he writes from Würzburg, seek 'unsre Absicht' — he means his cure — 'so wohlfeil als möglich zu erkaufen'[a] (September 20, 1800). The postal coach is standing outside the door, he writes on the journey, yet — and this is an entirely characteristic touch of Kleistean teasing[2] — he is taking his letter to Wilhelmine along with him, ever further away from her. For '. . . das Porto ist teuer und *wir beide* müssen für ganzes Geld auch das ganze Vergnügen genießen'[b] (September 4 (and 5), 1800). In a similar vein he regrets that a path has been constructed for easier access to a ruined castle on a rock: 'Man will sich den Genuß erkaufen, "wärs auch mit einem Tropfen Schweißes nur"' he comments, and, significantly, adds: 'Du bist mir noch einmal so lieb geworden, seitdem ich um Deinetwillen reise'[c] (September 3 and 4, 1800).

When Kleist divulges his intention to become a writer to his fiancée, he formulates this confession as follows:

> 'Ich selbst habe mir schon ein kleines Ideenmagazin angelegt . . . Ich vergrößere es täglich. Wenn Du auch einen kleinen Beitrag dazu liefertest, so könntest Du den Stolz haben, zu einem künftigen Erwerb auch etwas beizutragen. — Verstehst Du mich? —'[d] (November 16 and 18, 1800).

Is he talking literally or metaphorically? There is no saying.

Back from Würzburg, he receives a letter from Wilhelmine which pleases him especially because it is written 'aus Deinem Herzen zu meinem Herzen' — 'from your heart to mine'; and promptly proceeds to exhort her to continue improving herself and to rob him 'of that strange property', the heart, rather than force him to remain faithful to her for duty's sake, which would make him utterly wretched: 'Daher kann ein Wechsler die Echtheit der Banknote, die sein Vermögen sichern soll, nicht ängstlicher untersuchen, als ich Deine Seele'[e] (January 11 and 12, 1801).

What does such language signify? As Kleist hypostasizes abstract concepts, so too, he reifies relationships. Wilhelmine becomes an object to scrutinise and assess and possess like a collector's piece or a banknote. In fact, he decides not to study law because he has heard the question discussed whether contracts of love, being made in a state of passion, can be held to be binding.

Minchen, a capital we must have, and if it is not *money*, let it be *education*, since our bodies may well go without sustenance, but never, never our *minds* — and what are we to live by, if we do not save while we may?'

a 'to purchase what we are after as cheaply as we may'

b ' . . . the postage is costly and we must *both* enjoy our pleasure in full if we are to pay in full'

c 'One wants to purchase one's enjoyment, "were it but with a drop of sweat"' 'You have become twice as dear to me since I have begun to travel for your sake.'

d 'I myself have started on a little file of ideas which I enlarge day by day. If you, too, could add to it some small contribution, you would have the pride of knowing that you were contributing something towards a future income. Do you get my meaning?'

e 'Hence a money-changer cannot scrutinise the genuineness of the banknote which is to secure his fortune more anxiously than I scrutinise your soul.'

'und was soll ich von einer Wissenschaft halten, die sich den Kopf darüber zerbricht ob es ein Eigentum in der Welt gibt, und die mir daher nur zweifeln lehren würde, ob ich Sie auch wohl jemals auch mit Recht *die Meine* nennen darf? Nein, nein, Wilhelmine, nicht die Rechte will ich studieren, . . . an die Rechte meines Herzens will ich mich halten'[a], (beginning of 1800)

he protests like the fervent disciple of Rousseau that he is; yet it is precisely the doubts as to the legality of his proprietorship of her — his *Eigentum* — which have frightened him off the study of law. And we may well ask whether the need to experience the loved person as an object, a *Gegen-stand* or *Eigen-tum*, is not so pressing because it takes such a verifiable possession to confirm a self-hood which is but rudimentary and precariously established[3].

Our initial suggestion that Kleist's Kant letter operates with materials which derive from a phase prior to this particular catalyst, is beginning to gain some force. His whole spiritual and emotional stance is that of an obsessive collector and hoarder. And so too our initial hunch that his *cri de cœur*, in the same letter, that the treasures we have collected do not follow us into the grave is significantly different from the statement of *Ecclesiastes* seems to be justified. The distinctions so carefully observed by the biblical author between material and spiritual goods in the case of Kleist are consistently slurred. As abstract concepts are hypostasized, i.e. endowed with thing-character, so too persons and relationships are reified; and the result of diverse *immaterial values* being thus indiscriminately treated as though they were all alike *material goods* is the painful experience of their radical perishableness.

2.

Indeed, the full force of Kleist's wholesale reduction of ideas and feelings to the status of thinghood as yet remains to be explored. Turning over the pages of letters which concern themselves with his life's plan and intimations of the truth, one comes upon a standing and strangely static vocabulary in which words such as *gründen, sicher, unwandelbar, unterstützen* and indeed *Ziel* — to ground, secure, immutable, support, goal — figure with remarkable frequency, complemented on the other side by expressions such as *unsicher, schwankend* or *wankend, sinken* or *zweideutig* — insecure, wavering or tottering, sink, equivocal. They form the background of a verbal mosaic as it were, out of which the crucial sentence of the Kant letters 'Mein einziges, mein höchstes Ziel ist gesunken'[b] (22 March 1801), gradually materialises and meets our eye. And again we are struck by the static quality and the sheer physicality of his conception of the ideal: it might be roughly described as a sturdy and soaring column resisting wind and weather because it is driven deep into the ground, and secured by firm supports. Again his aspirations are compacted and exteriorised into an object, a *vis-à-vis*, from whose stable

---

[a] 'and what am I to think of a science that gives itself headaches in trying to decide whether there is such a thing as property in the world, only to make me doubt whether I may ever legitimately call you *mine*? No, no, Wilhelmine, I don't want to study law, . . . I want to abide by the rights of my heart'
[b] 'My sole, my loftiest goal is laid low'

'otherness' a very rudimentary self derives the maximal support. To appreciate the robustness and staying power of this ego prop, one would have to take note of the complementary images associated with water, which is unfailingly represented as *schwankend, wankend* or *sinkend* – mutable, wavering or sinking: the tie-up between this uncertain element and his own labile self is patent: 'In mir ist nichts beständig, als die Unbeständigkeit'[a], he is supposed to have said of himself; and so, too, we find him remarking to Wilhelmine: 'Sei zufrieden mit diesen wenigen Zügen aus meinem Innern. Es ist darin so wenig bestimmt, daß ich mich fürchten muß etwas aufzuschreiben, weil es dadurch in gewisser Art bestimmt *wird*'[b]. (June 3, 1801)

If ideals may justifiably be envisaged as stationary, relationships must maintain their identity in a more dynamic fashion, that is to say, through their capacity to respond to the changing demands of the moment. It is in his handling of the ebb and flow of emotional relationships that Kleist's need to create a stable object world around him which shall be a prop to a precarious self becomes most patently apparent.

He invariably treats beloved persons and the interplay of feelings between him and them as though they were stationary outside objects capable of being tested, scrutinised and measured, in exactly the way in which physical objects are investigated by the scientific method. In a cutting diatribe against all intellectual onesidedness – a strain that recurs persistently since the days of his close companionship with Brockes on the Würzburg expedition – he writes:

> 'Ich glaube, daß *Newton* an dem Busen eines Mädchens nichts anderes sah, als seine krumme Linie, und daß ihm an ihrem Herzen nichts merkwürdig war, als sein Kubikinhalt. Bei den Küssen seines Weibes denkt ein echter Chemiker nichts, als daß ihr Atem Stickgas und Kohlenstoffgas ist'[c]. (July 29, 1801.)

This is Kleist bitterly parodying an exhausted Kleist who has vivisected and scrutinised the wild life of love to the point where it is fragmented and he recoils in disgust, both from what he has thus destroyed and from his own alienated self. Let us look at some illustrations of this reduction of people to objects and of objects to smithereens and dust.

---

[a] 'nothing in me is immutable save my mutability'

[b] 'Rest content with these few signs* of what goes on within me. Everything there is so indeterminate that I am fearful of writing anything down, because by doing so it *becomes* determinate in a certain manner.'

[c] 'I fancy that *Newton*, looking at the bosom of a girl, saw nothing save its curvature, and that regarding her heart nothing was noteworthy to him bar its cubic content. A proper chemist, amidst his wife's kisses, thinks of nought but that her breath is nitrous oxide and carbon dioxide.'

---

* I am rendering the word 'Zeichen' as 'signs' rather than as, say, 'snatches' for the sake of consistency. 'Zeichen' is a most important and emotion-charged word in Kleist's use, always employed in implicit or explicit contrast to – unseen – significances, and had best be rendered throughout as 'sign', wherever possible, so as to preserve this association.

The first communication, dated beginning of January 1800, is addressed to Wilhelmine after a talk with her father, clearly to ask for her hand in marriage. It begins thus: [the beginning is lost] '. . . sichtbar die Zuversicht von Ihnen geliebt zu werden? Atmet nicht in jeder Zeile das frohe Selbstbewußtsein der erhörten und beglückten Liebe? – Und doch – wer hat es mir gesagt? Und wo steht es geschrieben?'[a] Kleist then goes on to describe the unmistakable change that has come over Wilhelmine's bearing since he spoke to her father – and he describes it with astute powers of observation, too – only to continue: '– ich frage, was soll ich aus allen diesen fast unzweifelhaften Zügen anderes schließen, was anderes, Wilhelmine, als daß ich geliebt werde?'[b] *Fast unzweifelhaft, Züge* – almost indubitably, sign (a word which assumes a crucial significance as a misleading perceptual clue in connection with the initialled diadem, in *Amphitryon* and else-where), *schließen* – infer: this is the legal vocabulary of a judge or a prosecutor, not of a young lover. This is how he continues:

> 'Aber darf ich meinen Augen und meinen Ohren, darf ich meinem Witze und meinem Scharfsinn, darf ich dem Gefühle meines leichtgläubigen Herzens, das sich schon einmal von ähnlichen Zügen [sic!] täuschen ließ, wohl trauen? Muß ich nicht mißtrauisch werden auf meine Schlüsse'[c]

etc. etc. Here, *in nuce*, we encounter that radical distrust of perception engendered by an undue reliance on perception in complex feeling-situations – an excessive reliance itself bred, as we shall see, of insecurity – which we have met a number of times: we have encountered it in the essay *On The Puppet-Show* in the anecdote of the beautiful youth who lost his grace, and in *The Broken Pitcher* in the figure of Ruprecht who would use his eyes to play tiddly-winks. It is a mistrust of, and a reliance on, perception which will recur, as we shall see, in exacerbated form in *Das Bettelweib von Locarno*, in Amphitryon's desperate anatomy of his senses or the Prince's nihilistic self-scrutiny, to mention only a few instances. We are entitled, indeed in a literary enquiry we are obliged, to trace back to its source, here, a reaction-pattern which assumes such importance in Kleist's poetic *opus* and which, moreover, may afford us a crucial clue to the poet's reception of Kant.

He tests Wilhelmine, distrusts her, paranoically thinks himself betrayed by her and Ulrike, scrutinises her worth as – he himself says so – one holds a banknote to the light, fearing that it might be a fake. In a letter written on 11 (and 12) January, 1801, protesting especial pleasure at a communication of hers 'aus Deinem Herzen zu meinem Herzen' – from your heart to mine – he reciprocates her spontaneity thus:

---

a '. . . visibly the assurance of being loved by you? Does not the happy consciousness of a reciprocated and blissful love breathe in your every line? And yet – who has told me so? And where is it written?'

b '– I ask, what should I infer from these virtually indubitable signs, what Wilhelmine, but that I am loved?'

c 'But may I trust my eyes and ears, may I trust my judgment and my wits, may I trust the intuition of my gullible heart which was once before deceived by signs such as these? Must I not distrust my own inferences?'

'. . . da ich Dich selbst nicht sehen und beurteilen kann, was bleibt mir übrig, als aus Deinen Briefen auf Dich zu schließen? . . . Daher ist mir jeder Gedanke, der Dich in ein schöneres Licht stellt, jede Empfindung, die Dich schmückt, teuer, wie das Unterpfand einer Tat, wie das Zeichen [sic!] Deines moralischen Wertes . . .'[a]

For all that he probes, like a detective, for circumstantial evidence instead of relying on the spontaneous voice of his feeling, these lines, if slightly ludicrous, are not outright offensive. But what are we to say when he continues thus:

'Ja, liebe Wilhelmine, wenn jemals die Erinnerung an Dich in mir immer kälter und kälter werden sollte, so bin ich in meinem heiligsten Innern überzeugt, daß es einzig Deine Schuld sein würde, nie die meinige. Nur dann könnte und müßte ich gleichgültig gegen Dich werden, wenn die Erfahrung mich lehrte, daß der Stein, den ich mit meiner ganzen Seele bearbeite, den Glanz aus ihm hervorzulocken, kein Edelstein wäre –'[b],

adding reassuringly, 'Ich würde Dich darum nicht verlassen, – denn warum solltest *Du* den Irrtum büßen, den *ich* beging? Aber unglücklich würde ich sein . . .'[c] (January 11 (and 12), 1801)? The naïvely vicious unconcern and egocentricity of this passage apart, it is the total reification of the woman he purports to love which is betokened by the image of the gem. Incidentally he has used the same image before, pleading: 'O lege den Gedanken wie einen diamantenen Schild um Deine Brust: *ich bin zu einer Mutter geboren!* Jeder andere Gedanke, jeder andere Wunsch fahre zurück von diesem undurchdringlichen Harnisch'[d] (10 (and 11) October 1800), which makes the business of conceiving something of a problem in the first place! We shall meet the image of the diamond time and again in Kleist's dramas, and always it is meant to signify integrity in relationship. But a stone is inanimate; and this particular stone, the diamond, reflects the light which glances off its facets rather than absorbing it: tokens of the profound unfeasibility of relatedness between two parties one of whom holds the other away from himself, transforming him or her into an object from whose impingement he hopes to have full immunity.

As Kleist staves off the impact of the other on himself by reifying him or her[4], so he manipulates his partner into total passivity. This becomes especially pronounced during his secretive trip to Würzburg. His requests to be trusted implicitly become ever more imperious; yet what he stimulates, by the morsels of information that he feeds into those he has left behind, is precisely that reliance on

---

a '. . . since I cannot see and assess you in person, what else can I do but draw inferences as regards you from your letters? . . . For that reason every thought of yours that makes you appear in a more favourable light, every sentiment that adorns you, is as dear to me as the pledge of a deed or as the outward sign of your inner, moral worth . . .'

b 'Let it be said, dear Wilhelmine, if ever my recollection of you were to grow colder and yet colder, I am convinced in the most sacred depths of my self that it would be your fault alone, not mine. I could and would be compelled to become indifferent *vis-à-vis* you only on one condition: if experience were to teach me that the stone on which I am working with all my soul, to make it shine, were not after all a gem.'

c 'Even so, I would not leave you, – for why should *you* pay for *my* mistake? But I'd be unhappy . . .'

d 'O place the thought upon your breast like a diamond shield: *I was born to be a mother!* Let every other thought and every other wish glance off this impermeable harness.'

circumstantial evidence which is so destructive a trait in himself and which can be
designed only to erode the spontaneity of the other's faith in him until it becomes
a mechanical cleaving to the letter of the truth. To Wilhelmine he writes that if
only he knew that his letters were not read by others, 'so könnte ich Dir schon
manches mitteilen, was Dir zwar eben noch keinen Aufschluß, aber doch Stoff zu
richtigen Vermutungen geben würde'ᵃ (September 20, 1800). Are *richtige Vermutungen* the stuff of which faith is made? Earlier on, he implores both his fiancée
and his half-sister to trust him blindly, 'selbst bei den scheinbar widersprechendsten Umständen'ᵇ as he has it in one instance (August 26, 1800) and, in the other,
'selbst bei dem widersprechendsten Anschein'ᶜ (August 14, 1800); a complexity of
circumstances he alone is responsible for engineering through his habit of dropping half-hearted and ambiguous hints – a form of teasing we shall find time
and again, in characters such as Jupiter, the Grand Elector, Graf Wetter vom
Strahl and others, not to mention the wilfully paradoxical structure of his plots.
Most striking in this context is his injunction to Ulrike, repeated all but verbatim
to his betrothed: 'Unterlasse alle Anwendungen, Folgerungen, und Kombi-
nationen. Sie *müssen* falsch sein, weil Du mich nicht *ganz* verstehen kannst. Halte
Dich bloß an das, was ich Dir gradezu mitteile. Das ist buchstäblich wahr'ᵈ.
(August 26, 1800). It is the letter of the truth, not living faith, which he tries to
instil in the objects of his affection. He looks for the jerky obedience of the
puppet whose every mechanical reaction he himself manipulates, rather than for
the spontaneous if unpredictable movements of true relatedness.

3.

What is the cause of such tortuous evasion of true relationship, of the reduction of
the other to an object held at arm's length, and the sterilisation of their living
response? To answer this question we must enquire into another image complex,
forerunner of the famous metaphor of the green glasses in the Kant letter and an
invaluable clue to its meaning. This is the image of the mirror.

The opening image of the series is benign enough. Kleist is at his Pygmalion-
game. He knows the worth of the matter he is fashioning – Wilhelmine – and he
will not ask more of it than its nature permits. Wilhelmine is pure ore with a strain
of gold. He will separate out the metal from the rock, warm it in the sun of his
love and in turn warm himself in the rays its mirrored surface will reflect back to
him. A reification as before, in a variant of the diamond metaphor, expressing
overtly a good deal of narcissism and, obliquely, the same basic unrelatedness we
have noted before. In any case, the mirror returns his own undistorted image to
the recipient, and that image is good.

ᵃ 'I could tell you a good many things, not enough to make you understand, it is true, but
   enough to base correct suppositions on.'
ᵇ 'even in the seemingly most contradictory circumstances'
ᶜ 'the most contradictory appearances notwithstanding'
ᵈ 'Desist from making any applications, inferences and combinations. They are *bound* to be
   misguided, because you cannot *wholly* understand me. Stick to what I tell you straight
   out. That is literally true.'

Later on in the same letter — dated October 10 and 11, 1800 and written from Würzburg — Kleist returns to the image in converse. Wilhelmine is to gaze at her self in the mirror of her consciousness and enjoy the beauty that is reflected back to her. Do not entirely neglect the looking-glass of the ballroom and its joys, he writes, but: 'Das Gefühl, *im Innern schön zu sein,* und das Bild das uns der Spiegel des Bewußtseins in den Stunden der Einsamkeit zurückwirft, das sind Genüsse, die allein unsere heiße Sehnsucht nach Glück ganz stillen können'[a].

This is a momentous utterance in the inner history of Kleist; one of several on this all-important trip to Würzburg, undertaken to cure him of some impediment which made him feel that he was not fit for marriage. The nature of this impediment is hinted at in the early laments to Ulrike over an inexplicable 'Beklommenheit' — sense of oppression — which seizes hold of him in company, the onset of which significantly coincides with his introduction into the Zenge-household (November 12, 1799). This ailment has been widely thought to be some speech defect: Kleist is known to have been prone to stuttering. If this was so, it is most likely to have been a displacement upward of some more deep-seated trouble. Kleist himself will prove his lively awareness of the connection between the zone of speech and the genital sphere in the wish he will place onto Amphitryon's lips at the end of the drama, when the general wishes for a son, in the words:

> Nein, Vater Zeus, zufrieden bin ich nicht!
> Und meines Herzens Wunsche wächst die Zunge.[b]

This deviation is necessary if we are to appreciate the unexpectedness of Kleist's stance in the last cited letter. For a young man plagued by self-consciousness — this much we may surely glean from the early letter to Ulrike, to be confirmed within a few months from the time of writing by the open laments to her and Wilhelmine (January 31 and February 5, 1801) — this praise of, and quest for, consciousness is nothing short of astounding. The future author of *Über das Marionettentheater* with its story of the youth who lost 'the paradise of innocence' as he beheld his likeness in the mirror of the lake, or indeed of *Käthchen,* that epitome of unconscious grace, is still well protected in his cocoon; it is the creator of *die Familie Schroffenstein* and especially of Sylvester whose sense of integrity is restored by 'nought beside my consciousness', who is speaking here. In the letter with which we are concerned, Kleist drives home his exhortation to Wilhelmine to enjoy her moral image by advising her to brush aside the distractions of ballroom-mirrors pandering to vanity and to return to the looking-glass of her soul: thus the heart will recover from dissipations, 'wobei . . . das Bewußtsein gleichsam ganz ausgelöscht war'[c]. A thoroughly positive image then, indicating however some slight fissure between the external and the inner self.

---

a The feeling of *one's inside being beautiful,* and the image which the looking-glass of our consciousness casts back to us in our solitary moments, those are the pleasures which alone can wholly quench our parching thirst for happiness.'

b No, Father Zeus, I am not satisfied/ And my heart's wish does issue in my tongue.

c 'in which . . . consciousness was, as it were, obliterated'.

The metaphor recurs, this time as an analogy, in one of those tedious quizzes Kleist devised for the betterment of his beloved. In the famous *Gewölbe*-letter, written after his return from Würzburg, he poses the problem:

'Gesetzt Du fändest . . . den Satz, daß die *äußere* (vordere) Seite des Spiegels nicht eigentlich bei dem Spiegel die Hauptsache sei, ja, daß diese eigentlich weiter nichts ist, als ein notwendiges Übel, indem sie das eigentliche Bild nur verwirrt, daß es aber hingegen vorzüglich auf die Glätte und Politur der *inneren* (hinteren) Seite ankomme, wenn das Bild recht rein und treu sein soll − − welchen Wink gibt uns das für unsere eigne Politur, und wohin deutet es?'[a] (November 18, 1800).

Here, for the first time, the mirror is seen as a distorting medium; and the distortion is located in its outer surface, precisely as, in the earlier passage, the ballroom-mirror reflecting the outer self was adjudged to be irrelevant and positively distracting. The fissure between what is within and what is without has widened; but now it is projected onto the reflecting object itself which is envisaged as an active and disruptive agency.

Wilhelmine's solution of the task set to her clearly gave much pleasure to Kleist. In his reply, he stresses the activity with which her mind has taken hold of the impression he had conveyed through his metaphor. 'Die Seele muß tätig sein' − 'the soul must be active', he writes; it must be busy interpreting phenomena which do not disclose themselves to 'the dead eye'; a Kantian thought evidently suggested to him by the ingenuity of Wilhelmine's answer. For he goes on to write − and here the active participation of the mirror (as of the mind) in response to what it receives is fully brought out into the open:

'Ganz vortrefflich, besonders dem Sinne nach, ist der Gedanke, daß es bei dem Menschen, wie bei dem Spiegel, auf seine eigne Beschaffenheit ankommt, wie fremde Gegenstände auf ihn einwirken sollen . . . Aber nun, mein liebes Kind, müssen wir auch die Lehre nutzen, und fleißig an dem Spiegel unserer Seele schleifen, damit er glatt und klar werde, und treu das Bild der schönen Natur zurückwerfe'[b](29 (and 30) November, 1800).

These words are poised, as it were, on the point of a needle. Kleist has eulogised over the joys of moral consciousness and here, in a metaphor which has gradually gained force, is the heartening thought that we are not mechanical reflectors of what is without, but masters of what the medium of our soul reflects back to us. So far so good. But at the back of our minds there lingers the recollection of the

---

[a] 'Suppose you came upon . . . the proposition that the *outermost* (frontal) aspect of the mirror is not the most important thing in a mirror, indeed, that it is nothing more than a necessary evil, in that it falsifies the true image; that, conversely, what matters are the smoothness and polish of its *innermost* (back) side, for the image to be unflawed and true − − what hint does that give us as regards our own polish, and in which direction does it point?'

[b] 'Your thought that, with a human being as with a mirror, its inherent quality determines the effect upon it of external objects, is quite excellent, especially in its implications . . . But now, my dear child, we must make use of this precept and assiduously grind away at the mirror of our soul, for it to become smooth and luminous, and able to cast back the true image of nature's beauty.'

growing fissure Kleist has discerned between our sensible self and our soul, between the outer, distorting, and inner surfaces of the mirror. Will he put two and two together? These confident sentences mark the lull before the storm.

And sure enough, in the very next sentence the storm breaks, as yet some distance from home. 'Wie mancher Mensch', he reflects,

> 'würde aufhören, über die Verderbtheit der Zeiten und der Sitten zu schelten, wenn ihm nur ein einzigesmal der Gedanke einfiele, ob nicht vielleicht bloß der Spiegel, in welchen das Bild der Welt fällt, schief und schmutzig ist? Wie oft stand nicht vielleicht ein solcher Mensch schon vor dem Spiegel, der ihm die lehrreiche Warnung zurief, wenn er sie verstanden hätte — ja *wenn er sie verstanden hätte*! —!'[a]

Ten weeks later, on February 5, 1801, lightning strikes. In a deadly flash Kleist perceives that he himself is the man whom the mirror has tried to warn. Meanwhile, we hear the rumble of distant thunder grow ever nearer and louder. For in these intervening months, the rift that has opened up between outer and inner, sense and soul — his soul and hers — becomes too deep and too wide to be overlooked. It is in these weeks, weeks of which we have already studied the documents, that his distrust of Wilhelmine reaches new dimensions; now he compares himself to a money-changer who anxiously scrutinises the banknote in his hands for its genuineness. If before, at the time of Würzburg, he had doubted her actions — would she betray his plan or keep it to herself? — it is her essential character and being which he now anxiously scrutinises under the magnifying glass of an imagination run riot. Has she entered into a new phase of her development as she ought to have done, through the catalyst of her love? Has she neglected her appearance, and through his fault as she suggests, or is something amiss with her appearance in a far deeper sense, as he had indeed suspected? This doubt is formulated following a grotesque caricature of two society ladies who — like his own Kunigunde — are all make-up and falsehood. Is his Wilhelmine a mere façade too, if in a less obvious fashion? Is something amiss, not with her clothes as she seems to think, but with her *Äußere* in a sense which language lacks words to convey, namely her whole phenomenal self, her very embodiment? '*Dieses* Äußere kann nicht zugeschnitten werden, wie ein Kleid, es gründet sich in der Seele, von ihr muß es ausgehen . . .'[b] (January 22, 1801). Now come outright offensive passages as well as that preposterous metaphor for their continued loving trust (he had already hinted at the cooling down of his emotional temperature): the metaphor of the icefloat which is safely carried past all impediments towards the sea. (January 21 (and 22), 1801.) And now comes the crowning statement, elicited by the hope that she has indeed entered a new epoch in her development: 'Ich

---

[a] 'How many a person would stop fretting at the wickedness of the times and its mores, if he tumbled to the idea but once that it is perhaps only the mirror, which catches the image of the world, that is flawed and sullied? How often such a one may have stood in front of the looking-glass imparting to him just this homily, if only he had understood it — nay, *if he had but understood it!* — !'

[b] '*This* exterior cannot be cut to measure, like a garment. It is grounded in the soul, and from the soul it must emanate.'

freue mich darauf, daß ich Dich nicht wiedererkennen werde, wenn ich Dich wiedersehe'[a] (January 31, 1801).

Let it be said in fairness that he adds the afterthought: 'Auch Du sollst besser mit mir zufrieden sein'[b]. For, clearly, a good deal of the abuse he heaps upon his unfortunate sweetheart is a projection of the growing nausea he feels *vis-à-vis* himself, about his own theorising and cerebrating, about his own dissection of every spontaneous impulse − his own and others' − about the secret business he carries on of reifying people into objects, and the resultant sense of icy alienation. Much implicit self-criticism is to be found in his eulogy of his friend Brockes, with his out-and-out scepticism against all cogitation and the unerringness of his *Gefühlsblick* − intuitive glance, which so tellingly contrasts with the sterility of Kleist's own mentations. It is in this connection that he essays the haunting − and haunted − description of himself which he will repeat almost verbatim to his step-sister, a description the import of which we have already analysed in the opening chapter of this book. He encourages his beloved to scrutinise herself, predicts that, especially by comparison with the perfect Brockes − another teaser − she will blush with shame at what she finds, and continues thus:

'Vielleicht hat die Natur Dir jene Klarheit, zu Deinem Glücke versagt, jene traurige Klarheit, die mir zu jeder Miene den Gedanken, zu jedem Worte den Sinn, zu jeder Handlung den Grund nennt. Sie zeigt mir alles, was mich umgibt, und mich selbst, in seiner ganzen armseligen Blöße, und der farbige Nebel verschwindet, und alle die gefällig geworfnen Schleier sinken und dem Herzen ekelt zuletzt vor dieser Nacktheit − O glück-lich bist Du, wenn Du das nicht verstehst'[c] (January 31 and February 5, 1801).

The compulsion to reify relationships, to reduce loved persons and love itself to an object of ruthless investigation, has borne its sad fruit: the percipient stands stripped, even as he has stripped all around him, disgusted at the fragmentation his peering eyes have revealed within and without and disgusted, above all, by the cynical alienation born of such self-consciousness[5].

The theme of self-consciousness is brought out more explicitly still in the letter written just over a month later to Ulrike in which he repeats the passage I have cited, omitting the earlier reference to the merciful mists and veils that have dropped, and instead continuing: 'Dazu kommt bei mir eine unerklärliche Verlegenheit, die unüberwindlich ist, weil sie wahrscheinlich eine ganz physische Ursache hat' etc. etc.[d] (February 5, 1801.) It is in this crucial letter, too, that Kleist, clearly already in the grips of the Kant-crisis, returns to the image of the

---

[a] 'I am looking forward to not recognising you when I next see you.'

[b] 'You, too, will find me more satisfactory.'

[c] 'Maybe Nature has been kind enough to deny you that lucidity, that wretched lucidity which in my own case spells out the thought behind every mien, the sense of every word, the reason behind every act. She shows me everything that surrounds me, and my own self, in all their threadbare nakedness, and the colourful mist disperses, and all the veils that pleasingly shroud things fall away and in the end the heart is revulsed by this naked-ness − O lucky you if you do not get my meaning.'

[d] 'Superadded to that, I suffer from some inexplicable self-consciousness which, stemming in all probability from a plain physical cause, is unsurmountable.'

mirror which has been lurking beneath his description of his wretched reflectiveness and cries 'mea culpa, mea culpa'.

He confesses that he is a misfit, the reason being that he does not like people.
'Ich weiß wohl', he continues,

> 'daß es bei dem Menschen, wie bei dem Spiegel, eigentlich auf die eigne Beschaffenheit
> beider ankommt, wie die äußern Gegenstände darauf einwirken sollen; und mancher
> würde aufhören über die Verderbtheit der Sitten zu schelten, wenn ihm der Gedanke
> einfiele, ob nicht vielleicht bloß der Spiegel, in welchen das Bild der Welt fällt, schief
> und schmutzig ist'[a].

In his own case, however, he freely concedes that the blame rests not on others,
but squarely on himself.

The dichotomy between sense and spirit, self and other, which we have seen
developing has become absolute. As Kleist has rejected the embodied self of
Wilhelmine − *das Äußere* in that special sense he found impossible to put into
words − so he rejects his own phenomenal self, lock, stock and barrel. His
dissecting and reifying of others as well as of his feelings towards them has made
him perceive the shabbiness of his own perceptual apparatus. It is his mirror
which distorts because, deep beneath the outer surface, it is flawed and soiled. If
we take into consideration that Kleist in this letter also laments that his efforts at
Bildung have crumbled, exclaiming twice in a strain bearing the closest resemblance to the image he will use some six weeks later in the notorious Kant letter,
'Selbst die Säule, an welcher ich mich sonst in dem Strudel des Lebens hielt,
wankt − ich meine, die Liebe zu den Wissenschaften'[b] (5 February, 1801), we
may say that we have inadvertently approached the burning centre of the so-called
Kant-crisis.

For clearly, the image of the soul's mirror which distorts whatever reality falls
upon its surface is but a slight variant of the simile of the green glasses in which he
will presently explain his predicament to Wilhelmine. Both inevitably distort our
vision. But if the simile of the spectacles − which we discussed in the preceding
chapter − leaves the option open as to whether the impairment of our vision is
inherent or extraneous, the metaphor of the soul's mirror gives us an unequivocal,
if strictly personal, answer. *This* man's vision is as distorted as he feels his own
soul to be; and but for a remedy of this inner flaw − to which we owe a poetic
opus of the very first rank[6] − his condition must be pronounced incurable.

4.

Let us summarise our findings so far in this chapter and then ask the crucial
question: 'what did the encounter with Kant mean to this man?'

---

a 'I am well aware of the fact that, as with a mirror, it depends on the intrinsic make-up of
   a man how external things affect him; and many a person would cease to pontificate about
   moral corruption if the thought came to him that it might be but the mirror which reflects
   back to him the image of the world, that is flawed and sullied.'
b 'Even the pillar to which I held fast in the vortex of life, sways − I mean my love for the
   Sciences'

In an analysis of the linguistic materials of these letters, we have noted the astonishingly consistent recurrence of images, such as of money, drawn from the economic sphere, and have observed that such metaphoric material is indiscriminately applied to the ideological and emotional spheres, often with no trace of any accompanying awareness on the part of Kleist that he is in fact still continuing to move on a figurative level of discourse. We have further traced a steady process of reification on the level of relationship, that is to say, a steady strengthening of the tendency to treat persons and relationships as though they were objects amenable to scientific analysis and verification; and we have noted that this need of Kleist's to view the other — and even his own feeling-material — as a stable *vis-à-vis* argues the experience of a self that is ontologically deeply insecure. Finally we have seen the emergence of Kleist's own image of himself in the metaphor of the *schiefe und schmutzige Spiegel* — the flawed and sullied mirror, and with it, the dawning insight that for all the need to experience the object as a pure *vis-à-vis*, a *Gegen-stand*, the self is inextricably and fatally involved in what it perceives.

Into this psychic constellation Kant must have crashed like a thunderbolt[7]. As I see it, the trauma Kant meant to Kleist was fourfold. First, Kant's epistemology finally eroded the belief, so indispensable to Kleist, that objects have an existence that is independent of, and ontologically prior to, the experiencing subject. That he did so in order to safeguard, and explain, the universality and necessity of our empirical knowledge, was of precious little use to the literal-minded Kleist. To one of his psychic structure, with a very rudimentary sense of self-hood — 'Eigentum' — it was the reliable 'thingness' of objects, their very quality of opaque 'otherness', that was all-important. He needed stable objects to guarantee a threatened sense of self, not mind-imbued objects as Kant envisaged them; for these partook in the precariousness of an identity they could do nothing to prop up from the outside, as it were. Thus Kant's 'Copernican Revolution' of the very concept of objectivity, that is to say, its shift from an ontologically independent world of objects to the subjective orders of coherent knowledge constituted by the synthesising mind, to Kleist was bound to be a movement into personal chaos, threatening in the extreme[8].

Secondly: the result of the 'Copernican Revolution', Kant's phenomenalistic account of knowledge, to Kleist was bound to be profoundly perturbing. Not merely because he needed the opacity of objects, their 'otherness', nor merely because the mind, which according to Kant 'constitutes' the objects of our experience, is involved in that process: as we have seen, for all Kleist's efforts to hold the object away from the experiencing self, he had gradually come to terms with the fact of this involvement and temporarily even welcomed the mind's participation in creating a worthy image of the world. No, the decisive reason that made Kleist shrink from the very thought of the mind's active role in the process of cognitive experience was his discovery of an ineradicable flaw lodged in the 'mirror of his soul'. To him, it — i. e. his embodied self — was a distorting and sullied medium. For this reason no doubt he reserved the compromising metaphor of the dirty mirror for Ulrike with whom he was more candid, and in communication with Wilhelmine switched over to the far less personal and emotionally incriminating metaphor of the coloured spectacles.

Thirdly, because of the dualistic dichotomy that had opened up in him between spirit and sense, self and other, Kleist saw himself caught on the horns of a dilemma. Experience, in Kant's eyes, is an act involving the knower in the known. What we perceive, and know, is inevitably modified by the knowing self. To Kleist, split as he was and chary of relationship, this phenomenalistic account of knowledge meant one of two equally disastrous alternatives. It meant either that we cannot experience without entering a context of relatedness (however far away from ourselves we push the object, we are involved with it in the act of knowing it, even as it is modified in and through that act); or, conversely, that we cannot enter into relatedness without coming up against the intervening context of our phenomenal experiencing. However much we strive for a direct communion between the self and another, we cannot circumvent the enveloping context of embodied selves conditioning, and modifying, the experience of both partners in the relationship. As Amphitryon cannot view the phenomenon Alkmene at a distance, without coming up against her noumenal, and indeed numinous, essence which has received the imprint of Jupiter, so Jupiter, in his turn, cannot reach out directly for the noumenal, and indeed numinous, essence of Alkmene, without coming up against her phenomenal self which is stamped through and through with the imprint of Amphitryon.

This dilemma persists throughout Kleist's epic and dramatic work where we shall encounter it in all the detail of its ramifications. I shall continue to call the attempt at experiencing without relating the objective fallacy, and the converse attempt to relate directly, jumping the guns of phenomenal experience, the subjective fallacy[9].

Fourthly and lastly, Kant's careful distinction between the diverse cognitive modalities must have been shattering to Kleist. As we have seen, he was wont to slur distinctions of consequence between literal and figurative forms of speech; and that semantic tendency in its turn reflects a more basic confusion in his intellectual household, a confusion between the sphere of perception and empirical enquiry on the one hand, and such higher, more complex and interpretative cognitive activities as are involved in the discernment of emotional and spiritual patterns of experience on the other. The boundaries between these for him were literally non-existent. In his anguished desire for the objective truth all the more sophisticated manifestations of the psyche, such as love, trust and faith, and the mode of apprehension appropriate to them, had become scaled down to the remorseless quest of a sharp pair of eyes bent on impartial enquiry. On *this* perceptual level at least he could hope to get a good and direct look at his object, whilst yet remaining essentially unrelated to it.

But Kant did not merely erode the object *per se*; he demonstrated the inextricable involvement of the mind even in the most basic perceptual act. More than that: he insisted on a hierarchy of our cognitive functions and denied to the one dearest to Kleist, the metaphysical urge towards knowledge of things as they are in themselves, any application in the realm of theory. As soon as they are hypostasized, the Ideas of Reason, such as that of the immortality of the soul so important to Kleist, become spurious and lead into a veritable labyrinth of antinomies. Hence Kant saw himself forced to deny the object-character of these ultimate termini of our thinking; we cannot 'have' them, as we have a treasure or a harvest. They are nothing but practical postulates, to be acted upon but not hoarded or 'speculated' about by the theoretical intelligence.

'I had to deny knowledge to make room for faith': this crucial Kantian message was 'the sharp point of his thought' which pierced the very heart of Kleist and wounded him in his 'heiligsten Innern' — 'in the innermost sanctuary of his self'. This was the scalpel that stripped everything around him, and himself, too, of its merciful veils and made him shudder at his nakedness. For the mental modality Kant here isolates as being distinct from all theoretical mentation and incapable of ever being supplanted by it, is the very modality in which Kleist, by the consistent witness of these letters, was radically unversed, and of whose very existence as something *sui generis*, apart from perceptual processes, he seems to have been unaware: the spontaneous movement of the mind towards the 'other' in empirically unsupported truth and faith.

This Kantian manifesto, the vital hinge between the two first Critiques, made all those false props crumble on which Kleist had leaned, unaware that they were pseudo-scientific if reassuring surrogates for that *Gefühlsblick* — intuitive glance — he so admired in his friend Brockes: those *Gründe* and *sichere* or *unwandelbare Stützen* and *Beweise* — grounds and secure or immutable supports or proofs — with which he had tried to cement the edifice of his ideals and of his happiness, collapsed beneath his feet. Worse than that, Kant's isolation of faith as a mode of apprehension *sui generis,* divided by an unbridgéable gulf from all perceptual and even from the more highly abstractive cognitive activities in the theoretical sphere, illuminated as with a piercing searchlight the very spontaneity (both in the Kantian and the present day sense of the word) of which Kleist knew himself to be utterly incapable, however much he tried to hide this basic defect by tortuous cerebrations and subterfuges: and in this brilliant illumination he now stood, shabby and naked, forever saddled with his insuperable self-consciousness and the shame of it. Here is the root of a suffering he was to transcend only in death, a suffering which paradoxically gave the world a rich harvest of great writing, not least the essay *Über das Marionettentheater.*

And now that he stands in the searchlight of Kant's beacon, self-conscious like a naked sinner caught *in flagranti*, the direction of his mind is all of a sudden reversed. Gone is the time when he craved the consciousness of his self as a prized reward of honest striving. Now we read: '. . . mich ekelt vor allem, was Wissen heißt'[a] (March 23, 1801); or: 'Meine heitersten Augenblicke sind solche, wo ich mich selbst vergesse'[b] (May 4, 1801); or again: 'Sonst waren die Augenblicke, wo ich mich meiner selbst bewußt ward, meine schönsten — jetzt muß ich sie vermeiden, weil ich mich und meine Lage fast nicht ohne Schaudern denken kann'[c]. (May 21, 1801.) And now begins the yearning, not only for religious faith as such, but for Catholicism for which he had had nothing but contumely even in his Würzburg days: 'Ach, Wilhelmine', he writes,

---

[a] 'Everything that calls itself knowledge revolts me'

[b] 'My happiest moments are those when I forget all about myself'

[c] 'The moments when I was conscious of myself used to be my loveliest ones — now I have to avoid them because I cannot think of myself and my predicament except with something approaching a shudder.'

'unser Gottesdienst ist keiner. Er spricht nur zu dem kalten Verstande, aber zu allen Sinnen ein katholisches Fest. Mitten vor dem Altar, an seinen untersten Stufen, kniete jedesmal, ganz isoliert von den andern, ein gemeiner Mensch, das Haupt auf die höheren Stufen gebückt, betend mit Inbrunst. Ihn quälte kein Zweifel, er *glaubt* – Ich hatte eine unbeschreibliche Sehnsucht mich neben ihn niederzuwerfen, und zu weinen – Ach, nur einen Tropfen Vergessenheit, und mit Wollust würde ich katholisch werden'[a]. (May 21, 1801.)

The encounter with Kant had cost this naïvest of realists 'the paradise of his innocence'. His defect was bared, he suffered and he wrote. Always he lingered and looked for the time when he might re-enter the lost home 'through a back-door', as he has in the essay *Über das Marionettentheater*; and always the cherub with the flaming sword drove him away, back into the agony of wakeful consciousness, of distrust, reification and literalism – a miraculously creative agony as it turned out in the event. Sometimes, he let some of his figures experience the bliss of being at home in the haven of faith from which he himself was debarred – Käthchen, the Prince of Homburg at the end, and – the four mad brothers in *Die heilige Cäcilie oder die Gewalt der Musik* who howl their grisly *Gloria in excelsis* like leopards or wolves bellowing into the night, having returned into 'the lap of the Catholic Church'.

Kleist remained his literal-minded self, shocked to the end that 'articles' of faith cannot be had, or handled, or hoarded, like material goods. A day or two before his death he wrote to his cousin Marie 'daß ich sterbe, weil mir auf Erden nichts mehr zu lernen und zu *erwerben** übrig bleibt' . Had he learned anything?

Yet he succeeded after all in retrieving the oblivion of unconsciousness, and 'to relapse into the estate of innocence' as the *Marionettentheater* so ambivalently has it, a formulation which sheds the faith of the Enlightenment in man's steady ascent towards the autonomy of reason like a desiccated husk. Of his double suicide he writes 'daß meine ganze jauchzende Sorge nur sein kann, einen *Abgrund tief genug** zu finden, um mit ihr hinab zu stürzen' . (November 19, 1811.) And just before he embarked on his 'große Entdeckungsreise', on the day of his death, he wrote these words: '. . . ich bin ganz selig. Morgens und abends knie ich nieder, was ich nie gekonnt habe, und bete zu Gott'[d]. (November 21, 1811.) And to be able to do so without blushing was all he could have wished for.

---

[a] 'Alas, Wilhelmine, our worship is no worship. It merely addresses itself to the cold understanding, whilst a Catholic service speaks to every one of our senses. Every time, some ordinary fellow knelt right in front of the altar, his head bent low over the higher steps, quite on his own, praying devoutly. No doubt tormented him, he has *faith* – I felt an unspeakable yearning to prostrate myself by his side, and to cry – Oh, but for one drop of obliviousness and I would rapturously embrace the Catholic faith.'

[b] 'that I am going to my death because there is nothing more to learn and to *acquire** on this earth.'

[c] 'I have but one exultant care: to find an abyss deep enough for her and me to plunge into.'

[d] '. . . I am in bliss. Every morning and every night I kneel down, a thing I was never able to do, and pray to God.'

---

* my italics

III   Embargo on Relatedness

Laß die Sprache dir sein, was der Körper den Liebenden. Er nur
Ist's, der die Wesen trennt und der die Wesen vereint.

Schiller

Wie soll ich meine Seele halten, daß
sie nicht an deine rührt? Wie soll ich sie
hinheben über dich zu andern Dingen?

Rilke

5 Sacred Centre: 'Amphitryon'

1.

Amphitryon, illustrious general of Thebes, has returned from a successfully concluded war. Having sent his servant Sosias ahead of him to announce his arrival to Alkmene, his young bride, he finds the commonsensical fellow in a state of inexplicable confusion, and worms the story of a strange encounter out of him which we, the readers, have witnessed. On approaching Amphitryon's palace, Sosias had seen himself − or one exactly like him − leaving the house, a truly *entgeisternder Anblick* − dementing sight: and by cajoling and cruelly beating him up, that other self had eventually forced him to cede his own identity. An unlikely story, as he himself admits,

> Ein Vorfall, koboldartig, wie ein Märchen,
> Und dennoch *ist* es, wie das Sonnenlicht.[a] (II, 1)

How had Mercury − for it was he, Jupiter's companion, who had posed as Sosias' double − prevailed upon the latter to give up his selfhood? By no means only through threats and wallops, but by the most extraordinary argumentation. One by one, he had recounted to Sosias events relating to his own life of which outsiders could have had little or no knowledge: that he had recently been jailed, had received a beating from his master for pilfering and, worst of all, that he had helped himself to a good chunk of ham and a draught of wine, secretly, while his compatriots were locked in battle tooth and claw. And as the other had proven his knowledge of him, piece by compelling piece, Sosias had grown increasingly uncertain of his selfhood, musing:

> . . . ohne daß man selbst
> Sosias ist, kann man von dem, was er
> Zu wissen scheint, nicht unterrichtet sein.
> Man muß, mein Seel, ein bißchen an ihn glauben . . .[b]

and:

> Ich fang im Ernst an mir zu zweifeln an.
> Durch seine Unverschämtheit ward er schon
> Und seinen Stock, Sosias, und jetzt wird er,
> Das fehlte nur, es auch aus Gründen noch.[c] (I, 2)

---

[a] A happening, impish as a fairy tale,/ And yet as plainly *there* as is the light of day.

[b] . . . without being/ Sosias, one cannot be informed/ Of what he seems to know. Upon my soul,/ One's forced to have a little faith in him . . .

[c] I seriously begin to doubt myself./ His cheek made him Sosias/ And his stick, and now he will, Heaven forbid,/ Become the same on reasonable grounds.

But what had finally undone him, was the other self's knowledge of his culinary indulgences:

> Denn aus dem Flaschenfutter trinkt man nicht,
> Wenn man, wie ich, zufällig nicht im Sacke
> Den Schlüssel, der gepaßt, gefunden hätte . . .:[a]   (*ibid.*)

A compelling piece of circumstantial evidence which leaves no option to Sosias but to surrender his identity, lock, stock and barrel. Later, he will in all seriousness confirm to Amphitryon that it was he himself, his other self, who foiled 'his' mission to Alkmene:

> Ich, ja. Ein Ich, das Wissenschaft
> Von allen unsern Heimlichkeiten hat,
> Das Kästchen und die Diamanten kennt,
> Dem Ich vollkommen gleich, das mit Euch spricht.[b]   (II, 1)

Clearly, the identity of this 'I' was not very securely established in the first place. Located in the anonymous region of the belly, it was capable of being dislodged on purely empirical outside evidence, and circumstantial evidence at that.

> Am I not wholly conscious of myself?   (I, 2)

Sosias had asked himself in his first surprise; but for all that Amphitryon had admonished him, saying:

> Gather together your five senses now . . .   (II, 1),

those very senses had let him down: he had seen, and heard, and his eyes had told him

> Daß ich, der einfach aus dem Lager ging,
> Ein Doppelter in Theben eingetroffen;
> Daß ich mir glotzend hier begegnet bin . . .[c]   (*ibid.*)

2.

It is shaken and annoyed by this inauspicious beginning that Amphitryon enters his wife's rooms and registers her surprise at his precipitate return. As she has just spent a matchless love-night with Jupiter, believing him to be Amphitryon, and is at that very moment preparing to offer a sacrifice for 'the best of husbands', we may legitimately assume her 'Ye gods! Amphitryon! . . . Already back?' to be an expression of incredulous delight. Yet Amphitryon reacts exactly as his servant had reacted: scanning an internal situation as though it were an extraneous event

---

[a] For no one drinks out of the bottle pouch,/ Save one who, like myself, has found/ The key that fits, inside the travelling bag.

[b] Yes, me. A me that has full knowledge/ Of all our secrecies,/ That knows the casket and the diamonds,/ Exactly like the me that speaks to you.

[c] That I who left this camp as one,/ Arrived in Thebes as one in duplicate,/ That I myself encountered, gaping, here . . .

and relying on observation and inference to interpret it for him[1]. Like a criminologist or a judge, he assesses her surprise as 'ein zweideutig Zeichen' – 'an ambiguous sign', and from there argues himself into suspecting that 'his calculations' were wrong, that she has 'taught him' that he has returned too early rather than too late for her liking, concluding, 'mit Befremden' – 'with surprise and alienation' –

> . . . daß ich
> Ein Überlästger aus den Wolken falle.[a]   (II, 2)

In his *The Will to Believe and other Essays*, William James has shown how faith can create fact, and has described the converse possibility thus:

> The previous faith on my part in your liking's existence is . . . what makes your liking come true. But if I stand aloof, and refuse to budge an inch until you shall have done something apt, as the absolutists say, *ad extorquendum assensum meum,* ten to one your liking never comes[2].

Amphitryon is one that thus 'stands aloof', refusing to advance Alkmene the credit of his loving, and insisting on taking a cool and unsentimental look at her predicament. He thinks – and, indeed speaks – in terms of marital 'claims', reminds her of the 'consequences' of what she so innocently divulges, alludes to 'certain reasons' which make him insist on a 'circumstantial account' of what precisely did happen during the night, scolds her for adducing 'proofs' in her own favour when she assures him of her inner peace of mind, resolves to call in witnesses to clear up the situation once and for all and, most of all, entrenches himself in the position that his 'honour' has been damaged and must forthwith be cleared: conceptions, all of them, that are singularly ill-fitted to illuminate an emotional tangle to which he is himself a party. For this requires, above all, trust in the beloved and the hypothesis of faith in the benignity of what at present appears to be an inscrutable fate. True, at one point he seems to have an inkling that it is faith which is required here, when he reflects:

> Ich habe sonst von Wundern schon gehört,
> Von unnatürlichen Erscheinungen, die sich
> Aus einer andern Welt hieher verlieren;[b]

but he is unable to sustain belief[3] – and belief, *fides,* is closely adjacent to trust, *fiducia* – and at once continues:

> Doch heute knüpft der Faden sich von jenseits
> An meine Ehre und erdrosselt sie.[c]   (II, 2)

---

[a] . . . that, thunderstruck,/ I fell, more than a nuisance, from the clouds.

[b] Before this I have heard of miracles,/ Unnatural events whose trail, emitted/ In some other world, has lost itself in our own;

[c] But on this day, the thread spun in the yonder,/ Entangled with my honour, strangles it.

The public stance and the public values have gained the day; and 'der öffentliche Geck' — 'the public charlatan' — (this is what Jupiter calls him) concludes the confrontation with his wife with the resounding declaration that he will avenge 'his bleeding honour' (Alkmene, characteristically, has spoken of her 'bleeding heart') by tearing up, with the help of witnesses and his own commonsense, 'this accursed web of falsehoods' in which he has been caught. How could he know? But this web, this thread, which entangles him is nothing other than the emanation of the Numinous which surrounds Alkmene since her divine visitation, making her incomprehensible to him. Tearing it will not help, only accepting her as the mystery that she has become; and to that his powers of imagination will not stretch.

Amphitryon is not a Sosias, nor indeed a Ruprecht. His rank and the acrid dignity of his bearing assure him his place in the domain of *haute tragédie*. Yet the reaction-pattern Kleist traces in this brittle man of war bears a more than coincidental resemblance to that of his more common folk. In a situation fraught with ambiguity, calling for the highest interpretative powers of an emotionally articulate mind, Amphitryon displays the same inner literalism that is familiar to us from the humbler of this poet's figures, indeed from their creator himself: holding the figure of the beloved, and the feeling-situation in which he is involved, at more than an arm's length, and refusing to take her to himself, he exchanges 'the life of faith' for 'the cold mechanism'[4] of a purely perceptual analysis and, in the last resort, reifies the 'wingèd life' of his love.

The basic obtuseness of such a stance — and its underlying aggressiveness — are mercilessly pinpointed by Mercury in his confrontation with the clueless general:

> Nun? bist du fertig? Hast du mich beschaut? [a]

he asks, and continues to describe him thus:

> Hast du mit deinen stieren Augen bald
> Mich ausgemessen? Wie er auf sie reißt!
> Wenn man mit Blicken um sich beißen könnte,
> Er hätte mich bereits zerrissen hier. [b] (III, 2)

The result of thus dissecting a feeling-relationship by means of a perceptual inquest is a profound sense of nausea directed against the perceptual apparatus which has so dismally failed him when it came to detecting what no five senses can detect: that same nausea which prompts Ruprecht, in *The Broken Pitcher*, to malign his eyes, and to which Kleist himself confesses in the two letters to his fiancée and his half-sister which we have been considering in the preceding chapter. Disgusted at his own disorientation, Amphitryon turns on the very organs upon which he has mistakenly relied, organs which have of necessity failed

---

a Well? Have you done then? Have you studied me?
b When will you leave off measuring me out/ With your eyes all agog?/ See how he tears them open!/ If looks could bite and bite and bite/ Why, he'd have torn me into shreds by now.

to guide him through the emotional and spiritual labyrinth in which he finds himself:

> In Zimmern, die vom Kerzenlicht erhellt,
> Hat man bis heut mit fünf gesunden Sinnen
> In seinen Freunden nicht geirret; Augen,
> Aus ihren Höhlen auf den Tisch gelegt,
> Vom Leib getrennte Glieder, Ohren, Finger,
> Gepackt in Schachteln, hätten hingereicht,
> Um einen Gatten zu erkennen. Jetzo wird man
> Die Ehemänner brennen, Glocken ihnen,
> Gleich Hämmeln um die Hälse hängen müssen.[a]   (III, 1)

If perception and the cold mechanism of the enquiring intelligence will make no guide in situations requiring the hypothesis of trust, how much less so will organs severed from their base? What does this gruesome post-mortem on the physiology of perception signify, if not the fragmentation of a mind which would know without being involved in the act of knowing, which cuts off the very tentacles through which the knower relates to the known? Amphitryon's desperate quest to know Alkmene and the feeling-truth they both share, independently of his experience of it, for fear of his experience falsifying its object and yielding up appearance; his violent dissociation from his very organs of perception lest they modify what he would apprehend in undilute objectivity, as it is in itself: this is Kleist's poetic answer to Kant's epistemology[5]; and it results, not merely in a radical alienation from the other, but in an equally radical fragmentation of the knowing self.

Experience, even perceptual experience, presupposes a positive act of relating, an assimilation of what is to be known to the knowing self. In his dread that by operating within the frame and with the categories of relatedness, he will be deceived into accepting Alkmene-as-she-appears-to-him, in lieu of discovering the scientific truth about Alkmene, Amphitryon seeks to jump the guns of relatedness and, in doing so, metaphorically cuts off his nose to spite his face. Here, in classic purity, we encounter what I have termed the objective fallacy. The result of such an obstinately empirical attack on a situation calling for the spontaneous movement of the mind to encompass the mystery of the other − 'des Geistes heitre Tätigkeit' as Alkmene has it − is twofold. The 'public charlatan' is left clutching in his clumsy hands the phenomenal husk of the person and the relationship he seeks to know, the noumenal essence of Alkmene and indeed her divine involvement having utterly eluded him. What is more, his selfhood, precariously anchored in the phenomenal domain of his public persona and unconfirmed by his

---

[a] To date, in rooms lit up by candlelight,/ One has not failed to recognise one's friends/ Equipped with five sound senses: eyes,/ Placed on a table, excised from their orbs,/ Limbs severed from their bodies, fingers, ears,/ Packed up and boxed, were good enough/ To recognise a spouse. Now one will have/ To brand a husband with an iron, and place/ A bell around his neck as though he were a ram.

relationship to his wife, splinters, less ridiculously it is true, but ultimately no less ignominiously than that of his servant Sosias.

> Begraben bin ich schon, und meine Witwe
> Schon einem andern Ehgemahl verbunden . . .[a]   (III, 3)

he bitterly muses as Mercury drives him away from his own doorstep; and for all that he calls upon his lieutenants' five sound senses to identify him, he is seen through as though he were made of glass and declared null and void. 'Squeezed out of the fortress of his consciousness', he *has* no deeper identity. As Sosias puts it in a less tragic strain, he is 'entamphitryonisiert' − 'deamphitryonised' − even as he, Sosias, was 'entsosiatisiert' − 'desosiasised' − by Jupiter's companion, Mercury. He is neither a noun, nor a subject, but a past participle, finished, obsolete. The crushed plume on his helmet is the only remaining sorry token of the identity of one who has opted out of sustaining relatedness; and the infantility of the deposed self is underpinned by the comic counterpoint of Sosias who concludes the matter, saying:

> Der ist der wirkliche Amphitryon,
> Bei dem zu Mittag jetzt gegessen wird.[b]   (III, 5)

3.

At the other end of the cognitive spectrum stands Jupiter, the extreme opposite of Amphitryon, or so it would seem[6]. To him Alkmene's inner worth is patent. He has no need of outward signs and tokens, as does his rival. When Alkmene shows him the tell-tale diadem with the exchanged initial, humbly awaiting his judgment, he brushes aside what to Amphitryon has been a piece of damning 'evidence', lightly saying:

> Mein schönes Weib! Werd ich den Stein ergreifen,
> Da solch ein Wert vor mir im Staube liegt?[c]   (II, 5)

Her beauty and her worth, he knows, lie in her 'unfehlbares Gefühl', that unerring purity of heart which transforms whatever approaches her into Amphitryon; in that unfailing capacity to hold what she loves in the embrace of her relatedness.

And yet Jupiter has his troubles, too. It is precisely what he knows to be her shining worth that worries him. Not merely is he compelled, in deference to her integrity, to appear to her as Amphitryon, a thoroughly unwanted embodiment: worse still, he must accommodate himself to the fact that she, too, is embodied, and is ensconced in the prison-cell of this, her human estate. It is Amphitryon she loves, and whatever to her is lovable, her sentience construes as Amphitryon.

---

[a] I am already buried, and my widow/ Is wedded to another . . .
[b] The true Amphitryon is doubtless he,/ At whose place dinner is now being served.
[c] My lovely wife! How could I grasp the gem,/ When such a jewel lies before me in the dust?

For Jupiter this is an intolerable constriction. He frets for a direct communion of souls, of his innermost self with hers, untainted by the intervention of any human context, his or hers. Time and again he labours to wean her soul of its conditioning, first by bidding her distinguish between the familiar figure of the husband and the — to her — equally familiar figure of the lover, later by disclosing his true identity as the god who demands her most fervent adoration, and finally by engineering a direct confrontation with his mortal double: an inordinately foolish quest in which he cannot win, since he is ever constrained to assume the mask of the man she loves and unwaveringly acclaims at his ideal best[7].

It is for a twofold reason that the god would wean Alkmene's 'befangner Sinn' — 'hidebound mind', her 'Gefühl, an seinem Nest gewöhnt' — 'her feeling as yet clinging to its nest', of its habitual trappings. Like Ottokar who would see Agnes 'ganz klar' — 'quite plainly', who can 'divine her unborn thoughts as though he were her god', Jupiter wants to have direct access to Alkmene's soul:

> Er will geliebt sein, nicht ihr Wahn von ihm.[a]   (II, 5)

He craves to strip her love of its phenomenal husk in order that he may see it as it is in itself. If Amphitryon refuses to *relate* for fear of finding what *he* himself has invested in *his* experience, so conversely Jupiter, with equal stubbornness, refuses to *be related to,* for fear of finding what *Alkmene* has invested in *her* experience. As Amphitryon pushes Alkmene away from himself lest the shadow of *his* trusting fall across their relationship and obscure her measurable worth, so Jupiter seeks to drive a wedge between Alkmene and her own loving, lest the shadow of *her* habituation fall across their relationship and obscure the quality of *her* passion *per se.* For all Jupiter's inwardness, for all his yearning to 'touch her soul' directly, by the sight of his 'unsterblich Antlitz' — 'immortal face', he too holds her away from himself the better to see her and to delight in what her feeling 'really' is like, viewed in a clinical void.

And what is the ultimate object of wanting to gaze at a soul that is as blank as a slate from which the writing has been wiped off, or, as Alkmene has it, as a white marble wall?

> In ewge Schleier eingehüllt,
> Möcht er sich selbst in einer Seele spiegeln,
> Sich aus der Träne des Entzückens widerstrahlen.[b]   (II, 5)

Jupiter does not merely want to see Alkmene's passion for what it is, taken by itself: in her, through the unalloyed image of him that she casts back, he wants to gaze upon himself as he 'really' is — the infinite, and infinitely narcissistic, lover.

In the last analysis, the extreme objectivity of Amphitryon and the no less radical subjectivity of Jupiter coalesce, even as — so we are told in the essay *On*

---

[a] 'Tis *he* that would be loved, and not her whim of him.
[b] Wrapped in eternal veils,/ He fain would be reflected in a soul,/ And grasp his mirrored image in a tear of joy.

the Puppet-Show — the *Gliedermann* and the god intersect somewhere in infinity. If Amphitryon seeks to know Alkmene's worth from the outside, by detached and distant observation, so does Jupiter endeavour to see his own worth reflected back, as through opera glasses reversed. However far they seem removed from one another, the objective fallacy evinced by Amphitryon and the subjective fallacy here exhibited by Jupiter coincide. Both want to know outside relatedness and outside the fixed boundaries of human experience what can only be known from within: the quality of the other, the self, and the relationship shared by both.

It will be seen that these two figures, seemingly polar opposites, are strictly complementary to one another; indeed we may say that they are the two obverse aspects of one and the same person. The one — the general — is phenomenality incarnate, accounting for things in terms of their appearances here and now and disregarding their noumenal essence; the other — the god — is pure numinous visitation directly apprehending the noumenal essence of things and repudiating his — and their — embodied appearance here and now. In rejecting 'the other' in himself, each remains a fragmentary self, equally precariously grounded in that each forfeits that wholeness of experience in which self and other, spirit and body, marry, engendering a partnership that transcends the shortcomings of severance within and without. Each, we may say, is an aspect of Kleist's own divided self, deeply insecure as well as narcissistic and in either case determined to jump the guns of relatedness in a quest for the naked unmediated truth.

4.

Such fullness of experiencing as is withheld from the rivals to the very end, Kleist has embodied in the lovely and tormented figure of Alkmene. Into that vessel a very sick mind has poured all his uncanny intimations of human wholesomeness and health. Alkmene's selfhood is secure, as secure as anyone's can be who is not tried beyond the limits of human endurance. It is secure in that it is built upon the firm foundations of relatedness[8]. First established in the relationship with the mother, a precious legacy which enables her to rely on

> dieses innerste Gefühl,
> Das ich am Mutterbusen eingesogen,
> Und das mir sagt, daß ich Alkmene bin . . .,[a]   (II, 4)

her selfhood is consolidated through her union with Amphitryon:

> Er wäre fremder mir, als ich![b]

---

[a] this inmost feeling which/ I suckled in at the maternal breast,/ And which informs me that I am Alkmene . . .

[b] He should be stranger to my self than I!/

she exclaims, and continues thus:

> Nimm mir
> Das Aug, so hör ich ihn; das Ohr, ich fühl ihn;
> Mir das Gefühl hinweg, ich atm' ihn noch;
> Nimm Aug und Ohr, Gefühl mir und Geruch,
> Mir alle Sinn und gönne mir das Herz:
> So läßt du mir die Glocke, die ich brauche,
> Aus einer Welt noch find ich ihn heraus.[a]   (*ibid.*)

Because Amphitryon has grown into her very heart, it is her heart that bleeds
when he renounces her:

> Es reißt das Herz sich blutend von dir los   (II, 2)
> — Bleeding, my heart does wrench itself from you,

as she has it.

Amphitryon is the alpha and the omega of her being. In Kantian terms — and
these are the only ones that are apposite here — he is the pure form of her
intuition, and the sole category of her understanding. She no longer needs to see
or feel or hear him — she herself has told us so: rather does she see or feel or hear
with him and *through* him. Her loving bears the form and features of
Amphitryon; he is the green filter, or the mirror, of her soul; and whatever she
receives, to her appears as Amphitryon, becomes the one and only, 'der Ein- und
Ein'ge'. Jupiter himself knows it — he says it often enough — and frets at it:

> Wer nahet dir, o du, vor deren Seele
> Nur stets des Ein- und Ein'gen Züge stehn?
> Du bist, du Heilige, vor jedem Zutritt
> Mit diamantnem Gürtel angetan.
> Auch selbst der Glückliche, den du empfängst,
> Entläßt dich schuldlos noch und rein, und alles,
> Was sich dir nahet, ist Amphitryon.[b]   (II, 5)

Thus Jupiter, to reassure her; and again:

> Was könntest du, du Heilige, verbrechen?
> Und wär ein Teufel gestern dir erschienen,
> Und hätt er Schlamm der Sünd, durchgeiferten,
> Aus Höllentiefen über dich geworfen,
> Den Glanz von meines Weibes Busen nicht
> Mit einem Makel fleckt er! Welch ein Wahn![c]   (*ibid.*)

---

[a] Take/ My eye, and I shall hear him; my ear, and I shall feel him;/ My sense of touch and I shall breathe him yet;/ Take eye and ear, take touch and sense of smell,/ Take all my senses, granting me my heart:/ And you will leave me with the bell I need/ To tell his presence in the whole wide world.

[b] Who could approach you, you, before whose soul/ The features of the one and only stand as etched?/ You, holy one, are shielded from all base/ Advances with a diamond belt./ Even the favoured one whom you receive,/ Releases you immaculate and pure,/ And all that comes to you is but Amphitryon.

[c] What crime could you commit, you holy one?/ And had the devil visited you yesterday,/ And from the depths of hell had spewed upon you,/ Slobbering, the very slime of sin,/ He

And again:

> *Ihn*
> Hat seine böse Kunst, nicht dich getäuscht,
> Nicht dein unfehlbares Gefühl! Wenn er
> In seinem Arm dich wähnte, lagst du an
> Amphitryons geliebter Brust; wenn er
> Von Küssen träumte, drücktest du die Lippe
> Auf des Amphitryon geliebten Mund.[a]   (*ibid.*)

And yet again, this time visibly irritated:

> Und müssen nicht sie [die Allgegenwärtigen] selber noch, Geliebte,
> Amphitryon sein und seine Züge stehlen,
> Wenn deine Seele sie empfangen soll?[b]   (*ibid.*)

And finally, with signs of smouldering anger:

> Ists nicht Amphitryon, der Geliebte stets,
> Vor welchem du im Staube liegst?[c]   (*ibid.*)

At the end, Jupiter plays his trump card: Suppose, he asks, I myself were this god of whose frustrated longing I have been telling you? His question, and the exchange that follows, is so interesting that I shall quote it in full:

> Jupiter: Wenn ich nun dieser Gott dir wär −?
> Alkmene: Wenn du
>   − Wie ist mir denn? Wenn du mir dieser Gott wärst
>   − − Ich weiß nicht, soll ich vor dir niederfallen,
>   Soll ich es nicht? Bist dus mir? Bist dus mir?
> Jupiter: Entscheide du. Amphitryon bin ich.
> Alkmene: Amphitryon −
> Jupiter: Amphitryon, dir, ja.
>   Doch wenn ich, frag ich, dieser Gott dir wäre,
>   Dir liebend vom Olymp herabgestiegen,
>   Wie würdest du dich dann zu fassen wissen?
> Alkmene: Wenn du mir, Liebster, dieser Gott wärst − ja,
>   So wüßt ich nicht, wo mir Amphitryon wäre,
>   So würd ich folgen dir, wohin du gehst,
>   Und wärs auch, wie Euridike, zum Orkus.[d]   (*ibid.*)

---

could not dim the radiance of/ My own wife's bosom by one single stain! What phantom fears!

a   'Tis *him*/ His base arts have deceived, not/ Your unerring sense! When he/ Conceived himself in your embrace, you lay/ At your beloved's breast, Amphitryon's; when he/ Dreamt of your kiss, your lips caressed/ Amphitryon's beloved mouth.

b   And must not they [the all-present ones] themselves, my love,/ Become Amphitryon and steal his very form/ For your soul to admit them?

c   Is it not always your own love, Amphitryon,/ To whom your knee bends, grovelling in the dust?

d   Jupiter: If then I were this god to you − ?/
      Alkmene: If you/ − What's coming over me? Were you that god to me/ − − I know not, should I bend my knee to you,/ Or should I not? Are you that one to me? You he to me?

This passage is enchanting, in that it shows Alkmene's total inability − a very Kleistean inability − to abstract from the dear ubiquity, to her, of Amphitryon[9]; an indivisible oneness of man and god which is underscored by Charis' pious posturing in the following scene, when she has 'reason' to believe that her churlish husband might after all be a churlish god, a very different matter indeed. But its touchingness apart, this scene is revealing for an overriding stylistic device the poet employs. Nine times, in this short exchange, do the partners use the ethical dative, with reference to Alkmene and 'her' Amphitryon: eloquent evidence that whatever filters through to her, whatever she receives, to-her-appears-as-Amphitryon, even as it is Amphitryon who has stamped her being through and through, who is the eyes she sees with and the sensibility with which she registers the world. Out of the manifold impressions that assail Alkmene − be it her husband, or the god, or the very devil Jupiter conjures up in her imagination − she unwaveringly construes Amphitryon, the beloved. She 'constitutes' his very selfhood in the way that the spontaneous synthesising mind, for Kant, constitutes the 'thingness' of objects. In this woman's capacity creatively to relate Kleist has, for once, found the triumphant answer to the tormented question 'ob das, was wir Wahrheit nennen, wahrhaft Wahrheit sei, *oder ob es uns nur so scheint.'* [a] In this figure, as perhaps nowhere else, Kleist transcended the trauma of Kant. What appears to Alkmene as Amphitryon, *is* Amphitryon, *wahrhaft wahr* − truly true, precisely because he-*appears-to-her* as such. The semantic pattern of this tell-tale passage is this poet's 'yes' to the wholesomeness of an epistemology which affirms the inextricable involvement of the knower with the known. Here, in this drama, the 'spontaneity' of the knowing subject is gloriously transposed from the theoretical level of Kant's first Critique onto the plane of feeling, and affirmed: Alkmene's unerring spontaneity creates, and sustains, the identity of the man who only through her steadfast relating to him is fitted to grow into a stable self.

Conversely, Alkmene's sensibility is also this poet's 'yes' to Goethe. As he, in the *Gegenständlichkeit* of his perceiving and thinking, permitted his mind to be imbued with the objects that entered into his ken, as his love poems are stamped through and through with the being of Friederike or Lili or Charlotte von Stein or Marianne von Willemer, so here: Alkmene not only creates 'her' Amphitryon: so sensitively has she assimilated herself to him as to be virtually his creation. She is permeated by the figure of her beloved, he is her eyes and ears, and it is this fine and unerring attunement to his sensibility which empowers her, herself his creature, to give him back to himself[10].

Jupiter: You must decide. I am Amphitryon.
Alkmene: Amphitryon −
Jupiter: Amphitryon, aye, to you./ But if I were, I ask, that god to you,/ Descended from Olympus full of love,/ What would you make of such a knowledge, speak?
Alkmene: If you, beloved, were this god to me −/ There would be no Amphitryon for me./ I'd follow you wherever you would go,/ Even to Orcus, like Euridice.

* my italics
a 'whether, what we call truth, is indeed the truth or whether it but appears to us as the truth.'

In this abounding capacity, both to relate and to be related to, Alkmene is all but unique amongst Kleist's figures; Kantian, Goethean, and wholly human. In her, for one glorious moment, the embargo on relatedness is lifted.

But how cruelly she is set upon by the rival lovers[11], the one denying the mystery of her noumenal self and with it any relationship in depth, the other repudiating the conditioning of her phenomenal self and with it, the whole apparatus of sensible experiencing. And even as they themselves are parts, so they tug and tear at her wholeness. The one would denigrate her to the status of an object, the other would elevate her to the dignity of a discarnate soul. And in their endeavour to reify her or to deify her, they both alike transgress the bounds of a humanity poised between those extremes in a most precarious balance.

Alkmene withstands these pulls, but only just. Even she endures a hideous crisis of identity when the pure phenomenal aspect and the pure noumenal aspect of the man in whom her self is vested, finally break asunder and both claim her allegiance. As they confront her, split, she experiences the vulgarity of the phenomenal *per se* and the intolerable beauty of the noumenal, indeed, the Numinous, in its unmediated onslaught. Yet, even in opting for Jupiter, she is faithful to Amphitryon and faithful to her own indivisible wholeness. For all she does is what she has ever done: she worships the god in the man.

As the vainglorious Amphitryon is forced upon his knees and constrained to acknowledge both the divine source of his being and the newborn certainty

> Des unerschütterlich erfaßten Glaubens,
> Daß er Amphitryon *ihr** ist . . .[a],

he not only receives back his eclipsed self: Alkmene receives back, from this gruelling test, a man whose hollowness has been filled by the influx of the Divine. This new wholeness of Amphitryon, together with the disembodiment of Jupiter, once again vouchsafes the integrity of an experiencing which had been all but rent apart by the warring claims of the rivals. Alkmene, blinded still by the dazzling visitation of the god, may once again return within the bounds of phenomenality and love the Divine-as-it-appears in the human. And that Amphitryon has become worthy of such a love is testified by his wish, which had been the god's wish, too, that he be granted a son like that of Tyndarus. From the marriage of sense and spirit, the material and the Divine, the demi-god is conceived.

But the purge has been terrible. The naked visitation of the god has all but annihilated the human vessels he has touched. After Jove's disappearance the sturdiest and most simple-minded of the officers, Argatiphontidas, comments Amphitryon's glory, saying:

> Du siehst durchdrungen uns —
> — You see us piercèd through and through.

---

* my italic
[a] Of the unshakable belief/ That he, to *her*, is but Amphitryon . . .

Little does he — do they — know what it was like to have been visited, and penetrated, by the living god. To those whom he called from their sleep, undid, and seared, once again to release them back into the mediacy of the human condition, there is nothing to say save 'Alkmene!' and that pregnant 'Ach!', echo of Alkmene's first shaken farewell from Jupiter, now heralding the blessings and the bleaknesses of the temperate days to come.

6 On the Horns of a Dilemma:
The Subjective and the Objective Fallacies

1.

In the preceding chapters I have endeavoured to identify two characteristic models of experiencing which I termed the subjective and the objective fallacies respectively. In the case of Kleist's first drama, we have seen the subjective and the objective fallacies exhibited turn by turn in the same figure, the youthful Ottokar. Having sought at first to reach out for a direct communion with Agnes in an empirical void, he soon comes up against the intervening individual context dividing him and her, and in turn seeks to assess her from the outside, overriding her concrete situation. In *Amphitryon*, conversely, Kleist has seemingly distributed these two modalities over different figures: the subjective inwardness of Jupiter clamouring for a direct communion standing at one end of the cognitive spectrum, whilst Amphitryon, backed by Sosias and his generals, stands at the other extreme, relying upon a detached perceptual analysis of a situation in which he is himself emotionally involved. Nevertheless, in this play, too, we have found these two models of experiencing to merge in their extreme ranges, both intrinsically and in that the two rivals are in fact aspects of one person.

In most of Kleist's poetic works we shall encounter these two complementary modalities as different phases of the same cognitive dilemma embodied in one and the same character. In one or two instances, however, it appears in classic purity, predominantly or even exclusively, in one of its forms. For this reason, and for the sake of greater clarity of exposition, I shall begin by treating these two interrelated modalities successively.

Of all Kleist's characters the purest example of the subjective mode is probably the figure of Count F., protagonist of the Marquise von O. At first sight, this hypothesis is going to meet with some resistance. Is he not the brutal rapist of an unknown woman with whom he cannot be conceded to have the least emotional rapport? We shall leave this question open for the time being and point out that the narrator, who from early on in the story gives us abundant clues as to the rapist's identity with the count, scrupulously refrains from attaching any blame to the latter, let alone from condemning him[1]. He seems more concerned to show a monstrous action compulsively flowing from an otherwise noble and blameless character than to unfold the character from the vantage-point of his deed. There is indeed a striking absence of all realistic psychological detail. Instead, this enigmatic figure is shown time and again in the almost frozen stance of his impetuous wooing; and the impression arises that the fierce intensity of his wish to be granted an immediate union is the primary feature of his character, and that it is intended to be understood as the cause of his otherwise unexplained deed rather than as its consequence[2].

This absence of all realistic detail, especially with regard to the motivation for his deed, is matched by the sustained suggestion that the count belongs to a higher order of beings altogether. At the beginning, just before the rape, and then again in the closing words of the story, he is likened to an angel, indeed at the end to a devil as well. At his first visit to the exiled Julietta he is described as 'schön wie ein junger Gott' — 'beautiful as a young god'. His swan dream links him to the myth of Jupiter visiting Leda, though in dreamlike fashion the figures are reversed — it is Julietta who appears as the swan — whilst in relation to himself, images of inviolate integrity ambivalently appear side by side with images of pollution. The numinous aura surrounding the count is very strong. And indeed, we are reminded of Kleist's Jupiter by the 'unerhörte Begebenheit' — the 'unheard of occurrence' — of the story, an event touched upon by the Leda motif: the visitation of a woman by a power gaining access to her in an unnatural, or supernatural, way. The biblical genesis of this motif — which Goethe spotted and condemned in Kleist's Greek comedy — here becomes an overt theme of discourse when the marquise asks the midwife whether she would concede the possibility of an 'unwissentlichen Empfängnis'[a][3] and receives the caustic reply 'daß dies, außer der heiligen Jungfrau, noch keinem Weibe auf Erden zugestoßen wäre'[b]; a religious allusion which in turn is strengthened by the characterisation of Julietta's father as a veritable doubting Thomas.

If, then, references to the numinous domain are central and recurrent, we must concede a more than incidental significance to the count's words when he first approaches Julietta in her state of dereliction. He protests his fervent belief in her innocence and describes himself as being 'so überzeugt, . . . als ob ich allwissend wäre, als ob meine Seele in deiner Brust wohnte'[c]. These might be Jupiter's words to Alkmene, fraudulent in that he is in fact fully aware of her innocence, yet also sincere in that the speaker behind the thin mask of ignorance does indeed seek nothing more ardently than a direct communion from soul to soul. To achieve such a communion is then, I would suggest, the overriding motive of the count who is ambivalently portrayed as superhuman and subhuman rather than human, except towards the end when he 'comes down to earth' and learns to respect, and fall in with, the emotional tempo of the woman he loves; and this impatience to penetrate to the essence of the loved one is the cause of his intrepid deed rather than the result of trying to make good for it. In the abbreviation of a pure poetic *chiffre*, without choosing to fill in the details of psychological motivation Kleist has, in this enigmatic figure, created the longing of one touched with numinosity

---

a 'of a conception of which she herself knew nothing'
b 'That save for the Holy Virgin this had happened to no woman on earth';
c 'so convinced, . . . as though I were omniscient, as though my soul resided in your breast.'

for mystical consummation. The fact that this consummation assumes the primitive form of a sexual penetration need not astonish us, let alone make us doubt our hypothesis. For this regression to a primitively physical plane is characteristically Kleistean, and no more incomprehensible than the first mortal couple's reaching out for an apple in their quest for moral knowledge, or indeed than Penthesilea's savagery when what she means is love. Here, *in nuce*, in this unmotivated 'unerhörte Begebenheit', is the secret point of coincidence between the subjective and the objective approaches to 'knowledge'. The count certainly degrades the marquise to the status of an object, that is to say, he reifies her at the moment of the rape. But Kleist in this mystery story has chosen to leave this incomprehensible reversal psychologically unmotivated so as not to detract from the air of numinosity surrounding the count and the total reception of the baffling event he has set in motion. In any case, there is no character from the pen of Kleist spiritual enough not to lapse, on occasion, into the physicality of Ruprecht's

> Was ich mit Händen greife, glaub ich gern,[a]   (9)

or indeed Charis'

> Man nimmt ein falsches Kleid, ein Hausgerät,
> Doch einen Mann greift man im Finstern.[b]   (II, 4)

2.

If in the case of the enigmatic lover of the Marquise von O. interpretation was bound to proceed indirectly and tentatively, we are on much firmer ground as we turn to the figure of Graf Wetter vom Strahl, the strange and dazzling protagonist of Käthchen von Heilbronn. Graf Friedrich Wetter vom Strahl is, as it were, the human brother of Jupiter; and paradoxically this signifies his being an exaggeration, almost a caricature, of the divine seducer's portrait. For whilst Jupiter is a god with all the mental reserves of his divinity behind him, Strahl is a mortal, and that same trend towards disembodied communion in the realm of essences on him represents an unnatural strain. Where Jupiter is at home in the Numinous, Strahl, by following its lure, temporarily becomes a dissociated human being. His very name, that high-voltage condensation of elemental forces − and much play is made of its significance − is of a frenetic sublimity which only just escapes the ridiculous. His *vis attrativa* is irresistible and his very appearance breathes the Numinous: 'Mensch, entsetzlicher, als Worte fassen, und der Gedanke ermißt: stehst du nicht rein da, als hätten die Cherubim sich entkleidet, und ihren Glanz dir, funkelnd wie Mailicht, um die Seele gelegt!'[c] (I, 1) How could that 'aura' of

---

[a] What I may grasp with hands I'd fain believe,/
[b] You catch hold of a garb, an implement that's wrong;/ But your own man you grab at dead of night.
[c] 'Man, more terrible than words can say and thought may fathom: do you not stand there verily as though the cherubs had taken off their robes and dressed your soul in their radiance, dazzling as the light on a May day!'

numinosity of which we have spoken be more precisely articulated than here, in Theobald's vision of his child's seducer?

Much has been made of Strahl's sadism, and understandably so. His extortionist method of cross-examining Käthchen and the whip that is ready at hand are evidence enough. Indeed, it would be easy to treat Strahl's sadistic tendencies, and Käthchen's corresponding masochistic ones, as case history material eminently lending itself to a depth-psychological analysis. The pathology of these mechanisms here as of other behaviour patterns elsewhere is patent and their investigation, with full use of critical tools, would compel one's admiration for Kleist's psychological acumen. Yet little would be gained by such an undertaking in a literary study which is not first and foremost biographical. For Kleist was to a remarkable degree unconscious of the mechanisms he portrays – except in *Die Familie Schroffenstein* which sets out to be a scrupulous anatomy of evil after the fashion of, say, Shakespeare's *Richard III* and as such is quite uncharacteristic of him. His creative empathy did indeed uncover pathological mechanisms in his characters such as were only to be discursively formulated in our own century; but such a portrayal lay outside the bounds of his artistic intentions and, on the whole, fails to illuminate them. And it is with these that the literary critic is concerned.

What, then, are we to make of Strahl's cruel testing out and exhibiting of Käthchen's love? It evinces an overpowering need to see that love *per se,* as it is in itself, to know its naked essence. To allow himself to be 'taken in' by Käthchen's devoted loving and relatedness would be to be content with a vision of it that takes its colouring from him, the beloved. And that would be the conditional knowledge of one who – and here the shadow of Kant rears its head again – is content with nothing save the absolute and unmediated truth.

This overweening drive it is which informs Strahl's interrogations of Käthchen, first before the secret tribunal and later, under the elderberry bush. The sleeping Käthchen is a totally accessible Käthchen, in that all the barriers and masks of consciousness are lowered. Indeed, we may say that Käthchen's gestic repertoire, her falls, faints and somnambulist states, are a function of Strahl's need to see through her, absolutely, without the distortions of her self-conscious reflectiveness. He wants to read her like an open book, as Ottokar wants to read Agnes and Jupiter Alkmene. He wants to see her love as it really is, not as it appears to Käthchen.

> *Er* will geliebt sein, nicht ihr Wahn von ihm . . . :[a]   (II, 5)

this self-revelation of Jupiter's, in *Amphitryon,* holds good here, too, in full force.

Strahl's powerful desire for communion with the beloved's essence is brought home in a spate of images which are strongly reminiscent of those of Ottokar or the god; and to establish his theme the poet has placed all but one of these in the

---

[a]   'Tis *he* that would be loved, and not her whim of him . . .

expository first act of the play. Weeks after her incomprehensible fall from the window in her father's house Strahl reports finding Käthchen again, on the way to Straßburg: '— da liegt sie mir, wie ich erwache, gleich einer Rose, entschlummert zu Füßen . . .'[a] (I, 1). He pretends to scold her for deceiving him,

> Mir, dessen Blick du da liegst wie die Rose,
> Die ihren jungen Kelch dem Licht erschloß . . .[b]   (I, 2)

and calls upon her to reveal the mystery of her passion to him, and to him alone:

> Willt den geheimsten der Gedanken mir,
> Kathrina, der dir irgend, faß mich wohl,
> Im Winkel wo des Herzens schlummert, geben?[c]   (I, 2)

In a final burst of mental possessiveness he decrees:

> Du rührst dich nicht!
> Hier soll dich keiner richten als nur der,
> Dem deine Seele frei sich unterwirft.[d]   (I, 2)

And indeed, Käthchen freely concurs with his claim upon her soul. Governed and guided by direct contact with the Numinous — it is a cherub that has appeared to her announcing her true love, and a cherub will guard her as Kunigunde's burning house collapses — she refuses to disclose the mystery of her love to anyone bar him:

> Den nenn ich grausam, der mich darum fragt!
> Wenn *du* es wissen willst, wohlan, so rede,
> Denn dir liegt meine Seele offen da![e]   (I, 2)

The wish to see her soul bared, essence to essence, has found its culminating — though hardly its most appealing — formulation in Strahl's monologue following the tribunal scene. He muses:

> Käthchen, Käthchen, Käthchen! Du, deren junge Seele, als sie heut nackt vor mir stand, von wollüstiger Schönheit gänzlich triefte, wie die mit Ölen gesalbte Braut eines Perserkönigs, wenn sie, auf alle Teppiche niederregnend, in sein Gemach geführt wird![f]   (II, 1)

Yet the voluptuous spirituality of such communion remains confined to Strahl's fantasies. In reality there are the kicks of his boots, and the lash of his whip and his tongue. In this split it is easy to recognise Kleist's own reaction pattern as we

---

a   '— as I awake, there lies she at my feet, like to a slumbering rose . . . '
b   To me who gazes on you as a rose,/ That has disclosed its maiden chalice to the light . . .
c   Wouldst thou give me the inmost secret of your thoughts,/ Which somewhere slumbers, Cathrin, mark my words,/ In some dark corner maybe of your heart?
d   You shall not stir!/ No man may judge you here save me alone,/ To whom your soul submits of its free will.
e   Him I call cruel who should ask me that!/ If *you* would know the answer, say so, pray;/ 'Tis you alone to whom my soul lies bared.
f   'Käthchen, Käthchen, Käthchen! You, whose young soul, standing there naked before me, veritably dripped voluptuous beauty, like the anointed bride of a Persian king when she is led into his chamber, showering down over all the rugs!'

know it from his letters: the pleasurable arousal caused by the increasing distance between him and Wilhelmine von Zenge on his Würzburg trip, the teasing in which he indulged, putting out feelers only to retract them again, raising expectations and then veiling himself in mystery. But over and above such biographical links, it is the embargo the count places on relatedness, under the guise of a stormy need to establish a direct communion, which concerns us in this section. Here again we encounter the same ambivalence we have isolated in the figures of Ottokar and Jupiter: an intense desire for absolute relatedness which yet shuns a fusion in a reality that is feared as being beset by appearances; a reaching out for the Absolute which yet shuns the phenomenality of embodied experience. Such *voyeurism* — for this is what the holding away of the other comes to — contains the seeds of that *Nervenfieber* which so frequently figures in Kleist's works. Here as always it signifies the fracturing of a personality that shrinks from having a very rudimentary self-hood confirmed by receiving its image back from a sustaining 'other'. It is only when Strahl permits himself to be 'taken in' by Käthchen's relatedness — incorporated into and assimilated by her emotional system, as it were — that the split in himself between body and spirit will heal. Meanwhile he whom the cherub in his nocturnal dream-vision bade 'Vertraue! vertraue! vertraue!' — 'Trust! trust! trust!' (II, 9) cannot but doubt and unrelatedly view what he cannot quite bring himself to trust, for fear, precisely, of being 'taken in'.

Needless to say, this imperious thrust for the absolute essence of another who is kept spellbound in the frozen stance of a surrender in a void, here too gives way to an equally extreme reliance on objective factual evidence. Not only is Käthchen reduced to an object of scientific scrutiny; not only does Strahl let himself be duped by Kunigunde, that synthetic conglomerate of falsehoods: even when he has begun to trust in the reality of his visionary love he tests the 'Wissenschaft, entschöpft dem Himmelsbronnen' — 'the knowledge drawn from the fount of heaven' (V, 1): ravaging the church registry, calculating the exact hour of Käthchen's conception and ferreting out 'mit verruchtem Witze' — 'with accursed perspicacity' (V, 1), the exact movements of the emperor on his visit to Heilbronn sixteen years previously. Is this the way to trust a cherub's annunciation? Here, as in *Die Familie Schroffenstein* and *Amphitryon*, the subjective fallacy is revealed for what it in fact is: the first cousin of its polar opposite.

3.

We have reached the halfway-house of our present enquiry. In the works that remain to be discussed, notably *Prinz Friedrich von Homburg* and *Penthesilea*, the subjective and the objective modes appear so inextricably entwined that they have to be treated side by side, rather than in succession. Before proceeding to that task, let us recapitulate the most characteristic features of the objective fallacy as we have isolated it so far, and demonstrate it in its unadulterated purity in two short narrative works.

In the opening chapter of this study we were concerned at some length with the fountain-head of the objective modality, the biblical myth of the Fall as related in Genesis 3. This was as it should be, seeing that the narrator of *Über das Marionettentheater* himself insists that our understanding of the human condition in the different phases of its development is contingent upon our knowledge of that opening chapter. Moreover, allusions to 'the paradise of innocence' and even the unhappy apple − the young dancer F. in the role of Paris is guilty of his worst girations as he hands the apple of contention to Venus − continue to make their appearance in the narrative, underpinning the central importance of the biblical motif. The primal Fall from grace, then, is envisaged as a mis-taking − Kleist's own word is *Mißgriff* − of a material and physically perceptible good − the apple − for an ideal and invisible one − our knowledge of moral truth. We have in our perusal of Kleist's letters seen how keen the danger of such a hypostasization was in the poet's own case. As the early church-father Irenaeus envisaged the church as a 'truth-bank', so he himself continually thinks, and speaks, of truth as a hoarding of material treasures capable of being taken with us into the grave, a misconception which turned the acquaintance with Kant into such a reverberating disaster.

This mis-apprehension of material goods for ideal ones has continued to play a central role in the works we have discussed; and everywhere the occurrence of this *erste Mißgriff* is accompanied by images of paradise, of falling and even of the ill-starred apple. The written contact of inheritance which is the root of the catastrophic distrust in *Die Familie Schroffenstein* is likened to the Fall and its presiding requisite, the apple. The *corpus delicti* in *The Broken Pitcher* is caused by a threefold fall; and as we saw, the nomenclature of the play as much as its preoccupation with 'the paradise of innocence' testifies to the centrality of the biblical motif. Trust and faith in this play are replaced by reliance on a dead requisite, an 'article of faith' in Kleist's reading of the word[4]: and what is believed is not merely what is seen but what can be grasped and handled − like the fruit of the forbidden tree. Already here we encounter that desperate assault on eyes not capable of discerning an emotional truth which is of its nature invisible, a motif which was to be sounded more tragically and more insistently in *Amphitryon*, a tragicomedy in which the cleaving to material surrogates for unsupported trust is taken to its all but tragic conclusion, in the annihilation of the Theban's false-self[5]. And it is amusing to note that this play too starts with a fall, if a metaphorical one: the 'fall' of the sobered general 'from the clouds' at his young wife's unexpected welcome which is the immediate occasion for his flight into unrelatedness.

Before embarking on the further pursuit of our theme in its more intricate forms, then, I should like briefly to allude to two narratives in which it is presented in unbetterable simplicity. The first of these is *Das Bettelweib von Locarno − The Beggar-woman of Locarno*. The masterly analysis Emil Staiger has accorded to this short story seems to leave the critic with little that is worth saying[6]. But what he has ignored in the specific context of his syntactical investigation is the story's actual theme: the failure of the two protagonists to comprehend a *spiritual* configuration by *perceptual* means. An impious act of the marquis has led to the death of an old woman. When he bids a beggar-woman who has sought shelter in his castle relinquish the bed of straw which has been assigned to her by his wife's compassion, the old woman slips, falls, and, after painfully traversing the room, perishes in a corner. The consequences of the marquis' action are visible; its essence – his hard-hearted lack of piety – is hidden from sight. But the psychic event leaves a trail in the physical universe: not a visible one, but one less material and addressing itself to the more defenseless of our sense-organs, the ear. 'Jemand, den kein Mensch mit Augen sehen kann' – 'one whom no mortal eye can see' – audibly traverses the room at midnight in the direction the old woman took and with the identical sounds. A prospective buyer of the castle – the marquis has meanwhile fallen on bad days himself – is surprised by the apparition and, terrified, leaves the castle without concluding the buy; and the rumour that the place is haunted begins to spread like wildfire. Anxious to sell the house, the impoverished marquis decides to investigate – *untersuchen* is the word the narrator uses – this incomprehensible matter. 'Unbegreiflich' is what it is three times aptly called, for a spectral apparition cannot be grasped; and three times, with rising terror, the marquis, joined later by his wife, stays in the room over-night to 'subject' the mystery to which only empathy and insight could give him a clue, to a 'kaltblütigen Prüfung' – a 'cold-blooded scrutiny'. The third occasion, related at length, proves to be decisive. Accompanied by their dog, man and wife sit, each on his bed, 'zwei Lichter auf dem Tisch' – 'two candles on the table', he armed with pistols. Waiting and whiling away the time, chatting uneasily, gazing into the void, they seek to see the invisible invasion from the realm of the Numinous. Instead they hear it, the dog backs in the direction of the noise, and while the marquis draws his sword 'und da ihm niemand antwortet, gleich einem Rasenden, nach allen Richtungen die Luft durchhaut'[a], his wife leaves the place, terror-stricken. Frantic, the marquis takes a candle – is it one of those with which he had tried to illumine the invisible? – sets fire to the room at all four corners, and perishes in the conflagration, 'müde seines Lebens' – 'weary of his life'.

This story scarcely requires to be commented upon. In its extreme concentration which Staiger has so beautifully analysed, it is the story of the apple all over again. An invisible moral reality requiring a differentiated interpretation is perceptually scrutinised and physically attacked as though its material manifestation were its super-sensible significance; and a wide-eyed fool, disgusted like Ruprecht and Amphitryon with his crude sense-apparatus *vis-à-vis* a metaphysical reality he cannot grasp, destroys himself with the very light which had shone on his obtuseness.

---

[a] 'and, as no one replies, like one raving cuts through the air in every direction'

The second story is an even terser narrative. It is a chronicle-style anecdote told in the context of a review of Werner's fate-tragedy *Der vierundzwanzigste Februar*. Its title: *Von einem Kinde, das kindlicher Weise ein anderes Kind umbringt* — *Of a Child which Murders another Child in a Childlike Fashion*. A group of small children play 'butcher and cook'. Before they begin, they distribute the roles each is to play. One is 'to be' the butcher, another one the cook, a third one a sow. Two little girls are 'to be' cook and assistant cook, the latter being told to catch the blood of the little boy that is 'to be' the sow in a vessel, to make sausages with. The game begins and the cook, 'verabredetermaßen' — 'as previously agreed', cuts the throat of the little boy who 'is to be the sow', whilst the assistant cook catches his blood in her little vessel. The unhappy butcher is brought before the town-council, who are at a loss what to do about the murder, 'denn sie sahen wohl, daß es kindlicher Weise geschehen war'[a]. A wise old counsellor suggests a Solomonic solution. The supreme judge is to hold out to the child a Rhenish florin in one hand and a 'schönen, roten Apfel' — 'a bright, red apple' — in the other. If the child takes the money, it is to be killed; if it takes the apple, acquitted. The child, merrily laughing, reaches for the apple and goes unpunished.

This extraordinary story will engage our attention once more in a later chapter. In the present context it is enough to show that the theme we are concerned with, which we have traced in *Das Bettelweib von Locarno*, is here taken to that logical conclusion we shall meet again in *Penthesilea*. The clue to the story is to be found in the judgment; more precisely in the role assigned to the apple. We are back at the beginning, in the first chapter of the world as related in Genesis 3. The playing children do not distinguish between appearance and reality, between visible signs and their invisible significances. They do not agree to *enact* the cook and the butcher and the sow, but to *be* these things. Thus they *act out* literally, in brute reality, what they do not have symbolic gestures to represent, even as Eve, seeking knowledge, takes the visible — and edible — sign of knowledge, the apple, offered to her by the serpent. The regression from seeing to grasping and eating which is entailed in the hypostasization of an immaterial good, its reduction to object status, is complete, both in the biblical myth and Kleist's grisly anecdote.

The judgment puts the developmental phase of the culprit to the test. If he takes the coin, he is in fact able to distinguish between signs and significances. For the coin signifies a value over and above signalling it. It may be worth more than its weight or less than its looks. The apple is an apple, a discrete object and a symbol only to the post-paradisical intelligence which has learned that truth cannot be plucked from a tree and eaten. The child choosing the apple, 'lachend' — 'laughing', testifies to a primal innocence incapable of that differentiation between abstract and concrete goods which is ushered in by the Fall. Thus it is acquitted, and rightly so, in Kleist's estimate of the matter.

---

[a] 'realising as they did that it had been a childlike action'

4.

We seem to have drifted from a world pregnant with the Numinous into a pre-human domain instinct with bestiality. This movement of my argument is quite deliberate. It marks the huge span between the extremes of the subjective and the objective modalities which, seemingly poles apart, yet lie adjacent to one another, intermingled, in one and the same person. Of such an intermingling of opposites I now propose to give two illustrations, one example being *Prinz Friedrich von Homburg*, the other *Penthesilea*.

Has the prince slipped back into the Garden of Eden by that backdoor through which, so the dancer in *Über das Marionettentheater* tells us, we are forever seeking to gain access to that place? Or did he never leave it? 'Im Garten hinten' – 'at the back of the garden' – deeply regressed into the unconsciousness of sleep, he sits, winding himself a laurel wreath[7]. The grand elector is called to witness this strange spectacle; and with the clairvoyance of a god sees straight into the dreamer's soul –

> – was gilts, ich weiß,
> Was dieses jungen Toren Brust bewegt –[a]   (I, 1)

and deftly and ruthlessly draws its mystery to the light. As the sleeping prince receives from Natalie's hand the elector's golden chain, all the love and trust and faith and ambition that lie dormant in him are disclosed. Here indeed is a direct communion from soul to soul. To the prince, the cavalcade that moves before his sleep-bound eyes is a veritable vision, a visitation from above, essentially religious in character and more real than reality itself[8]. This is how he describes his apparition:

> Mir war, als ob, von Gold und Silber strahlend
> Ein Königschloß sich plötzlich öffnete,
> Und hoch von seiner Marmorramp' herab,
> Der ganze Reigen zu mir niederstiege,
> Der Menschen, die mein Busen liebt . . .[b]   (I, 4)

There follows his curious dithering as to who it was that held out the chain entwined with the wreath to him; he grasps at it,

> in unaussprechlicher Bewegung,
> Die Hände streck ich aus, ihn zu ergreifen:[c]   (I, 4)

but the ramp itself evades him, seemingly stretching to the gates of heaven:

---

a – what will you bet, I know/ What goes on in the soul of this young fool –
b Methought I saw the palace of a king,/ Gleaming with gold and silver, open suddenly/ And from its marble ramp on high/ The cavalcade of those my bosom loves/ Descended one and all . . .
c To grasp it I stretch out my hands,/ Moved beyond words:

Ich greife rechts, ich greife links umher,
Der Teuren einen ängstlich zu erhaschen.
Umsonst! Des Schlosses Tor geht plötzlich auf;
Ein Blitz der aus dem Innern zuckt, verschlingt sie,
Das Tor fügt rasselnd wieder sich zusammen:
Nur einen Handschuh, heftig, im Verfolgen,
Streif ich der süßen Traumgestalt vom Arm:
Und einen Handschuh, ihr allmächtgen Götter,
Da ich erwache, halt ich in der Hand![a]   (I, 4)

But what to the prince seems an invasion from the Numinous is threatened, and in more ways than one: 'the elector, with the brow of Zeus' is viewing him, indeed manipulating him, impartially, to see into the bottom of his soul; and the response he elicits from the dreamer is unleavened in the extreme. Worldly goods and love and faith lie intermingled in his mind, each and all confused in one vague and overwhelming vision of immortal glory. His conscious mind does not even know the name of the woman who appeared to him as in an aureole – and we know that the name of a person is much more than

die freundliche Erfindung
Mit einer Silbe das Unendliche
Zu fassen –:[b]   (*Fam. Schroffenstein*, II, 1)

it may mean a whole hostile world intervening between two lovers, as it does for Romeo and Juliet, and for Ottokar and Agnes. Nor yet does his conscious mind know of the conditions under which glory is to be attained, which are the law and discipline of the state and those battle orders he so totally ignores except for the one that plays in with his excited imagination:

Dann wird er die Fanfare blasen lassen![c]   (I, 3)

His vision takes place in a dream, that is to say in a contextual void. Impetuously, without knowledge or care of the complexities of life, he reaches out for the ultimate to lay hold of it and grasp it.

And grasp, physically, at what his blind eyes have seen, he does. He snatches at Natalie's glove –

Dies Stück des Traums, das ihm verkörpert ward,[d]   (V, 5)

a first *Mißgriff* which ushers in his fateful disorientation[9] – as he will snatch at fortune's own winged orb: things and abstract ideas, material tokens and the immaterial goods they symbolise, to this untried mind seem commensurable and

---

[a] I reach out to the right, now to the left,/ Seeking to clutch one of the dear ones, anxiously./ In vain: the castle's portals open suddenly;/ A flash from its interior swallows them,/ The portals close, loud clanking, and fall to:/ A single glove, in vehement pursuit,/ snatch I from the sweet apparition's arm,/ And ye almighty gods, it is a glove/ I hold, on waking, in this very hand!

[b] the sweet device/ To grasp the infinite within the confines of/ One syllable –:

[c] Then he will bid the fanfare to be sounded!/

[d] This piece of dream that put on flesh for him,/

are freely exchanged one for the other: a process of hypostasization we know well enough from Kleist's own letters. *Streifen, greifen, erhaschen* and finally *stürzen* − brush, grasp, snatch and toss − these are the words in which the poet describes the prince's quest for the vision he has glimpsed, first in action and stage direction, then in his retrospective account of the apparition to Hohenzollern, and finally in his apostrophe to fortune in which the first act culminates and on which it concludes[10].

But between that first instinctive snatching at what his sleep-bound eyes perceive and desire and those later re-enactments there occurs − a resounding fall:

> Da liegt er; eine Kugel trifft nicht besser![a]   (I, 4)

Thus Hohenzollern glosses the dreaming Adam's fall into consciousness from that paradise of innocence where the Absolute had beckoned to him in the shape of a lady's glove and been triumphantly carried off by him in this guise; a lapse into a phenomenal world requiring distinctions between signs and things signified such as this lyrical mind, roused now to semi-consciousness, will not, one knows, be able to sustain.

The test comes when the Absolute the young visionary had beheld, eye to eye and soul to soul, withdraws itself from sight and the remorseless machinery of causes and consequences blocks the Numinous out from view. The war tribunal has pronounced its verdict of guilty. The prince argues − and here we must attend to the familiar imagery of the corona the poet has put onto his lips[11] − that the elector would not let the judges go so far,

> Dächt er, mit einem heitern Herrscherspruch,
> Nicht, als ein Gott in ihren Kreis zu treten . . .[b]

and urges:

> Nein, Freund, er sammelt diese Nacht von Wolken
> Nur um mein Haupt, um wie die Sonne mir
> Durch ihren Dunstkreis strahlend aufzugehn . . .[c]   (III, 1)

Still he bases his certainty 'Auf mein Gefühl von ihm!' − 'Upon the verdict of my heart!' − but only just. The sun of the elector's caring remains shrouded in its own impenetrable atmosphere − the state, the law, obedience. When Hohenzollern shatters the prince's simplistic expectation of a renewed immediacy of vision and assures him that the legal machinery is taking its predictable course, the prince's faith falters and baulks before the first opaque barrier of phenomenality. Incorrigible rationalist that he is, Hohenzollern has found a credible reason for the elector's anger. He has his political schemes and, in courting Natalie, the prince has crossed them. He wants peace with the Swedes and Natalie's hand is the 'bewußte Preis' − 'the price that we both know' − in that barter.

---

[a] There he lies; no bullet could do better!/
[b] Did he not mean to step into their midst/ With the serene pronouncement of a god . . .
[c] No, friend, he gathers these nocturnal clouds/ About my head for nought but radiantly/
To rise above their misty banks . . .

This low-key pragmatic reading of the elector's withdrawnness strikes at the heart of the prince's untried faith. 'Jetzt ist mir alles klar' — 'Now I see all plainly', he proclaims; and from that moment on he that has been so lyrically and extravagantly subjective lapses into the crudest forms of the objective fallacy[12]. Shying at an impermeable situation, he at once opts out of the emotional context in which he has hitherto existed and views his own life, and the relationships that have made up its weave, with the cold and cynical eye of an outside observer. Natalie to him becomes a barterable object to be sold or exchanged at will; so does her blue-eyed son — a consolation prize he dreams up for her, to be purchased with cash; and honour, service, country, respect and self-respect are likewise jettisoned by one who has at one stroke become totally unrelated. Viewing the mystery of his life empirically, cold-bloodedly, he arrives at a naked vitalism which is nothing short of nihilistic and jumps onto the senseless merry-go-round of survival for survival's sake:

> Ich will auf meine Güter gehn am Rhein,
> Da will ich bauen, will ich niederreißen,
> Daß mir der Schweiß herabtrieft, säen, ernten,
> Als wärs für Weib und Kind, allein genießen,
> Und in den Kreis herum das Leben jagen,
> Bis es am Abend niedersinkt und stirbt.[a]   (III, 5)

Here as always, the death of creative vision is accompanied by an acute awareness of those organs which are presiding over the perceptual anatomy of a complex spiritual predicament: his eyes, those fragile and fallible guides on which, in his disorientation, he places an excessive reliance. And what his eyes tell him is literal extinction — his and their own — and the pitiableness of such dereliction:

> Ach! Auf dem Wege, der mich zu dir führte,
> Sah ich das Grab, beim Schein der Fackeln, öffnen,
> Das morgen mein Gebein empfangen soll.
> Sieh, diese Augen, Tante, die dich anschaun,
> Will man mit Nacht umschatten, diesen Busen
> Mit mörderischen Kugeln mir durchbohren.
> Bestellt sind auf dem Markte schon die Fenster,
> Die auf das öde Schauspiel niedergehn,
> Und der die Zukunft, auf des Lebens Gipfel,
> Heut, wie ein Feenreich, noch überschaut,
> Liegt in zwei engen Brettern duftend morgen,
> Und ein Gestein sagt dir von ihm: er war![b]   (III, 5)

---

[a] I shall repair to my possessions by the Rhine,/ There I shall build things and demolish them again,/ Until the sweat drips from my brow, shall sow, shall reap/ As though for wife and child, alone enjoy,/ And whip life in a constant roundabout,/ Until at eventide it flags and dies.

[b] Alas! As I came here, upon my way to you,/ I saw my grave by torchlight being dug/ Which, come the morrow, is to hold my bones./ Look, Aunt! these very eyes that gaze on you/ They mean to dim with night, and pierce/ This bosom with their murderous lead./ The windows on the market place which give/ Upon this desolate sight are booked,/ And

As he looks at himself, so, in the dislocated schizoid world he now inhabits, everything looks at him, impartially, remorselessly, even the gun barrels[13]. As Natalie has it:

> Der denkt jetzt nichts, als nur dies eine: Rettung!
> Den schaun die Röhren, an der Schützen Schultern,
> So gräßlich an, daß überrascht und schwindelnd,
> Ihm jeder Wunsch, als nur zu leben, schweigt . . .[a]   (IV, 1)

The nadir in this atomisation of the personality is reached in the prince's monologue which precedes the arrival of Natalie in prison. The prince has done as Natalie had bidden him: returning to his place of arrest, he has taken a cool look at his grave; and his eyes have reported to him total and utter extinction. Homburg is at this point no longer concerned with the impenetrable stance of the elector. He has come up short against the impenetrable mystery of life itself, its patent finiteness which the gun barrels and his grave proclaim, and against the sheer paradox of any notion of immortality held in the teeth of such evidence. 'Die Wunder ruhn, der Himmel ist verschlossen'[b]: the sun of the Absolute is behind its bank of clouds, the paradise of the prince's direct communion with what now seems so unattainably remote is forfeited; all his eye meets preaches mortality:

> Das Leben nennt der Derwisch eine Reise,
> Und eine kurze. Freilich! Von zwei Spannen
> Diesseits der Erde nach zwei Spannen drunter.
> Ich will auf halbem Weg mich niederlassen!
> Wer heut sein Haupt noch auf der Schulter trägt,
> Hängt es schon morgen zitternd auf den Leib,
> Und übermorgen liegts bei seiner Ferse.
> Zwar, eine Sonne, sagt man, scheint dort auch,
> Und über buntre Felder noch als hier:
> Ich glaubs; nur schade, daß das Auge modert,
> Das diese Herrlichkeit erblicken soll.[c]   (IV, 3)

This is vision contracted to a pin-point. Pledged to see what is invisible and to quantify what is immeasurable, the prince, in his quest for the detached objective truth, sees the vast expanses of life as through opera glasses reversed. The immensities of lived space and time become pared down to the scale of the

---

he that, on life's summit still today,/ Gazes upon a future like a dream,/ Will, fragrant, lie between two narrow boards tomorrow,/ A tombstone telling you of him: he was!

a He does not think save one thing now: salvation!/ The barrels at the gunners' shoulders look at him/ So horribly that, taken by surprise and dazed,/ His every wish is silenced save to live . . .

b 'Miracles are suspended, Heaven's closed'

c The dervish looks on life as on a journey,/ A brief one, too. In truth/ From two short spans above the earth/ To two short spans beneath it./ I'll sit me down, now half way mark is reached!/ Today, whoever bears his head upon his shoulders,/ Tomorrow hangs it trembling on his chest,/ And the day after it is laid beside his heels./ They say, 'tis true, a sun does shine there, too,/ And over gayer pastures yet than here:/ I'll grant it. A thousand pities, though, the eye must rot,/ Which all this splendour is supposed to see.

perishable body, and to a consciousness that can encompass today, tomorrow and the day after that; but only just. And in this mercilessly materialistic scrutiny of the human condition perceived from the outside we once again encounter the characteristic Kleistean turn against organs of perception which so patently fail to bring to the light significances that do not meet the eye and complexities that must be felt to be understood; only the rage has been drained out of the profound weariness of the prince's 'Ich glaubs'.

The low ebb of the objectifying stance is reached; it will be transcended through a renewed communion with the Numinous, here in total eclipse, a communion which, in a synthesis of the subjective and the objective modalities, relinquishes sensory perception as an organ of knowing altogether. But to say this is looking ahead to a later chapter[14].

5.

It is not until the central scene of *Penthesilea*, the fifteenth, that the exposition of the drama is completed, as the queen recounts to Achilles the history of the Amazon state and the meaning of the bizarre rites he and the Greek prisoners have incredulously witnessed. And here it becomes fully evident that the Amazons' paradoxical tactics in this protracted war against Greeks and Trojans alike spring from a religious source, and that Penthesilea's inane pursuit of Achilles in particular is a sacred legacy laid upon her by her dying mother.

The account she gives to Achilles of their first meeting bears all the marks of a religious experience. Indeed, we seem to know her words almost verbatim from the prince's recollection of his nocturnal visitation.

> Wie aber ward mir,
> O Freund, als ich dich selbst erblickte —!
> Als du mir im Skamandros-Tal erschienst,
> Von den Heroen deines Volks umringt,
> Ein Tagstern unter bleichen Nachtgestirnen!
> So müßt es mir gewesen sein, wenn er
> Unmittelbar, mit seinen weißen Rossen,
> Von dem Olymp herabgedonnert wäre,
> Mars selbst, der Kriegsgott, seine Braut zu grüßen!
> Geblendet stand ich, als du jetzt entwichen,
> Von der Erscheinung da — wie wenn zur Nachtzeit
> Der Blitz vor einen Wandrer fällt, die Pforten
> Elysiums, des glanzerfüllten, rasselnd,
> Vor einem Geist sich öffnen und verschließen.[a] (15)

---

[a] But what befell me then,/ O friend, when I beheld your self —!/ When you appeared to me in the Skamandros vale,/ Surrounded by the heroes of your race,/ A morning star 'midst pale stars of the night!/ I would have felt like that if he/ Had thundered down, direct, from Mount Olympus' heights/ With his two snow-white steeds,/ Ares himself, the god of war, to greet me as his bride!/ When you escaped me then, I stood all dazed,/ The apparition gone — as though at dead of night/ A lightning flash struck by the wanderer's feet,/ The portals of Elysium, filled with radiance, clanking,/ Before some spirit opened and then closed.

Indeed on first hearing that Achilles was hers, Penthesilea had in very similar strains ordered the rose-feast to be prepared:

> An euer Amt, ihr Priesterinnen der Diana:
> Daß eures Tempels Pforten rasselnd auf,
> Des glanzerfüllten, weihrauchduftenden,
> Mir, wie des Paradieses Tore, fliegen![a]   (14)

And an answering echo in the same visionary terms had come from Achilles, at his first greeting of the Queen of the Amazons.

> O du, die eine Glanzerscheinung mir,
> Als hätte sich das Ätherreich eröffnet,
> Herabsteigst, Unbegreifliche, wer bist du?[b]   (15)

We can be in no doubt, then, that Kleist in this play as in the other works already touched on in this chapter is concerned with a face to face encounter of two numinous entities[15]; nor indeed but that in this tragedy this encounter has a more direct and annihilating force than in any other we have so far discussed. From the beginning, Penthesilea is characterised in cosmic and elemental terms rather than in human ones. Divine and bestial in one, she seems to belong to some mysterious order outside the ken of humanity. And so, too, her assault upon the Absolute she has gleaned in 'des Ägiers schimmernder Gestalt' — 'the Aegian's iridescent form' — is something more — or less — than human in its savage intensity. She has seen the representative of Mars who, so her mother had confided to her, is destined to be vanquished by her in love; and pursues him, as Theobald has it of Käthchen, 'geführt am Strahl seines Angesichts, fünfdrähtig, wie einen Tau, um ihre Seele gelegt'[c]. (I, 1) Like one sleepwalking with open eyes, blinded by desire, she follows him, at first trying to reach him up the rock face of a vertical drop, then chasing his quadriga as he makes his escape. Finally she meets him in a head-on clash of arms —

> Jetzt, eben jetzt, da ich dies sage, schmettern
> Sie, wie zwei Sterne, aufeinander ein —[d]   (7)

we hear, and:

> Achill und sie, mit vorgelegten Lanzen,
> Begegnen beide sich, zween Donnerkeile,
> Die aus Gewölken in einanderfahren —:[e]   (8)

---

a Back to your stations, Dian's priestesses:/ And may the clanking portals of your shrine,/ With radiance filled and incense-fragrant clouds,/ Spring open for me, e'en like Heaven's gates!

b O you who does descend to me, a dazzling dream,/ As though ethereal realms had opened up,/ O you impossible to comprehend, say, who are you?

c 'lead by the ray of his face twisted round her soul, rope-like, with five wires'.

d Now, even now, as I am saying this,/ They crash into each other, like two stars —

e She and Achilles, with their lances couched,/ Meet one another, like twain thunder-bolts,/ Roaring into each other from their clouds —

and each time the tempestuousness of her assault upon the Absolute she has glimpsed is punctuated by − a resounding fall[16].

We know why she so falls, indeed we know the biblical ancestry of the fall she suffers. Like the first woman, Penthesilea stretches out her hand physically to grasp what is an immaterial good: the consummation of her thirst for the Absolute[17]. Like Eve before her Fall, Penthesilea has no means of distinguishing between the Absolute she so vehemently assaults and its material surrogates; and, like Eve, she is driven out of the paradise of her innocence as she senses the terrible inadequacy of the tools with which she has sought to grasp the mystery. This is at the end of the drama, when she 'falls' into consciousness, when, in a breathlessly rapid process of maturation, she comes to understand the difference between material signs and their significances and rises to full human stature, forging for herself a symbol strong enough to kill. But now, chasing the Numinous as a she-wolf pursues its prey, she is still in the mythological, prehuman, pre-symbolic state in which religious awe and hot desire, lyrical love and the ghastly pomp of war lie incongruously intermingled[18]:

> das Chaos war,
> Das erst', aus dem die Welt sprang, deutlicher.[a]   (3)

The impact of the Numinous on Penthesilea is overwhelming, greater by far than is the corresponding experience of her fellow-Amazons. This is not just because she is Penthesilea to whom all assumes more colossal dimensions than to her more moderate 'sisters': from the beginning there is a directness about Penthesilea's relation to Achilles which is absent in the case of the other Amazons. For where they engage in battle with whomever the god sends as his representative and accept the anonymous character of their wooing[19], Penthesilea herself does not. By a fatal break of the Amazons' law, Penthesilea's mother, Otrere, has divulged to Penthesilea the identity of her man; and it is he himself, not the anonymous symbol of Mars, whom she seeks to meet and mate in an encounter which from the beginning is direct and instinct with passion. How religiously overwhelming the meeting with Achilles is to her has already been seen from the visionary language she employs in recollecting it. We may add two descriptions of the *Göttersohn*, first as he appears to us and then as he appears to Penthesilea, seen through her own eyes as it were and surrounded by an aura of numinosity. This is how we ourselves come face to face with him at the beginning of the third scene.

> Seht! Steigt dort über jenes Berges Rücken,
> Ein Haupt nicht, ein bewaffnetes, empor?
> Ein Helm, von Federbüschen überschattet?
> Der Nacken schon, der mächtge, der es trägt?
> Die Schultern auch, die Arme, stahlumglänzt?
> Das ganze Brustgebild, o seht doch, Freunde,
> Bis wo den Leib der goldne Gurt umschließt?

---

[a] The primal chaos,/ Mother of our world, was plainer far.

> . . .
> Jetzt, auf dem Horizonte, steht das ganze
> Kriegsfahrzeug da! So geht die Sonne prachtvoll
> An einem heitern Frühlingstage auf!a (3)

We have witnessed a cosmic event; and already here Achilles is likened to the sun, a metaphor which in Penthesilea's mind will take on the disastrous force of literal truth.

The second description of Achilles actually accompanies the decisive head-on collision of these 'two luminaries':

> Seht, seht, wie durch der Wetterwolken Riß,
> Mit einer Masse Licht, die Sonne eben
> Auf des Peliden Scheitel niederfällt!
> . . .
> Auf einem Hügel leuchtend steht er da,
> In Stahl geschient sein Roß und er − der Saphir,
> Der Chrysolith, wirft solche Strahlen nicht!
> Die Erde rings, die bunte, blühende,
> In Schwärze der Gewitternacht gehüllt;
> Nichts als ein dunkler Grund nur, eine Folie,
> Die Funkelpracht des Einzigen zu heben!b (7)

This is Kleist's nature imagery at its most magnificent; and here as always such grandeur is at the poet's bidding when he treats of the direct apparition − Erscheinung − of the Numinous in its consuming glory and thunderous overproximity[20].

But for all the tempestuousness of Penthesilea's wooing for direct communion with the Absolute across all the chasms of nature's or men's designing, that quest is from the very outset flawed. It is the frightening physicality of the imagery used by and about her that warns us of danger ahead; or, rather, the incongruous interlacing of mental and physical events in the language the poet deploys to characterise her. The frequent occurrence of animal imagery − the very first speech sports 'die Verbißnen' − is too well known and too fully commented to

---

a Does not, o look! across the ridge of yonder hill/ Appear a head, an armèd head?/ A helmet, overshadowed by its plumes?/ And now the mighty column of its neck?/ The shoulders now, the arms, agleam with steel?/ And now the chest, o come and look, ye friends,/ Down to the golden girdle round the waist?/
. . .
Now, etched on the horizon, wholly plain,/ The warrior's chariot stands! Thus splendidly/ The sun does rise on a fine spring morn!

b See, see, how, through the cleft in yonder thunderclouds,/ The sun e'en now does pour/ A mass of light upon the brow of Peleus' son!/ . . . He stands on yonder hillock, all agleam,/ His charger sheathed in steel and he − the sapphire,/ The chrysolite lacks rays as those he casts!/ The ground around him, blossoming and gay,/ Shrouded in inky hues of storm-swept night;/ Nought but a sombre backcloth to enhance/ The sparkling splendour of the only one!

require our renewed consideration here. What I would note is the ominous intermingling of the mental and the physical spheres in a simile like this:

> Rasch einen Blick den Pfad schickt sie hinan;
> Und dem gestreckten Parder gleich, folgt sie
> Dem Blick auch auf dem Fuß;[a]   (2)

where the figure of speech 'auf dem Fuß' — she is in fact on horseback — sucks the mental event of looking into the orbit of the metaphor with its unmitigated physicality. Again, there is the description of her centaur-like figure,

> Wie sie, bis auf die Mähn herabgebeugt,
> Hinweg die Luft trinkt lechzend, die sie hemmt . . .[b]   (3)

or:

> Mit jedem Hufschlag,
> Schlingt sie, wie hungerheiß, ein Stück des Weges,
> Der sie von dem Peliden trennt, hinunter![c]   (3)

or:

> An seiner Seite fliegt sie schon! Ihr Schatten,
> Groß wie ein Riese in der Morgensonne,
> Erschlägt ihn schon![d]   (3)

Drinking, eating and slaying the object of her intense and religious longing: here, *in nuce*, the poet intimates on the plane of imagery what Penthesilea will presently do in gruesome, literal fact.

And indeed, an object Achilles increasingly becomes in her frenetic imagination: the same Achilles who, like a zigzag flash of lightning, to her is sheer numinous essence in scarce embodied form. This drift towards reification significantly sets in when, shocked by her second fall, Penthesilea begins to feel the incommensurability of her dawning love with the martial conventions enjoined by her estate. Disorientated, she complains:

> Wo sich die Hand, die lüsterne, nur regt,
> Den Ruhm, wenn er bei mir vorüberfleucht,
> Bei seinem goldnen Lockenhaar zu fassen,
> Tritt eine Macht mir hämisch in den Weg.[e]   (5)

She sends a hasty look along the path,/ And, like a panther at full stretch,/ Her foot does follow where her look did speed;

[b] How, bent o'er her charger down unto its mane,/ She, panting, drinks the intervening air . . .

[c] With every hoof-beat/ She hungrily devours a piece of road/ That separates her self from Peleus' son!

[d] There she comes flying by his side! Her shadow,/ Huge like a giant in the morning sun,/ Does slay him even now!

[e] Whenever wantonly the hand does stir/ To grasp, as he is flying past,/ At fame's fair locks,/ Some power, sneering, spiteful, bars my way.

Even earlier, at the very beginning of that scene, she has likened victory over Achilles to the radiance of 'a thousand suns, smelted into one ball of molten gold'. When she rides out to meet Achilles in battle it is

> Als ob sie, heiß von Eifersucht gespornt,
> Die Sonn im Fluge übereilen wollte,
> Die seine jungen Scheitel küßt!ᵃ   (7)

After the third and decisive fall in the head-on collision with Achilles, her reification of him becomes complete and, with it, tragedy unavoidable. Prothoe articulates the confusion in the queen's soul when she exonerates her passion in the famous words:

> Was in ihr walten mag, das weiß nur sie,
> Und jeder Busen ist, der fühlt, ein Rätsel . . .,ᵇ   (9)

incongruously continuing:

> Des Lebens höchstes Gut erstrebte sie,
> Sie streift', ergriff es schon: die Hand versagt ihr,
> Nach einem andern noch sich auszustrecken. − ᶜ   (9)

These words are usually interpreted at their face value, as an objectively valid comment upon the enigma of Penthesilea's fierce wooing. But such an interpretation ignores the ominous intermingling of mental and physical events, the palpable grasping at an immaterial mystery as though it were an extraneous material object which is familiar to us from Kleist's last drama. Prothoe's words do not reflect the judgment of the poet, merely her empathy with her friend. For presently the sun metaphors which have been gathering momentum for a while altogether cease to be metaphors: and Penthesilea begins in stark reality to confuse the golden orb and the lover that have maddeningly eluded her.

> − Wo steht die Sonne?
> − Where is the sun?

she asks, restlessly; (9) and while Prothoe dreams of the vanquished Achilles, Penthesilea − and the stage-direction reads '(die während dessen unverwandt in die Sonne gesehen)' − abstractedly muses:

> Daß ich mit Flügeln weit gespreizt und rauschend,
> Die Luft zerteilte −!:ᵈ   (9)

and what follows in the next page or two is the inane identification of the luminary with the beloved man[21]. She laments that 'he' − and this 'he' is equivocal − is

---

ᵃ As though she, spurred on by hot jealousy,/ Meant to outpace in flight the very sun/ That kisses his young head!

ᵇ None but she knows what passes in her soul,/ And every heart that feels is but a mystery . . .

ᶜ She strove for life's most coveted possession,/ Brushed past it, even grasped it: her hand/ Will not now reach for yet another good. −

ᵈ Would that I cleft the air with pinions/ Spread-eagled wide and rustling −!

> Zu hoch, ich weiß, zu hoch –
> Er spielt in ewig fernen Flammenkreisen
> Mir um den sehnsuchtsvollen Busen hin.[a] (9)

She wants to follow him via the rocky route; for

> Da komm ich ihm um soviel näher.[b] (9)

She calmly announces that she wants to pile Mount Ida upon Mount Ossa

> Und auf die Spitze ruhig mich bloß stellen.[c] (9)

Asked what she would do when she has accomplished this gigantic task, she replies:

> Blödsinnige!
> Bei seinen goldnen Flammenhaaren zög ich
> Zu mir hernieder ihn –
> Prothoe: Wen?
> Penthesilea: Helios,
> Wenn er am Scheitel mir vorüberfleucht![d]

And, gazing into the river, she exclaims:

> Ich, Rasende!
> Da liegt er mir zu Füßen ja! Nimm mich – [e] (9)

and making as if to plunge into the river to grasp the sun's reflected orb, unconsciously collapses.

In an important sense, this scene is unique in the whole of Kleist's work. For here, and virtually here alone, the subjective and the objective modalities are not shown in succession, but totally entwined in unabated intensity. Penthesilea is in direct touch with the Absolute, the numinous character of which is unmistakable. But that Absolute to her appears totally objectified, as a thing to be reached for and grasped[22]. It is crucial to be alive to the clue afforded by the stage-direction: at this point of maximal inner stress – for her feelings are at odds with the reification enjoined by the law of the Amazon-state to whom the god is scarcely more than a stud – Penthesilea is described as *unverwandt* – abstracted; and this means that she is not merely absent-minded, but, over and above that, profoundly unrelated. And unrelatedness is the hallmark of both the subjective and the objective modalities which here coalesce. The Kleistean character who lapses into the subjective fallacy in his quest for the other's noumenal essence, seeks to jump the guns of

---

[a] Too high, I know, too high –/ He hovers round this lonely, longing breast/ In ever distant circles made of flames.
[b] I would get closer to him by that much./
[c] And, quiet, mount the summit, nothing more./
[d] You idiot, you!/ I'd pull him down to me, the golden,/ By his flaming hair –
Prothoe: Whom?
Penthesilea: Helios,/ When he is brushing past my very brow!
[e] Fool that I am!/ There he is lying at my feet! Take me –

phenomenal experiencing; and this Penthesilea assuredly does in her hunt for the unattainable Absolute. Conversely, the Kleistean character in the grips of the objective fallacy exclusively relates to the phenomenal being of the other: and again this is what Penthesilea, confusing the invisible essence of Achilles with the sun of the physical universe, is unquestionably doing here. Achilles to her is an *Erscheinung* in two mutually contradictory senses of the word: he is absolute noumenal visitation and sheer phenomenal delusion in one; a fatal intermingling which causes the catastrophic violence of her emotional swings, first in one direction and then in the other. At no point is Achilles an *Erscheinung* in the third meaning of the word, that is to say, a human manifestation of the Divine, a *Phänomen* in Goethe's and even in Kant's sense, a material and transient *symbol* which is yet instinct with the Divine and anything but delusory[23]. To Kleist, an *Erscheinung* in that humanistic sense of the word was a virtually unknown modality of knowledge; and here, in Penthesilea's experience of Achilles, pure Absolute and sheer delusion in one, we come upon the crowning formulation of a paradox which is thoroughly characteristic of the structure of this poet's mind altogether and goes a long way towards explaining the intrinsic violence of his art. Penthesilea's incapacity to experience in symbols is a primitive streak[24] we shall encounter time and again; and it will eventually force us to raise the fundamental question asked by this book, namely, whether Kleist himself possessed the capacity that is so strikingly absent in the creatures of his imagination and, if the answer be in the negative, how his poetry works *qua* poetry.

The further course of the drama is contained *in nuce* in what we have seen, save for the fact that the process of reification becomes ever more palpable, on the reality-plane of the lovers' exchanges. When Penthesilea, at her most heart-meltingly lyrical, wreathes the surrendered Achilles as though he were a young dove, assuring him that

> . . . die Gefühle dieser Brust, o Jüngling,
> Wie Hände sind sie und sie streicheln dich . . .,[a]   (15)

she is in fact beginning to act out what she had dreamed of before:

> Nicht eher ruhn will ich,

she had said,

> bis ich aus Lüften,
> Gleich einem schöngefärbten Vogel, ihn
> Zu mir herabgestürzt;[b]   (6)

and that process of withdrawal into unrelatedness and reification is doubly underscored: by her inability to recognise the wild and lonely warrior of her

---

a   The feelings in this breast, O beauteous youth,/ They are like hands and they are stroking you . . .

b   I will not rest until from up on high/ I've tossed him at my feet, like to a bird/ Of lovely hue;

dreams in the gentle youth who is reposing at her feet — she relies on his armour to establish her lover's identity! — and by the disclosure of her background: the mutilated breast which is 'der Sitz der jungen, lieblichen Gefühle' — 'the seat of youthful, gentle feelings' — and indeed the mediator of the first relationship, that with the mother[25], and the incongruity of one as impulse-driven as she belonging to a state which assesses the need for loving 'according to annual calculations'. (15) Those caressing hands, in one as untried as she is in feeling and as dependent on material surrogates, are ominous. And when we learn of the savage Bacchanalia by which her tribe annually replenishes its numbers, when we hear the final duet between the lovers and listen to the unrelated religious fervour of her 'Themiscyra' pitted against his human plea for 'Phtia', we cannot but foresee the end. A Penthesilea bestialised by the trauma of a divine visitation turning — or so she thinks — into the most monstrous deception, will lie amongst her hounds, her teeth sunk into the flesh of the beloved of whom she made an object to be ruthlessly grasped in an absolute thrust which is itself destructive from the start[26]. A bitch amongst her pack, she at last reaches what was unattainably remote as long as she tried to reach it with her arrow,

> Und stürzt — stürzt mit der ganzen Meut, o Diana!
> Sich über ihn, und reißt — reißt ihn beim Helmbusch,
> Gleich einer Hündin, Hunden beigesellt,
> Der greift die Brust ihm, dieser greift den Nacken,
> Daß von dem Fall der Boden bebt, ihn nieder![a]   (23)

Penthesilea herself cannot credit that the catastrophic 'mis-taking' of her vision for a reified Absolute forced her to do as she did:

> Was! Ich? Ich hätt ihn —? Unter meinen Hunden —?
> Mit diesen kleinen Händen hätt ich ihn —?
> Und dieser Mund hier, den die Liebe schwellt —?
> Ach, zu ganz anderm Dienst gemacht, als ihn —!
> Die hätten, lustig stets einander helfend,
> Mund jetzt und Hand, und Hand und wieder Mund —?[b]

If she did what words fail her to pronounce — and what words could she find to name her deed? — if she did savage the loved one to death,

> So war es ein Versehen . . .   (24)
> It was an oversight . . .

Thus she will wrily say, gruesomely chastising the literalness of her apprehension of a mystery, as we have seen Ruprecht and Amphitryon and Prinz Friedrich von

---

[a] And flings herself — with her entire pack, O Diana!/ Herself upon him, tears — yes, tears him by his crest,/ Like to a bitch surrounded by her dogs,/ This grabs his chest, that grabs him by the neck,/ She drags him down, upon the quivering ground!

[b] What? I? Him I'm supposed to —? 'Mid my hounds —?/ Him should I have —? And with these tiny hands —?/ These very lips here, which are swelled by love —?/ Made for a service other than to — him?/ They should have, like a bunch of merry mates,/ Lips now and hand, and hand and lips again — ?

Homburg do. With a deadly wit she will say:

> Küsse, Bisse,
> Das reimt sich, und wer recht von Herzen liebt,
> Kann schon das eine für das andre greifen.[a]   (24)

In her atavistic regression from desiring to seeing to grasping and thence to eating, this somnambulist figure does no more or less than retrace the footsteps of God's first woman. She honestly completes the terrible fall into literalism which Kleist's major figures have to endure time and again on their painful awakening to consciousness, in a world too complex for their seeing. Of her as of them all what Ruprecht says is true:

> Was ich mit Händen greife, glaub ich gern.[b]

---

[a] Bites and love-rites,/ That makes a rhyme, and he who loves deep from the bottom of his heart,/ May well get hold of one and miss the other.
[b] What I may grasp with hands, I'd fain believe.

IV Through a Glass, Darkly

> For now we see as through a glass, darkly; but
> then face to face; now I know in part; but
> then I shall know as also I am known.
>
> St. Paul

> . . . the existence of a God could not be intellectually more
> evident without becoming morally less effective; without
> counteracting its own end by sacrificing the life of faith to the
> cold mechanism of a worthless because compulsory assent.
>
> Coleridge

7 Faulty Medium:
'Penthesilea' and 'Die Verlobung in St. Domingo'

1.

In a previous chapter I treated of Kleist's disastrous encounter with Kant. My tools were those of literary criticism, in that I proceeded by way of analysing the verbal precipitate this encounter had left in Kleist's letters of the period. Two metaphors stood out clearly from a wealth of material, and these were seen to be milestones on Kleist's road to the self-understanding of his predicament. They were the metaphors of the 'warped and sullied mirror' in the letter of February 5, 1801 to his step-sister Ulrike, and the corresponding one of the 'green glasses' in which he explains his heartache to his fiancée Wilhelmine on March 22 of that year.

While both metaphors clearly suggest a basic flaw in our perceptual apparatus which makes it impossible for us to know whether we do indeed apprehend the truth, we have found the image the poet uses *vis-à-vis* his half-sister a good deal more candid than that in which he explains himself to his fiancée. And this is not only because in the image of the warped and sullied mirror of the soul the impairment of our perception is squarely attributed to the sensuous medium in which the knower is embodied, whilst the image of the green glasses leaves open the possibility that it is due to the faultiness of an extraneous adjunct: the greater candour of the mirror-image itself is reflected, and vouchsafed, by the context in which it is placed. For in the letter to Ulrike the deprecatory reference to himself as a warped and dirty mirror is revealingly embedded in the overt confession that he dislikes people, and that he feels as uncomfortable in their company as in his own. 'Ach, liebe Ulrike,' he writes, 'ich passe nicht unter die Menschen . . . und wenn ich den Grund ohne Umschweif angeben soll, so ist es dieser: sie gefallen mir nicht.'[a] This initial avowal is followed by the metaphor of the mirror which in its turn gives rise to that description of his profound uneasiness in his own skin and in the company of others which, in correspondence with his fiancée, is reported in a far less telling context in a letter dated January 31, 1801.

Indeed, how revelatory the letter to Ulrike is may be seen from a late echo. In one of his last letters to Marie von Kleist, written on November 10, 1811, at a time when his suicide is already a certainty, he once again couples his acute sense of discomfort *vis-à-vis* himself with his dislike of others; and in this heartrending document we are once again struck by the sheer physical vehemence of his disgust.

---

[a] 'Alas, dear Ulrike, I am a misfit amongst my fellow-men . . . and if, without humming and hawing, I am to say why, it is because I do not like them.'

Of himself he writes: '. . . meine Seele ist so wund, daß mir, ich möchte fast sagen, wenn ich die Nase aus dem Fenster stecke, das Tageslicht wehe tut, das mir darauf schimmert.' Of others: 'Mir waren die Gesichter der Menschen schon jetzt, wenn ich ihnen begegnete, zuwider, und nun würde mich gar, wenn sie mir auf der Straße begegneten, eine körperliche Empfindung anwandeln, die ich hier nicht nennen mag.'[a][1] We may safely supplement Kleist here and say that it is that *Ekel* — nausea — of which he speaks in the above mentioned communications to Wilhelmine and Ulrike, a word which incessantly reverberates through the letters written during the acute phase of the Kant-crisis then about to break.

In this chapter I wish to treat of this characteristic revulsion from the medium of embodied existence as Kleist articulated it in two works of art patently moulded by the Kant experience: *Penthesilea* and *Die Verlobung in St. Domingo*.

2.

As is well known, Kleist wrote to his cousin Marie that in *Penthesilea* he had embodied 'mein innerstes Wesen . . .': 'der ganze Schmutz zugleich und Glanz meiner Seele'[b] are incarnated in this figure (Late autumn, 1807). *Glanz* and *Schmutz* — these epithets take us back to the image of the mirror which so frequently figures in the letters dating from between the Würzburg trip and the Kant-crisis, some six to seven years earlier, to begin with seen as radiant and true and later, in ever increasing measure, as 'warped and sullied'. If that association be legitimate, we may venture the hypothesis that in the enigmatic figure of his heroine Kleist is once again exploring the predicament, highlighted by the encounter with Kant, of a sentience which is radically and incurably flawed, by virtue of the bad sense-medium in which it is embodied.

That Penthesilea is a figure of shining radiance we have seen. The fierceness of her quest for the Absolute, however misguided in the means she chooses, and the throat-catching, childlike sweetness of which she is capable, are eloquent witnesses to that. But in what sense are we to understand Kleist when he attributes to her the *Schmutz* of his own soul? Again it would be tempting, and easy, to essay a depth-psychological interpretation of Penthesilea whose psychic structure is characterised by a profound fear of what in recent analytical literature is termed 'implosion' of any given 'other', together with the obverse tendency to devour that other[2]. Such a reading, stressing the dominant need to devour, would certainly be correct, and would offer an explanation of Penthesilea's pathology — her *Schmutz* — in currently acceptable terms. Yet, as a literary critic concerned with words, I

---

[a] '. . . my soul is so sore that, dare I say it, when I stick my nose out of the window, the daylight that shines upon it hurts. Even then I could not stomach the faces of the people I encountered, and were I to meet them in the street now, this would produce a physical sensation I would rather refrain from naming.'

[b] 'my innermost being . . .': 'all the filth and radiance of my soul'

prefer once again to stay closer to Kleist's own frame of reference; and in the present case this means offering a reading of the term which bears on Kleist's strikingly similar use of it in the context of the Kant-crisis.

The mirror of Penthesilea's soul is flawed and sullied, we would accordingly say; and that signifies that she is a bad sensory medium reflecting back an incurably distorted picture of the world. In this connection, we must consider the society in which she is embedded, which has in the first place shaped and conditioned her perception of the world. This society is the answer of a tribal group of women to a corporate outrage committed against them in the past. Vanquished by the Ethiopians, the widowed Scythian women were subjected to the indignity of being raped by their conquerors. To free themselves from this yoke, they killed their tormentors one and all and resolved to found a self-sufficient — *mündiger* is the word Kleist uses — state of women,

> Der das Gesetz sich würdig selber gebe,
> Sich selbst gehorche, selber auch beschütze . . . :[a]   (15)

words in which we cannot fail to recognise a direct echo of Kant's conception of autonomy. To be able to protect themselves efficiently, the women, following the example of Tanais their queen, amputated their right breasts so as not to be impeded in their use of bow and arrow. Hence their name: 'Amazon' means 'bosomless'[3]. They resolved to replenish their race whenever, 'nach jährlichen Berechnungen' — 'according to annual calculations', this seemed indicated, making war on such virile and virtuous tribes as might be shown to them by Mars, the presiding deity of their state. Whatever tribe the god so designates to the *Marsbräute* — Mars' brides — is attacked,

> Und wie die feuerrote Windsbraut brechen
> Wir plötzlich in den Wald der Männer ein,
> Und wehn die Reifsten derer, die da fallen,
> Wie Samen, wenn die Wipfel sich zerschlagen,
> In unsre heimatlichen Fluren hin.[b]   (15)

As their initial choice is anonymous[4] — the men are the *Stellvertreter* of the god of war and every Amazon 'marries' the one Mars has destined her to vanquish in battle — so is their fiercely male wooing and the ensuing consummation of their union.

> Es schickt sich nicht, daß eine Tochter Mars'
> Sich ihren Gegner sucht, den soll sie wählen,
> Den ihr der Gott im Kampf erscheinen läßt . . .[c]   (15)

---

a Which would prescribe its own law worthily,/ Itself obey and so protect itself . . .

b Abruptly, like a flame-red gust of wind,/ We break into the forest of the men,/ Blowing the ripest ones of the defeated,/ Like seeds of tree-crowns crashing all around,/ Toward the pastures of our native land.

c It is not meet and right that one of Ares' daughters/ Seek out her foe, him she must choose who, at the god's own bidding,/ Appears to her upon the battlefield.

Penthesilea explains to the incredulous Greek. Thus, having ensured the survival of the women's race in protracted religious rites, the prisoners are released and sent home as soon as progeny is on the way.

This unlikely story — a story of the grossest systematised unrelatedness — Penthesilea recounts to a wide-eyed Achilles, paradoxically and tragically at the very moment when his own ability to relate has made him bow to what he thinks is a whim of the enchanting enigma before him and, abrogating all male pride, has permitted her to fancy that it is she, the Amazon, who has vanquished him[5].

Only in one respect, and a crucial one, does Penthesilea differ from her fellow-Amazons. To her Otrere, her mother, has divulged the identity of the man she will conquer in battle; and him she loves with a love that from the beginning is fiercely personal. Yet she too is a member of her women's state; and in this autonomous state — a spiritual progeny of Kant's, as we saw — the relation between the sexes is envisaged, we might say, through categories of the utmost unrelatedness. As Alkmene experiences the world through the category of Amphitryon which is the sole category at her disposal, so, analogously and paradoxically, the Amazons and their queen with them, experience love through the category of aggression[6]. This is the flawed and sullied spot on the mirror of their soul, and the physical token of it is — the mutilated breast. For as we know, and as Kleist himself knew very well, the maternal breast is the first and prime 'other' to and through which the infantile self learns to relate; and this powerful teacher in the Amazons, 'the bosomless ones', is missing. How radical the ensuing distortion of emotional values is we may gauge from the fact that Penthesilea, suspecting that it is she who has in truth succumbed to Achilles, hides from this sign of feminine surrender as though it were a stain and immerses herself in her fantasy world, seeking ablution 'wie ein besudelt Kind' — 'like to a sullied child'.

Thus it is through the flawed and sullied mirror of a soul conditioned to unrelatedness that Penthesilea is forced to perceive her love, and the figure of her beloved. She perceives him shaped by the only category that is at her disposal, that is to say, as one profoundly unrelated himself. This compulsive drift into unrelatedness becomes apparent in her endowing him with a string of ever fiercer attributes, successively naming him

> Den Lieben, Wilden, Süßen, Schrecklichen,
> Den Überwinder Hektors![a] (15)

She herself articulates that process of filtering his image through the pure form of *her* intuition, the category of *her* understanding. For this is how she continues:

> O Pelide!
> Mein ewiger Gedanke, wenn ich wachte,
> Mein ewger Traum warst du! Die ganze Welt
> Lag wie ein ausgespanntes Musternetz
> Vor mir; in jeder Masche, weit und groß,

---

[a] The dear, the wild, the sweet, the fearful one,/ The slayer of Hector!

> War deiner Taten eine eingeschürzt,
> Und in mein Herz, wie Seide weiß und rein,
> Mit Flammenfarben jede brannt ich ein.[a]   (15)

What she so perceives through the meshes — *Musternetz* — of her sensibility is the ruthless, utterly unrelated warrior:

> Bald sah ich dich, wie du ihn niederschlugst,
> Vor Ilium, den flüchtgen Priamiden;
> Wie du, entflammt von hoher Siegerlust,
> Das Antlitz wandtest, während er die Scheitel,
> Die blutigen, auf nackter Erde schleifte;
> Wie Priam flehnd in deinem Zelt erschien —
> Und heiße Tränen weint ich, wenn ich dachte,
> Daß ein Gefühl doch, Unerbittlicher,
> Den marmorharten Busen dir durchzuckt.[b]   (15)

In such a world as this, the Amazons' and Penthesilea's in particular, there is hardly a gesture, indeed hardly a word, that does not betoken the exact opposite of what it is intended to convey. How deliberately tasteless and false — synthetic, we would say — is the sixth scene, with its cloying exchanges between the chief priestess and her 'geliebten, kleinen Rosenjungfraun' — 'beloved little rose-maidens'![7] How contrived — and this has not been appreciated — is even Prothoe's famous 'Gewölbe'-speech, with its incongruent metaphor of breath quickening mortar and stone. When these Amazons speak of love they cannot but speak falsely. And how riddled with ambiguity is Penthesilea's own lament when Achilles first unseats her:

> — Ists nicht, als ob ich eine Leier zürnend
> Zertreten wollte, weil sie still für sich,
> Im Zug des Nachtwinds, meinen Namen flüstert?
> Dem Bären kauert ich zu Füßen mich,
> Und streichelte das Panthertier, das mir
> In solcher Regung nahte, wie ich ihm . . .[c]   (9)

Penthesilea exclaims, unconscious that in her turn of phrase she is both the lyre and the fiend who tramples it underfoot, the bear and the panther as well as the trusting soul that strokes them. True, she has been smitten by love's arrow —

---

a O Peleus' son!/ I ever thought, when wakeful,/ I ever dreamt of you! Before my eyes/ The vast world, like a patterned net,/ Lay stretched; into its every ample mesh/ I knit one of your deeds,/ And every deed, with colours made of flame,/ I etched into my heart, as white and pure as silk.

b Now I would see you as you smote him down,/ The fleeing son of Priamus, by Troy;/ How you, incensed by lust of victory, turned back,/ And dragged along his blood bespattered brow/ Upon the naked ground; how Priamus/ Came begging to your tent —/ And stinging tears I shed, remorseless one,/ When pondering that some feeling after all/ Swept through your bosom, adamant as stone.

c Is it not as though I would, enraged,/ Stamp on a lyre whispering my name/ All quietly and to itself, in the nocturnal breeze?/ I'd crouch down by the feet of any bear/ And stroke the panther coming up to me/ With such a feeling as I bear for him . . .

> Vom giftigsten der Pfeile Amors sei,
> Heißt es, ihr jugendliches Herz getroffen.[a] (7)

Yet, when an unarmed Achilles comes toward her to woo her on her terms, she

> . . . spannt . . .
> Den Bogen an, daß sich die Enden küssen,
> Und hebt den Bogen auf und zielt und schießt,
> Und jagt den Pfeil ihm durch den Hals . . .[b] (23)

True, she would fetter him with the bond of love

> Wie Blumen leicht, und fester doch, als Erz,[c] (15)

she dons 'das erzene Gewand der Hochzeit' — 'the iron wedding garb'

> (Weil ich mit Eisen ihn umarmen muß!)[d] (5)

only to draw him gently to her breast; yet, when he follows her bidding, she calls upon Ares, 'dich Schrecklichen' — 'thou dread one', to send — and she repeats this twice —

> O! — — deinen erznen Wagen mir herab![e] (20)

to grind her love to atoms. True, her feelings are like hands that stroke Achilles and wreathe him like a young dove. Even before meeting him she has in the same imagery pledged herself not to harm him:

> Hebt euch, ihr Frühlingsblumen, seinem Fall,
> Das seiner Glieder keines sich verletze.
> Blut meines Herzens mißt' ich ehr, als seines . . .[f]

she said and continued thus:

> Nicht eher ruhn will ich, bis ich aus Lüften,
> Gleich einem schöngefärbten Vogel, ihn
> Zu mir herabgestürzt; doch liegt er jetzt
> Mit eingeknickten Fittichen, ihr Jungfraun,
> Zu Füßen mir, kein Purpurstäubchen missend:[g] (6)

then let the gods descend to help us celebrate the feast of roses! But even here the beloved's wings are broken: and when Achilles has vanquished her and spared her in a sudden burst of tenderness, the self-same Penthesilea whose feelings, in that

---

[a] They say her youthful heart is smitten/ By the most venomous of Amor's darts —

[b] . . . tenses/ Her cross-bow till its ends do kiss/ Then lifts the bow, takes aim and forthwith shoots/ And sends the arrow whizzing through his neck . . .

[c] As light as flowers, yet more firm than ore,

[d] (Because it is with iron I must clasp him!)

[e] O — — send your iron chariot down to me!

[f] Rise, O ye flowers of spring to stay his fall,/ Lest any of his limbs be bruised./ I'd rather shed my heart's blood than his own.

[g] I will not rest until, from up on high,/ I've tossed him down to me, a bird of lovely hue;/ But maidens, once he crouches at my feet,/ His pinions crushed, with not a purple speck brushed off:

central love scene, would wreathe him with garlands of roses like an unharmed bird, will in the self-same images wish wreck and ruination upon the four corners of the cosmos:

> Daß der ganze Frühling
> Verdorrte! Daß der Stern, auf dem wir atmem,
> Geknickt, gleich dieser Rosen einer, läge!
> Daß ich den ganzen Kranz der Welten so,
> Wie dies Geflecht der Blumen, lösen könnte![a]   (9)

The same Penthesilea who would not brush a single particle of coloured dust off her lover's wings will meticulously dry and curl and smoothe the plumage of the arrow with which she has shot him, brutally, through his slender neck. Worst of all: the same Penthesilea who had wept at the thought of Achilles showing compassion to Hector's father Priamus, will turn on her lover like a Fury when, in a supreme gesture of tender empathy, he challenges her in deference to the Amazons' law, 'eine Grille, die ihr heilig . . .'[b], as he has it. (21)

Unrelatedness is the law of Penthesilea's society as of her being, the 'category' with which nature and nurture have conditioned her to approach the phenomenon of love between the sexes. No human words can penetrate this aura by which she is surrounded[8], this bond that fetters her with laws which, to her, are sacred, this very medium in which her Amazon self is embodied, through which she perceives the world. The mirror of her soul is warped, it is flawed and sullied. And paradoxically and tragically, it is the Greek's endeavour to relate to her which ushers in the final catastrophy. Not only does she view his challenge in the terms of her own alienation, as one meant to kill, even though he has already spared her once; unrelated as she herself is, she does not *want* another to understand her and to break through the barriers within which she has learned to live. As Jupiter rejects Alkmene's fine attunement to him so as to see her as she is, in herself; as Strahl repudiates Käthchen's empathic relatedness to him and lets her surrender spend itself in a painful void, so Penthesilea cannot brook the tender lover who leaves behind all that is his − his camp, his companions, his values and conventions and, indeed, his warrior's honour − in order to see life through the beloved's eyes and follow her to Themiscyra. This ultimate threat to her unrelatedness she has no option but to kill.

There is no reaching across to a figure whose vision is thus warped. For herself, there is no way of shedding the distorting mirror that is built into her very being save to shed that body itself which has proved to be a bad bond and a faulty medium.

---

a   May all the springtide/ Wilt away! And may the star on which we breathe and live,/ Like one of these rose blossoms here, be crushed!/ I'd tear apart the garland of all worlds/ As I undo this wreath of flowers now!

b   'A whim that to her is sacred . . .'

3.   .

The novella *Die Verlobung in St. Domingo* is similarly concerned with a people
that is victimised at the hands of another race, and its ensuing brutalisation and
unrelatedness. This time, however, the physical basis of the failure of communication is — colour.

The scene is set at the time of the insurgence of the black natives of St. Domingo
against their French governors. The blacks have suffered much injustice and
ill-treatment at the hands of their white masters and have now risen to retaliate in a
like manner. Hounded down on all sides, the whites seek to entrench themselves
in Port-au-Prince, their last French stronghold on the island. A young Swiss
refugee, Gustav von der Ried, comes to the lonely house owned by a specially
vicious negro, Congo Hoango by name. This 'terrible' man, 'der in seiner Jugend
von treuer und rechtschaffener Gemütsart schien'[a], has killed his former white
master, a magnanimous man, and has since continued to murder whites whenever
the occasion offers itself. For this purpose his mistress, a mulatto woman named
Babekan, and her young daughter Toni, a mestizo, are especially useful. By virtue
of their lighter complexion — Toni is distinguished by an 'ins Gelbliche gehenden
Gesichtsfarbe' — 'a yellowish complexion' — these two halfcast women are able to
act as baits enticing whites into Hoango's plantation where they are duly done
away with. Young Gustav, begging for asylum at dead of night, is in the absence
of Hoango taken in by the two women, who have every intention of making a
catch of him as well as of his family sheltering in a nearby forest. At first Toni
uses her calculated tricks to charm the stranger; before the evening is over,
however, these skirmishes give way to a real emotional involvement between the
two young people who end up by spending the night together. Toni pledges
herself to save the stranger, whom she considers as her betrothed, and his family
from the cruelty of her adoptive father, and from her mother's machinations. She
resolves to make a clean breast of her past misdeeds and her initial intentions, but
is prevented from doing so because, entering her lover's room the following night,
she finds him fast asleep. Guarding Gustav's sound sleep with fervent love, she is
surprised by Hoango's precipitate return. Toni is desperate at being found in a
compromising situation with a white which will make it impossible for her to
manœuvre for his life, and in a sudden brainstorm ties her sleeping sweetheart to
his bed, so as to avert the suspicion of having any collusion with him. Hoango is
duly fooled by this trick and Gustav's family, called to the scene by Toni in the
nick of time, succeed in getting the better of Hoango and his men by tying him
and the old Babekan to a table and threatening to take the life of his two
illegitimate children whom they hold as hostages, likewise tied. They succeed in
freeing the roped Gustav and are preparing to beat their retreat when Gustav,
incensed and disconsolate at Toni's seeming betrayal of him, shoots her down and

---

[a] 'This terrible man who in his youth appeared to be of a faithful and stalwart disposition'

puts a bullet through his own head. The bereaved family escape unscathed with the help of their small hostages, having exchanged the rings on the lovers' hands and buried them on the island.

The brutalisation of the two warring races is shown to be equal on both sides, and the narrator scrupulously refrains from making an evaluative judgment. On the one hand there are the excesses of Hoango; but the narrator's comment on his original character — so curiously reminiscent of the opening gambit of *Michael Kohlhaas* — shows him to be conditioned by his unfortunate experiences and exonerates him, at least in part. Besides, his viciousness is balanced by the indignity done to the old Babekan who — and this is related twice — was cruelly beaten up by the white father of Toni and, as a consequence, contracted tuberculosis. And in a strange quest for symmetry on the narrator's part this atrocity is in its turn balanced by the story Gustav recounts of a young black woman who, to avenge herself for the harshness of her former master, had slept with him to give him the yellow fever she had herself contracted, calling out: 'geh und gib das gelbe Fieber allen denen, die dir gleichen!'[a] 'Would you do such a thing to me?' Gustav had testily asked Toni, who had replied in the negative with every sign of confusion.

It is against such a background of mutual hatred and suspicion that the encounter of Gustav and Toni is played out. Neither is free from the distrust towards the other's faction that taints its own race. Toni freely employs the ruses she has learned in the remorseless war against the enemy, first against the white stranger and later on his behalf. Gustav in his turn sends along his ring with the negro boy who is despatched to contact his stranded family, as an earnest of his honesty, a reliance on an objective 'article of faith' which is a characteristically Kleistean index of distrust.

It is in such a general climate of unrelatedness that the endeavour of the young ones to relate across the barriers of colour is played out. The scene is set predominantly at night and envisaged in sombre monotones. An anxious white youth spends two foul and tempestuous nights in the company of two halfcasts whose sallow complexions envelop him in a kind of uncertain semi-dark. Gustav's first question, before ever he enters the house, is: 'seid Ihr eine Negerin?'; and his dread of a black world is shrewdly summed up by Babekan's reply: 'Nun, Ihr seid gewiß ein Weißer, daß Ihr dieser stockfinstern Nacht lieber ins Anlitz schaut, als einer Negerin! Kommt herein'[b]. Eventually the door is opened for him by the young Toni, who cleverly illuminates her fair complexion with the lantern she holds without however dispelling the shadow cast over her face by her hat. 'Wer bist Du?' — 'Who are you?' — Gustav asks, 'sträubend' — 'bristling', alike attracted by the girl and repulsed by the sallowness of her face.

---

[a] 'go and give the yellow fever to all the likes of you!'
[b] 'Are you a negress?' 'Well, you are sure to be a white, seeing that you'd rather face this inky night than a black! Come in.'

The conversation that ensues is about the racial affiliation of the two women, the true nature of whose relation to him Gustav endeavours to discover. These exchanges are ambiguous in the extreme. Asked the whereabouts of his family, Gustav, after some hesitation, replies: 'Euch kann ich mich anvertrauen; aus der Farbe Eures Gesichts schimmert mir ein Strahl von der meinigen entgegen.'[a] Babekan, simulating sympathy for his plight and disapproval of black violence, in the course of the conversation cleverly takes up Gustav's cue and asks: '"Was kann ich . . . für den Schimmer von Licht, der auf meinem Antlitz, wenn es Tag wird, erdämmert?"'[b] And she goes on to assure Gustav that, as halfcasts, she and her daughter share the Europeans' plight, and that the only hope of survival for them lies in the cunning of the defenceless: '"der Schatten von Verwandtschaft, der über unsere Gesichter ausgebreitet ist, der, könnt Ihr sicher glauben, tut es nicht."'[c] Like the uncertain light of the lantern in the surrounding gloom, these shifting allusions to their all-important complexions, now likened to the fallow light of the dawning day, now to a pall spread over their faces, themselves cast flickering shadows over the scene. It is Toni who picks up the lingering doubts in the stranger's mind by admitting in his hearing that she had done her best to illuminate her fair hue at the welcome: 'Aber seine Einbildung . . . war ganz von Mohren und Negern erfüllt; und wenn ihm eine Dame von Paris oder Marseilles die Türe geöffnet hätte, so würde er sie für eine Negerin gehalten haben.'[d]

In these words I would suggest that Toni is putting her finger on the sickness at the heart of this story. This chary and puzzled youth, she is in effect saying, is wearing the tinted spectacles of distrust; and in his fear of blacks the whole world, to him, is wearing their colour. Through these adroit words — as indeed through the ones Babekan addressed to Gustav as he stood outside the window — Kleist is, I suggest, reformulating what may well be the crucial message of his first tragedy:

> Das Mißtraun ist die schwarze Sucht der Seele,
> Und alles, auch das Schuldlos-Reine, zieht
> Fürs kranke Aug die Tracht der Hölle an . . .[e]   (I, 2)

Certainly — and this may be more central in our present context — he is reformulating here, through the sensibility of his heroine, at the beginning of a narrative of unalleviated gloom, his own anguished question to Wilhelmine von Zenge about the possibility of certain knowledge: given that what human beings experience is from the start vitiated by the green glasses of their subjectivity, the unanswerable riddle arises 'ob ihr Auge ihnen die Dinge zeigt, wie sie sind, oder

---

[a] 'To you I can entrust myself; the colour of your face reflects a ray of my own.'
[b] '"Is it my doing that a ray of light dawns upon my face as day breaks?"'
[c] '"the shadow of kinship on our faces doesn't do it, you may rest assured."'
[d] 'But his imagination . . . was crammed full with negroes and blackamoors; if a lady from Paris or Marseilles had opened the door to him, he would have thought her a black.'
[e] Distrust is the black addiction of the soul,/ And all, even the innocent and pure,/ To the diseasèd eye puts on the garb of hell.

ob es nicht etwas zu ihnen hinzutut, was nicht ihnen, sondern dem Auge gehört'[a].
(March 22, 1801)[9].

The sickness at the heart of this story is certainly bilateral. Whites as well as
blacks have their vision of the other distorted by the tinted glasses of their
subjectivity; and indeed it is the halfcast Toni whose 'schöne Seele' — 'beautiful
soul' — alone of all characters transcends the barriers of colour and prejudice and
in the midst of soul-destroying hatred and unrelatedness rises to a deed of radical
trust, for her lover's sake sacrificing 'alles, Eltern und Eigentum' — 'all, parents
and property'. Nevertheless Kleist has chosen to symbolise that perceptual flaw,
which vitiates our very experiencing at the sheer bodily level, in the colour of the
roused natives and in the fear inspired by it. Toni's uncertain hue constitutes the
same physical barrier to true perception which in the case of Penthesilea has found
expression in the mutilated breast. With one important difference: Because of the bad
medium in which she is embodied, Penthesilea is prevented from perceiving truly;
Toni, by an analogous handicap, is prevented from *being* perceived as she truly is.
It is the white Gustav's vision which, if anything, is flawed, not that of the
stigmatised halfcast: a complication adding to the ambiguity which from the
beginning shrouds this uncanny story like a sinister pall.

The poet has articulated that uncertainty which, with the inevitability of a
Greek tragedy, leads to disaster, in four symbolisms. Together, these define the
impossibility to relate in the face of the radical distortion of our experience which
is brought about through the faultiness of our bodily medium. Of the first and
most telling of these symbolisms, colour, we have already treated. It is supported
by three others which have to do with relatedness on a deep and primitive level:
food; the linking of hands as a token of trust; and tying. Against the background
of prevailing distrust and hostility Kleist has deployed these basic symbols of
relatedness with an ambiguity and a tantalisingly inconclusive symmetry which, in
the view of this writer, makes this story one of the greatest, if also gloomiest,
triumphs of his narrative art.

It is in fact the symbolism of colour which initiates the motif of food. Gustav is
anxious for his relatives in the forest to be saved from starvation, and after
protracted discussions Babekan despatches a basket with provisions to them, in
the hope of having Congo Hoango catch them and their valuables on his return. It
is in this context of food being employed as a bait that Gustav, looking into the
lit-up face of Toni, exclaims: 'Hätte ich dir . . . ins Auge sehen können, so wie ich
es jetzt kann: so hätte ich, auch wenn alles Übrige an dir schwarz gewesen wäre,
aus einem vergifteten Becher mit dir trinken wollen'[b]. This motif has already been
sounded in *Die Familie Schroffenstein* when Agnes, suspecting that Ottokar wants

---

a 'whether their eye shows them things as they really are, or whether it superadds something to them, which does not pertain to them, but to the eye itself.'

b 'If I had . . . looked you in the eye as I am doing now, I would have drunk from a
poisoned cup with you, had you been black all over.'

to poison her, drinks the water he offers her in his hat. It is no less ambivalent here. These are the protestations of a youth who will presently relate the story of the negress who deliberately gave her yellow fever to a white, and ask the girl before him whether she would do likewise; who for all Toni's attractiveness is repulsed — so we are told repeatedly — by her yellow complexion. The milk that is to be offered to Gustav in the morning turns out to have been poisoned by the old Babekan; and if she withholds it, it is not from compassion but so as to catch him the more surely now that she knows Toni will side with him. The poisoned drink — and of all things milk, that first of all foods through which the infant learns to relate to, and trust, what is outside his self — is a symbol of relationships which are through and through vitiated by hatred, uncertainty and distrust.

The same ambiguity attaches to the symbolism of linked hands, a motif incomparably more richly developed in this story. Taking a person by the hand signifies a gesture of relatedness on the most basic physical level. In the world of Kleist, whose primitive and perplexed characters continually seek for palpable modes of reassurance, the importance of such a gesture can hardly be exaggerated. And indeed, in this comparatively brief narrative hands are linked and stroked and kissed no less than twenty-one times. But even this primordial token of tenderness cannot be interpreted at its face-value. For one thing, these spontaneous acts are embedded in a vast network of references to hands — again more than twenty in number — in which they frequently appear as hostile agents, snatching, injuring or themselves being injured, or pantomimically enact the abstracted puzzlement of unspoken doubt. In such a context even the overt act of linking hands means different things at different times, the signification of which as often as not remains ambiguous. Babekan and Toni seize Gustav's hand three times — *ergreifen* and *fortreißen* — 'grab' and 'pull away' are the words the narrator uses — to drag him into a home which is to be his deathtrap. In such a climate, Gustav's responses — he too reaches out three times, first from the outside through the open window, then drawing the hand of the old woman to his heart and finally, showering it with kisses — are not expressions of trust, but tokens of an uncertainty that swings from anguished doubt to fearful hope. Most undermining of all is an early diatribe of the old mulatto-woman in which she seeks to gain Gustav's confidence by condemning the violence practised by the blacks: "'Ja, diese rasende Erbitterung", heuchelte die Alte. "Ist es nicht, als ob die Hände *eines* Körpers, oder die Zähne *eines* Mundes gegen einander wüten wollten, weil das *eine* Glied nicht geschaffen ist, wie das andere?"'[a] The reassuring meaning of Babekan's message is drowned in its tell-tale imagery. Hands are ominously linked with teeth — we cannot but think of Penthesilea — and, as if such a fraternity were not enough, teeth are set warring one against the other,

---

[a] "'This inane hatred, indeed! Is it not as though the hands of *one* body or the teeth of *one* mouth were to make war one against the other, because they were not created the same?'"

gainsaying Babekan's pretence that she is in truth thinking of blacks and whites as members of one encompassing organism.

With the credibility of this basic act thus multiply eroded, how can it carry conviction and dispel distrust? Gustav is asleep when Toni, fortified by prayer, slinks into his room during the second night and, kneeling by his bedside, 'covers his dear hand with kisses'. He will wake when her hands are busied tying his own hands and feet with a rope; and for all that his uncle, Herr Strömli, believes her explanation of this all but incomprehensible act and himself leads her into Gustav's room by his hand, the faith of the youth is shattered and he shoots her in despair. Toni's outstretched hand cannot reach across the gulf of distrust. ' "Ach!" rief Toni, und streckte, mit einem unbeschreiblichen Blick, ihre Hand nach ihm aus . . . Aber sie konnte nicht reden und ihn auch mit der Hand nicht erreichen'[a]. In the end, it is the lovers' dead hands that will be linked as their rings are exchanged, before they are committed to the earth.

The motif of tying is an extension of the symbolism of linked hands. As a modern psychiatrist has convincingly shown, tying is a typical expression of possessive love mingled with hostility[10]. This motif too, ambivalent in itself, is here used with a vast spectrum of significances ranging from sheer brutality or defensiveness to the most unalloyed love. It is introduced in a patently negative context. 'Der Wahnsinn der Freiheit', Gustav reflects thoughtfully, . . . 'trieb die Negern und Kreolen, die Ketten, die sie drückten, zu brechen, und an den Weißen wegen vielfacher und tadelnswürdiger Mißhandlungen, die sie von einigen schlechten Mitgliedern derselben erlitten, Rache zu nehmen'[b]. When Toni relates her predicament to Herr Strömli the latter has the hands of Hoango's illegitimate boy Nanky tied, 'aus Vorsicht, als eine Art von Geißel'[c]. Presently Hoango, hit over the hand by a swordblow, is also tied, together with Babekan, 'mit Stricken am Gestell eines großen Tisches'[d]; an arrangement which is made more secure later on when both are bound to the door post. To force the negro's hand, his youngest little boy Seppi (whom Toni is shrewd enough to produce, having roused him from his sleep) is likewise tied and retained, together with his older brother, as a hostage by the whites. Against such a foil of hostility and ambivalence, how can Gustav — roused from his sleep like the child Seppi — comprehend the motives of Toni's inane act? 'Sie umschlang den Jüngling, vielfache Knoten schürzend, an Händen und Füßen damit' — that is to say, with a rope she had seen — 'und nachdem sie, ohne darauf zu achten, daß er sich rührte und sträubte' ('Wer bist Du?' Gustav had earlier asked her, 'sträubend' — 'bristling', as she had appeared in

---

a ' "Alas!" Toni cried and with an indescribable look stretched out her hand towards him . . . But she could not speak, nor could her hand reach him.'

b ' "The delirium of liberty goaded on the negroes and the creoles to break the chains oppressing them and to avenge themselves on the whites for the many and reprehensible instances of maltreatment they had suffered at the hands of some." '

c 'by way of a precautionary measure, as a kind of hostage'

d 'with ropes, tied to the frame of a large table';

the doorway!), 'die Enden angezogen und an das Gestell des Bettes festgebunden hatte: drückte sie, froh, des Augenblicks mächtig geworden zu sein, einen Kuß auf seine Lippen, und eilte dem Neger Hoango, der schon auf der Treppe klirrte, entgegen'[a].

Needless to say, her public comment on her deed is ambiguous in the extreme: '"da liegt der Fremde, von mir in seinem Bette festgebunden; und, beim Himmel, es ist nicht die schlechteste Tat, die ich in meinem Leben getan!" '[b] To which we may add that Gustav's rope is later on tightened by Hoango and his men, just as the negro and Babekan are re-tied by the whites against a doorpost. Awful symmetry.

No, Toni's deed was not the worst she had done in her short life. In fact, it was as radiantly loving a deed as that of Gustav's former fiancée Mariane, who had sacrificed herself for him, protecting him from the fury of the French Revolutionaries by denying any acquaintance with him. '"diesen Menschen kenne ich nicht!"' – 'I do not know this man!' she had cried at the foot of the guillotine, and had gone to her death in her beloved's stead.

These are the words of Peter as he denied Christ, as the poet well knew. Here, in this world of an unrelatedness so total as to permit no communication between lovers, these archetypal words of betrayal need to be deployed to signify the ultimate act of fidelity, even as in Kleist's tragedy of unrelatedness we must take Penthesilea's word for it that her bites were meant to signify caresses. Where unrelatedness is the sole category at the disposal of human beings, foul murder and fiendish roping up are the only fitting signs left to hint at love. As Penthesilea's grief no longer reaches the mangled corpse of Achilles, so Toni's 'Ach! . . . dich, liebsten Freund, band ich, weil – –!'[c] is left helplessly dangling in mid-air, and only the last tie of all, the exchanged rings, makes patent the pity of it all.

As so often, Kleist has in his first tragedy found words to express the horror and nausea at the thought of the bad medium in which we are embodied, which corrodes all the certainty and truth signalled from one human being to another:

> Es hat das Leben mich wie eine Schlange,
> Mit Gliedern, zahnlos, ekelhaft, umwunden.
> Es schauert mich, es zu berühren. – [d]   (II, 3)

This is the unending cry of Kleist's tormented souls.

---

[a] 'She tied the hands and feet of the youth with the rope, repeatedly knotting it, and having tightened the ends and fastened them to the base of the bed, oblivious of the fact that he was stirring and resisting, she sealed his lips with a kiss, happy to have mastered the moment, and hurried towards the negro Hoango who was already clattering up the stairs.'

[b] '"there the stranger lies, tied by me to his bed; and, Heaven knows! it is not the meanest deed I have done in my life!"'

[c] '"Alas! . . . dearest friend, I tied you, because . . ."'

[d] In its embrace life clasps me like a snake,/ With toothless limbs, and nauseatingly./ I shudder, horrified, to touch it. –

8 The Turn of the Screw: Structures of Ambiguity in Kleist's Narrative and Dramatic Art

1.

In the foregoing chapters of this book we have repeatedly made the acquaintance of the type of character with whom Kleist predominantly peopled his poetic cosmos: Simple Simons all and sundry in one basic respect, even after making due allowance for the vast differences between them with regard to social station and intellectual rank. They are simple, even simplistic, in that they invariably assail the situation into which they are placed with a kind of mothlike religious zeal: desiring nothing short of the Absolute — absolute trust, absolute communication, absolute truth — under whatever conditions[1].

There are a very few exceptions to this rule, and these are for the main part in the shape of unprincipled characters such as Adam in *The Broken Pitcher* or Sosias and Charis in *Amphitryon*. These figures know how to accommodate themselves to the vital rhythms of life. In order to survive and to enjoy the bodily pleasures of existence, they will, without excessive scruples, change the law of the land or even their identity; and it is easy to recognise them as deriving from an ancient comic lineage of which Aristophanes is the fountain-head.

But such characters are few and far between. The overwhelming majority of the figures that Kleist has created lack that resilience and adaptability which make for the survival of the tougher members of our species. They are exposed and vulnerable in that, with an unbending religious vehemence, they want to understand and be understood, to know and be known[2], to believe and be believed unconditionally, in conditions which are, to say the least, singularly unpropitious. Unpropitious, to begin with, because such fanaticism is implanted in beings with an extraordinarily primitive mental endowment. For, as we have seen, these characters insist on bashing their way through to the ultimate truth with the aid of cognitive tools which are lamentably unequal to the kind of spiritual challenge they are made to encounter. Like Adam and Eve in the opening chapter of the human race, they assail complex moral configurations requiring subtle powers of differentiation with an intellectual equipment which is simply not harnessed to such eventualities: seeking to come by the abstract knowledge of good and evil as though such knowledge were an apple to be plucked from the nearest tree.

In our opening chapter we explained this progressive deterioration into, and of, the perceptual mode — a fallen state if any — by the inadequacy of the.primitive model of being Kleist puts before us in the essay *On the Puppet-Show* to the exacting demands entailed by the *condition humaine*. It takes perception innocently geared to divinely directed instinct to bring forth that unconscious grace beside which the most complicated feats of cerebration pale into insignificance. A configuration such as this, however, is a utopia which cannot be realised in a *gebrechliche Welt* — a fragile world —

> Auf die nur fern die Götter niederschaun.[a]   (*Penthesilea*, 24)

And yet it is with the selfsame perceptual tools, now controlled from an unhinged centre of gravity, in a singularly complicated world from which God has withdrawn out of sight, that figures as widely different as Frau Marthe and Ruprecht at one end of the mental spectrum and the Theban General, the Amazon Queen or Prinz Friedrich von Homburg at the other seek to blaze their way to certainty notwithstanding the labyrinthine complexity of their respective predicaments.

But it is not only the profound obtuseness of these characters whose materialistic literal-mindedness is ill-matched to their religious thirst for things ultimate, which accounts for the tragic or near-tragic issue of every play or story from Kleist's pen. It is the combination of such dim-witted fervour with situations of the most exquisite complexity which is the truly characteristic feature of Kleist's narrative and dramatic art; and to the ambiguous and ultimately paradoxical structure of his highly wrought plots we must now turn.

2.

The fabric of Kleist's plots is spun, as it were, of a dense web of ambiguities some though not all of which are experienced as such by the reader no less than by the characters themselves. It is, however, with the ambiguity encountered by the characters themselves that we shall principally concern ourselves at this point.

We may single out four main areas of incomprehension *vis-à-vis* which the Kleistean figure finds himself brought up short. These are, first, an inexplicable fact or event; second, the concealed motivation of another character or characters; third, his own character which is, or becomes, problematic to him; and fourth, the meaning of his total experience which is thus multiply obfuscated and, arising from that, the enigmatic nature of the world into which he is placed.

These areas of obscurity for the most part overlap and interlace so that, in the end, the nature of the world itself, a web of the most varied kinds of ambiguities, becomes inscrutable. As an outstandingly clear example of such a conflation we may cite *Das Erdbeben in Chili*, where the incomprehensible event, the earthquake — and an earthquake at the precise moment that is to terminate the lovers' lives — combines with the incomprehensible change of their co-citizens' characters and a dreamlike blurring of the protagonists' sense of their own standing in the kaleidoscopic scene, to bring about that culminating awe at, and tentative interpretation of, the total concatenation on the part of the surviving Fernando.

---

[a] On which the gods gaze down but from afar/

There is scarcely a play or a story in which there does not figure an inexplicable fact, event or chain of events. We may cite the two supposedly murdered children in *Die Familie Schroffenstein* and the strange mutilation of one of them; the nocturnal visitations (real or imputed) in *Der zerbrochene Krug, Amphitryon, Der Zweikampf, Die Marquise von O.*: visitations, all of them, which cruelly mock the innocence of the women who experience them, but which are in every instance attested by a *corpus delicti*: the broken pitcher, the initialled diadem, the ring and, in the case of Julietta, her own mysteriously changing body. The incomprehensible *donnée* of *Das Käthchen von Heilbronn* is the total subservience of the heroine to Strahl, and his own mesmerised collusion in this bewildering bond. In *Die heilige Cäcilie oder die Gewalt der Musik* it is the performance of the choral work by one who lies dying and the miraculous efficacy of this performance which holds the centre of the story; whilst in *Penthesilea* it is the illogical war strategy of the Amazons who make war on Trojan and Greek alike which constitutes the shifting ambivalence at the centre of the plot. In *Prinz Friedrich von Homburg*, finally, the enigma that propels the action onward is the lost victory, a giddying contradiction underscored by the prince's possession of the glove, that token seemingly snatched from the very hands of fortune.

The puzzlement Kleist's characters experience in relation to one another is so universal a feature of this poet's plays or stories that it is all but impossible, and perhaps not even desirable, to essay an exhaustive enumeration. In Kleist's first tragedy everyone is perplexed by everyone else (and this includes the lovers); a state of affairs which is still complicated by Rupert's obfuscating adoption of an evil role. In that quartet of women singled out for erotic visitations – in *Der zerbrochene Krug, Amphitryon, Der Zweikampf* and *Die Marquise von O.* – the ambiguous position of the heroines becomes the source of unbounded stupefaction for those associated with them, i. e. Frau Marthe and Ruprecht, Amphitryon himself, Littegarde's brothers and Trota's mother and the marquise's family; whilst the women in turn are baffled by the behaviour and motivation of those that sue or pursue them. That bewilderment culminates in the trials of Alkmene who is alternately adored and vilified by what to her seems the same person. In *Die Verlobung in St. Domingo* and in *Penthesilea* we have seen the erosion of plot and verbal fabric by an ambiguity so total as to make for the incomprehensibility of every figure to every other one. As Achilles and Penthesilea are an enigma to one another, so they are to their own and the opposing camp. Except perhaps for Prothoe, there is no one on the side of the Greeks or the Amazons who understands Penthesilea, and even Prothoe's understanding of her erratic friend is confined, precisely, to the knowledge that she is an undecipherable riddle. Again, Toni is as incomprehensible to Gustav as she is to her own clan. The four brothers in *Die heilige Cäcilie* are an inexplicable mystery to the world around them; so is Nicolo, and for that matter his adoptive mother Elvire with her clandestine worship of one dead and gone. Hermann der Cherusker who protests that he wants nothing more than to lose Germany to the Romans – 'Schritt vor Schritt

. . . das Land der großen Väter verlieren'[a] (I, 3) − presents an impenetrable mask to his own followers no less than to Varus[3]. Robert Guiscard, that tower of strength who is suspected of having contracted pestilence, is as inscrutable to those around him as is the elector to his entourage and officers, and to none more so than the prince. Kohlhaas becomes increasingly undecipherable, first to his wife, then to Luther, and finally to the Elector of Saxony.

In a number of instances, the contradictory pulls tugging away at a mind are so fierce that he appears as an enigma even to himself[4]. Sylvester, torn between his own sense of integrity and the seemingly well founded accusations that are levelled against him, in his own eyes becomes a mystery; and the towering rage that gradually seizes this benign and patient man for us, too, has something of the ineluctable boiling up of an elemental cataclysm. So does Penthesilea's irrational behaviour, into which neither she nor those around her have any insight; and Achilles, in his contumely of his countrymen's blithe rationalism and the deep abstractions into which he lapses, is all but her match. Alkmene, Littegarde and Julietta, accused of what they know to be an untruth, yet convinced by external evidence that it must have happened, threaten to disintegrate under the strain of such internal contradictions, and become a mystery from which they themselves shrink in alienation. Käthchen to her conscious self is never anything but a mystery; and Graf Wetter vom Strahl, thunderstruck at his own doubled self, totters on the brink of madness when he learns of the coincidence between Käthchen's dream-vision and his own. The prince's sleepwalking self and its transports are certainly an enigma to him which is extended into waking hours blurred by the riddle of the fateful glove.

The withdrawnness into secrecy is so dense in some of Kleist's figures that we cannot even say whether they are a mystery to themselves as they indubitably are to others. Among these we may cite Robert Guiscard and of course Jupiter, Hermann der Cherusker and the Grand Elector; in the stories figures that spring to mind are the Graf F., Nicolo the foundling, Sister Antonia in *Die heilige Cäcilie* and, marginally, the mysterious figure of the old gipsy woman in *Michael Kohlhaas*.

In the end, the fog of all these ambiguities thickens, as it were, into a pall which envelops the whole cosmic scene. Sylvester is the first Kleistean figure to voice the incomprehensibility of the powers that have tangled the threads of his destiny.

Ich bin dir wohl ein Rätsel?[b]

he says to Jeronimus, and continues:

. . . Nun, tröste dich, Gott ist es mir.[c]   (II, 3)

---

[a] 'Step by step . . . to lose the land of our illustrious ancestors'
[b] I guess I am a riddle to your mind;/
[c] . . . Take comfort, man, for God is one to me./

Prothoe's famed words of the fragile world

Auf die nur fern die Götter niederschaun[a]   (24)

are echoed by similar passages in *Die Marquise von O.* and *Michael Kohlhaas*. *Das Erdbeben in Chili* and *Der Zweikampf* end on a delicately and deliberately inconclusive note; and the peace that descends over the final scenes of *Amphitryon*, *Die heilige Cäcilie* and *Michael Kohlhaas* releases the reader, uncertain what to make of endings which are more of a smiling riddle than a definitive resolution. The endings of *Die Familie Schroffenstein, Die Verlobung in St. Domingo, Der Findling* and *Penthesilea*, finally, although refraining from any explicit judgment about the ultimate nature of things, ring down the curtain upon a world in which God, if he exists, is indubitably felt to be a *deus absconditus*[5]. Of all of them Jeronimo's words in *Das Erdbeben in Chili* hold true: '. . . und fürchterlich schien ihm das Wesen, das über den Wolken waltet'[b].

Undoubtedly, such structures of ambiguity as Kleist creates in his dramatic and narrative art have their equivalents in his biography. In his letters it is easy to see how he imports elements of doubt and ambiguity into situations which, but for such concerted activity on his part, might have been regarded as being perfectly innocuous. This trait is especially apparent on his trip to Würzburg. In his communications to his fiancée and his half-sister, he continually and altogether unnecessarily harps on the fact that he harbours a secret; he keeps drawing their attention to it, interminably veiling his movements and interminably pointing out that this is what he is doing, until the gulf he has torn up between him and them is so great that he must beg them for their unconditional, 'literal' trust. What of all things he can least bear is the tranquil reliance upon him of those who love him, *in* their ignorance. That ignorance he waylays from all sides, dropping hints as to his motives, insinuating the presence of dark doubts in their hearts, and not resting until he has stirred up anxiety and sown suspicion where before there was neither. It is then that he will imperiously decree 'trust me absolutely' and 'above all, remain calm'. Having irreversibly manoeuvred himself and those he has left behind into such an ambiguous position, he eventually adopts the stance that he is 'ein unbegreiflicher Mensch' − 'an incomprehensible person'; and it is impossible to miss the deep gratification that accompanies this statement at least to begin with when he is, as it were, trying out a role he has long been busy preparing for himself.

Much could be said about these patterns from the point of view of depth-psychology. There is a great deal of sado-masochistic teasing and testing out here, and this points to a deep-rooted sense of insecurity. Moreover, he is clearly under some inner compulsion to produce tension-fraught situations in order to 'feel' himself at all, a mechanism about which we shall have to say more in an aesthetic and semantic context.

---

[a] On which the gods gaze down but from afar/
[b] '. . . and the being that rules above the clouds to him seemed terrible'.

What stands out in these machinations above all else, however, is Kleist's profound need for unrelatedness; and this unrelatedness, this alienation, is precisely what his many-layered use of ambiguity engenders in his fictional characters: alienation from the stream of events that carries them along, from their fellow characters, from themselves and from life in its totality[6]. To pursue this need for unrelatedness in depth-psychological terms would be untimely at this point: my study as a whole will, it is hoped, offer a comment on this as on other aspects of this poet's personal make-up. What is of interest here is that this doubtless deeply pathological person has transmuted a character trait which, seen in itself, is destructive and a severe handicap, into an artistic plus[7], a power enabling him to devise plots that are nothing short of masterly in their structure. And this tightening of his plots into a relentless structure of ambiguities, contradictions and, indeed, paradoxes by ever renewed turns of the screw we must single out for investigation in the following sections of this chapter.

3.

At many points in Kleist's stories and plays the − merciful − veil of mere ambiguity is rent and his stupefied characters find themselves face to face with the spectre of a flagrant contradiction. In simple characters − and we have seen how simple these figures for the most part are in their relation to the truth − such an experience does more than usher in a crisis of credibility: it erodes the whole plausibility structure within which their minds operate, and leaves them suspended in a tormenting dilemma. What is Jeronimus, witnessing the holy communion that is being held at Rossitz, to make of this ceremony? He comes from Warwand,

> Wo Sylvester, den
> Ihr einen Kindesmörder scheltet,
> Die Mücken klatscht, die um sein Mädchen summen . . .;[a]   (I, 1)

that is to say, from a place thriving in the deepest peace, in which Sylvester will presently ask the herald after his cousins in a manner suggesting that their most trifling concerns are his own:

> als, wie groß der Älteste,
> Wie viele Zähn der Jüngste, ob die Kuh
> Gekalbet, und dergleichen, was zur Sache
> Doch nicht gehöret . . .[b]   (I, 2)

Here, in Rossitz, this same Sylvester is branded as a foul infanticide; and Rupert's wife, Eustache, is told to pledge herself to exterminate her own kith and kin by taking the host:

---

[a] Where Sylvester, whom/ You brand as being a foul killer of a child,/ Swats gnats that hum around his girl . . .;

[b] Such as: how tall the eldest,/ How many teeth the babe, whether the cow/ Has calved and more such trifles which are hardly/ To the point . . .

Würge
Sie betend.[a]   (I, 1)

Again, in *Der zerbrochene Krug* how are the villagers to face the enormity that their own revered judge, dispenser of the law as they know it through his embodiment, is an unscrupulous rogue, the very criminal that is sought? What are the Thebans to make of two Amphitryons, when a man can only be in one place at one time, not to speak of Alkmene's stupefaction at such a doubling? What are those born logicians, the Greeks, to make of the Amazons' flouting of nature's very law, appearing here, there and everywhere? And what are they to believe of the raving Penthesilea with her tiny hands, 'halb Furie, halb Grazie' – 'half Fury and half Grace'? How are Theobald and the people of Heilbronn to reconcile their image of the demure burgher's child who is devoted to her father with Käthchen's brazen pursuit of a strange knight, not to mention the rumour Strahl has spread that this incomprehensible hussy is the emperor's own child? As for the German princes, how can they be expected to understand a leader who solemnly pledges himself to lose their country to the Romans, assuring them that 'alles zu *verlieren* bloß die Absicht ist' – 'to lose all is the sole intent'? (I, 3) And those Romans themselves, how can they make rhyme or reason of one known to be an astute warlord when he masks himself behind the *bonhomie* of a tribal chieftain from the jungle? A society lady placing an ad. in the local paper to ascertain the father of her child – how is such a flagrant flouting of all accepted standards of etiquette going to be received by her family and the worthies of her town? And that other noblewoman, accused of adultery and pronounced guilty in a solemn ordeal – what is the world to make of her? How can her lover look into the gulf that opens up beneath his feet and not be giddied by the demands on his credulity? What are the populace of Chile to think of a novice giving birth on the steps of their cathedral as the bells toll in the solemn rites of Corpus Christi? And finally: How can the Elector of the State of Brandenburg 'cope' with a senior Prussian army officer who, the night before a decisive battle, is busy winding his own wreath of a victory as yet to be gained, trying it on as a girl would her bonnet and whispering sweet nothings? How can he 'believe' in a warrior whose teeth chatter at the sight of his grave?

In such instances – and they could be multiplied – a vast gap of credibility is seen to open up. Such incongruities of situation or action as the poet has seen fit to invent challenge the most ingrained values, attitudes and expectations of those who are called upon to judge and understand them[8]. We have seen in earlier chapters how unfitted Kleist's characters are intellectually and emotionally to handle cognitive situations in which outward and familiar signs belie the significances that are concealed behind them, in which truth and appearance gape apart. We have seen with what misbegotten confidence they will cleave to simple perception or, at best, to scientific scrutiny to spell out such ambiguous signs,

---

[a] Strangle them/ in your prayer.

inevitably 'mis-taking' them in a situation which takes 'des Geistes heitre Tätigkeit' — 'the mind's serene activity' — for them to shed their preconceptions and
relate to the other in spontaneous empathy. In the previous chapter we saw,
moreover, how such disinterested vision of relatedness is encumbered — no, more:
vitiated — by the obstinately distorting medium of the percipient's enveloping
subjectivity shrouding him like a corona. By placing such formidable obstacles in
the way of their understanding, the poet is erecting impenetrable barriers to these
simple minds' apprehension of the absolute truth which — as we have seen — they
pursue with the incorrigible fervour and stupidity with which Penthesilea pursues
the alien apparition of Achilles.

And yet this poet — a poet who liked to torment himself and others, who liked
to think of himself as incomprehensible — twists the screw even further, to the
point where common contradiction turns into that most opaque of cognitive
stumbling-blocks: a flagrant paradox.

We may for our present purpose distinguish three different uses of the word
paradox. We employ it firstly, and somewhat loosely, vis-à-vis a statement
asserting the coexistence of two facts, or concatenation of events, felt to be
incompatible with one another and thus mutually exclusive. In that sense Kleist
frequently employs paradoxical statements to mark the fact that the mind of his
character is stretched to the very limit of what it can comprehend as elements
cohering together in one complex configuration. Such a sense of the paradoxical is
expressed by Natalie when she describes the prince's mental frame to the elector,
saying — and the stage direction reads 'zaudernd':

> Der denkt jetzt nichts, als nur dies eine: Rettung!
> Den schaun die Röhren, an der Schützen Schultern,
> So gräßlich an, daß überrascht und schwindelnd,
> Ihm jeder Wunsch, als nur zu leben, schweigt:
> Der könnte, unter Blitz und Donnerschlag,
> Das ganze Reich der Mark versinken sehn,
> Daß er nicht fragen würde: was geschieht?
> — Ach, welch ein Heldenherz hast du geknickt![a]   (IV, 1)

The incommensurable disparity between the prince's real character — his *Helden-
herz* — and its present manifestations is most tellingly pointed by the consistent
use of 'der', a demonstrative not altogether free from contempt, however
compassionate in intention here. Again, there is a strong paradoxical element in
the conditions Hermann stipulates *vis-à-vis* his chiefs if he is to lead their
confederation:

---

[a] He does not think save one thing now: salvation!/ The barrels at the gunners' shoulders
look at him/ So horribly that, taken by surprise and dazed,/ His every wish is silenced
save to live:/ That one might see, 'midst thunderclaps and lightning,/ The whole realm of
the Mark be blown to smithereens,/ Without so much as asking: what's amiss?/ — O
Uncle, what a hero's heart you've crushed!

> Kurz, wollt ihr, wie ich schon einmal euch sagte,
> Zusammenraffen Weib und Kind
> Und auf der Weser rechtes Ufer bringen,
> Geschirre, goldn' und silberne, die ihr
> Besitzet, schmelzen, Perlen und Juwelen
> Verkaufen oder sie verpfänden,
> Verheeren eure Fluren, eure Herden
> Erschlagen, eure Plätze niederbrennen,
> So bin ich euer Mann −:[a]   (I, 3)

The incomprehensibility of this seemingly ludicrous strategy − incidentally curiously reminiscent of Kohlhaas' liquidation of his home − is pointed up by Hermann's most perceptive follower, Thuiskomar:

> Das eben, Rasender, das ist es ja,
> Was wir in diesem Krieg verteidigen wollen![b]   (I, 3)

As a third illustration of an incongruity containing a strong paradoxical element we may cite Kohlhaas' obdurate insistence that his blacks be bodily restored to their original condition, an obstinacy which exactly parallels that of Frau Marthe *vis-à-vis* her broken jug. Her final

> Soll hier dem Kruge nicht sein Recht geschehen?,[c]   (*Letzter Auftritt*)

in its absurd disregard for the wider issues and their significances that have come to light, is echoed in greatly intensified form by Kohlhaas' stiffnecked cleaving to a couple of half-dead knacker's horses 'um derethalben der Staat wankte' − 'for whose sake the state was tottering': and the measure of such a paradoxical conflation of incommensurables is the ridicule with which the demands of both these figures are at this moment received.

We may in this connection mention the fact that not infrequently a plot will, in its entirety, make a paradoxical statement which addresses itself directly to the reader. This is so in the cases of *Penthesilea* and *Die Verlobung in St. Domingo*, both of which articulate the paradox of relatedness as envisaged through the categories of unrelatedness; it is patently so in the novella *Der Findling* where paternal compassion is eroded by filial viciousness to the point where it paradoxically turns into its contradictory opposite. The orphan Nicolo who impassively cracks open nuts between his teeth as the bereaved stranger takes him to his heart, is paradoxically mirrored at the end as his own adoptive father crushes his skull between his naked hands.

We employ the term 'paradox' in a second, and narrower, sense to designate − I am here quoting from the Oxford English Dictionary − a statement or propo-

---

a In short, if you will do as I have said before,/ Snatch up your children and your wives/ And dump them on the right bank of the Weser,/ Smelt dishes you possess of gold or silver,/ Barter or pawn your pearls or jewellery,/ Lay waste your fields, clobber your cattle,/ Set fire to your homesteads,/ Why, I am your man −:
b 'Tis that, you madman, 'tis those very things,/ We'd launch this war in order to defend!
c Is not my pitcher to receive its due?/

sition that is 'self-contrary, or contradictory to reason or ascertained truth, and so essentially absurd and false'. As an introductory example we may adduce Odysseus' assessment of the Amazons' incomprehensible strategy, warring alike against the Trojans and the Greeks, themselves known to be implacable enemies:

> So viel ich weiß, gibt es in der Natur
> Kraft bloß und ihren Widerstand, nichts Drittes.
> Was Glut des Feuers löscht, löst Wasser siedend
> Zu Dampf nicht auf und umgekehrt. Doch hier
> Zeigt ein ergrimmter Feind von beiden sich,
> Bei dessen Eintritt nicht das Feuer weiß,
> Obs mit dem Wasser rieseln soll, das Wasser,
> Obs mit dem Feuer himmelan soll lecken.[a]   (1)

To characterise the irrational, indeed the incredible behaviour of the Amazons, Odysseus is here invoking the law of contradiction in something like the following form: if two entities are absolutely contradictory to one another, then a third which is like one of them, will be absolutely contradictory to the other, too[9]. At one stroke Kleist is here underscoring the hidebound rationalism of the Greek who relies on perception and commonsense –

> Was er im Weltkreis noch, so lang er lebt,
> Mit seinem blauen Auge nicht gesehn,
> Das kann er in Gedanken auch nicht fassen – [b]   (21)

and pinpointing the perverseness of a behaviour pattern which stretches the comprehension beyond its normal span. The same imagery has already occurred in a more threatening vein in *Die Familie Schroffenstein*. It is used by Sylvester who, accused of infanticide, credits the good faith of those who level the charge against him, yet knows that this possibility, for all that it is reinforced by the appearance of things does not, and in his case cannot conceivably, apply. This is Sylvester's response to Aldölbern's challenge of blood vengeance:

> Nein, halte – Nein, bei Gott, du machst mich bange.
> Denn deine Rede, wenn sie gleich nicht reich,
> Ist doch so wenig arm an Sinn, daß michs
> Entsetzet. – Einer von uns beiden muß
> Verrückt sein; bist dus nicht, *ich* könnt es werden.
> Die Unze Mutterwitz, die dich vom Tollhaus
> Errettet, muß, es kann nicht anders, *mich*
> Ins Tollhaus führen. – Sieh, wenn du mir sagtest,
> Die Ströme flössen neben ihren Ufern

---

[a] For all I understand, Nature knows only/ Force and counterforce, and nought besides./ What quenches fire's glow, will not cause water to/ Evaporate in steam, nor the reverse. But here/ We meet a bitter enemy of both,/ One at whose coming fire does not know/ Whether to course with water, nor yet liquid/ Whether to lick the Heavens with the flames.

[b] What his blue eyes have failed to see/ 'Twixt Heaven and earth, as long as he has lived,/ He can no more encompass with his thoughts –

> Bergan, und sammelten auf Felsenspitzen
> In Seen sich, so wollt — ich wollts dir glauben;
> Doch sagst du mir, ich hätt ein Kind gemordet,
> Des Vetters Kind —[a]   (I, 2)

With his flair for seeing things dispassionately, through the eyes of the other party, as it were, Sylvester does not dismiss the charge against him out of hand. A child has been murdered and the aspersions cast upon him by a man he honours suggest that there must be some serious indications that he himself is the murderer. In his rectitude he is bending over backwards to be fair. Nevertheless,

> Wer kann das Unbegreifliche begreifen?   (I, 2)
> The unintelligible, who can grasp it?

In the light of his consciousness this possibility, though real, is self-contradictory. The disparity between outward signs and inward significances — his own sense of integrity — is too great for his mind to encompass; and thus it gives, and he retreats into a faint.

In this, his first play, Kleist has used a turn of the screw he will be employing time and again. A real possibility or actual certainty is played out against a sensibility which discerns the absolute incompatibility of this possibility or certitude with its innermost self. The respect for material evidence which is so deeply ingrained in Kleist's characters, forbids them to discount what fatally undermines their image of themselves[10]; and thus, unable to entertain a possibility they cannot or dare not gainsay, their vision of the truth — their own most intimate truth — is occluded and eclipsed.

The same metaphor of natural laws being turned topsy-turvy recurs yet again in the analogous plight encountered by Amphitryon. Confronted with his divine double, he is unable to sustain the paradoxical notion that there should be two of them, that 'he' could exist in more than one place at one and the same time. Yet the *Augenschein* — a favourite word of Kleist's — is patently against him: Amphitryon number two stands there, in the eyes of the bystanders evidently more real than he. Here again the external reality he cannot but seriously entertain forces him 'aus des Bewußtseins eigner Feste'[b]. (III, 10) This is how he pleads in what he senses to be a lost cause:

> Ich wußt es wohl. Ihr sehts, ihr Bürger Thebens,
> Eh wird der rasche Peneus rückwärts fließen,
> Eh sich der Bosphorus auf Ida betten,

---

[a] No, hold it — No, you frighten me, by God,/ Because your speech, though not exactly rich,/ Is yet so little poor in sense that I am/ Horrified — One of us two must be/ Insane, and if it is not you, *I* could become it./ The ounce of commonsense which saves you from/ The madhouse must take *me* to the madhouse/ Of necessity. — Look, if you told me/ Streams flow uphill, next to their dried up beds,/ And gather into lakes on rocky peaks,/ I would — I would believe you;/ But tell me I'm the killer of a child,/ My cousin's child —

[b] 'out of the fortress of his consciousness.'

> Eh wird das Dromedar den Ozean durchwandeln,
> Als sie dort jenen Fremdling anerkennen.[a]   (III, 11)

Amphitryon's mind is not a match to the cognitive challenge he encounters, and if it boggles under the insupportable strain of it this is because, like Ruprecht and Frau Marthe, he cannot differentiate between distinct levels of reality. The paradox of there being two Amphitryons at the same time is only apparent. It is dispelled as soon as the general learns that the other belongs to a different order of existence altogether. In reply to the question as to who he is, the god ironically, and impressively, answers:

> Amphitryon! Du Tor! Du zweifelst noch?
> Argatiphontidas und Photidas,
> Die Kadmusburg und Griechenland,
> Das Licht, der Äther, und das Flüssige,
> Das was da war, was ist, und was sein wird.[b]   (III, 11)

As soon as Jupiter informs him of his numinous nature and – this comes to the same thing – teaches the phenomenal Amphitryon to acknowledge that he too partakes of the noumenal realm, the apparent paradox that held good in the empirical realm vanishes. Yet for a Kleistean character riveted on the literal yet bent on the discernment of the ultimate truth, such an exercise in differentiation is an all but annihilating experience.

In much the same way, and for similar reasons, Graf Wetter vom Strahl finds himself face to face with a paradox which strains his mind beyond its proper limits. Knowing himself to have been confined to his sickbed and imagining that he had merely dreamed of his future wife, Käthchen's somnambulist revelations cause him to realise that he in fact visited her in her chamber, that is to say, was in two places at one and the same time.

> Nun steht mir bei, ihr Götter: ich bin doppelt!
> Ein Geist bin ich und wandele zur Nacht![c]   (IV, 2)

he exclaims; and:

> Was mir ein Traum schien, nackte Wahrheit ists:
> Im Schloß zu Strahl, todkrank am Nervenfieber,
> Lag ich danieder, und hinweggeführt,
> Von einem Cherubim, besuchte sie
> Mein Geist in ihrer Klause zu Heilbronn![d]   (IV, 11)

---

[a] I knew it well, you see, you Theban men,/ Peneus will more likely speed upstream,/ And Bosporus will bed itself on Ida,/ The dromedary walk across the sea/ Than she will recognise this stranger there.

[b] Amphitryon! You fool! You doubt it still?/ Argatiphontidas and Photidas,/ The Kadmus castle and the whole of Greece,/ The light, the ether and the waters,/ That which once was, which is and which will ever be.

[c] Ye gods, now help me! I am double!/ I am a spirit and I walk at night!/

[d] What seemed to me a dream, is naked truth:/ In Castle Strahl I lay, sick unto death/ With typhoid fever, and by a cherub led/ My spirit went to see her/ In her closet at Heilbronn!

Again the perception of a paradox — his doubleness — rests on the negation of his twofold nature. What Strahl significantly, because pejoratively, calls *'nackte Wahrheit'* — *naked* truth — is nothing less than the noumenal, indeed the numinous part of him which, predestined for the love of a humble child, he steadfastly and arrogantly disclaims. As soon as he outgrows his submission to appearance —

> meine Seele,
> Sie ist doch wert nicht, daß sie also heiße!
> Das Maß, womit sie, auf dem Markt der Welt,
> Die Dinge mißt, ist falsch . . . — a   (V, 6)

his mind will cease to totter 'an des Wahnsinns grausem Hang umher' — 'on the dread cliff of insanity', and by accepting his own numinous legacy in Käthchen, he will be one and whole.

4.

The use of paradox as an index of a character's inability to see that he belongs at one and the same time to different orders of reality: with this definition we have inadvertently come to the third, and culminating, meaning this logical structure assumes in Kleist's dramatic and epic work: this is its employment to express an essentially religious mode of awareness.

As we saw in the chapter on Kleist's comedy Frau Marthe, in recounting the vicissitudes of her broken pitcher, is blithely unaware of the different categories — legal as well as aesthetic — under which her shattered object of contention may be subsumed, over and above its sheer facticity. This incapacity to distinguish between different orders of significance and discourse has found its culminating expression in her inability to discern the supernatural properties of her jug. The erstwhile owner of the jug, the tailor Zachäus, broke his neck when he threw himself out of the window; well and good, but what happened to the jug when he did likewise to it?

> Und dieser irdne Krug, der Krug von Ton,
> Aufs Bein kam er zu stehen, und blieb ganz . . . b   (7)

This she reports in the most matter-of-fact way, as though to have remained in one piece in such shattering circumstances were the most ordinary thing ever. We have seen that her account is absurd, precisely in that she is unaware of the absurdity of what she is saying, at least on the face of it. It would have ceased to be so the moment she had tumbled to the paradoxical nature of her statement; and that statement, in turn, would have ceased to be paradoxical the moment she might have distinguished between the natural and the supernatural dimensions of

---

a My soul,/ It's scarcely worth to be so called!/ The yardstick which it uses in the market of the world/ To measure things, is false . . . —

b This earthen jug, this pitcher made of clay,/ It landed on its foot and stayed intact.

her jug. But to the span of such a differentiation her mind does not even remotely stretch.

Kleist has subjected his characters to a battery of paradoxes of this kind: paradoxes, that is to say, which require the mental distinction between the phenomenality in which a given fact or event is embedded in all its incontrovertible concreteness, and its invisible essence which reaches into, and partakes of, the noumenal order of things[11]. Yet as we have seen, the figures of whom he demands this interpretative feat of differentiation are literal-minded and simple to a fault, and quite unable to rise to the mental exercise required of them. Let us give some examples.

When first the Marquise von O. seeks the doctor's counsel, she finds herself in the grips of a paradox to which no supernatural solution is anywhere in sight. A physical change is taking place in her the signs of which are quite unequivocal. Yet her own conscience exonerates her from having had any part in the erotic encounter that must be assumed to have taken place to account for her symptoms. In more senses than one, this is a diabolical conception. In it, the poet is making use of his characters' congenital susceptibility to material evidence. But whereas in the overwhelming majority of cases such evidence — say, of Eve's transgression — is circumstantial and extraneous, here it is rooted in the depths of the marquise's bodily being. She does not believe it: she knows it with the certainty with which we know hunger, cold or pain. Yet she also knows herself not to have been near any man. How can she believe what her own body contradicts? The doctor who smilingly assures her that she is 'quite well' and diagnoses her condition is dispatched with contumely. Next the midwife is sent for. 'Ein reines Bewußtsein, und eine Hebamme!' — 'A clear conscience, and a midwife!', her mother comments. In the ensuing conversation the real, religious issue is hinted for the first time. '. . . ob die Möglichkeit einer unwissentlichen Empfängnis sei?'[a] Julietta asks; and again the midwife smiles, as the doctor did, and assures her that this is not the case in her 'Fall'; taken aback, the marquise says she merely wants to know in general terms 'ob diese Erscheinung im Reiche der Natur sei'; for that is where she locates the deadly paradox. 'Die Hebamme versetzte, daß dies, außer der heiligen Jungfrau, noch keinem Weibe auf Erden zugestoßen wäre.'[b]

Neither the marquise nor we, the readers, are asked to believe for one moment that she has been overshadowed by the Holy Ghost. What she and we are meant to rise to is a belief of an analogous nature: the unsupported belief in a psycho-spiritual reality which is totally and hopelessly at odds with the whole of actuality arrayed against her, the voice of her own body included[12]. The marquise must learn to feel in tune with her noumenal, indeed her numinous, essence which, in

---

a '. . . whether the possibility existed of her having conceived without having any knowledge of it?'

'whether this phenomenon existed in the realm of nature' 'The midwife replied that, the
b Holy Virgin apart, this had not happened to any woman on earth.'

secret league with her own unconscious[13], has been sought out by the impetuous count; and that means accepting her strange condition *and* feeling pure in one. For a Kleistean character, with their deep rootedness in the literal and material, and their clamouring for direct access to the truth, this sustained paradox is the most cruel test this poet could have devised; and it is perhaps due only to his uncanny (since biographically totally unsupported) insight into the strange resourcefulness of motherhood that he is able to find the motivation for Julietta's fortitude[14]. Banished by her own family she takes away her children, 'diese ihre liebe Beute'; and: 'Ihr Verstand, stark genug, in ihrer sonderbaren Lage nicht zu reißen, gab sich ganz unter der großen, heiligen und unerklärlichen Einrichtung der Welt gefangen.'[a]

It is perhaps no accident that this most 'incarnate' of poets, so utterly enmeshed in the concretion of existence in all its physicality, should at one and the same time have subjected a character to the most gruelling test of living with this paradox, and found one of his most triumphantly humane and convincing resolutions in her acceptance of it: for he is here dealing with the very mystery of incarnation; and a fate which might have seemed diabolic in any other poet's hands to this, his character, flesh of his own flesh and blood of his blood, feels sweet and angelic as well.

The fact that we are not far out in according a religious reading to the marquise's paradoxical plight is attested by another vital biblical allusion. Julietta's father, as literal-minded as she is herself, scorns the testimony of his daughter's conscience flatly contradicted as it is by the evidence of his — and her — senses. And this father is lovingly nicknamed a doubting Thomas by his wife: 'Nein, solch ein Thomas! sprach sie mit heimlich vergnügter Seele; solch ein ungläubiger Thomas! Hab ich nicht eine Seigerstunde gebraucht, ihn zu überzeugen. Aber nun sitzt er und weint.'[b] 'Unless I shall see in his hands the prints of his nails and put my finger into the place of the nails and put my hand into his side, I shall not believe': thus St. Thomas, according to the Gospel of St. John. Perhaps we are well advised not to see yet another erotic aberration in this father's vehement lovemaking with his daughter, but to recognise it as being the religious transport of one of this ineradicably physical poet's characters as he touches the truth that has been so cruelly hidden, bodily, with his lips and his hands and his lips again: a well deserved respite for one so simple who has to live with so abstruse a paradox.

Littegarde, on the same charge of having an illicit erotic adventure, yet bereft of the fount of strength that comes from the depth of the physis, does not rise to Julietta's serene acceptance. Confronted with the paradox of unequivocal material and even divine evidence mercilessly pitted against a spotless conscience, her mind

---

a 'her precious booty;' 'her mind, strong enough not to give in this extraordinary situation, wholly surrendered itself to the great, sacred and inexplicable ordinance of the world.'

b 'Dear me, what a Thomas! she said with secret relish in her soul, such a doubting Thomas! Did it not take me one full hour by the clock to convince him. And now he sits there, crying.'

gives. It cracks beneath the crushing weight of the signs that are arrayed against her, and her vision of herself in its ultimate truth is blotted out. '"Schuldig, überwiesen, verworfen, in Zeitlichkeit und Ewigkeit verdammt und verurteilt!" rief Littegarde, indem sie sich den Busen, wie eine Rasende zerschlug: "Gott ist wahrhaftig und untrüglich; geh, meine Sinne reißen . . ."'[a]. Nothing could be more characteristically Kleistean than this deferential dependence on material and circumstantial signs — in this instance the fateful ring Rotbart produces as a token of their love-tryst — this devastating reliance on the absolute truth as it becomes, or seems to become, directly manifest through the outcome of the ordeal. It is Trota who will teach Littegarde to transcend the intolerable paradox with which she has to live through a faith in her own integrity and their love which is unsupported by any material tokens whatever. But of that later.

Needless to say, Alkmene's problem is closely similar to that of Littegarde and, even more so, to Julietta's. Her situation is even closer than that of the Marquise von O. to the biblical myth. She has in fact been overshadowed by the divine presence and has conceived. But — typically Kleistean trait — it is not a ghostly presence she has received, but the god she has held in her unsuspecting arms, flesh and blood in the embodiment of her own husband Amphitryon. She lives with a paradox of which she is quite unaware except indirectly, through the flagrant contradictoriness in the behaviour of what she thinks is one and the same being. She has to wake up and learn the nature of that paradox: it is that of the divine hypostasis, the mystery of one being who is at one and the same time wholly god and wholly man. If Jupiter frets at the depth of his incarnation in her and yearns to step out of it, it is not only, as I have argued in a previous chapter, so as to gain a view of her loving as it is in itself, unobscured by her attunement to its particular object: it is also because, to become fully human and adult, Alkmene has to stretch her mind and, in differentiating between the physical and the spiritual[15], the material sign and its invisible significance, the phenomenal and the Numinous, must learn to bear the blessed paradox for which divine favour has singled her out. What she so learns to distinguish all but annihilates her by the incomprehensibility of its mystery; but like Julietta, she too is fortified in the depths of her maternal self by the visitation she endures. She conceives, and the glory of that physical event may well reverberate in the final 'Ach!' with which she bows before her incarnate mystery.

Curiously enough, it is the least sophisticated character of that group, Eve, who is most articulate about her predicament. Indicted by formidable evidence and repudiated by lover and mother alike, she turns to Ruprecht and demands the all but impossible of him:

> Pfui, Ruprecht, pfui, o schäme dich, daß du
> Mir nicht in meiner Tat vertrauen kannst . . .[b]   (9)

---

[a] '"Guilty, convicted, cast out, condemned and judged in time and eternity!" Littegarde cried, beating her breast like one raving: "God is true and unerring! Go away, my mind is taut to snapping . . ."'

[b] Fie, Ruprecht, fie, o shame on you/ Who could not trust me in my very deed . . .

she blazons out at him: *in meiner Tat* — a stipulation that neither Amphitryon nor Gustav nor Penthesilea could have met. And fiercely, she articulates the full span of the spiritual challenge meted out to Ruprecht, and the only proper way to surmount it:

> Und hättest du durchs Schlüsselloch mich mit
> Dem Lebrecht aus dem Kruge trinken sehen,
> Du hättest denken sollen: Ev ist brav,
> Es wird sich alles ihr zum Ruhme lösen,
> Und ists im Leben nicht, so ist es jenseits,
> Und wenn wir auferstehn, ist auch ein Tag.[a]   (9)

Eve knows and here puts into words what neither the marquise nor Littegarde nor Alkmene realise: that there are some paradoxes for which there is neither room nor resolution 'im Reiche der Natur' — 'in the realm of nature', as Julietta has it. She of all people, who unsuspectingly exposed herself to indignity and shame for the sake of the benighted 'Schein' — 'certificate' — she had sought to obtain for her beloved's safety, tears the web of appearances asunder and shows her Simple Simon the only way to that absolute truth he in common with all Kleistean characters so ardently desires and so clumsily 'mis-takes': through the sheer paradox of ungrounded faith. But then this is easier seen than done. Besides, Eve figures in a comedy, and in the relaxed idiom of this genre the poet has spared his characters the most cruel turns of the screw.

5.

Amidst the throng of figures who, enmeshed in physicality yet drawn by the lure of the Absolute, endure the dark paradoxes in which they are trapped, there are a few shining ones capable of transcending them in maturity of vision and the freedom of total faith. Amongst these are the mother of Julietta and the chamberlain Trota, friend and lover of the hapless Littegarde. Frau von G. . ., Julietta's mother, has read the anonymous newspaper advertisement requesting her daughter to come to a rendezvous with the unknown father of her child. At that point the scales fall from her eyes. 'Frau von G. . .', we read, 'sagte, nach einer nochmaligen Überlesung des Zeitungsblattes, daß wenn sie, von zwei unbegreiflichen Dingen, einem, Glauben beimessen solle, sie lieber an ein unerhörtes Spiel des Schicksals, als an diese Niederträchtigkeit ihrer sonst so vortrefflichen Tochter glauben wolle.'[b] She resolves the contradictoriness of her daughter's situation by giving her free credence to that one of the conflicting facts which stands bereft of

---

a   And had you spied me through the keyhole/ Drinking with Lebrecht from the jug,/ You should have said: Eve is a good girl,/ All will come out all right and do her credit,/ If not in this life, in the next one then,/ The day will dawn when we shall rise again.

b   'After once more perusing the paper, Frau von G. said that, if of two incomprehensible things she was to put her faith in *one*, she would prefer to believe in some preposterous trick of fate than in such baseness of an otherwise excellent daughter.'

all external props and has on its side nothing save her faith in Julietta's unevidenced integrity. Of two incomprehensible options she chooses the one that is by far the less comprehensible, in the teeth of improbability, indeed of impossibility, with no support bar the small voice of a faithful heart.

A closely similar choice is made by Trota. Defeated in the divine ordeal, condemned by the incriminating facts that have come to light regarding Littegarde's past, and bitterly mocked for his criminal credulity by his own mother, he receives his beloved's solemn assurance of her innocence. And: "'O Gott, der Allmächtige!'", he cries, kneeling before her: "habe Dank! Deine Worte geben mir das Leben wieder; der Tod schreckt mich nicht mehr, und die Ewigkeit, soeben noch wie ein Meer unabsehbaren Elends vor mir ausgebreitet, geht wieder, wie ein Reich voll tausend glänziger Sonnen, vor mir auf!"'[a] Then come the decisive words, the same words almost as those spoken by Julietta's mother, only more radiantly free: "'Laß uns, von zwei Gedanken, die die Sinne verwirren, den verständlicheren und begreiflicheren denken, und ehe du dich schuldig glaubst, lieber glauben, daß ich in dem Zweikampf den ich für dich gefochten, siegte!"'[b] That belief, so movingly and absurdly flung into the face of facts, can only be the more understandable and comprehensible of the two for a man whose spirit has emancipated itself from the bondage of fetishes and facts, even from those facts which appear to make manifest the divine judgment in an immediate and material manner. Trota is capable of what scarcely another character from this poet's pen accomplishes: he *interprets* an all but impenetrable cognitive situation in which faith and fact are radically at odds, in the spirit of trust, unswervingly alive to its hidden significance and undeterred by any outward token, be it even of divine origin. To do so requires the prior hypothesis of faith, and reverence for that element of ambiguity shrouding the divine incognito which alone can ensure the life of faith. As Pascal has it: 'He so regulates the knowledge of Himself that he has given signs to those who seek him, and not to those who seek him not. There is enough light for those who desire to see, and enough obscurity for those who have a contrary disposition'. Alone amongst Kleist's figures Trota is free and faithful enough not to demand the immediate and intellectually compelling revelation of the truth. That he is right is proven by his gradual recovery and his rival's slow mouldering towards extinction. His faith will be vindicated by the imperial amendment of the statutes obtaining to a divine ordeal: "'überall wo vorausgesetzt wird, daß die Schuld damit *unmittelbar** ans Tageslicht komme"'

a '"O God Almighty! . . . thanks be to Thee! Your words give me back my life; death holds no more terrors for me and eternity, stretching before me like an ocean of unfathomable misery until a moment ago, is once again shining upon me, like a realm ablaze with a thousand suns!"'

b '"Of two thoughts confounding the mind let us think the more intelligible and comprehensible one, and rather than have you believe yourself guilty, believe that I was victorious in the ordeal I fought on your behalf!"'

* my italics

the clause is to be inserted: ' "wenn es Gottes Wille ist." '[a] Such mature acceptance of the ineluctable mediacy of the Absolute strikes a new and mellow note in this vehement poet's world[16].

It yet remains for us to follow Kleist in the transcendence of the darkest paradox of all, the paradox surrounding the question of death and life immortal. This, we have seen, was the rock on which his own untried faith foundered in the days of his youth; and this arena it is in which his mature art reaps its finest triumphs. And as we touch on these ranges, the mind is imperceptibly transported to the last exchanges between Christ and his little band of followers in the intimacy of the upper room, those still moments before the rabble breaks loose.

Let us go back to the beginning. In a previous chapter we discussed the conversation in Kleist's first play between the young heroine and her blind grandfather Sylvus. This conversation, we saw, turned upon Agnes' dead brother, Philipp. Agnes had come up sharp against the paradoxical assurance of the priest that Philipp was alive and well. Her commonsense, indeed her very eyes, had made her doubt the meaningfulness of this assertion. For

> Ich seh es, wo er ist, am Hügel. Denn
> Woher, der Hügel?[b]

True, noting Sylvus' confidence that the priest was right after all, she had thought that there might be more between heaven and earth than her eyes were able to make out:

> Denn woher
> Die Zuversicht?[c]

But with the realism of youth she had rested within the confines of her mechanistic approach, operating with causal categories which could, by definition, yield up no answer bar one valid in the empirical sphere. Still, for a short childish moment between crying and laughing she had faced up to the paradox of death.

In this same play, Kleist has envisaged a response to that riddle which is vastly more primitive even than that of young Agnes. In his search to discover a clue as to how his own young brother came to meet his death, Ottokar happens on a peasant's dwelling and finds an old and a young woman stirring a gruel over a flame amid strange incantations. It turns out that it was they who mutilated young Peter, they that cut the little finger off his hand; for a dead child's finger, they explain,

> . . . tut nach dem Tod mehr Gutes noch,
> Als eines Auferwachsnen ganze Hand
> In seinem Leben. –[d]   (IV, 3)

---

[a] ' "wherever it is presumed that it will *directly* bring the guilt to the light of day" ' – ' "if it be God's will." '

[b] I see where he is from the mound. For/ Whence the mound?

[c] For whence/ The confidence?

[d] . . . does more good after death,/ Than does a grown up's whole hand/ Throughout his life. –

The magic finger, properly prepared and cooked, together with the right incantations, will conquer death and ensure final resurrection. This is the prayer
Barnabe chants on behalf of her dead father:

> Ruh in der Gruft: daß ihm ein Frevlerarm nicht
> Über das Feld trage die Knochen umher.
> Leichtes Erstehn: daß er hoch jauchzend das Haupt
> Dränge durchs Grab, wenn die Posaune ihm ruft.
> Ewiges Glück: daß sich die Pforte ihm weit
> Öffne, des Lichts Glanzstrom entgegen ihm wog.[a]   (IV, 3)

This for her mother:

> . . .
> Leben im Tod: daß ihr kein Teufel die Zung
> Strecke heraus, wenn sie an Gott sich empfiehlt.[b]   (ibid.)

For all we know, this luridly melodramatic scene may have had the young poet
in stitches when he tried to read his tragedy to his friends; and understandably so.
Yet for us it is important in that it depicts the primal, one is inclined to say the
prehuman, attitude to the phenomenon of death and resurrection. There is no
awareness of paradox here, no sense even of the different areas of experience that
blend into our response to it: the grossly physical, the intellectual, the spiritual
and the magic are all mixed up in the brew of one featureless conflation. This
unleavened physicality and lack of differentiation presents an admittedly grotesque
caricature of what is nevertheless a characteristically Kleistean trait: for here we
find all the reliance on the material, the palpable – the cut off finger is the first of
Kleist's many 'articles of faith' – the reification of living process and the
hypostasization of the unsubstantial, which are familiar features of his imagination, in and out of his poetry. For all the barbarism of the scene we are not far
from Ruprecht's and Frau Marthe's world, not far even from Amphitryon's
imagined vengeance on his limbs or indeed from Penthesilea's magic introjection
of Achilles'.

It is against the foil of such primitiveness that we must assess the poet's mature
handling of his theme. The Prinz von Homburg is spared none of the horrors of
dying and death. Like Agnes with her young brother, he *sees* his grave and,
looking ahead with his physical eye, asks, as she did:

> Ich seh es, wo er ist, am Hügel. Denn
> Woher, der Hügel?[c]   (*Fam. Schroffenstein*, I, 2)

---

[a] Rest in your grave: let no wanton arm/ Scatter his bones across the field./ Easy rising:
let him exultant press his head/ Through the grave, when the last trumpet summons him./
Eternal happiness: let the portals open wide/ For him, and bathe him in a shining stream
of light.

[b] . . ./ Life in death: let no devil stick out his tongue/ At her when she commends her soul
to God.

[c] I see where he is from the mound. For/ Whence the mound?

Only he says:

> Und ein Gestein sagt dir von ihm: er war![a]   (*Homburg*, III, 5)

He too says, like Agnes, 'Ihm sei wohl' — 'that all was well with him' — and: 'der Pater freilich solls verstehn' — 'the Pater of course should know these things' (*Fam. Schroffenstein*, I, 2); only he puts it differently:

> Ich glaubs; nur schade, daß das Auge modert,
> Das diese Herrlichkeit erblicken soll.[b]   (*Homburg*, IV, 4)

But how weary is this 'ich glaubs'; what hope can there be of immortality so long as it is in the smallest part interlaced with our perishable self? Yet perishableness is all the prince's eyes report. It is these physical fetters he casts off when, at the elector's words, he sees himself as the ghostly lover of Natalie and his spirit 'tot vor den Fahnen schreitend' — 'striding dead before the flags' (V, 8); when, with his physical eyes closed and his new spiritual eyes open[17], his new spiritual body grows and he wings his way above the one-time sensuous world. Thus, dead to the world and to his old self, cleansed of all bondage save the bonds of loyalty and love, he is ready to receive immortality now, in the midst of a transfigured life.

> Was ich besitze, seh ich wie im Weiten,
> Und was verschwand, wird mir zu Wirklichkeiten . . .[c]

writes Goethe; and Kleist responds, asking:

> Nein, sagt! Ist es ein Traum?[d]

and answering:

> Ein Traum, was sonst?[e]   (V, 11)

We have spoken of the selfless deed of Mariane, Gustav's dead fiancée who sacrifices herself by denying him, saying with Peter, '"diesen Menschen kenne ich nicht!"' — '"I do not know this man!"' — and of Toni's answering deed: actions of luminous fidelity which, in a misshapen world, must hide themselves behind the mask of paradox. And is not Fernando's pretence that 'this worthy man', Jeronimo, is a stranger who is magnanimously coming to his aid, a similar act of costly loyalty clothed in paradoxical denial? Does not Jeronimo's stepping forth, defying, so the narrator has it, 'die ganze im Tempel Jesu versammelte Christenheit'[f] and saying: '"Wenn Ihr den Jeronimo Rugera sucht: hier ist er! Befreit jenen Mann, welcher unschuldig ist!"'[g] echo the light and unearthly freedom from

---

a And but his tombstone says of him: he was!/
b I'll grant it; a thousand pities though the eye must rot,/ Which is supposed this splendour to behold.
c What I possess, my eye as distant sees,/ And what had gone grows to realities . . .
d No, say! Is it a dream?/
e A dream, what else?
f 'the whole of Christendom foregathered in the temple of Jesus'
g '"If you seek Jeronimo Rugera: I am he! Let that man go, for he is innocent!"'

incarnate life of Christ when he steps forward, asking 'Whom seek ye?', and answering 'I am he: if therefore ye seek me, let these go their way'? Is not the two friends' protectiveness of one another which costs the life of one and the best part of the other's, a re-enactment of those quiet words in the upper room, absurd and paradoxical words, too, in the eyes of those that cleave to life: 'Greater love has no man than this, that a man lay down his life for his friends'? And what of that culminating paradox, sounded in those hauntingly lovely words on which this grim and glorious story concludes: 'und wenn Don Fernando Philippen mit Juan verglich, und wie er beide erworben hatte, so war es ihm fast, als müßt er sich freuen.'[a]? Was the earthquake a divine scourge, or was it the swift flowering of a redemption bound to wither away as soon as life was once again within secure grasp?[18] With the most delicate ambiguity — and ambiguity is the prerequisite of freely offered living faith — these words leave both options open; but the balance gently inclines towards tenderness and joy. These are the final words about a man who gave his only son to blot out the evil perpetrated by a 'satanic mob' and their prince. Perhaps it is more than a quirk of the narrator's fancy to have called him 'dieser göttliche Held' — 'this divine hero'.

---

[a] 'And when Don Fernando compared Philipp with Juan and reflected on how he had acquired them both, something in him told him, almost, to be glad.'

V Paradise Regained

Joy and woe are woven fine
Clothing for the soul divine; . . .
Man is made for joy and woe
And if this we rightly know
Safely through the world we go.
Blake

If a man could pass through Paradise in a dream, and have a flower presented to him as a pledge that his soul had really been there, and if he found the flower in his hand when he awoke — Aye, and what then?
Coleridge

9 'Das Erdbeben in Chili': A Heaven on Earth?

1.

In a late and unusually high-spirited little essay entitled *Allerneuester Erziehungs-plan* — *The Latest on the Educational Front* — Kleist bases some illuminating observations regarding emotional and moral behaviourpatterns in the human realm upon the law of contradiction as exhibited in the field of experimental physics. An electrically neutral body, brought into proximity with one that is electrically charged, will, he reports, at once take on the opposite pole.

> Es ist als ob die Natur einen Abscheu hätte, gegen alles, was, durch eine Verbindung von Umständen, einen überwiegenden und unförmlichen Wert angenommen hat; und zwischen je zwei Körpern, die sich berühren, scheint ein Bestreben angeordnet zu sein, das ursprüngliche Gleichgewicht, das zwischen ihnen aufgehoben ist, wieder herzustellen. Wenn der elektrische Körper positiv ist: so flieht, aus dem unelektrischen, alles, was an natürlicher Elektrizität darin vorhanden ist, in den äußersten und entferntesten Raum desselben, und bildet, in den, jenen zunächst liegenden, Teilen eine Art von Vakuum, das sich geneigt zeigt, den Elektrizitätsüberschuß, woran jener, auf gewisse Weise, krank ist, in sich aufzunehmen; und ist der elektrische Körper negativ, so häuft sich, in dem unelektrischen, und zwar in den Teilen, die dem elektrischen zunächst liegen, die natürliche Elektrizität schlagfertig an, nur auf den Augenblick harrend, den Elektrizitätsmangel umgekehrt, woran jener krank ist, damit zu ersetzen. Bringt man den unelektrischen Körper in den Schlagraum des elektrischen, so fällt, es sei nun von diesem zu jenem, oder von jenem zu diesem, der Funken: das Gleichgewicht ist hergestellt, und beide Körper sind einander an Elektrizität, völlig gleich.'[a]

And so it is, Kleist continues to argue, with human beings, especially in the moral sphere. Not only will one whose condition is indifferent cease to be so as soon as he comes into contact with one that is determinate in any given fashion: more than that, his being will swing to the opposite pole; such that he will exhibit plus when his partner is minus, and minus when his counterpart is plus.

---

[a] 'It is as though nature had an abhorrence of anything which, through some concatenation of circumstances, has taken on an excessive and unbalanced charge; and there seems to be some endeavour as between two bodies that touch one another to restore the initial equilibrium between them that has been disturbed. If the electric body be positive, all the natural electricity that is in the neutral one withdraws into its farthest and remotest corner, forming a kind of vacuum in the portions adjoining the other which readily absorbs the excess of electricity that is, as it were, ailing it; if the electric body be negative, the natural electricity in the neutral one accumulates ready for discharge in those portions that adjoin the electric one, waiting to supplement the electrical deficiency ailing its opposite number. If one moves the neutral body into the electric field of the one that is charged, the spark will jump, be it from the latter to the former or *vice versa*: the equilibrium is restored and both bodies are identical in their electrical charge.'

It is easy to see this law in operation in, say, *Das Käthchen von Heilbronn* and in its 'algebraic obverse', *Penthesilea*[1]. Where Käthchen herself is 'plus', Strahl, by some secret law, seems compelled to be 'minus'; whilst Penthesilea, in oscillations that are predictable in their very unpredictability, always adopts the counterpole to the one represented by Achilles. While he pursues her in deadly earnest, she spares his life and dotes on him. As soon as he woos her according to her wont, she swings over to the negative pole of implacable and murderous hatred.

In the moral realm, however, Kleist has nowhere worked according to the law of contradiction as consistently and as relentlessly as in the novella that is our concern in this chapter: *Das Erdbeben in Chili (The Earthquake in Chile)*. Natural events spark off reactions in the human sphere which contradict their causes, even as such reactions contradict one another, in a perpetual see-saw motion. Let us begin by recounting some instances of the first, the oscillating events in the human sphere sparked off by the great cataclysm the reverberations of which, immediate as well as distant, the narrator traces in this story.

A violent earthquake, a destructive event if any, saves life; more than that, it seems spontaneously to generate life. By its intervention, two lovers who think that their last moments have come are rescued: Jeronimo Rugero at the precise moment when he is about to make an end to a life he does not want, and Josephe Asteron within seconds of being executed. Jeronimo is released from his place of captivity through the strange circumstance that the crashing walls of his prison and those of the building opposite in their very fall form a temporary archway through which he escapes unhurt[2]. The encroachments of annihilation all around perversely whip him on, from danger to danger to safety. Similarly, Josephe enters the collapsing convent in which her baby son has been left behind and emerges with him safely, 'gleich, als ob alle Engel des Himmels sie beschirmten' − 'as though all the heavenly hosts were shielding her'. The places associated with her guilt and prosecution − the cathedral on the steps of which she gave birth, the vice-king's palace, the court of law in which she was sentenced to death, her parental home in which her transgression was met with remorseless vindictiveness − they are all razed to the ground. The archbishop who persecuted her most bitterly is being drawn, crushed to death, from beneath the ruins. The very tremors that shake the town give her renewed strength to run for her life, for her baby's sake. And that operation of the law of contradiction on the microcosmic plane is shown to be but an instance of its more general rule: immediately following the first and greatest shock, the whole town is reported to have been full of women going into labour and delivering in full view of the other sex.

Such incongruities on the bare biological level are complemented by reactions in the moral domain which are nothing short of the paradoxical. A veritable hell − the Dantesque quality of the description of the disappearance of Josephe's paternal home has been noted[3] − gives way to an idyll not experienced this side of the Garden of Eden. A society rent by selfishness, malice or mutual indifference whilst existing in unthreatened peace, through the catastrophe seems for the first time to live up to its promise, in the midst of shambles. The calamity and the terror of it have created *one* large family where before there were unsurmountable barriers of rank, sex and class; and the universal distress has liberated all the survivors' capacity for heroism and love. The very culprits of yesterday are loved and honoured members of today's primal community. The narrator sums up Josephe's thoughts to that effect, stating: 'Und in der Tat schien, mitten in diesen gräßlichen Augenblicken, in welchen alle irdischen Güter der Menschen zu Grunde gingen, und die ganze Natur verschüttet zu werden drohte, der menschliche Geist selbst, wie eine schöne Blume, aufzugehn.'[a] Paradox of paradoxes, this flowering of life, physical and moral, as the immediate result of a death-dealing blow!

But, as I have indicated before, this polarisation between a natural event and its effects in the human domain is not the only, nor indeed the principal, manifestation of the law of contradiction as Kleist traces it in this story. It is but the grand backcloth against which the polarisation between one human reaction and its opposite is played out. On this polar rhythm Kleist's story focuses, and it is to this reaction pattern that we must devote our attention.

2.

Jeronimo, we said, is liberated from a life he does not desire since it has brought about the certain death of his beloved. On hearing this supposition confirmed he wishes, so he recounts later, for a renewed tremor to destroy him and resolves 'nicht zu wanken, wenn auch jetzt die Eichen entwurzelt werden, und ihre Wipfel über ihn zusammenstürzen sollten.'[b] That wish is from the beginning subtly undermined. For 'wanken' in this story as, indeed, everywhere in Kleist's writings, designates surrender to calamity; and Jeronimo's resolve here expresses the unconscious desire to stand up to it. So, too, the image of the oak tree – as also the narrator's earlier one of the sustaining arch – both of which are familiar to us from *Penthesilea*, intimate secret resources of strength meeting, and matching, the onslaught of disaster. And sure enough, the resolve to die contrarily revives the desire to live 'since . . . amid searing tears hope had once again returned to him'. He duly gets up and scours the countryside until he finds Josephe.

Quite similarly, Josephe's own 'first horrified steps' are retraced as she remembers her little boy; and the sight of Jeronimo's shattered prison, for all that it heralds a swoon, in her consciousness is blotted out by a tremor the very terror

---

a 'And truly, in the midst of these terrible moments in which all the earthly goods of these people perished and the whole of nature threatened to be choked beneath debris, the human spirit itself seemed to open up, like a beautiful flower.'

b 'not to waver even if the oak trees were to be uprooted and their crowns were to crash above his head.'

of which whips her into renewed action at the thought of the baby in her arms: 'sie küßte das Kind, drückte sich die Tränen aus den Augen, und erreichte, nicht mehr auf die Greuel, die sie umringten, achtend, das Tor.'[a]

Such violent oscillations within the lovers are matched by the contrast of their reactions to the surrounding misery. Alive to the sufferings of the bereaved, they slink into the thicket so as to hide 'the secret exultation of their souls'. The very sight of so much wretchedness seems to enhance their bliss, almost as much as the nocturnal scene in its limpid beauty − Kleist has never exceeded the pure lyricism of this description − seems uncannily to belie the horrors nature spewed before[4].

The most paradoxical reversals, however, are saved up to characterise the swings of mood on the part of the populace in its interplay with the lovers. It is a giddying kaleidoscopic succession of shifting images and complementary after-images: divisiveness in peace, peace amidst devastation and renewed hatred sparked off at the veriest prospect of a return to normality. The sardonic depiction of the gossips gloating, together with their 'sisters', over Josephe's impending execution − the dismantling of roofs the better to see is a bitter parody of the leper's story recounted in St. Luke 5, 18−20 − abruptly gives way to sagas of universal lovingkindness, a change Jeronimo and Josephe themselves register uneasily, even as their hearts warm to the welcome extended to them by Don Fernando's party. It is at this point in the story that the action, suspended by the temporary lull in the night, the morning's shared meal and individual meditations, gathers momentum again and we are drawn into a violent vortex of oscillations, following one another like the very shocks of the earth which still continue to reverberate. News of the planned thanksgiving service reaches the party: Donna Elisabeth's cautions spark off Josephe's and Elvire's answering enthusiasm, Elisabeth's renewed warnings only serving to fire the resolve of Fernando, whose face flushes with a wave of anger. The atmosphere of veneration in the church − the boys perched high up on the walls recall the story of Zacchaeus climbing the sycamore tree (Luke 19, 2−9) − is electric. 'Niemals schlug aus einem christlichen Dom eine solche Flamme der Inbrunst gen Himmel, wie heute aus dem Dominikanerdom zu Sankt Jago; und keine menschliche Brust gab wärmere Glut dazu her, als Jeronimos und Josephens!'[b] Yet, minutes later, 'the whole of Christendom foregathered in the temple of Jesus' will cry − and this cry is significantly directed towards the innocent − '"Stone them! stone them!"' The sermon, beginning with 'glorification, praise and thanksgiving', turns into apocalyptic visions of the Last Judgment and an annihilating denunciation of the lovers. And now the law of contradiction is given full rein, heroic love and bestiality firing and steadily enhancing each other, shock by countershock, almost as from one sentence to the

---

a 'She kissed the child, wiped the tears from her eyes and, ignoring the horrors that surrounded her on all sides, reached the gate.'

b 'Never did such a flame of devotion rise to heaven from a Christian minster as today from the Dominican cathedral at St. Jago; and no human hearts contributed a more ardent glow than Jeronimo's and Josephe's.'

next. Fernando's saving ruse is followed by the first brutal assault on Josephe; this by his protective embrace of her and by Josephe's anguished identification of the child she is carrying as Fernando's; the child's seeking of his father's arms by the crowd's '"Stone them! stone them!"'; that by Jeronimo's heroic — and Christ-like — self-revelation and plea for Fernando; the ensuing tumult by Fernando's noble covering up of his friend's identity; this in turn by Meister Pedrillo cornering Josephe; that by the trapped Josephe's marvellous 'save both your children', and her resolve to sacrifice herself; Fernando's deeply paternal accept-ance of both children, the strangers' as well as his own, by Rugero's cudgelling down of his own son; Donna Constanze's supplication '"Jesus and Mary"' by the murderous '"whoring nun"'; the bystanders' compassionate horror at the con-fusion by Pedrillo's monstrous '"Warum belogen sie uns! . . . sucht die rechte auf, und bringt sie um!"'[a]; Josephe's subsequent self-offering and death, finally, by Meister Pedrillo's bestial murder of the wrong child; and that, in the renewed lull after this climax, by Fernando's 'ineffable grief' rippling away into the noiseless void that has formed around him.

3.

The teleological judgments — explicit or implicit — to which such a turbulent succession of events gives rise, follow and contradict one another with much the same speed and vehemence as do the events themselves[5]. The opening episode — a man being saved who is unwilling to live — communicates an air of senselessness. Prayerful trust and hopelessness alternate in the young man's soul, until despair at this 'vale of misery' gains the upper hand. After a miraculous escape prompted by the blind will to live Jeronimo's consciousness is all but blotted out as he falls into a deep faint. Feeling on his recovery the pleasurable sensation of being alive, he bows down to the ground 'to thank God for his miraculous deliverance', weeping for sheer joy. Immediately afterwards, he remembers the more distant past and Josephe's fate: and 'sein Gebet fing ihn zu reuen an, und fürchterlich schien ihm das Wesen, das über den Wolken waltet.'[b]

Josephe's early steps are similarly dogged by ambivalence. Her rescue of their baby son from the burning and collapsing convent seems miraculous enough: 'as though all angelic hosts were shielding her'. But the note of caution sounded in the narrator's 'as though'[6] presently issues in a reversal as the heroic Mother Superior, together with most of Josephe's sister-nuns, is crushed by a falling parapet 'in an ignominious manner': an epithet reflecting Josephe's own horrified reaction. 'Within a few steps' the indignity of this sight is counterbalanced by Josephe's learning of the rightful death of the archbishop, the most implacable enemy of her

---

[a] '"Why did they lie to us! . . . look for the right one and do her in!"'
[b] 'He began to regret his prayer, and the presence that rules above the clouds to him seemed terrible.'

love, and the dereliction of all the places associated with her prosecution. Gratitude for the child 'whom Heaven had given back to her' alternates with grief at her lover's death, when at long last the two find one another again and with it, 'find a bliss as though this were the valley of Eden'. Again we are struck by the proviso lingering about this 'als ob' − 'as though'.

The brief and blissful union of the lovers ushers in a series of teleological judgments seen increasingly through Josephe's eyes and exhibiting a progressively higher degree of disinterested generality. The first of these is as yet entirely geared to the lovers' own miraculous escape: 'und [sie] waren sehr gerührt, wenn sie dachten, wie viel Elend über die Welt kommen mußte, damit sie glücklich würden!'[a] Significantly, this naïvely self-centred reading[7] of a cosmic cataclysm is followed by plans for their future security; an egocentric concern which in its turn − and equally significantly − gives way to Josephe's wholly selfless feeding of Fernando's child. It is this action which inaugurates the bonds of friendship between the lovers and Fernando's family, especially between the child's mother Elvire and his present nurse. At this juncture, as Josephe is encouraged to share her nightmarish experiences with the sympathetic Elvire, she ventures on her second interpretation of the cataclysmic event: 'Josephe', we read, 'dünkte sich unter den Seligen. Ein Gefühl, das sie nicht unterdrücken konnte, nannte den verfloßnen Tag, so viel Elend er auch über die Welt gebracht hatte, eine Wohltat, wie der Himmel noch keine über sie verhängt hätte.'[b] We note the subjunctive, and the narrator's seeming concurrence − again cautiously phrased in terms of 'schien' − with her sentiments. This is contained in the immediately following paradoxical statement which I have quoted earlier on: 'Und in der Tat schien, mitten in diesen gräßlichen Augenblicken, in welchen alle irdischen Güter der Menschen zu Grunde gingen, und die ganze Natur verschüttet zu werden drohte, der menschliche Geist selbst, wie eine schöne Blume, aufzugehn.'[c] A strange metaphor, this. Not only are all material foundations shattered: nature itself seems buried beneath its own debris; and the lovely flower of humanity seems to open up in mid-air, ungrounded in any soil that could conceivably have nurtured it. And this is precisely the tenor of the description that follows of deeds surmounting any natural causation, transcending even the doers' natural capacities: deeds 'von freudiger Verachtung der Gefahr, von Selbstverleugnung und der göttlichen Aufopferung, von ungesäumter Wegwerfung des Lebens, als ob es, dem nichtswürdigsten Gute gleich, auf dem nächsten Schritte schon wiedergefunden würde.'[d][8]

---

[a] 'and [they] were greatly moved when they mused how much misery had to come upon the world for them to be happy!'

[b] 'Josephe thought she was amongst the blessed. Some voice inside her which she could not suppress called the past day, for all the wretchedness it had loosed upon the world, a blessing the like of which Heaven had never yet ordained to grant to her.'

[c] Cf. p. 161 (a).

[d] 'deeds testifying to joyful disregard of danger, to self-denial and divine self-sacrifice, to an

It is in reflecting on this phenomenon of human self-transcendence that Josephe ventures upon her third, and by far the most disinterested and sensitive interpretation of the baffling event: 'daß sich . . . gar nicht angeben ließ, ob die Summe des allgemeinen Wohlseins nicht von der einen Seite um ebenso viel gewachsen war, als sie von der anderen abgenommen hatte.'[a] This statement – and it is borne out by the concluding words of the story – is an affirmation of some mysterious and incomprehensible balance; as such it is cast in the apodeictic mood of the indicative. It is interesting to see, however, that Josephe cannot maintain herself at the level of generality to which her mind has momentarily risen: the narration continues with the lovers' renewed considerations of how best to secure their good fortune, and with their adopting the shrewder of two possible courses[9]. This renewed concern is immediately followed by the introduction of the final motif, the party's disastrous attendance at the thanksgiving service, where Josephe's ardent desire to revere her creator's 'unbegreifliche und erhabene Macht' – 'inscrutable and sublime power' – is overtaken by the rush of mutually contradictory events each one of which contains its own immanent teleological judgment, as paradoxically polarised as are the events themselves.

4.

Do the attempted evaluations then cancel each other out by the same law of contradiction which so clearly governs the train of the external events? Is a return to an indifferent balance, which is the result of the encounter between polarised electric bodies, all this story has to offer in the moral domain? And if so, is the verdict of indifference not synonymous with a negative verdict adjudging the concatenation of paradoxical events to be ultimately meaningless?[10]

At this point it may be useful to turn our attention to the enigmatic figure of Donna Elisabeth, whose secret thoughts on two occasions obtrude themselves upon the sensibilities of the reader when the lovers' souls, and especially Josephe's, are on the high crest of happiness and trust. Of all the participants in the story whose consciousness of the past is blotted out by the idyllic present, Donna Elisabeth alone remembers.

> Es war, als ob die Gemüter, seit dem fürchterlichen Schlage, der sie durchdröhnt hatte, alle versöhnt wären. Sie konnten in der Erinnerung gar nicht weiter, als bis auf ihn, zurückgehen. Nur Donna Elisabeth, welche bei einer Freundin, auf das Schauspiel des gestrigen Morgens, eingeladen worden war, die Einladung aber nicht angenommen hatte, ruhte zuweilen mit träumerischem Blicke auf Josephen; doch der Bericht, der über irgend ein neues gräßliches Unglück erstattet ward, riß ihre, der Gegenwart kaum entflohene Seele schon wieder in dieselbe zurück.[b]

---

unhesitating tossing away of life, as though it might be picked up again one step further, like some worthless good.'

[a] 'that it was impossible to say whether the sum of the general well-being had not increased on the one side by as much as it had decreased on the other.'

[b] 'It was as though all minds were reconciled since that terrible blow which had reverberated through them. They could not recollect anything preceding it. Only Donna Elisabeth who

Donna Elisabeth knows. She remembers and she foresees. And that foreknow-ledge of disaster, in a world where the old ledger of good and evil has been wiped off the slate and the forces making for either are once again poised in the pristine balance that obtained in the primordial paradise of innocence, is treachery. The words of warning she proceeds to 'hiss' into Fernando's ears, are the words of the wily serpent. To presume to know where the face of providence is veiled is godless and blasphemous. With this one word, *zischeln* — *hiss*, which echoes 'the sharp tongues' that in the beginning lashed out their merciless condemnation of Josephe's loving, the narrator and with him the poet repudiate knowledge, and knowledge pieced together from empirical evidence at that, as a fruitful response to the mystery that is being enacted. In the end it is Fernando's baby who pronounces poetic judgment. Held out to Donna Elisabeth, he cries and from her sterility turns to the fount of life and love, Josephe, who has given him the milk of human kindness.

What then is the poet's verdict upon a world in which love and hatred, life and devastation, good and evil are so inextricably and seemingly mechanically inter-laced? A clue to the answer is, I think, to be found in a strange narrative ploy an otherwise meticulously precise chronicler adopts in this novella. There is a curious haze, or blur, he has spread over some facts and human configurations. Donna Elisabeth reminds the party 'with evident anxiety, of the disaster that had befallen the church the previous day'. Yet it is the cathedral that was destroyed, and we have been expressly told a sentence or two before that the Dominican church was the only one to remain intact. Similarly, Don Fernando's sisters-in-law have but been introduced generically. The reader is left, with some difficulty, to identify them as the two donnas who are later mentioned by name, and to differentiate them from Donna Elvire, Fernando's wife. Finally, the little procession Fernando forms on the way to church represents a curious mingling of the parties whose interlocking tricks the imagination. One has to remind oneself who walks with whom. This is precisely because of the original separateness of the respective couples and the fact that they are now welded together in one shared fate overriding that separateness in their own view, though not in that of the populace which continues to think of them in terms of their family-affiliations and to interpret their identities along the lines of simple familial patterns. Fernando walks with Josephe, she holding his child; Jeronimo, leading his own son, follows with Donna Constanze. It is little Juan reaching out, from Josephe's arm, to his own father who causes Fernando to be taken for Jeronimo; it is Donna Constanze's walking by Jeronimo's side which causes her to be mistaken for the 'whoring nun' and cudgelled to death; and finally Fernando, holding both 'his' children, loses his

---

had been invited by a friend to see the spectacle of the previous morning, but had declined to do so, now and then dreamily gazed at Josephe; but the report of some new blood-curdling disaster catapulted her soul back into a present it had barely succeeded in escaping.'

own, instead of the child of love. '"Despatch the bastard to go to hell with her!"', the shoemaker shouts as Josephe falls, and seizes Donna Elvire's baby son.

Surely this blurring, against the backcloth of the populace's merciless if misled efforts at identification, is deliberate and contains the clue to the baffling narrative. It is the interlacing of strangers 'als ob das allgemeine Unglück alles, was ihm entronnen war, zu *einer* Familie gemacht hätte'[a], which is being palpably enacted here. Interlocked and all but anonymous in their chosen solidarity, each partners a stranger in a weird dance of destiny and shares what befalls the other. Before this mutual self-giving all original allegiances pale into insignificance, all divisive and individual claims to survival and security are silenced. A sacrificial rite is enacted which is as simple as Josephe's offering her breast to the little stranger and as solemn as a ceremonial procession. All teleological arguments are muted before a mutual self-giving which transcends the limits of human nature itself and allows an ungrounded faith, to which the grateful heart may give its absolutely free assent, to flower from devastation. 'Und wenn Don Fernando Phillipen mit Juan verglich und wie er beide erworben hatte, so war es ihm fast, als müßt er sich freuen'[b]. Living with ambiguity and revering it as God's own *incognito*: such enfranchisement from the death of doubt and intellectual certainty, to one as beholden to both as was Kleist, in the end meant heaven on earth. For, as Hölderlin has it in his *Hyperion*: 'Das schafft dem Menschen sein Elysium und seine Götter, daß seines Lebens Linie nicht gerad ausgeht, daß er nicht hinfährt, wie ein Pfeil, und eine fremde Macht dem Fliehenden in den Weg sich wirft. Des Herzens Woge schäumte nicht so schön empor, und würde Geist, wenn nicht der alte stumme Fels, das Schicksal, ihr entgegenstände'[c].

---

[a] 'as though the universal disaster had knit all that had escaped it, into *one* family.'
[b] 'And when Don Fernando compared Phillip with Juan and reflected on how he had acquired them both, something in him told him, almost, to be glad.'
[c] 'This gives man his Elysium and his gods that he does not conclude his life's course in a straight line, that he does not fly straight like a dart, but that an alien power obstructs his flight. The wave of the heart would not so splendidly foam, nor turn to spirit, were it not for the old mute rock, his destiny, opposing it.'

10 The Children of Grace:
Context and Text of 'Prinz Friedrich von Homburg'

1.

At the beginning of this study we started, together with Kleist, on the journey around the world of which the essay on the puppet-show speaks as a necessary step in the evolution of human kind. We have seen something of the pitfalls with which this path is strewn: of the basic simplicity of the characters destined to undertake it as well as of their zest for the Absolute that is ill-matched to the intricacies of a world

. . .
On which the gods gaze down but from afar . . .,

in which they are supposed to find their labyrinthine way.

It is time now to trace the final stage of that particular journey, the return 'home' to which Kleist, in his essay, makes such intriguing allusion. He has intimated that a 'relapse' into the estate of innocence, a repetition of the primal transgression − the eating off the tree of knowledge − would be necessary to blot out the first one. And we have been bound to ask ourselves whether by such a re-enactment he means a return to the unconsciousness of the bear or the puppet[1] or, indeed, whether such an ostensible regression marks a secret progression to somewhere the other side of that disastrous event when Adam's and Eve's eyes 'were opened' by the 'subtle' serpent.

Before proceeding to complete the round to journey's end, however, I propose to recapitulate, and to expatiate on, the principal landmarks we have encountered during its first half. Everywhere, we have come upon a resounding fall placed at the beginning of the respective drama or novella, a fall from a primal state of unconscious grace into the depths of reflective self-consciousness and reality. This fall has been occasioned by the characters' coming upon a situation requiring intellectual differentiation where, before, there has been no need for such an exercise; and this necessity to differentiate between material signs and their hidden significances has engendered a rigid reliance on those very perceptual tools which have been a good enough guide in simpler situations but prove disastrously inadequate now.

Adam and Eve, desiring knowledge and instead eating apples, in their fallen state have become riveted on perceiving their own perceiving and in the dismal self-consciousness of such a state have forfeited their grace; and so has the youth in Kleist's essay on the puppet-show. The descendants of that first couple and Ruprecht, in *The Broken Pitcher*, have literally as well as metaphorically fallen into complexities in which the *Augenschein* of things to which they cleave, and notably the *Schein* produced by the wily judge to exempt Ruprecht from army service, have tricked and tortured them. In *Die Familie Schroffenstein*, mutual suspicion and an excessive reliance on testing out and seeing have been ushered in by the contract of inheritance between the two branches of the family which marks their lapse from innocence 'as surely as the apple marks the Fall'.

> Du sollst mit deinen Händen nichts ergreifen,
> Nichts fassen, nichts berühren, das ich nicht
> Mit eignen Händen selbst vorher geprüft . . .[a]   (II, 3)

Gertrude frenetically admonishes the young Agnes. Amphitryon 'falls from the clouds' and it is the unexpectedness of his wife's reception and the duplicity of the situation into which he stumbles which inaugurates the general's wide-eyed inspection of a truth no five senses, however sound and sharp, can help him disentangle. Käthchen falls repeatedly from the heights of her dreamy vision, first as, encountering her idol in sober reality, she flings herself from a window of her father's house, then when Theobald comes to take her back home again, and finally when she has seen the naked corruption of Kunigunde face to face. The whole earth totters in *Das Erdbeben in Chili*; and the arch that remains standing to afford Jeronimo's escape from prison paradoxically holds because, as Kleist has it in a letter, 'every stone wants to tumble down at one and the same time'[2]. The old woman in *Das Bettelweib von Locarno* falls and dies: and it is this mishap that inaugurates the misled ocular inspection conducted by the marquis. Trota trips up and falls, significantly as he pays heed to public opinion instead of being true to his own intuition; and here again it is this accident which ushers in the endeavours to 'see' the blueprint of the invisible truth in the material outcome of the ordeal. The Marquise von O. falls and faints when first she encounters her rescuer and rapist, Graf F., and then again collapses, 'faint unto death', after the joint verdict of the doctor and midwife that she is in fact pregnant. Of the Elector of Saxony finally, a weak man without fibre or sustaining vision, we hear that he falls from one faint into the next.

After her blind-eyed chase of Achilles —

> Hier diese flache Hand, versichr' ich dich,
> Ist ausdrucksvoller als ihr Angesicht —[b]   (1)

Penthesilea crashes, and from that shamed moment on seeks to see, and reach, and seize, the Absolute teasing her senses, as though it were a lifeless thing. True, in her confused pursuit she seems time and again to take wing —

> Numidian arrows are no speedier! —   (3)

---

[a] You must not seize a morsel with your hands,/ Nor grasp, nor touch aught I have not/ Beforehand tested with my own . . .

[b] Here this flat palm, let me impress 't on you,/ Bears more expression than her face.

but such images of frantic flight remain object-bound and centrifugal; and her union with Achilles is persistently and ominously envisaged as a falling and indeed a felling:

> Ich nur, ich weiß den Göttersohn zu fällen.
> Hier dieses Eisen soll, Gefährtinnen,
> Soll mit der sanftesten Umarmung ihn
> . . .
> An meinen Busen schmerzlos niederziehn . . .[a]   (5)

she announces; and:

> Nicht eher ruhn will ich, bis ich aus Lüften,
> Gleich einem schöngefärbten Vogel, ihn
> Zu mir herabgestürzt . . .[b]   (*ibid.*)

Indeed, to her the very dream of love has a paralysing, venomous quality; and no wonder, since it is at odds with the path for which she is destined. She feels herself to be 'palsied . . ., smitten at the very core' at Achilles' sight; Prothoe declares her as little fit to continue the war

> . . . wie, sich mit dem Spieß zu messen,
> Der Löwe, wenn er von dem Gift getrunken,
> Das ihm der Jäger tückisch vorgesetzt . . .;[c]   (5)

at the most soaring height of the pursuit she is said to have been hit 'by the most venomous of Amor's darts' (7), and then again to be 'the aim of feathered arrows soaked in poison' (7); vanquished by Achilles, she remembers feeling 'constricted in her every limb' (14), unable to lift her arm to defend herself; and to check her deluded transport, Prothoe feels tempted

> dir das Wort zu nennen,
> Das dir den Fittich plötzlich wieder lähmt . . .[d]   (14)

The serpent and the Fall belong together; and it is not surprising to find images of a divided vision side by side with those of venom, and especially of venom paralysing those implements of careless flight, the wings. This is how we find the image complex deployed in Kleist's *Hermannsschlacht*. The Romans, with their degenerate vision, helplessly sink into the mire of the land they seek to subjugate.

> Wir können keinen Schritt fortan,
> In diesem feuchten Mordgrund, weiter rücken![e]

---

[a] None but myself knows how to fell the goddess' son./ This iron here, my playmates and my friends, shall/ Draw him, painless, to my bosom, with the gentlest clasp . . .

[b] I shall not rest till, from the air,/ Like to a bird of beauteous hue, I shall/ Have tossed him down to lie here, by my feet . . .

[c] . . . as is the lion to withstand the spear/ When he has drunk the venom which the hunter/ Has treacherously planted on his trail . . .;

[d] to name the word to you/ That instantly will lame your wings again . . .

[e] We cannot get a move on, not one step,/ In the humidity of this accursèd bog!

one of their generals complains:

> Er ist so zäh, wie Vogelleim geworden.
> Das Heer schleppt halb Cheruska an den Beinen,
> Und wird noch, wie ein bunter Specht,
> Zuletzt, mit Haut und Haar, dran kleben bleiben.[a] (V, 1)

After the nocturnal encounter with the Alraune, Varus wearily concedes:

> Sie hat des Lebens Fittich mir
> Mit ihrer Zunge scharfem Stahl gelähmt![b] (V, 5)

Such associations render us suspicious of Ventidius' protested passion for Thusnelda. Can it in truth be nourished by an honest vision to which all of him is committed, when he speaks of it in telltale terms such as these?

> Was für ein Strahl der Wonne strömt,
> Mir unerträglich, alle Glieder lähmend,
> Durch den entzückten Busen hin . . .:[c] (II, 5)

This is a love heavily tainted with the venom of consciousness; indeed, as it turns out, it is no more than a show of love masking his very realistic ulterior motives. As against this, Thusnelda's collapse after her revenge on the Roman youth — Gertrud adumbrates her faint, in words strongly reminiscent of those used of Penthesilea and Käthchen, saying

> Du selbst, wenn nun die Tat getan,
> Von Reu und Schmerz wirst du zusammenfallen![d] (V, 16)

— signifies the total if temporary eclipse of a vision that has been as ruthlessly betrayed as it is now being cruelly avenged.

What is the meaning of all these faints and falls[3]? Do they not designate, in the great majority of these instances, a loss of unreflecting spontaneity in the face of a reality the sphinx-like duplicity of which shatters the victim's unquestioning intuition of his very self, his belief in another, or in the integrity of the total configuration of which he forms part? Brought up short against an incongruity in his primal vision of things which was concealed before, the whole man ceases to move at once: he boggles and becomes conscious of his responding; and that fumbling response, floodlit by doubt and the shame of doubt, becomes progressively more splintered and uncertain, and less equal to the exigencies of a delicate situation calling above all for 'the spirit's serene activity'. 'Fall' and 'venom', in the world of Kleist, mean precisely that loss of spontaneous *élan*, that profound uncertainty and self-doubt which, crippling his figures' emotional stance, drives

---

a It has become as glutinous as lime./ The troups drag half Cheruska by their feet/ And, like some gay-hued woodpecker, will end/ By getting stuck in it,/ Skin, hair and all.

b The keen edge of this woman's tongue/ Has paralysed the pinion of my life!

c What is this surge of bliss/ which past endurance palsies every limb/ and spurts through my intoxicated heart . . .

d You will yourself, once you have done the deed,/ Collapse from excess of remorse and pain! —

them into frantic cerebration and makes them cling, incongruously and fetish-istically, to such material surrogates of authentic knowing as they are able to lay hands on: broken jugs, initialled diadems, a child's cut off finger, a ring or − a glove.

To characterise this condition a little more closely, we may refer back to Kleist's early letters where it is pinpointed with remorseless clarity. I mean the image of the warped and sullied mirror of his soul, warped and sullied not primarily because he feels that he is bad, but because it is a *mirror* and as such undermines the unreflecting flow of sensation. It is the fact that there *is* a mirror throwing him back onto his self which dogs him with that 'traurige Klarheit' − 'bleak lucidity' − of which he complains − Adam and Eve's bleak clarity once they start perceiving themselves − which shows him his self and everything around him 'in seiner ganzen armseligen Blöße, und dem Herzen ekelt zuletzt vor dieser Nackt-heit' (5 February, 1801).[a] We may also recall the twice recounted description of Kleist's musical transports, which are relevant in the present context. We remember his account of how he heard whole concerts in his mind's ear at dusk, by the river Rhine, walking into the evening breeze; concerts as meltingly soft and ravishing as the music of the spheres. The whole visionary experience, related in significantly synaesthetic terms, would at one stroke be destroyed by awareness: '. . . aber sobald ein *Gedanke* daran sich regt, gleich ist alles fort, wie weg-gezaubert durch das magische: disparois! Melodie, Harmonie, Klang, kurz die ganze Sphärenmusik'[4][b].

As I have argued in the opening chapter of this book this, no more, no less, is what ails Kleist and his characters: the mirror of self-reflectiveness which intervenes between them and their own trance-like immediacy.

It is in the context of our discussion of the imagery of falling, and the associated imagery of paralysing venom, that we may take a look at the fragment *Robert Guiscard*. From the extant portion of the work it is clear that the towering figure of the hero has succumbed to the pestilence that rages through his camp. The Norman and Guiscard's own nephew Abälard give the game away, and the most telling bit of pantomime shows the exhausted ruler sitting down on a kettledrum provided by the empress for his support. But what is the underlying meaning of this heroic fight of a born leader against a killer that has attacked him? Here the imagery Kleist uses, with which we have become familiar, serves as the only reliable pointer. The pestilence, we hear,

> Geht . . . durch die erschrocknen Scharen hin,
> Und haucht von den geschwollnen Lippen ihnen
> Des Busens Giftqualm in das Angesicht.[c] (1)

---

[a] 'in all its shabby bareness, until at long last the heart is revulsed by such nakedness.'

[b] 'But no sooner the veriest *thought* of it stirs than everything is gone, conjured away, as it were, by the magic: disparois! Melody, harmony, sound, in short, the whole music of the spheres.'

[c] Strides . . . through the terror-stricken hosts/ Breathing from swollen lips/ Into their faces venom from her breast.

Images of paralysis persistently recur. Twice Abälard divulges that Guiscard lay in his tent 'unable to control a single limb'. (7 and 9) He reports him to have said that he would have to call in the giants

> To move, by one iota, this slight hand.   (7)

And it may be more than coincidental that Robert, his son, cuts short the traitor's first intimation of Guiscard's true condition, exclaiming:

> Daß dir ein Wetterstrahl aus heitrer Luft
> Die Zunge lähmte, du Verräter, du!ᵃ   (6)

In such a context Guiscard's own protestations that, surely, he looks like one 'who is the master of his every limb . . .' (10) seem forced; and the leader's concluding expostulation that pestilence has heinously waylaid him 'on your speedy flight', and that, even if he be uninfected himself, his people,

> . . . deiner Lenden Mark,

are

> Vergiftet, keiner Taten fähig mehr,
> Und täglich, wie vor Sturmwind Tannen, sinken
> Die Häupter deiner Treuen in den Staub.
> Der Hingestreckt' ists auferstehungslos,
> Und wo er hinsank, sank er in sein Grab . . .,ᵇ   (10)

carry a greater weight of conviction than the forced stance of Guiscard's own serenity.

What this play was to be 'about' there is no saying. What is certain is that it is 'about' a deep and unadmitted loss of immediacy and verve. Could this play, conceived as an aftermath of the Kant-crisis — and we know what the Kant-crisis meant to Kleist — in its entirety be 'about' little besides the paralysis visiting a mind that is divided against itself? And could it be that, being so direct and unmediated an expression of the poet's own predicament, it was bound to remain a fragment, much as Goethe's *Natürliche Tochter* which is likewise concerned with the poet's profound distrust of his own creative processes, was destined to prove abortive?[5] We can only guess.

2.

We have accompanied Kleist's characters on their journey through the world and we know something of the content of that middle chapter. It is a chapter he wrote many times over. He gave utterance to it in Eve and Ruprecht's history, in the heart-searchings of Littegarde and Alkmene, in Amphitryon's and Gustav's

---

ᵃ Would that a thunderbolt, from sunny skies,/ Palsied your tongue, you treacherous villain, you!

ᵇ . . . the marrow of your loins/ Is poisoned, impotent, and day by day/ Your faithful servants sink into the dust/ As pine trees are uprooted by a storm./ He that is felled is resurrectionless,/ And where he sank, he sank into his grave . . .

torments, in the black suspicion dividing the Schroffenstein family and in the tragic disorientation of Penthesilea, who endeavours to reach an hypostasized Absolute by piling up cosmic furniture or by pinning it down with her arrows and thence, by the actual incorporation of the living mystery her mind has reified yet failed truly to 'take in'.

Loss of the 'paradise of innocence', unrelated watching, assessing and bodily mis-taking of what began by being a vision: this, in one or other of its tragic variants, is the content of the second chapter of the world. And always the act of seeing is paramount; an uncreative seeing — so far removed from that unerring *Gefühlsblick* Kleist envied his friend Brockes — which atomises what it would grasp, and itself in the process.

It is up to this point that we have hitherto taken our analyses, for the most part. Yet the essay on the puppet-show assures us that this is not the end. Always fallen man lingers outside the gate of Eden, desirous to re-enter it and to have his primal innocence restored; and always the cherub bars the entrance with his sword. But renewed grace, so the dancer intimates, lies the other side of consciousness and knowledge. '"Mithin . . . müßten wir wieder von dem Baum der Erkenntnis essen"', muses the speaker, '"um in den Stand der Unschuld zurückzufallen?"' '"Allerdings"', the dancer replies: '"das ist das letzte Kapitel von der Geschichte der Welt"'.[a]

To this last chapter of the history of the world it is now our business to turn. Kleist has poetically implemented it many times; and always he has done so through symbolisms that are the obverse of the Fall which ushers in the painful journey through the world. When he speaks of paradise regained, he does so through the symbols of soaring or flying, and through that of blindness. That he should do so is scarcely a matter for surprise. For soaring and flying are the motions by which, like the dancing puppets, we transcend the gravity which is our primal failing; and blindness is the condition of which we partook before the 'subtle' serpent treacherously tempted us to see, a guilty seeing which, we may suspect, conceals a deeper blindness.

In Kleist's first tragedy the recovery of the lost vision is excitingly coupled with imagery expressing the transcendence of gravity. Having discovered the story — unlikely but innocuous enough — behind the amputated finger, Ottokar imagines himself unseeing and on a swing. In an aside, he says:

> Wiege
> Mich, Hoffnung, einer Schaukel gleich, und gleich
> Als spielt' geschloßnen Auges schwebend mir
> Ein Windzug um die offne Brust, so wende
> Mein Innerstes sich vor Entzücken. — Wie

---

[a] '"Thus . . . we would have to eat once again off the tree of knowledge in order to relapse into the estate of innocence?"' . . . '"Quite so; and that is the final chapter of the history of the world."'

> Gewaltig, Glück, klopft deine Ahndung an
> Die Brust! Dich selbst, o Übermaß, wie werd
> Ich dich ertragen – . . .[a] (IV, 3)

The soaring, the closed eyes, the synaesthesia – we shall find it all again, in snatches here and there, and then in its wholeness in Kleist's last drama, *Prinz Friedrich von Homburg*. Meanwhile here, in this first fruit of Kleist's genius, the motif of blindness persists. As the lovers find each other in the gloom of the cave, Ottokar says:

> Es kommt, du weißt,
> Den Liebenden das Licht nur in der Nacht . . .[b] (V, 1)

And guessing that Agnes blushes and asked by her whether the dark protects so little, he poignantly replies:

> Only against the eye, my little fool – (V, 1)

the sick, suspicious eye that had brought all the misery over their divided clan. In the end it is Sylvus, the blind grandfather, who sees the truth, the same who undistracted by the eye's false report had from the beginning opted for faith, saying:

> Agnes, der Pater hat doch recht. Ich glaubs
> Mit Zuversicht.[c] (I, 2)

Käthchen's unwavering vision is from the beginning associated with blindness and with flying. Whenever she is in touch with her dream-vision, her eyes are unseeing. She is blindfolded in the hearing before the tribunal, and in the encounter with Strahl under the elderberry-bush her lids are firmly closed, although seeing as she does with her mind's eye, she herself significantly thinks them to be 'wide open, my sweet Lord, as wide as e'er I may' (IV, 2); again, if on New Year's night when the two met she saw –

> Looked at me big-eyed, with black eyes

as the count reminds her – the answer is

> Yes, because I thought it was a dream. (IV, 2)

At the very end, when the count confounds her vision by pretending that it is Kunigunde he is about to marry, that disturbance has once more found expression through the imagery of sight and blindness. 'Why do you weep?' Strahl asks her, to which she touchingly replies:

> I do not know, my most reverèd Lord.
> Something, methinks, has settled in my eye. (V, 12)

---

[a] Cradle,/ O hope, me like a swing and e'en as though,/ Eyes firmly closed, a floating breeze caressed my barèd breast,/ Let my heart in my bosom turn for bliss. – How/ Vehemently, good fortune, does thy coming pound against/ This breast! And thou, excess, how shall I bear thy wealth?

[b] You know't, to those that love/ The light shines but at night.

[c] Agnes, after all, the Father's right. I believe't/ With full confidence.

From the beginning these two lovers, destined to live out a vision Käthchen accepts and Strahl repudiates, stand under the tutelage of a cherub; Käthchen always, and Strahl when voluntarily or by a secret compulsion he is in touch with his inner truth. This is how, at the outset of the play, Theobald describes his daughter's primal grace: she is 'gesund an Leib und Seele, wie die ersten Menschen, die geboren worden sein mögen; . . . Ein Wesen von zarterer, frommerer und lieberer Art müßt ihr euch nicht denken, und kämt ihr, auf Flügeln der Einbildung, zu den lieben, kleinen Engeln, die, mit hellen Augen, aus den Wolken, unter Gottes Händen und Füßen hervorgucken'[a]. (I, 1)

Fetched home by her father to enter a convent, Gottfried admits having expected that 'an dem Kreuzweg, wo das Marienbild steht, würden zwei Engel kommen, Jünglinge, von hoher Gestalt, mit schneeweißen Fittichen an den Schultern'[b], to take Käthchen on her way to God. (III, 1) Such symbolism actually turns into reality — the reality of a fairytale — when Käthchen appears in the porch of the burning house, 'hinter ihr ein Cherub in der Gestalt eines Jünglings, von Licht umflossen, blondlockig, Fittiche an den Schultern und einen Palmzweig in der Hand'[c]. (III, 14) Seeing her as she has emerged from the collapsing building, alive and unharmed, Strahl exclaims:

> Why, God and his hosts surround your every step! (III, 15)

But Strahl too, the obstreperous knight errant, is firmly associated with the image of the cherub. This is how Theobald who has reason in plenty to malign him, apostrophizes this demonic figure: 'O du — Mensch entsetzlicher, als Worte fassen, und der Gedanke ermißt: stehst du nicht rein da, als hätten die Cherubim sich entkleidet, und ihren Glanz dir, funkelnd wie Mailicht, um die Seele gelegt!'[d] (I, 1)

It is on New Year's night that the paths of these two chosen ones converge in a joint vision which takes place under the guidance and by the light of cherubic

---

[a] 'sound in body and soul, like the first humans that saw the light of day; . . . you could not imagine a being more tender, pious and dear, even if the wings of fancy carried you to the dear little angels which, bright-eyed, peep out of the clouds, from beneath God's own hands and feet.'

[b] 'at the crossroads, where the picture of Our Lady stands, two angels would come, tall youths with snow white pinions at their shoulders'

[c] 'behind her a cherub in the shape of a youth, bathed in radiance, with blond locks, pinions at his shoulders and holding a palm branch in his hand.'

[d] 'O you — being more dreadful than words can say and thought may fathom: do you not stand there, in truth*, as though the cherubim had shed their raiments and had laid their radiance, sparkling like the light of May, around your soul!'

---

* The word 'rein' here is equivocal. It may be a mere colloquialism, in the way in which it would be in the sentence 'er hat sich rein wahnsinnig benommen', meaning 'absolutely'. On the other hand — and what follows strongly suggest this — it also means 'pure'. Whether or not Kleist intended this *double entendre* it is difficult to say. I have sought to cover both meanings as best I can by rendering 'rein' as 'in truth'.

presences. Old Brigitte relates how the count, sick to death, had been visited by an angel bidding him 'Trust! trust! trust!'; how he had been led to Käthchen's chamber and saw her in the dark until 'the wretched servant-maid . . . had come in with a candle and the whole apparition had vanished as it had come, at her entry'. (II, 9) Käthchen herself confirms the miraculous event:

> Ein Cherubim, mein hoher Herr, war bei dir,
> Mit Flügeln, weiß wie Schnee, auf beiden Schultern,
> Und Licht − o Herr, das funkelte! das glänzte! −
> Der führt', an seiner Hand, dich zu mir ein.[a]   (IV, 2)

In the end it is the emperor who corroborates the cherubic connections of each and both of the lovers and concedes that it is for him to make good their guiding vision. He will have to acknowledge having fathered Käthchen, if Strahl, 'this intimate of the elect', can leave off Kunigunde: 'unless I risk the cherub coming down to earth a second time!' (V, 2) And of Käthchen he says:

> Die einen Cherubim zum Freunde hat,
> Der kann mit Stolz ein Kaiser Vater sein![b]   (V, 11)

We must yet take note of another image pattern associated with Käthchen, that of the siskin. Driven away by the infuriated Strahl, she recounts how she had wandered to the gate there to bed herself, exiled,

> am zerfallnen Mauernring
> Wo in süßduftenden Holunderbüschen
> Ein Zeisig zwitschernd sich das Nest gebaut.[c]   (I, 2)

Requested by Strahl to be sensible and go home, she had sent him the message:

> Den Zeisig littest du, den zwitschernden,
> In den süßduftenden Holunderbüschen:
> Möchtst denn das Käthchen von Heilbronn auch leiden.[d]   (I, 2)

It is beneath the same elderberry bush that Strahl finds the sleeping Käthchen and elicits from her the story of New Year's Eve. And it is there,

> . . . wo der Zeisig sich das Nest gebaut,
> Der zwitschernde, in dem Holunderstrauch,[e]   (V, 12)

that Strahl, true to his vision at last − but it *had* to be confirmed in writing by the emperor! − promises to build Käthchen a house to domicile and receive her exiled vision. The image of the bird, an innocent and winged thing of nature, weaves

---

a A cherub, noble Lord, was close to thee,/ With pinions, white as snow, at both his shoulders,/ And light − O Lord, it sparkled and it shone! − / 'Twas he that led thee by his hand to me.

b To her that has a cherub for a friend,/ An emperor may with pride a father be!

c by the ruined ringwall/ Where in sweet-smelling elderberry shrubs/ A siskin, twittering, built himself his nest.

d The siskin thou didst suffer, him that chirps/ In sweetly fragrant elderberry shrubs:/ Would that thou bearest with Käthchen of Heilbronn.

e . . . where twittering, the siskin built its nest/ Amidst the branches of the elderberry bush,

what is perhaps the central symbolism in this play: for as Kleist has developed it, it means that Strahl is at long last willing to relinquish viewing his vision detachedly as it lies there before him, denuded and in the void, and instead truly to receive Käthchen who had so truly harboured him. For us this image complex is important because it is a strongly synaesthetic one and because the bird is a symbol of gravity transcended which we shall meet again in *Penthesilea, Die Hermannsschlacht* and in *Das Erdbeben in Chili.*

In fact, in *Penthesilea* the symbolism of the bird is the one in which the poet has entwined the two incompatible and mutually destructive visions of the lovers. Achilles, we have seen, to the Amazon is 'like a bird of lovely hue' she wants to toss down, 'with his pinions crushed'; he is a dove she would enchain in flowery snares and caress — ominous sign — with feelings which are as soft as hands; he is the swallow whose wings she had wanted to lame

> In such a fashion that the wing will mend.   (24)

In all these images the need to destroy his vision in order to enslave him to her own is only too apparent. And yet she is his fellow creature. Her visions of Themiscyra — and Themiscyra is the magic word which sums up her vision — are opium-heavy with images of nightingales' song:

> . . . bergt euch
> In Hecken von süß duftendem Holunder,
> In der Gebirge fernsten Kluft, wo ihr
> Wollüstig Lied die Nachtigall dir flötet,
> Und fei'r es gleich, du Lüsterne, das Fest,
> Das deine Seele nicht erwarten kann.[a]   (5)

Such is the challenge she malignantly flings at Prothoe who has got her man when she, Penthesilea, has not; and thus, too, she nostalgically explains the conditions of her wooing to Achilles:

> Nicht . . .
> . . .
> Darf ich mir den Geliebten ausersehn;
> . . .
> Nicht in dem Nachtigall-durchschmetterten
> Granatwald, wenn der Morgen glüht, ihm sagen,
> An seine Brust gesunken, daß ers sei.[b]   (15)

At the end, and paradoxically immediately after the report of her lying on the ground, her teeth sunk deep into Achilles' flesh, these voluptuous associations of

---

[a] . . . lay yourselves down/ In sweetly smelling elderberry shrubs/ There, in these hilly regions' farthest dale/ Where nightingales flute their voluptuous song/ And forthwith, lecher, celebrate the feast/ For which your soul cannot in quiet wait.

[b] Not I . . ./ May choose who is to be my love;/ Not I may, in the nightingale-resounding/ Pomegranatewood, at sunrise, tell him,/ Snuggled to his breast, that it is he.

soaring and warbling love are once again taken up: and this time, Penthesilea is herself identified with such a loving:

> Sie war wie von der Nachtigall geboren,
> Die um den Tempel der Diana wohnt.
> Gewiegt im Eichenwipfel saß sie da,
> Und flötete, und schmetterte, und flötete,
> Die stille Nacht durch, daß der Wandrer horchte,
> Und fern die Brust ihm von Gefühlen schwoll.[a]   (23)

This is the poetic apotheosis of a vision an unseeing Penthesilea will in the end herself reaffirm and avenge, in all its sweet and fierce integrity.

The very thoughts of Hermann, the visionary, are said to soar lustily:

> Soweit im Kreise mir der Welt
> Das Heer der munteren Gedanken reichet,[b]   (I, 3)

he aims at nothing but to lose the contest with the Romans, he protests; and the very image he uses belies the overt meaning of his statement. Asked whether the German warlords would not make common cause with him, he replies:

> Meinst du, die ließen sich bewegen,
> Auf meinem Flug mir munter nachzuschwingen?
> Eh das von meinem Maultier würd ich hoffen.[c]   (IV, 3)

Vis-à-vis the Romans this consummate role player will gaily ironise himself to mask his high-flying thoughts. Marbod, he concedes to Ventidius, is a mighty warrior,

> Whereas, you know, a gentler aim is mine: (II, 1)

to be a worthy husband to his wedded wife and a good father to his 'sweet' children. With sham modesty he thanks Varus for protecting the oak trees that are sacred to the 'the doughty natives' — tongue in cheek this virtuoso of symbols advises him to put up some obscure 'picture-sign to warn them off'! — demurely saying:

> You quite outsoar,
> Quintilius, the wishes of your slave.   (III, 5)

But Hermann knows that the fight between the Romans and the Germans is one of vision against vision, the one more finely differentiated, the other embryonic but potentially nobler: and to this conflict he gives eloquent expression in recurrent imagery of birds: until the balance between the two peoples is righted, he argues,

---

a She was as though born of the nightingale,/ That lodges near the temple of Dian./ Rocked by the oak tree's crown she sat,/ Fluting and carolling and fluting/ Throughout the quiet night; the wanderer would hearken, rapt,/ And from afar his heart, enthralled, would swell.

b As far as in the orbit of the world/ The army of my nimble thoughts may roam,

c You think, the likes of these could e'er be moved/ To wing away as I do, merrily?/ I would more likely hope that of my mule.

> Kann es leicht sein, der Habicht rupft
> Die Brut des Aars, die, noch nicht flügg,
> Im stillen Wipfel einer Eiche ruht . . .,[a]   (I, 3)

an image which is taken up in a sombre minor key in the concluding words of the play, with only the splendid 'erschwingt' adding a ray of hope. The greater vulnerability and spirituality of the Germans' vision is subtly underpinned by the introduction of yet another symbolism − that of soaring sound. On hearing that the Roman legions are headed by a heraldic sign in the shape of an eagle wrought in metal, Thusnelda muses:

> Wie jedes Land doch seine Sitte hat!
> − Bei uns tut es der Chorgesang der Barden.[b]   (III, 6)

Images of angels and cherubs extend into the novellas, and wherever they occur, they designate a vision upheld and inwardly sustained against extreme odds[6]. Josephe emerges from beneath the porch of the collapsing convent 'as though shielded by all the heavenly hosts'. Later, during the night of reunion, the voluptuous song of the nightingale high up above the lovers tells its tale; and later still, the flame of devotion soaring heavenward from the church betokens a populace united for one brief, inspired moment.

As Littegarde and Trota descend from the pyre on which they are to be burnt to death, the emperor exclaims: '"Why, an angel guards every hair upon your head!"'. On being shown the newspaper announcement answering the marquise's own, the *Kommandant* devours it three times 'as though he did not trust his eyes'. And well might he begin to do so. The very words he finds to malign his daughter belie his doubts: '"Solch eine Miene!"', he laments: '"Zwei solche Augen! Ein Cherub hat sie nicht treuer!"' [c]. The marquise's mother, in turn, has seen the light. Hiding her tearful face, she exclaims: '"Dann begreife, . . . o du Reinere als Engel sind, daß von allem, das ich dir sagte, nichts wahr ist; daß meine verderbte Seele an solche Unschuld nicht, als von der du umstrahlt bist, glauben konnte . . ."'[d][7]. When Michael Kohlhaas lays down his patience and takes up his mission, we read: 'Thus the angel of judgment descends from Heaven'; and even in his unhinged claim that he is a plenipotentiary of the archangel Michael we may detect a trace of the narrator's concealed affection for the incorrigible visionary.

What then, we may ask, does this persistent symbolism of soaring and flying and blindness signify? Surely it betokens the transcendence of that earthbound gravity which set in with the act of self-conscious seeing, that primordial sin which meant expulsion from 'the paradise of innocence'. Liberated from the shackles of a

---

a It may well happen that the goshawk plucks/ The eagle's young which, not yet fledgling,/ Rest in the quiet crown of some old oak . . .

b How every land has its own native ways!/ − With us, it is the chorus of the bards.

c '"Such a mien! Two such eyes! A cherub's could not be truer!"'

d '"Understand then, O you, purer than angels, that nothing of what I said to you is true; that my wicked soul could not believe in such innocence as surrounds you like a halo . . ."'

bleak knowledge which has separated them from their primal vision, the spontaneity of Kleist's figures is regenerated and, with their eyes closed to an empirical reality that has tricked them into disbelief and suspicion, they soar aloft on the wings of an undivided faith, in themselves, in the other, and in the mysterious power that reigns above the clouds. To fly, blindly, is to be at one with their genius.[8] '"These words were music to my ears!"', Trota exclaims when Littegarde acknowledges her innocence: '"Say them again!"'. Here is an echo of Kleist's own musical trances; but now, at this stage of his characters' journeying through the world, no thought *that* they are experiencing heavenly harmonies – and such a thought inevitably engenders the further one *whether* they are doing so in truth – interrupts the stream of sensation. The magic 'disparois!' is banished once and for all, in the assurance of creative inspiration. The spontaneous mind, set free, wings its way towards the other, the Absolute, even as the *Gloria in Excelsis* performed by the patron saint of music carries the souls of the faithful 'on wings through all the spheres of harmony'. The cherub who guarded the gates of Paradise has become a friend, and it is he who guides Kleist's lost figures into sight of God's own face, 'gesund an Leib und Seele, wie die ersten Menschen, die geboren worden sein mögen'[a].

But still we have not answered the question Kleist poses at the end of his essay on the puppet-show. What is the meaning of the final return to the estate of grace? What are the marks the journey 'through an infinity of knowledge' has left on the travellers? Is theirs a new kind of innocence? What does the repeated eating off the tree of knowledge betoken? A renewed seeing, signifying a renewed fall into blindness and confusion? Or a blindness that is a kind of deeper seeing? And, most important of all, in what sense is the 'ringförmige' – 'ring-like' – return to the beginning of the trip a relapse, a *Zurückfallen*? To answer these questions we must turn to Kleist's last drama, *Prinz Friedrich von Homburg*, in which, indeed, beginning and end meet to interlock in a perfect circle.

2.

Did Kleist know Schiller's distich *das Höchste – the Highest*?

> Suchst du das Höchste, das Größte? die Pflanze kann es dich lehren.
> Was sie willenlos ist, sei du es wollend – das ists![b]

And did he know that remarkable passage from *Etwas über die erste Menschengesellschaft nach dem Leitfaden der mosaischen Urkunde* which so closely bears on his own argument in the essay *On the Puppet-Show*? This is what Schiller has to say about our exile from 'the paradise of innocence', a bare twenty years before Kleist wrote his essay and penned his last, and greatest, play:

---

a 'sound in body and soul, like the first human beings that saw the light of the day.'
b Seek you the highest, the greatest? The plant can teach you a lesson./ What it unwittingly is, consciously will it – that's it!

An dem Leitbande des Instinkts, woran sie jetzt noch das vernunftlose Tier leitet, mußte die Vorsehung den Menschen in das Leben einführen und, da seine Vernunft noch unentwickelt war, gleich einer wachsamen Amme hinter ihm stehen.

Aber der Mensch war zu ganz etwas anderm bestimmt . . . Er sollte den Stand der Unschuld, den er jetzt verlor, wieder aufsuchen lernen durch seine Vernunft und als ein freier, vernünftiger Geist dahin zurückkommen, wovon er als Pflanze und als eine Kreatur des Instinkts ausgegangen war; aus einem Paradies der Unwissenheit und Knechtschaft sollte er sich, wär es auch nach späten Jahrtausenden, zu einem Paradies der Erkenntnis und Freiheit hinauf arbeiten . . . wo er dem moralischen Gesetze in seiner Brust ebenso unwandelbar gehorchen würde, als er anfangs dem Instinkte gedient hatte, als die Pflanze und die Tiere diesem noch dienen . . . Sobald seine Vernunft ihre ersten Kräfte nur geprüft hatte, verstieß ihn die Natur aus ihren pflegenden Armen, oder richtiger gesagt, er selbst, von einem Triebe gereizt, den er selbst noch nicht kannte, und unwissend, was er in diesem Augenblicke Großes tat, er selbst riß ab von dem leitenden Bande, und mit seiner noch schwachen Vernunft, von dem Instinkte nur von ferne begleitet, machte er sich auf den gefährlichen Weg zur moralischen Freiheit. Wenn wir also jene Stimme Gottes in Eden, die ihm den Baum der Erkenntnis verbot, in eine Stimme des Instinktes verwandeln, der ihn von diesem Baum zurückzog, so ist sein vermeintlicher Ungehorsam gegen jenes göttliche Gebot nichts anderes als – ein Abfall von seinem Instinkte – also erste Äußerung der Selbsttätigkeit, erstes Wagestück seiner Vernunft, erster Anfang seines moralischen Daseins. Dieser Abfall des Menschen vom Instinkte, der das moralische Übel zwar in die Schöpfung brachte, aber nur um das moralische Gute darin möglich zu machen, ist ohne Widerspruch die glücklichste und größte Begebenheit in der Menschengeschichte . . . denn der Mensch wurde dadurch aus einem Automat ein sittliches Wesen[a9].

Lucky Schiller! How straight and linear is his attack, how firmly rooted in the soil of the Enlightenment! For him, that is for sure, man's emancipation from the

---

tutelage of instinct — equated with nurse Nature and with God — is a good thing; it is man's loftiest achievement. Leaving behind his primordial fellowship with the animal and the plant, those automatons of nature, he works his way upward in a steady if laborious ascent to the paradise of knowledge and to a fully conscious moral autonomy. A 'relapse' into the state of innocence — the very thought of it to Schiller would have been meaningless and offensive. A second innocence, yes. But one that is 'willed — that's it!'; a condition which it is difficult if not impossible to reconcile with the involuntary grace of plant-life. In any case, the step to morality implies recognition of the moral law, an obedience to be rated infinitely more highly than the plant's instinctive obedience to the law of its growth, or even man's to a God who forbade him to eat from the tree of knowledge. The plant is an individual, anarchic. Adult man is a member of a society that prescribes, and obeys, the law of its own making.

How far we seem to be from the world of Kleist's last play which, even in form, is a perfect circle made of concentric rings, or so it seems. For in this drama the end is in its beginning, with the prince in the garden, turned in upon himself, and Natalie holding out to his unseeing eyes a laurel wreath of his own winding, laced about with the elector's chain. If he falls at the start, on being shocked out of his magic sphere —

> There he lies; no bullet could do better! —

so he does at the end. As his eyes open to the vision before him, the same vision he saw at the outset of the play, he falls into a faint. Has he 'lapsed back' into the selfsame 'paradise of innocence' out of which he was so rudely jolted at the sound of his own name? Has there been no development, no change?

More puzzling still, beginning and end interlace, in that both are associated with the motif of plants and flowers[10]. The elector wonders, in the opening scene, what foliage the prince might be winding into a wreath. It is laurel, he is told. Where did he find such an outlandish plant in the sandy soil of his Mark Brandenburg? God only knows;

> Vielleicht im Garten hinten, wo der Gärtner
> Mehr noch der fremden Pflanzen auferzieht . . .,[a]   (I, 1)

a courtier suggests. At the end, on his way to his execution, the prince smells the sweet fragrance of what he thinks are dame's violets. They are gillyflowers and pinks, he is told. 'How do they get here?' he asks, very much as the elector did in the opening scene. 'I do not know; a girl has planted them, maybe.' 'May I give you a pink?'

> Lieber! —
> Ich will zu Hause sie in Wasser setzen . . .[b]   (V, 10)

is the prince's reply.

---

[a] Maybe at the far end of the garden, where the gardener/ Rears more of such exotic plants . . .
[b] I'll place them into water, Friend, back home . . .

This last episode has been eulogised and has come under heavy critical fire. The prince's response is 'sweet' in its 'near-idiocy'[11], one critic tells us, whilst another points out that, role player that he is, he is so preoccupied with his immortal part that he altogether skips the uncomfortable intermediate stage of having first of all to die[12]. We in our turn shall refrain from assigning any particular significance to this strange — yet patently poetic — interlude and content ourselves with pointing out that, in this piece too, beginning and end significantly interlace, and that the 'near-idiotic' yet endearing and precious association of the prince with the involuntary grace of the plant finds its enhanced — and deliberate — echo at the very close. What has become of Schiller's noble notion of man's ascending from the 'unconsciousness and servitude' of the Garden of Eden to 'a paradise of knowledge and freedom', in which the yoke of instinct to which plant and beast remain subject, is imperiously cast off? Does the prince remain the exotic plant with which he was associated at the start? What, if anything, happens between that beginning and that end?

This much is clear: the prince is repeatedly, and centrally, associated with the imagery of plant life, and for that matter with that of the animal and — the child[13]. He himself sees his being in this light when he assures Hohenzollern of the elector's love for him. Rejecting the very thought that he intends to execute the writ of law, he asks:

> Schien er am Wachstum meines jungen Ruhms
> Nicht mehr fast, als ich selbst, sich zu erfreun?
> Bin ich nicht alles, was ich bin, durch ihn?
> Und er, er sollte lieblos jetzt die Pflanze,
> Die er selbst zog, bloß, weil sie sich ein wenig
> Zu rasch und üppig in die Blume warf,
> Mißgünstig in den Staub daniedertreten?[a]   (III, 1)

At the beginning of the fourth act after the prince's nocturnal visit to Friedrich-Wilhelm's wife, Natalie, pleading with the elector, picks up and confirms the prince's words. She freely owns that she loves him; but it is not to save him for herself that she is running her errand of mercy:

> Ich will nur, daß er da sei, lieber Onkel,
> Für sich, selbständig, frei und unabhängig,
> Wie eine Blume, die mir wohlgefällt . . .[b]   (IV, 1)

And the lovers' voices are united in one single metaphor of flowering and growth when they think the elector has been killed in battle. The last support of her fortune's vine has fallen, Natalie laments; to which the prince replies:

---

[a] The growth of my young fame, did he not relish it/ More almost than I did myself?/ Am I not everything I am through him?/ And such a one should, loveless, stamp the plant/ He himself nurtured, back into the dust, aggrieved because/ It flowered too profusely and too fast?

[b] Dear Uncle, I want nought but that he is,/ Just for his own sake, independent, free,/ As I would want a plant I like to thrive . . .

> Schlingt Eure Zweige hier um diese Brust,
> Um sie, die schon seit Jahren, einsam blühend,
> Nach Eurer Glocken holdem Duft sich sehnt![a] (II, 6)

Similarly, the young dreamer who so innocently betrays his innermost longings is associated with the estate of childhood. He himself beseeches the elector's wife to save him for his mother's sake at whose deathbed she has promised to be a second mother; and what is his desperate counsel to Natalie?

> Get thee
> . . .
> A fair-locked boy who looks like me, (III, 5)

press him to your breast, teach him to say — 'babble' is the word he uses — 'mother', to love and to close the eyes of the dead: what is this if not a fantasy of patent self-commiseration? Natalie in her turn draws on this fantasy — and imagery — when she speaks to the elector of

> . . . this error, fairhaired with blue eyes, (IV, 1)

— the prince has been obsessed with his eyes, and this, too, Natalie has picked up —

> Den, eh er noch *gestammelt** hat: ich bitte!
> Verzeihung schon vom Boden heben sollte:
> Den wirst du nicht mit Füßen von dir weisen!
> *Den drückst du um die Mutter schon ans Herz,*
> *Die ihn gebar**, und rufst: komm, weine nicht . . .[b]

It is indeed a very small child for whom Natalie here goes to plead.

But where and how is the prince connected with the imagery of animals? Natalie has spoken of his *Fehltritt*; so too has the prince:

> Er könnte — nein! so ungeheuere
> Entschließungen in seinem Busen wälzen?
> *Um eines Fehls**, der Brille kaum bemerkbar,
> In dem Demanten, den er jüngst empfing,
> In Staub den Geber treten?[c] (III, 1)

We have come upon this word before, in the touching story of Froben's self-sacrifice[14]. The stable master has procured a 'radiantly white' charger for the elector with which the latter has set out into battle. Seeing that 'dieses Schimmels

---

a Entwine your branches here, around this breast,/ Which, blooming many a lonely moon,/ Yearns for the gentle fragrance of your bells!

b Whom tender mercy should raise from the dust,/ Before he ever stammered 'Pity, pray!'/ O such a one you will not kick with feet!/ But for his mother's sake, who bore him, you/ Will press him to your heart, and cry: hush, do not weep . . .

c He could — it can't be true! — turn o'er/ Such monstrous resolutions in his mind?/ Could kick into the dust the donor of/ The diamond he recently received, for nought/ But for a flaw no spectacles can spot?

* my italics

Glanz' — 'this steed's brilliance' — attracted the enemies' attention as well as their bullets, Froben has begged his master to change horses and to let him break the shy animal in. Quietly smiling, the sovereign has replied:

> "Die Kunst, die du ihn, Alter, lehren willst,
> Wird er, solang es Tag ist, schwerlich lernen.
> Nimm, bitt ich, fern ihn, hinter jenen Hügeln,
> Wo seines *Fehls** der Feind nicht achtet, vor". [a] (II, 8)

As soon as Froben mounts the splendid steed, we know that he is shot; 'a victim of his loyalty'.

We note the fact that the words used of the horse — *strahlend* — radiant, *Glanz* — brilliance, and even the *Gold* Sparren indignantly reiterates, are the very ones in which the prince has recounted his dream-vision, and we go on to ask what link between him and the wayward steed could possibly exist. At this point we remember that the prince fell off his horse twice, before the battle and during it. An officer reports that he fell at night-time — 'he fell?' Kottwitz asks — yes, he fell because

> His black did shy at yonder mill (II, 1)

but he did not come to any harm, sliding gently down the animal's flank. And then we hear that he has fallen a second time, immediately after the story of the elector's escape has come to light, and immediately after the elector has announced that whoever led the cavalry will be sentenced to death, thoughtfully enquiring,

> — The Prince of Homburg was not in command? (II, 9)

The ensuing story that the prince was thrown off his horse — this time a chestnut one — and was badly injured, is important if only because the elector is assured that it is not his young nephew he has impulsively condemned to die. It is important, also, because it firmly associates the dreamer with horses that shy and horses he cannot, quite, control[15].

But there is more to it. Is not the *Fehl* of the white horse which shies in the glare of the battle that of the vulnerable somnambulist who is dazzled and distracted by the sudden din of the day? Does not that young visionary too need gentle breaking in

> Where no adversary will spot his flaw . . .? (II, 8)

The help of a Kottwitz for instance who, for all that he is too old to dismount from his own, knows that he can take his wayward young master's horse in tow, if need be, and teach him a thing or two? Indeed, Kottwitz perfectly understands the prince in his vegetative and incorrigibly personal mould. He is ready to die for the Kurfürst, but as an anarchist who would happily repeat the prince's trans-

---

[a] The art, old chap, you would instruct him in,/ He scarcely will pick up while it is day./ Take him in hand, I beg you, far beyond those hills,/ Where no adversary will spot his flaw.

* my italics

gression if occasion arose. He would die for him as that unique individual, 'Hans Kottwitz from the Priegnitz' who has the irresistibly naïve dignity to say:

> Als mich ein Eid an deine Krone band,
> Mit Haut und Haar, nahm ich den Kopf nicht aus . . .[a]   (V, 5)

And when he repudiates all motives of gain and affirms the nature of his allegiance to his sovereign, saying:

> Was! Meine Lust hab, meine Freude ich,
> Frei und für mich im Stillen, unabhängig,
> An deiner Trefflichkeit und Herrlichkeit,
> Am Ruhm und Wachstum deines großen Namens!:[b]   (V, 5)

do not these words forge a secret link with Natalie's about her vegetable love, the third of the anarchists who are the bane and saving of the crown[16]? And when the elector decides:

> Doch weils Hans Kottwitz aus der Priegnitz ist,
> Der sich mir naht, willkürlich, eigenmächtig,
> So will ich mich auf märksche Weise fassen:[c]   (V, 2)

and gently taking him by one of his *silberglänzige* locks, leads him back to his barracks where he belongs: does not the epithet *silbergänzig* — silvery — tie in this splendid if wayward veteran with the capricious white charger and with the fairy castle of the prince's dream?

The plant, the child, the horse: with those 'creatures of instinct', those 'automatons' of unconscious and involuntary grace the prince remains firmly coupled right to the end; and well may we ask whether he has developed at all from his somnambulist beginnings. But then we know that he has. We have in an earlier chapter seen him 'fall' from the assurance of his instinct and lapse into that tormented and clueless dissection of a reality the meaning of which escapes him, a degeneration into a perceptual mode he shares with so many other figures from Kleist's pen. How has this dislocation of his intuition come about, and in what manner does he rise above it?

To answer the first question, we might turn to Goethe's *Egmont*, that other sleepwalker in German literature, a play the importance of which for Kleist's last drama has been repeatedly remarked[17]. In his encounter with Alba, Egmont stakes his claim for the kind of freedom to which he and his fellow-countrymen are pledged and ready to respond: 'Leicht kann der Hirt eine ganze Herde Schafe vor sich hertreiben, der Stier zieht seinen Pflug ohne Widerstand', he explains: 'aber

---

[a] When, by an oath, I pledged me to your crown,/ Hair, skin and all, I did not save my head . . .

[b] Why, nonsense! 'tis my pleasure, my delight/ Quite quietly to smile, just for myself,/ On your magnificence and eminence,/ The fame and growth of your distinguished name!

[c] But since it is Hans Kottwitz from the Priegnitz/ Who comes uncalled, anarchic and self-willed,/ I'll take myself in hand the native way:

dem edeln Pferde, das du reiten willst, mußt du seine Gedanken ablernen, mußt nichts Unkluges, nichts unklug von ihm verlangen'[a].

Like the elector's white charger, the prince is such a noble and sensitive creature. He shies, as any sleepwalker would, at the abrupt transition from night to day, from dream to battle, from fantasy to sober fact. Harshly jolted out of his private visionary world — and how immersed he is in it, how voluptuously it is experienced in a state of synaesthesia! — into the light of the common day, his genius baulks. He has been called by name, his mind reflects what he has unconsciously performed, and at one stroke 'the magic disparois!' paralyses him. Sensa bewilderingly invade his vision: the goodbye from the ladies, the battle orders and, most importantly, the glove,

> Dies Stück des Traums, das ihm verkörpert ward,[b]   (V, 5)

as Hohenzollern so succintly has it. His instinct, inviolate in the closed circle of his dream, now becomes attached to and enmeshed in the material sphere; and thus rechannelled and erroneously aroused, becomes a turbid stream of naked aspiration. He now wants to *have* what he *saw*; and brutally overriding all caution and regard, charges into battle and proposal.

It is customary to maintain that the ruthless self-assertion which seizes hold of the prince in action is prefigured in his vision[18]. But this is not quite true. His vision, conceived in the lap of night —

> With golden hair, and drenched in fragrances —   (I, 4)

is, above all, a private one of immortality and love. 'Like his own posterity' he winds himself his laurel-wreath, and

> Sterngucker sieht er, wett ich, schon im Geist,
> Aus Sonnen einen Siegeskranz ihm winden.[c]   (I, 1)

This is not the near vision of one who is tomorrow's hero. It is the distant vision of one long since dead whose name alone, immortal, is inscribed in the stars.

> The whole procession . . .
> Of those loved by me   (I, 4)

descends to him who stands there, 'in unspeakable emotion', ready to go onto his knees. Only later, when the involuntary flow of fantasies is ruffled and a sense-object violently intrudes upon his vision and materialises it, does his confused and naked instinct begin to run amok[19].

However, it is true to say that what his vision has held out to him is the glory of immortality achieved *together* with the possession of all that he loves — a

---

a 'The shepherd may without trouble drive along a whole flock of sheep, the steer pulls the plough without resistance: but you have to learn the thoughts of the noble horse you want to ride, and demand of it nothing unreasonable, nor in an unreasonable fashion.'
b This piece of dream that put on flesh for him,
c I'll bet he sees star-gazers in his mind/ Winding his victory wreath from galaxies of suns.

possession he will pursue as ruthlessly and materialistically as Penthesilea pursues Achilles. This hypostasization, as innocent and entertained in good faith as the Amazon's, will presently be challenged by his conflict with the law of state.

4.

The state: in his seminal essay *Über die allmähliche Verfertigung der Gedanken beim Reden (On the Gradual Fashioning of Thought in the Process of Conversing)* Kleist vividly describes the predicament of students who are faced, without inner preparation, with the request to explicate abstract concepts such as: 'was ist der Staat? Oder: was ist das Eigentum?'[a] Had they had time to become attuned to such thoughts through preliminary discussion, they might easily have found the answer, Kleist writes. As it is, they baulk before a challenge flung at them with such abruptness, as a horse will baulk before a sudden ditch.

This is precisely the situation of the prince. In the direct communion vouchsafed to him in his dream-vision he has known the meaning of the concepts *Staat* and *Eigentum* perfectly well, in the highly personal and particularised idiom which is as characteristic of him as of his creator. '. . . nicht *wir* wissen, es ist allererst ein gewisser *Zustand* unser, welcher weiß'[b] ,Kleist remarks in the essay of which we have just spoken. The prince's visionary condition has known the state in the sacred embodiment of its sovereign, and has known the ineffable delicacy of possessing in love. Now, rudely stripped of all he thinks of as belonging to him and checked against the barrier of the law, his genius falters for a second time and he dissects what in its cold abstractness he has ceased to comprehend. As Adam and Eve boggle at their own naked selves, so he boggles at what his stunned and shocked senses report. Vision has become conscious confrontation and conscious confrontation has made a shambles of his mind.

Like the plant, the child and the horse, the prince is an incorrigibly personal creature. The elector whom he loves, in whose person he reveres the state, has withdrawn behind the impersonal and, to him, utterly impenetrable barrier of the law. But this law, adamant and cold, does not speak to him, any more than the remorseless law of natural mechanisms spoke to Job, or the unexceptional law of the Pharisees spoke to Christ. To him 'the *letter*[*] of the elector's will' − Kott-witz coins this phrase − in meaningless. He wants the *spirit* of it, in love, as he beheld it in his vision, that primal vision 'im Garten hinten', which is his 'paradise of innocence'. He cannot but shrink from the unimpeachable sentence decreed by a sovereign who, to him, has become a *deus absconditus*. What he needs is a human sentence, a word addressed to him in the direct idiom of personal speech. It is the absence of that communion which prompts his cry of dereliction. If he

---

[a] 'What is the state? or: what is property?'
[b] 'It is not *we* who know, to begin with, it is a certain *state* in us that knows'
[*] My italics

'fleht um Gnade' — 'begs for mercy' — as he does, it is for the gift of grace he asks as much as for mere pity. Only, here again, 'it is not *we* that know; to begin with, it is a certain *state* in us that knows'.

That personal communication comes to him in the shape of the letter from the elector who has, I think, intuitively grasped the nature of the prince's need and who expresses this understanding in the — for him — surprising formulation:

> Die höchste Achtung, wie dir wohl bekannt,
> Trag ich im Innersten für sein *Gefühl** . . .ᵃ   (IV, 1)

It is not a matter of the elector pardoning the prince, either because he is not even worthy of being judged by a law he repudiates[20], or from a freakish impulse of mercy[21]; it is not even a matter of trying to educate the prince by appealing to his 'better self'[22]. What is here at stake for the prince is the experience of personal grace versus the impersonal abstract law; of the spirit versus the letter; and what is happening between these two men is that the remote sovereign understands and meets the need of 'his son'.

To make the nature of the issue clearer, let me quote a passage from a letter written by Hugo von Hofmannsthal to Richard Strauss, in which the poet explains the music he requires for a ballet on the Joseph legend: 'Sein Gottsuchen, in wilden Sprüngen nach aufwärts', Hofmannsthal writes,

> ist nichts anderes als ein wildes Springen nach der hochhängenden Frucht der Inspiration. Auf Bergeshöhen, in klarer funkelnder Einsamkeit ist er gewohnt, sich durch ein Noch-höher! Noch-höher! in einer einsamen reinen Orgie emporzuwerfen und aus einer un-erreichbaren Klarheit über ihm . . . einen Fetzen des Himmels herabzureißen, in sich hereinzureißen — diesen höchsten, flüchtigsten Zustand nennt er Gott, und der so er-schaute Gott ist es, den er mit emporgereckten Armen sich zu Hilfe zwingt . . . Ein Höheres, funkelnd, war oben und wollte herabgezwungen sein: das ist Josephs Tanzᵇ[23].

This is the inner gesture of the prince as, disconsolate before the women he seeks out at night, he gives them this message to take to the sovereign:

> Um Gnade fleh ich, Gnade! Laß ihn frei!ᶜ   (III, 5)

This is precisely what the elector's letter does. It is a token of grace at the moment of ultimate dereliction, and it sets the prince free because it commutes the impersonal sentence into human speech, into a sentence that addresses itself to him in person. The gracious judge places himself into the hands of the petitioner. This

---

* my italics
ᵃ Most true respect, as you will doubtless know,/ My inmost self does for his feeling bear.
ᵇ 'His seeking for God, in impetuous upward leaps, is nothing other than an impetuous leaping towards the fruit of inspiration hanging high up here. On mountain peaks, in the clear sparkle of his solitude he is wont to thrust himself upward with a higher-yet! higher-yet! in a pure and lonely orgy and to tear off a piece of sky from out of an unreachable luminosity above him, to suck it into himself — this loftiest, most evanescent state he calls God, and it is God so envisaged whom his outstretched arms force to his aid . . . Some-thing higher, gleaming, was above wanting to be forced down: that is Joseph's dance.'
ᶜ I come to ask for mercy, mercy! Set him free!

direct communion with the Absolute gives the prince back to himself. And where his intelligence has baulked before the abstract concept of the state and the intricate machinery of justice, free grace can now set in to do its work. Refusing to haggle over the question of legal right or wrong, the prince is liberated to respond to his 'father' in autonomous faith, in total reliance on a grace that has revealed itself independently of what the empirical outcome of his 'pater, peccavi' may be[24].

'The beautiful flower of humanity' which the sovereign's unreachable remoteness had 'crushed' − Natalie's word − has opened and come into bloom. How far we have moved from Schiller's world, where autonomy means the autonomy of consciousness and moral will, the snapping of the bond of instinct, of the fellowship with the world of plant and animal and child, with God. The genius of this fiercely personal figure, the prince, is restored as his plant-like self feels the benignity of the soil − the *mütterliche Boden* − maternal soil − as he has it − in which he was nurtured. The hidden God has shown his face and has renewed the ancient covenant with him, at his ardent wooing: 'for the written code kills, but the spirit gives life'[25].

5.

But it still remains for the prince to come to terms with that other abstraction: *Eigentum*. Once the glove has intruded into his gossamer vision and dragged it down into the material sphere, he has arrogantly appropriated what no man may claim for his own. Immortality has become materialised into victory snatched impetuously from fortune's cornucopia, it has become hypostasized into honour and glory, Natalie, fulfilment here and now. And even as his disturbed instinct has snatched at these goods, immaturely and frantically, so he has shed them all again, in obedience to the most powerful instinct of all, the instinct for survival.

Now, in the face of the gunbarrels and his open grave, he truly meets the challenge of immortality, and, with it, that of the meaning of *Eigentum*. Now, close to death, he understands the paradox that we must have as though we had not, and the greater paradox that in faith he, a dead man, will be the ghostly lover of the woman who has kept him faith and that his disembodied spirit will lead his loyal armies 'striding dead ahead of the flags'. In one indivisible act he affirms his solidarities and surrenders his possessions: and in this act of joint commitment and self-emptying − *Paradosis*, handing over, is what St. John calls it − his true self is born. Now he may say:

> Nun sieh, jetzt schenkest du das Leben mir! (V, 8)
> Come, see, 'tis you now gave my life to me!

and call seraphic blessings upon the elector's head. Now he is free to take the fragrance of an unseen flower on his way to his execution, and to call the place to which he is going, 'home'.

> Ich will zu Hause sie in Wasser setzen.[a] (V, 10)

---

[a] I'll place them into water when I get back home.

In one of his last letters Kleist wrote of Henriette Vogel that she gave him the ineffable joy 'sich . . . so leicht aus einer ganz wunschlosen Lage, wie ein Veilchen aus einer Wiese, heraus heben zu lassen'[a][26]. This is the spirit in which the prince, fulfilled and emptied, lightly lifts his life, like the flower he cups in his hand, out of the maternal soil that has nurtured it, to hand it over in a wholly sacrificial self-offering[27].

And now that his vision of immortality in love, immeasurably mellowed and deepened, has come to fruition, he may say:

> Nun, o Unsterblichkeit, bist du ganz mein!
> Du strahlst mir, durch die Binde meiner Augen,
> Mit Glanz der tausendfachen Sonne zu!
> Es wachsen Flügel mir an beiden Schultern,
> Durch stille Ätherräume schwingt mein Geist;
> Und wie ein Schiff, vom Hauch des Winds entführt,
> Die muntre Hafenstadt versinken sieht,
> So geht mir dämmernd alles Leben unter:
> Jetzt unterscheid ich Farben noch und Formen,
> Und jetzt liegt Nebel alles unter mir.[b]   (V, 10)

He that was blind and stumbled as soon as he began to see, is blinded again. The multifarious world, which has distracted him, which he has loved and offered up again, is faded out. But through his unseeing eyes he perceives the sun of immortality with new eyes of the spirit[28]. 'Lord, I believe,' he says with the newly cured blind man of St. John. All his senses are alive – he feels the breeze and he will presently smell the fragrance of the pink[29] – yet they do not enmesh him in physicality. They are the new senses of the new ethereal body he feels growing.

For now he that fell three times has metamorphosed into a cherub, soaring and floating in the unencumbered flight of genius, related yet free, carrying the full freight of his humanity yet weightless. The journey around the world is accomplished.

It was not many months after penning these glorious lines that the poet, bidding farewell to the world, wrote: 'Wir, unsererseits, wollen nichts von den Freuden dieser Welt wissen und träumen lauter himmlische Fluren und Sonnen, in deren Schimmer wir, mit langen Flügeln an den Schultern, umherwandeln werden'[c][30].

---

a   'of allowing herself to be lifted from a condition totally devoid of desire, like a violet from a meadow'.

b   Now, O immortal life, you are all mine!/ You greet me through the cloth upon my eyes/ With radiance of suns a thousandfold!/ At my two shoulders pinions grow,/ My spirit soars through still, ethereal realms;/ And as a ship, by gentle winds seduced,/ Loses from sight the merry bustle of the port,/ So, too, for me, all life is dimmed by haze:/ As yet I may discern its hues and shapes,/ But now all lies beneath me, wrapped in mist.

c   'We, for our part, want none of the joys of this world and only dream of heavenly pastures and suns in whose radiance we shall walk, with long wings at our shoulders.'

VI Hazards of Abstraction

Er nennt's Vernunft und braucht's allein,
Nur tierischer als jedes Tier zu sein.

St. John

Except I shall see in his hands the print of the nails and put
my finger into the place of the nails and put my hand into his
side, I will not believe.

St. John

11   Exercises in Humanity:
'Die Heilige Cäcilie' and 'Die Hermannsschlacht'

1.

We have already made mention of that revealing, and seminal, essay *Über die all-mähliche Verfertigung der Gedanken beim Reden*[a] in which Kleist is treating of the importance of the dialogue-situation for the formulation of nascent thought. Even concepts rehearsed beforehand, to be reanimated in the mind and become meaningful again, require the fructifying tension engendered by the spoken exchange. To illustrate his point, Kleist gives the doleful example we have already referred to: of academic examinations in which, without any preparation or intro-ductory skirmishes, the candidate is peremptorily asked to define abstract concepts such as 'what is the state?' or: 'what is property?' or suchlike.

For us, this illustration has a continued and twofold interest. First, *Staat* and *Eigentum* are the very concepts which as we shall see define the gravitational field of *Die Hermannsschlacht* which will centrally occupy us in the present chapter, and its obverse, *Michael Kohlhaas,* of which we shall treat in the chapter following. In both works, these two concepts between them plot the intellectual area covered by their respective themes as, indeed, we have seen them do in *Prinz Friedrich von Homburg*. But over and above that, Kleist's example is revealing in that it illustrates not merely the problem of the hypothetical student, but his own.

The difficulties this poet experienced *vis-à-vis* abstract thought have often been critically noted[1]. They are only too apparent from the descriptions, in his early letters, of his attempting to come to grips with pure philosophy and pure mathematics which, obstinately and perversely, he chose to pursue towards the end and after the conclusion of his career as an army officer. And a *cri de cœur* like the following is entirely characteristic of the strain and exhaustion caused by such exercises in abstraction. 'Wenn man sich so lange mit ernsthaften abstrakten Dingen beschäftigt hat', the poet writes to his half-sister Ulrike,

> wobei der Geist zwar seine Nahrung findet, aber das arme Herz leer ausgehen muß, dann ist es eine wahre Freude, sich einmal ganz seine Ergießungen zu überlassen; ja es ist selbst nötig, daß man es zuweilen ins Leben zurückrufe. Bei dem ewigen Beweisen und Folgern verlernt das Herz fast zu fühlen . . . Daher ist es wohl gut, es zuweilen durch den Genuß sinnlicher Freuden von neuem zu beleben; und man müßte wenigstens täglich *ein* gutes Gedicht lesen, *ein* schönes Gemälde sehen, *ein* sanftes Lied hören − oder ein herzliches Wort mit einem Freunde reden, um auch den schönern, ich möchte sagen den mensch-licheren Teil unseres Wesens zu bilden[b][2] (November 12, 1799).

---

a *On the Gradual Fashioning of Thought in the Process of Conversing*
b 'When one has been so long preoccupied with profound abstract matters which feed the mind but leave the poor heart without sustenance, it is a real luxury to abandon oneself to one's

In our discussion of these letters and the Kant-crisis we have seen the strange mutations the concept of *Eigentum* underwent at Kleist's hands; the literal and almost physical complexion with which he would endow it even in indubitably abstract contexts[3]. It is of his tussle with the conceptual displacement of the words *Eigentum* — property — and, indeed, *Staat* — state — that we shall largely treat in this and the following chapter; and, arising from that, of the almost crippling hazards the exercise of abstraction *per se* presented for this strangely literal mind. By way of introduction, I propose to take a look at the story *Die Heilige Cäcilie oder die Gewalt der Musik*.

2.

This extraordinary story treats of the dismal fate of four young iconoclasts whose intentions to wreck the cathedral of Aachen on the day of Corpus Christi are foiled by the mysterious power of an ancient Italian mass performed for this occasion. Relapsing into the religious rites of their native Catholic faith, the four brothers live out the rest of their lives in a state of quiet madness, speechlessly worshipping a crucifix of birch wood twigs made by their own hands, and breaking their silence only at midnight at which hour, like leopards or wolves, they nightly howl the very *gloria in excelsis* which cut short their misguided zeal.

The story is set at the end of the sixteenth century, at a time when Protestantism, still a young and vital movement, was kept on tiptoe by the backlash of the Counter-Reformation. Without going into intricate theological detail, we might roughly describe the principal contention of the new creed as being two-pronged: coupling the repudiation of the doctrine of transubstantiation with a renewed emphasis on faith geared to the Word, as opposed to the belief in the redemptive power of actions or 'works'[4]. The doctrine of transubstantiation, or of the transformation of the essence and substance of the bread and wine offered at mass into the body and blood of the Saviour, became a focal point in the doctrinal war between the two churches. It was transplanted by the much more enigmatic Protestant doctrine that in the Sacrament the natural eucharistic substances of bread and wine are present, mysteriously and paradoxically, *together with* the body and the blood of the Saviour, in much the same way in which Christ himself was envisaged as being at once wholly God and wholly man, in the mystery of the hypostasis[5].

A crucial doctrinal article of the new Protestant creed, it would explain the iconoclasts' choice of Corpus Christi for the violent profession of their faith; for

---

effusions once in a while; indeed, it is a necessity now and then to resuscitate the heart in this manner. With all one's endless proving and concluding the heart quite forgets what it is like to feel . . . For which reason it is an altogether good thing occasionally to revive it by the enjoyment of sensuous pleasures; one should read at least *one* good poem a day, see *one* beautiful painting, hear *one* soothing air or exchange a heartfelt word with a true friend, in order to educate the more beautiful, I would venture to say, the more human part of our being.'

Corpus Christi celebrates the institution of the mass, that is to say, the total and substantial conversion of the eucharistic elements into the body and blood of Christ. In attacking this main-pillar of the Catholic doctrine they were, by the same token, declaring war on the worship of minor sacraments and sacramentals, such as making the sign of the cross, for claiming to possess more than an instructional function and efficacy. In this way, and to this purpose, the four young brothers would quite naturally decide to initiate their protest by wrecking cathedral windows depicting biblical stories and no doubt attracting the worshipful devotion of a Catholic congregation.

What was it, we may well ask, that drew the poet to compose his story around this abstruse doctrinal issue, and furthermore, by what token did the music performed on the occasion of this holy feast bring about the conversion of his protagonists, a change of heart resulting in their life-long madness? The first question is more readily answerable than the second. My reading of the poet's meaning here is along the lines I have consistently argued in the foregoing chapters of this book. The Catholic faith in general, and the doctrine of transubstantiation in particular, make considerably fewer demands on the layman's powers of intellectual differentiation than their Protestant counterparts. The material host and wine are not envisaged as mysteriously coexisting with a substance of a different spiritual and indeed supernatural order. They themselves *are* or *become* that substance in incarnate form. As a leading Catholic theologian of our time, Romano Guardini, has it: 'Wenn Er zu ihnen sagt: "Das ist mein Leib" und "das ist mein Blut", dann "ist" es eben das und "bedeutet" es nicht bloß'[a][6]. The windows painted with biblical stories do not *symbolically represent* the sacred events they depict. They *are* their sacral re-enactment, themselves sacred. The little wooden figure with the outstretched arms nailed to a cross bar is not a *replica,* itself profane and one of millions like it, of Christ crucified: it is the *embodiment* of that eschatalogical event and to handle it is not merely instructional: it is to be in palpable and immediate communion with it and to partake of its significance and redemptive efficacy. Once the unequivocally sacramental status and dignity of these holy things is challenged, their relation to what they signify becomes immeasurably more tenuous and complex to apprehend. As tenuous and complex, in fact, as is the relation of Frau Marthe's shattered object of contention to its legal, moral and religious significance and, indeed, to the question of Eve's integrity. The broken pitcher *signals* the event that preceded its dereliction, i. e. the breakage; yet this event, and the consequences it ushers in, turn out to be no more than ambiguous and utterly misleading pointers to its real and concealed *significance.* The jug is broken where Eve is intact.

The young iconoclasts who are significantly said to be incensed by *Schwärmerei,* in fact seek to eradicate that irresistible tendency towards hypostasization and

---

[a] 'When He says to them: "This is my body" and "this is my blood", then this "is" it; it does not merely "signify" it.'

reification which we have seen to be so marked a feature not only of Kleist's characters, but of their creator himself. In repudiating, on Corpus Christi, the event of the transubstantiation which is being celebrated as the core of that day's mass, they affirm the original sacrifice at and after the last supper, yet sharply differentiate it from its subsequent commemoration in which − according to current late sixteenth century Protestant doctrine − Christ's body and blood were spiritually but not physically present[7]. We have seen that for Kleist himself no less than for his fictional characters, to sustain such a distinction between a literal and material event on the one hand, and its invisible spiritual significance on the other, was an extremely taxing psychic feat. I suggest that the four young *Schwärmer*, in trying to grope their way toward such a differentiation, exceed their own mental and psychic capacities and break under the strain. Led by their friend, the *Prädikant*, who reels off 'the whole row of prayers he had scoffed at but a little while earlier', they presently relapse into those spiritually less taxing forms of worship from which they have endeavoured to emancipate themselves. '. . . in ihre Wohnungen angekommen, binden sie sich ein Kreuz, sinnreich und zierlich von Birkenreisern zusammen, und setzen es, einem kleinen Hügel von Wachs einge-drückt, zwischen zwei Lichtern . . . auf dem großen Tisch in des Zimmers Mitte nieder . . . und schicken sich still, mit gefalteten Händen, zur Anbetung an'[a]. The narrator's precision in describing the physical properties of the object the brothers prepare for their worship is surely significant. They adore the very wood and wax in which the mystery of the crucifixion now resides; and all their mental efforts to abstract from graven images and to cleave to the unsubstantial, unhypostasized significance behind the material signs dismally collapse.

And the Word which is the mainstay of the revolutionary creed? Silently they sit, day in day out and through most of the night. Only once in every twenty-four hours, on the stroke of midnight, do they break their ghostly silence, to sing, 'schauderhaften und empörenden Gebrülls' − 'blaring horribly and outrageously', the *gloria in excelsis* which hit them like lightning in the hour of their attempted intellectual emancipation. 'So mögen sich Leoparden und Wölfe anhören lassen, wenn sie zur eisigen Winterzeit, das Firmament anbrüllen: die Pfeiler des Hauses . . . erschütterten, und die Fenster, von ihrer Lungen sichtbarem Atem getroffen, drohten klirrend, als ob man Hände voll schweren Sandes gegen ihre Flächen würfe, zusammen zu brechen'[b].

---

a '. . . on their return to their lodgings, they ingeniously and nimbly tie together a cross of
   birch twigs, and, having pressed it into a small mound of wax, place it between two
   candles on the large table in the middle of the room . . . and, with their hands folded together, quietly make ready to adore it.'
b 'Wolves and leopards may sound like that when they howl at the firmament in the icy
   winter: the pillars of the house . . . shook, and the windows, hit by the visible breath
   from their lungs, clattered, threatening to break, as though handfuls of heavy sand were
   being hurled against their panes.'

In their terrible regression the brothers do not only betray the incarnate Word; their barbaric din, their very breath, become visible, and the rattling window panes reverberating as from a physical assault involuntarily mock language itself, that most highly articulated, abstractive and quintessentially human of all human gifts. Nameless, they have relapsed into the savagery of animals; yet, true Kleistean figures that they are, they still continue to howl *de profundis* to the greater glory of God; and their mother, soon after seeing them, returns, broken, 'into the lap of the Catholic church . . .'.

As in his drama *Penthesilea* and so often elsewhere, Kleist has in this short and difficult story treated of the eclipse meted out to human minds in the face of the challenge to differentiate and to abstract; he has remorselessly traced their regression into a prehuman state where mime takes the place of words. We shall have more to say about this degenerative process in another chapter[8].

We have yet to broach the question suggested by the title of the story: in what sense was it, as the iconoclasts' mother has it, 'die Gewalt der Töne . . ., die, an jenem schauerlichen Tage, das Gemüt ihrer armen Söhne zerstört und verwirrt habe'[a]? And what is the connection between this event and the director of the performance who, so the Mother Superior of the convent assures the unfortunate woman on the highest authority, could have been none other than St. Cecilia herself?

To answer these questions we might take our cue from the visual impression which the iconoclasts' mother − who later on will so sensitively respond to the very sight of the musical score − receives of the cathedral in which, years before, her sons were ruined 'as though by invisible lightning'. It is an awe inspiring and thunderous vision even now. Struck first by 'die prächtig funkelnde Rose im Hintergrund der Kirche'[b], the mother and her companion see

Viele hundert Arbeiter, welche fröhliche Lieder sangen, . . . auf schlanken, vielfach verschlungenen Gerüsten beschäftigt, die Türme noch um ein gutes Dritteil zu erhöhen, und die Dächer und Zinnen derselben, welche bis jetzt nur mit Schiefer bedeckt gewesen waren, mit starkem, hellen, im Strahl der Sonne glänzigen Kupfer zu belegen. Dabei stand ein Gewitter, dunkelschwarz, mit vergoldeten Rändern, im Hintergrunde des Baus; dasselbe hatte schon über die Gegend von Aachen ausgedonnert, und nachdem es noch einige kraftlose Blitze, gegen die Richtung, wo der Dom stand, geschleudert hatte, sank es, zu Dünsten aufgelöst, mißvergnügt murmelnd in Osten herab'[c].

---

a 'the power of music . . . which had, on that awful day, destroyed and confounded her poor sons' minds'

b 'the rose window magnificently gleaming at the back of the church',

c 'Many hundreds of workmen, merrily singing, . . . busied on slender and intricate scaffoldings to raise the spires by a good third, and to cover their roofs and turrets which up to now had only been encased in slate, with strong bright copper which gleamed in the rays of the sun. While this was going on, storm-clouds of an inky black hue, gilded at their rims, glowered behind the building; the tempest had spent its force over the region of Aachen, and having hurled some last feeble bolts in the direction of the cathedral, was vanishing across the horizon in an easterly direction, angrily grumbling and dissolving into a haze.'

Like the first maiden's magnificent description of the gleaming Achilles against a thunder-crested hill, indeed like that of the cathedral in *Das Erdbeben in Chili* where the rose window is said to glow 'like the evening sun itself which illuminated it', this scene here is one heavily pregnant with the Numinous. The cathedral is not an object; it is like a large looming animal, magically lit up by the sun breaking through an angry sky. Thunder, the turrets soaring with their freight of believers, *glänzig* – a word in Kleist's idiosyncratic vocabulary reserved to designate a higher, angelic order – all this combines to mark out this spectacle as the visible scene of a numinous visitation[9]. And that visitation, re-enacted by the heavens themselves at the mother's approach now, strikes home in the shape of St. Cecilia, by a kind of transubstantiation replacing the earthbound and dying Sister Antonia, and in the shape of the musical mass she conducts.

We know that Kleist was intensely musical, indeed that he considered music and, in particular, the figured bass as the root or 'algebraic formula' of all arts and especially of poetry[10]. In his letters he reports on two occasions that he has the ability to hear, in his inner ear, whole concerts, 'die Melodie und alle begleitenden Akkorde, von der zärtlichen Flöte bis zum rauschenden Kontra-Violon. Das klang mir wie eine Kirchenmusik,' he writes, 'und ich glaube, daß alles, was uns die Dichter von der Sphärenmusik erzählen, nichts Reizenderes gewesen ist, als diese seltsame Träumerei'[a][11]. Such concerts, Kleist goes on to explain in the earlier of the two letters, he can reproduce and prolong at will: 'aber so bald ein *Gedanke* daran sich regt, gleich ist alles fort, wie weggezaubert durch das magische: disparois! Melodie, Harmonie, Klang, kurz die ganze Sphärenmusik'[b].

It is evident that for Kleist music, like the unerring poise of the puppets, the bear, and the Grecian youth, is a cypher for that preconscious, unreflecting state of grace, that 'paradise of innocence' which is ravaged by the advent of destructive self-consciousness. Here is a state in which the Kleistean character, like his somnambulist Käthchen, is tuned in to the Numinous and walks in its direct illumination. It is their breach of this primordial harmony, through the disruptive force of a reflective consciousness that severs signs from their significances, the material from the divine, which is visited home on the iconoclast brothers. As with invisible lightning, the Numinous strikes them down in the music, the tenuous edifice of their cleft minds is brought low, and they turn into grotesque prehuman caricatures of the primordial harmony they have violated. The mother *sees* these violated harmonies in the 'unbekannten zauberischen Zeichen, womit sich ein

---

[a] 'the melody and all accompanying chords, from the tender flute to the thunderous bass viols. It sounded like some church music,' . . . 'and I believe that what the poets tell us regarding the music of the spheres, can have been no more ravishing than this strange reverie.'

[b] 'but as soon as the veriest soupçon of a *thought* intervenes, all is gone, conjured away, as it were, by the magic: disparois! Melody, harmony, sound, in short, the whole music of the spheres.'

fürchterlicher Geist geheimnisvoll den Kreis abzustecken schien'[a] – and here we must remember that the seventeenth century was rife with pansophic speculations as to the secret concord of musical and cosmic harmonies – and bows to the disastrous dispensation of Providence under the impact of what she thus directly discerns.

We may add an ironic and revealing rider: Kleist offered this homiletic tale showing the ravages of consciousness being visited upon its aspirants as a baptismal gift for Adam Müller's baby daughter Cäcilie. '. . . warum ist es so schwer?' the four brothers seem to whisper to the sleeping child, and: 'Jede erste Bewegung, alles Unwillkürliche, ist schön; und schief und verschroben alles, sobald es sich selbst begreift. O der Verstand! der unglückselige Verstand!'[b][12]

3.

Die Hermannschlacht has been so persistently read as a violent and unhinged poetic comment on the immediate political German scene that my readers may well be incredulous to find it being treated under a section entitled 'Hazards of Abstraction' and in a context such as has been progressively established by the reading offered in the preceding pages. Needless to say, this play represents a desperate call for national unity in the contemporaneous political scene. Yet, at the risk of being charged with a wanting historical consciousness, I venture to assert that on its deeper levels it is concerned with the inevitability of large abstractions degenerating into bestiality in the process of realisation: with the all but inhuman tension engendered by the formulation of such an abstract concept as *Germania*, or Hitler's thousand year *Reich*, or Palestine, or Ireland, even in the phase of its inception. It is the battle cry of one whose mind would go blank at the analytical explication of *Eigentum* – property, and *Staat* – state, to whom the very framing of the concept 'nationhood' represented a strain so severe as to make its retention a feat purchased at great spiritual, intellectual and emotional price, to be defended with the last available ounce of blood.

Not unlike the protagonist of *Wallenstein* – a drama Kleist treasured from early on and to which he made significant allusion in the late phase of his poetic career[13] – Hermann der Cherusker is conceived as a superb political role player. But whereas Wallenstein finds it all but impossible to make the transition from *Spiel* to *Ernst* – from play to concerted action – in Hermann's case the lineaments of his true concern are discernible even while he pretends to make common cause with the Romans. Obsessively and bewilderingly, he insists that it is his aim to lose everything to the enemy. His followers interpret these enigmatic professions

---

[a] 'in the unfamiliar magic signs, with which some terrible spirit mysteriously seemed to demarcate its circle'

[b] 'why is it so hard? Every initial movement, everything spontaneous, is beautiful; and all becomes askew and tortuous as soon as it becomes conscious of itself. Alas and alack for reflection! wretched reflection!'

as being part of the mask he will cast off when he discloses his true intention to
fight Varus. But this is not so. 'Disengaging himself' and 'breaking off', he cuts
short their enthusiastic acclaim and once again stipulates his strange vision in more
alienating terms even than before. To lose what he holds and possesses is and
remains his avowed goal. And it is to his strange professions that he will do so,
both before his disclosure that he will fight and after it, that we must turn.

The first of his baffling declarations of policy comes at a point when he is still
pretending to make common cause with the Romans, against Marbod:

> So weit im Kreise mir der Welt
> Das Heer der munteren Gedanken reichet
> Erstreb ich und bezweck ich nichts,
> Als jenem Römerkaiser zu erliegen.
> Das aber möcht ich gern mit Ruhm, ihr Brüder,
> Wies einem deutschen Fürsten ziemt:
> Und *daß* ich das vermög, im ganzen vollen Maße,
> Wie sich's die freie Seele glorreich denkt –
> Will ich allein stehn, und mit euch mich –
> – Die manch ein andrer Wunsch zur Seite lockend zieht, –
> In dieser wichtgen Sache nicht verbinden.[a]   (I, 3)

The meaning of these words is far from obvious; yet they ring true. They evince
that sovereign serenity which distinguishes Hermann's utterances – he even plays
with the sombre truth, 'wie ein Abderit'; for

> – Warum soll sich, von seiner Not,
> Der Mensch, auf muntre Art, nicht unterhalten? –[b]   (III, 4)

– except *vis-à-vis* the Romans towards whom he adopts the *bonhomie* of a
cheerful savage. Especially striking are the references to his free soul and to the
'army of lively thoughts' he harbours. This last named military metaphor is far
from being coincidental. Hermann broods upon the comparison of the haphazard
German war bands with the splendid organisation of the Roman army; of his own
chiefs,

> – an eines Haufens Spitze,
> Zusammen aus den Waldungen gelaufen,
> Mit der Kohorte, der gegliederten,
> Die, wo sie geht und steht, des Geistes sich erfreut . . .[c]   (I, 3)

---

[a] So far as in the orbit of the world/ The army of my lively thoughts may roam,/ My goal
and purpose are exclusively/ To lose out to that Roman emperor./ But this I would fain
do with honour, brothers,/ As is befitting to a German prince:/ And *to accomplish* that,
as fully, wholly,/ As my free soul does gloriously demand –/ I must stand by myself, and
in this weighty matter/ Seek no alliance friends, with you,/ – Whom many a private
wish lures off the goal –.

[b] Why should a man not in a cheerful way/ Speak of his dire plight? –

[c] Leading their motley crowds,/ Haphazardly assembled from the woods,/ With the cohort,
the nimbly organised/ Which is instinct with mind where'er it move . . .

Could he be modelling his own intellect on this glory of the Roman mind, articulated, mobile, in every particle infused with the spirit which informs the whole? Could he disdain the fellowship of companions incapable

> Merrily to accompany me on my flight   (IV, 3)

because the bearskinned bands they lead betoken a mentality that is clumsy, undifferentiated and devoid of all inner freedom of movement? This is certainly the implication of his rejoinder to Selgar's startling comment that nobody could say that

> Arminius has set his sights inordinately high!   (I, 3)

to which he cuttingly replies

> So! —
> Ihr würdet beide euren Witz vergebens
> Zusammenlegen, dieses Ziel,
> Das vor der Stirn euch dünket, zu erreichen.[a]   (I, 3)

What subtle irony, juxtaposing the army of agile thoughts at his command with this dim-witted effort of two brains put together — one thinks of monkeys contriving sticks long enough to reach bananas on a tree, or indeed of Penthesilea wanting to pile Ida upon Ossa to get at the sun — to reach an aim into which they all but bash with their thick German skulls!

Against these blockheads he insistently pleads that the call of the hour is to lose everything he might call his[14]. He would be happy, he concedes, to fight alongside such stouthearted men as they are

> If I were out for any earthly *gain* . . .   (I, 3)

As matters stand, however, a pact is out of the question,

> . . . because to *forfeit* everything
> Is my sole aim —.   (I, 3)

He warns the optimistic Thuiskomar that

> Already the entire Germany is lost . . .,   (I, 3)

for good measure brutally recounting the four thrones that have already tumbled. Asked whether he really intends to surrender Germany without making a stand for his country, he cryptically replies:

> Behüte Wodan mich! Ergeben! Seid ihr toll?
> Mein Alles, Haus und Hof, die gänzliche
> Gesamtheit des, was mein sonst war,
> Als ein verlornes Gut in meiner Hand noch ist,
> Das, Freunde, setz ich dran, im Tod nur,
> Wie König Porus, glorreich es zu lassen![b]   (I, 3)

---

a   Ah now! You two would vainly put together/ Your wits to jointly reach up to this goal which you/ Think positively knocks at your thick skulls.

b   Wotan forbid! Surrender! Are you mad?/ My all, my house and home, the whole/ Of what I used to own in its entirety,/ Now but a forfeit idling in my hands,/ I stake not to let go of it again,/ Save gloriously, in death, as did King Porus once!

Quizzed as to whether he sees no hope of prevailing over the Romans in open
battle, he replies — and we shall come back to these words —

> No! step by step I want to lose the land
> Of our illustrious ancestors — . . .   (I, 3)

All this is before he has declared his true intent. He tops it after its disclosure,
following Wolf's impulsive acclaim. 'Disengaging himself', he abruptly stipulates
his conditions for accepting the leadership of the German lords. These are his
seemingly preposterous terms:

> Kurz, wollt ihr, wie ich schon einmal euch sagte,
> Zusammenraffen Weib und Kind,
> Und auf der Weser rechtes Ufer bringen,
> Geschirre, goldn' und silberne, die ihr
> Besitzet, schmelzen, Perlen und Juwelen
> Verkaufen oder sie verpfänden,
> Verheeren eure Fluren, eure Herden
> Erschlagen, eure Plätze niederbrennen,
> So bin ich euer Mann —:[a]   (I, 3)

The heated exchanges that follow are so revealing and so Kleistean that I shall
quote them here.

> Wolf: Wie? Was?
> Hermann: Wo nicht —?
> Thuiskomar: Die eigenen Fluren sollen wir verheeren —?
> Dagobert: Die Herden töten —?
> Selgar: Unsre Plätze niederbrennen —?
> Hermann: Nicht? nicht? Ihr wollt es nicht?
> Thuiskomar: Das eben, Rasender, das ist es ja,
>   Was wir in diesem Krieg verteidigen wollen!
> Hermann *abbrechend*:
>   Nun denn, ich glaubte, eure Freiheit wärs.
>   *Er steht auf.*[b]

All along, Hermann has been in earnest. He is resolved to forfeit everything,
every material possession and every emotional bond, to gain — freedom. But, we

---

a   In short, if you will do as I have said before,/ Snatch up your children and your wives/
    And dump them on the right bank of the Weser,/ Smelt dishes you possess of gold or
    silver,/ Barter or pawn your pearls or jewellery,/ Lay waste your fields, clobber your
    cattle,/ Set fire to your homesteads,/ Why, I am your man —

b   Wolf: How? What?
    Hermann: Unless —
    Thuiskomar: We lay waste our fields?
    Dagobert: Clobber our cattle —?
    Selgar: Set fire to our homesteads —?
    Hermann: No? no? Your answer's no?
    Thuiskomar: 'Tis that, you madman, 'tis those very things,/ We'd launch this
                   war in order to defend!
    Hermann (*breaking off*): Ah well, I thought 'twas freedom you were after.
                                                    (*Rises*).

must ask, what sort of freedom is it that he seeks, and to gain it, why must he lose all that the others would defend? Is it the freedom of his country from the Roman yoke? That this is his ultimate goal there can be no doubting. But in the first instance something different is at stake. The freedom for which he here proposes to strip himself to the marrow is a preliminary, mental freedom: it is the freedom that will enable him to formulate, and hold, his vision of *Germania*. It is the prohibitive remoteness of this vision that he trains his eye to hold unwavering, in the face of all distractions: after reiterating his intention to be routed 'according to his plan', he reflects:

> — Welch ein wahnsinniger Tor
> Müßt ich doch sein, wollt ich mir und der Heeresschar,
> Die ich ins Feld des Todes führ, erlauben,
> Das Aug, von dieser finstern Wahrheit ab,
> Buntfarbgen Siegesbildern zuzuwenden,
> Und gleichwohl dann gezwungen sein,
> In dem gefährlichen Momente der Entscheidung,
> Die ungeheure Wahrheit anzuschauen?[a]   (I, 3)

To his chieftains in their forest dwellings and their animal skins, the plight of a non-existent Fatherland is a nebulous notion, too precarious and too vast to fit into their skulls. Theirs are simple minds

> Whom many a private wish lures off the goal.   (I, 3)

Indeed, the opening exchanges of the play have provided a lively illustration of the fact that their vision does not extend beyond the ken of their immediate sphere of interest. Dagobert and Selgar are seen bickering about a narrow strip of land on the banks of the river Lippe. Both claim their right to it; and each professes his firm intention to stay out of a common war against the Romans unless the issue be settled in his favour. As Selgar has it:

> Eh ich, Unedelmütgem, dir
> Den Strich am Lippgestade überlasse,
> Eh will an Augusts Heere ich
> Mein ganzes Reich, mit Haus und Hof verlieren![b]   (I, 2)

But it is not only the dim-witted ones whose mental horizons are thus narrowly bounded. There is Aristan too, an intelligent man and the real villain of the play, who obdurately and cynically clings to his own partisan interest. Asked whether he did not read Hermann's proclamation to all the German tribes on the day of the decisive battle, he retorts — and the stage-direction reads *keck* — impudently —

---

a What a raving fool I'd be,/ Were I to let myself and those I lead/ Divert our gaze from this appalling truth/ And feast on visions, gay, of victory,/ To be constrained, when all is said and done,/ At the most dire moment of decision,/ To face the awesome truth?

b I'd sooner forfeit my entire realm,/ With house and home, to that Augustus' armies,/ Rather than cede to you, mean-minded cad,/ The strip of land on river Lippe's banks!

> Ich las, mich dünkt, ein Blatt von deiner Hand,
> Das für Germanien in den Kampf mich rief!
> Jedoch was galt Germanien mir?[a]   (V, 24)

It is not so much Aristan's insolence that incenses Hermann, but rather the cynical refusal of a good mind to liberate himself from the blinkers of his self-sufficiency and to give a larger vision, as yet unborn, his loyal and intelligent allegiance. Hermann's reply to Aristan is plain enough:

> Ich weiß, Aristan. Diese Denkart kenn ich.
> Du bist imstand und treibst mich in die Enge,
> Fragst, wo und wann Germanien gewesen?
> Ob in dem Mond? Und zu der Riesen Zeiten?
> Und was der Witz sonst an die Hand dir gibt; . . .[b]   (V, 24)

We may begin to suspect that what is at stake between the Cheruscan and his fellow-chieftains is nothing other than the problem we have at length discussed in a previous chapter, the one entitled 'Faulty Medium'. As in the works treated there, the issue on which our present drama opens and conludes is that of the percipient's subjectivity occluding and vitiating his vision of the truth. As Penthesilea discerns her relation to Achilles through glasses, darkly, through the categories of aggression which are all she has at her disposal; as Gustav perceives Toni through the tinted spectacles of his colour-prejudice: so Dagobert and Selgar and Aristan and the other chieftains glimpse the vision of a united *Germania* dimly or not at all, enveloped as they are in the corona of their own particular *milieux*. He who would put that vision on the map must strip himself of all his native conditioning, of all the particular interests and personal sentiments in which it is embedded: and the one figure able to perform such a feat of abstraction is Hermann.

To introduce our analysis of Hermann's quest, I shall quote a relevant passage from a contemporary philosopher. In her *Philosophy in a New Key*, Susanne K. Langer makes the following observations:

> *That which all adequate conceptions of an object must have in common, is the concept of the object* . . . A concept is all that a symbol really conveys. But just as quickly as the concept is symbolized to us, our own imagination dresses it up in a private, personal *conception*, which we can distinguish from the communicable public concept only by a process of abstraction. Whenever we deal with a concept we must have some particular presentation of it, *through* which we grasp it. What we actually have 'in mind' is always *universalium in re*. When we express this *universalium* we use another symbol to exhibit it, and still another *res* will embody it for the mind that sees through our symbol and apprehends the concept in its own way[15].

---

a I read, I think, a leaflet from your hand,/ Requesting me to battle for Germania./ But then, what was Germania to me?

b I know, Aristan. I know this way of thinking./ You are quite capable of trapping me,/ Of asking where Germania was and when?/ A lunar land? or in the giants' age?/ Or else whate'er your fancy might cast up; . . .

This passage describes perfectly the difficulties Hermann is encountering with his fellow-chieftains. They all harbour some nebulous concept of *Germania*. But each of them 'dresses it up' in a conception that is private and personal to him: Dagobert in the conception of his tribal kingdom, Selgar in that of his own, and so on. For both, the public concept *Germania* has been swallowed up in the private conception of the 'Strich . . . an dem Gestad der Lippe' − 'the strip of land on River Lippe's banks'; but even that is different in the different contexts of their thinking, representing for the one a strip, say, south of his native land, whereas it forms the northern border of the other's kingdom. Each may just 'see through' the other's embodied conception, his *res,* and understand that they mean the same: but even on that common bit of mental ground they quarrel. Is either likely to glimpse, let alone to retain, the public concept behind these impenetrably individual conceptions, the abstract concept conveyed by the as yet unborn symbol *Germania*?

Susanne Langer continues her argument as follows:

> The power of understanding symbols, i. e. of regarding everything about a sense-datum as irrelevant except a certain *form* that it embodies, is the most characteristic mental trait of mankind. It issues in an unconscious, spontaneous process of *abstraction,* which goes on all the time in the human mind: a process of recognizing the concept in any con-figuration given to experience, and forming a conception accordingly. That is the real sense of Aristotle's definition of man as "the rational animal". *Abstractive Seeing* is the foundation of our rationality . . . It is the function which no other animal shares. Beasts do not read symbols . . .[16]

I suggest that in the figure of Hermann, a figure placed at the dawn of German history, Kleist has portrayed the painful birth of that 'most characteristic mental trait of mankind', the power to envisage and create a symbol; and that in Hermann's strange quest to lose what is his the poet has traced that process of abstraction which, unconscious and spontaneous in others, to this primordial mind represents a strenuously conscious and exhaustingly unspontaneous mental labour.

To liberate the others' − and his own − unequivocal, universal and commu-nicable concept of *Germania* from the blurred, private and unshareable con-ceptions beneath which it is buried: this is the freedom Hermann craves. To attain this mental freedom and help his fellow-Germans attain it, he ruthlessly strips it of all the accidentals that clutter it up and distort it. Asking them to 'lose' everything they cleave to − wives and children, silver and gold, fields and flocks − means asking them to divest their conception of everything that is irrelevant and personal, and to penetrate through the total chance-configuration offered to their experience to the form it embodies: *Germania*. It means dismembering their individual conceptions, cutting across the haphazard mental conglomerates in which these are buried, as it were, excising them from their concrete embodiment, uprooting them from all 'grown' and organic contexts, and then building them up again in such a manner that the conception of each shall transparently exhibit the single and fully public concept: *Germania*.

Such a universal concept is not only stringent; it is also invariably over-simplified. To say this is no more than to concede its abstract character. It will never be congruent and coextensive with any given concrete situation, with the bewildering and contradictory variety of the data that go into its making. In everyone's experience, there will always be the good Roman who disproves the general validity of the concept of Romans as universally bad, and, conversely, the bad German who explodes the claim held out on behalf of the concept of *Germania* as the one and only to be entertained. There is the Roman centurion,

> Der junge Held, der, mit Gefahr des Lebens,
> Das Kind, auf seiner Mutter Ruf,
> Dem Tod der Flammen mutig jüngst entrissen . . .,[a]   (IV, 9)

to be set against the other Roman's deed who bashed a baby's skull against its mother's head. There are the narrow-minded and cowardly German princes − the Gueltans and the Fusts − to be set against such figures as Hermann and Thuiskomar and Wolf. And of course, there is Ventidius. But once this complexity of data is tolerated, no clean-cut concept will ever be formed. Impression cancels out impression. This is the relevant context in which we must view Hermann's most repellent trait: his demagogic suppression of one set of facts which might be favourable to the Romans, his fabrication and inflation of others designed to erode their prestige, as well as his analogous umbrella action shielding and forgiving all Germans, the traitors even who will be the best

> As soon as vengeance on the Romans is the cry! −   (V, 14)[17]

Hermann is not Kleist, who conscientiously pointed up all these pros and cons and granted Septimus and Varus an honourable enough exit[18]: but equally the poet shows his protagonist Hermann labouring in a painful birth-process of abstraction from all that is 'irrelevant' and accidental to evolve *universalium in re*, a concept of *Germania* that shall be recognisable, universal and viable. This means omission of detail and omission of detail in turn means oversimplification and distortion. 'Verwirre das Gefühl mir nicht!' − 'Do not confuse my instinct!' − (V, 14), Hermann characteristically exclaims when a complex and dilute interpretation of justice is offered to him such as might erode his clear-cut concept of *Germania*. In a political context the exercise of abstraction, that quintessentially human activity, may easily and tragically swing over into the savagery of terrorism.

We have come upon an eminently Kleistean, and modern, paradox: the paradox whereby 'the most characteristically mental trait of mankind', the power to conceive symbols and to see abstractively which is 'the foundation of our rationality', coalesces with the maximal bestiality to be found in literature on the far side of our own century's documentation of concentration camps. It is no good slurring over that truth; but to accord it a simplistic explanation in terms of Kleist's

---

a   The youthful hero who, at peril of his life,/ Dared snatch a child from certain death in
    flames,/ A day or two ago, heeding its mother's cries . . .

hysterical chauvinism will not do either. It is the immense difficulty experienced by Kleist's characters in rising to 'abstractive seeing' at all which accounts for the ugliness of Hermann's demagogism and the enormity of Thusnelda's revenge on Ventidius, not to speak of the repellent use to which Hermann puts the corpse of the raped virgin Halli, of which I shall treat presently.

Let us for a moment consider the subplot which is centred on Thusnelda and the hapless Roman youth. At first sight it may look as though Ventidius were another Amphitryon or Homburg, and Thusnelda another Penthesilea. Both comparisons are erroneous. Ventidius, it is true, *seems* to grasp at Thusnelda's lock of hair as Homburg grasps at Natalie's glove:

> Die einzge Locke . . .
> Die, in dem Hain, beim Schein des Monds,
> An meine Lippe heiß gedrückt,
> Mir deines Daseins Traum ergänzen soll![a]   (II, 5)

But whereas to the naïve prince the glove is a *sign* of fortune, pregnant with numinosity, the lock, to the realistic Roman, is a *sample* to gratify his empress' vanity, callously snatched with a *Werkzeug* − an implement. He is well able to differentiate between material signs and their − existent or non-existent − spiritual significances, but he chooses to pretend to having a primitive frame of mind that has not yet tumbled to such a distinction; and therein lies his cynicism. And Thusnelda?

> − Er hat zur Bärin mich gemacht!
> Arminius' will ich wieder würdig werden![b]   (V, 15)

These words − her last before Ventidius meets the she-bear in her stead − are not the words of one who in all unconscious innocence mistakes *Bisse* for *Küsse*: they are the words of one whose very humanity has been called into question, and who consciously avenges her nascent concept of outraged humanity − a concept grown on bitter soil − by exhibiting it in an aptly chosen *symbol*: the symbol of the beast which she chooses to *represent* her[19]. The she-bear has no idea of the highly abstractive process of using lock and key −

> Come now! she will not press the handle?
> − Here's the key! −:   (V, 17)

Thusnelda has; and therein lies the difference[20].

If Thusnelda has created a symbol of humanity outraged − for, however bestial, a fully-fledged symbol it is − Hermann must devise a symbol that will carry and exhibit the ruling concept of his life: defiled *Germania*. This must be simple enough to be unequivocal, and abstract enough to be universally understood. And again only Kleist could have dreamed up a symbol at once as devastating in its

---

[a] The one and only lock/ Which, pressed to feverish lips/ In yonder moonlit grove,/ Must supplement my dream of your existence!

[b] Into a she-bear he has turned my soul!/ I would be worthy of Arminius again!

concreteness and as abstract in its anonymity as is Hermann's propaganda weapon: but a symbol it is, the first one, we may say, in the second chapter of the world's history, to speak in the terms of the essay *Über das Marionettentheater*.

A young Cheruscan girl has been conveniently raped by Roman soldiers. *She*, over whose veiled figure 'the people' lament

> O des elenden, schmachbedeckten Wesens!
> Der fußzertretnen, kotgewälzten,
> An Brust und Haupt, zertrümmerten Gestalt . . .[a]   (IV, 5)

she is the inner form of the total confused configuration of a splintered and conquered land; *she* is the symbol that offers itself to Hermann for the purpose of exhibiting the concept of defiled and downtrodden *Germania* in its quintessential *Gestalt*[21]. Killed by her father, the maiden's ravaged corpse is to be cut into as many pieces as there are German tribes, and bodily sent to them in a final appeal to rebel.

> Wir zählen funfzehn Stämme der Germaner;
> In funfzehn Stücke, mit des Schwertes Schärfe,
> Teil ihren Leib, und schick mit funfzehn Boten,
> Ich will dir funfzehn Pferde dazu geben,
> Den funfzehn Stämmen ihn Germaniens zu.
> Der wird in Deutschland, dir zur Rache,
> Bis auf die toten Elemente werben:
> Der Sturmwind wird, die Waldungen durchsausend,
> Empörung! rufen, und die See,
> Des Landes Ribben schlagend, Freiheit! brüllen.[b]   (IV, 6)

Thus Hermann to Teuthold, Halli's father. And:

> Rebellion! Vengeance! Freedom!   (IV, 6)

the people of Germany respond. And no wonder. The obsessively ritualistic character of the initiation ceremony would be hard to miss: a religious symbol has been fashioned from the anonymity of human carrion, public, universally understandable, yet utterly concrete. The German mind has been mobilised. Not an element but will fail to respond, that is not instinct with the vision of the whole. Can we wonder that in his next words Hermann will enquire of Septimus whether the German forces have been, 'the Roman way',

> Divided into smaller maniples?   (IV, 7)

---

[a] O for the wretched shape bedecked with shame!/ Trampled with feet and rolled in stinking mire,/ A shattered figure, head as well as chest . . .

[b] Of fifteen tribes Germania consists;/ Go, cut her body into fifteen parts/ With the keen sword, and fifteen messengers,/ I shall assign you fifteen horses for the job,/ Speed it to our fifteen German tribes./ That corpse shall wreak your vengeance through Germania,/ Recruiting allies from the inert dust;/ The gale shall, roaring through the forests, cry/ Rebellion! and the sea, drumming against/ The ribcage of the land, shall bellow Freedom!

And now Hermann has done all that was in his power. Halli's dismembered body will be despatched: his own young sons, together with his proposals, his homage and a dagger, have been sent as an earnest of his integrity, to be killed if Marbod finds fault with his letter − another symbolic action. He has crossed the Rubicon and cut his losses in advance. At this point Kleist has inserted a monologue − Hermann's sole monologue in the play − and this is so telling that I shall quote it in full:

> Nun wär ich fertig, wie ein Reisender.
> Cheruska, wie es steht und liegt,
> Kommt mir, wie eingepackt in eine Kiste, vor:
> Um einen Wechsel könnt ich es verkaufen.
> Denn käms heraus, daß ich auch nur
> Davon geträumt, Germanien zu befrein:
> Roms Feldherr steckte gleich mir alle Plätze an,
> Erschlüge, was die Waffen trägt,
> Und führte Weib und Kind gefesselt übern Rhein. −
> August straft den Versuch, so wie die Tat![a]   (IV, 8)

We cannot miss the similarity of this speech to that of Amphitryon as he envisages his dismembered sense organs stored away 'in Schachteln'. Yet we are at the extreme opposite of the Kleistean spectrum of experience. This is the point where the two ends of the world, the puppet and the god, interlace, *ring-förmig* − in the manner of a ring; this is the borderland where the objective and the subjective modalities coalesce. Amphitryon, distrusting the noumenal visitation and unaware of his own involvement in it, is undilute phenomenality. Hermann, having stripped himself of all the phenomenal context in which his life was warmly embedded, is undilute noumenality. In him, conception and concept are as one. He sees 'die ungeheure Wahrheit' − the awesome truth − face to face. He embodies nothing but the pure *Gestalt* of the concept of liberation to which he is pledged. He has uprooted and liberated himself from all the personal associations through which that concept was symbolised; all that he was attached to, that has carried him, has been dismembered, liquidated, neutered, stored. Possessions, material and emotional, have become so many exchangeable counters, anonymous and fully negotiable:

> Um einen Wechsel könnt ich es verkaufen.
> − I could sell it for a banker's cheque.

He is wholly free, wholly able to manœuvre, like a traveller; and like one that is homeless his relation to what he has thus liquidated, his relation even to his unattached self, is impersonal and abstract. He is a pure cypher, a symbol, public,

---

[a] Now I am ready, like some traveller./ Cheruska seems, in its entirety,/ As though 'twere tucked away inside some chest./ Why, I could sell it for a banker's cheque./ For if the news leaked out that I had ever dreamt/ Of liberating our German lands,/ Rome's general would set our homes on fire,/ Would cudgel down whoever is in arms,/ Abduct their bonded kin across the Rhine. −/ Augustus punishes intent no less than deed.

negotiable and utterly mobile, like money — that amazing and most quintessentially human currency next to the great semantics of pure numbers and
speech.

But the price of becoming thus objectified is prohibitive. The strain of
abstractive seeing, of creating the symbol that shall rally his countrymen, has been
superhuman; and it is an alienated Hermann who survives in a chill zone
bordering hard on the inhuman. But he knows it.

> Take him away!
> What can he say that is not known to me?   (V, 24)

he wearily replies to Aristan's appeal for his compassion. And indeed, what is
there left to say? He who has murdered the warmth of compassion for others and
for himself, who has remorselessly excised the 'Sitz der jungen, lieblichen Gefühle' — 'the seat of youthful, sweet emotion' — to be loyal to the enormity of his
concept, can find no trace of pity in his stony breast. For he has died a thousand
deaths himself. 'Alas and alack for reflection! unhappy reflection!'[22]

12 *Universalium in Re:* 'Michael Kohlhaas'

1.

In the preceding chapter we witnessed the attempt of one of the most intellectually sophisticated of Kleist's figures to excise a vast and abstract concept — *Germania* — from out of the personal and limited conception in which it was embedded and to exhibit it in a symbol 'simple, sensuous and passionate' enough to act as its carrying-medium. We saw that, paradoxically, the strain of dismembering that living conception by a continual process of abstraction in the world of a Kleist is so enormous as to cause the resultant symbol — Halli's dismembered body — to degenerate into a parody of the superior humanity which the power of abstraction betokens.

In *Michael Kohlhaas* Kleist has once again broached the problem of abstraction, but this time from an angle that is more familiar to us. We are catapulted back to the range of problems that engaged our attention in the preceding section. There, in two successive chapters, we discussed the plight of characters assailing, with what I called a mothlike zeal, an Absolute which is triply shrouded from their sight: through the simplicity of their mental endowment, through the distorting medium, the corona as it were, in which both they themselves and the object of their visions are shrouded, and through the diabolical ambiguities by which such dim-witted and refracted visions as theirs are continually tricked. It is this triad of factors we must keep in mind as we deal with Kohlhaas' ill-starred endeavour to meet the Absolute of Justice face to face.

Michael Kohlhaas is a brother of Eve, Alkmene, Littegarde and the Marquise von O., as of Penthesilea and Toni, to mention only some of his vast clan. Like them, he is steeped in a concrete configuration colouring his conception of the Absolute he pursues; and like them, he wants to understand, and be understood, 'in meiner Tat'. As Eve and Alkmene and Littegarde and Julietta want their integrity to be recognised within the highly ambiguous situation in which they are placed; as Penthesilea wants to grasp the Absolute of Love and to be understood by Achilles within her distorted conception of it; as Toni wants to make her faithful intent understood within the semantic of treachery which is at her disposal: so Kohlhaas wants to vindicate the Absolute of Justice within the ineluctably concrete configuration into which ill luck or fate have levered him[1].

Most striking of all, it need hardly be said, is his resemblance to Eve's mother, Frau Marthe. What the broken pitcher is to her, his two emaciated blacks are to him: *corpora delicti* embodying his concept of justice with the same obdurate literalism and inflexibility of mind which is familiar to us from that earthy creation of Kleist's youth. As Frau Marthe wants her actual jug to be mysteriously brought back to its original state rather than be indemnified for it in some equivalent way, so Kohlhaas wants his horses restored to the pristine condition in which he was forced to abandon them. And the absoluteness of his claim is reflected in his accompanying desire to penetrate to, and be understood by, that absolute guarantor of justice, the sovereign of his country[2], a desire marked by Frau Marthe's resolution to take her claim to the high court in Utrecht.

From the beginning Kohlhaas evinces the liveliest conception both of justice and of the manner in which the wrong done to him can and must be righted[3]. His blacks have been ruined. His servant Herse has lost his bundle of clothes, his money, his health and finally his life, as a consequence of trying to protect Kohlhaas' rightful property. It is these items for which Kohlhaas claims reparation; actual repair for all but Herse's life, and compensation for the latter, which even this literal-minded man concedes to be irreparably lost, in the form of a monetary indemnification to go to Herse's old mother.

It will readily be seen that Kohlhaas' conception of justice is one of *universalium in re*. That is to say, it is a strictly private and personal conception, wholly governed by, and geared to, that actual configuration of facts which his untoward experience presents to him. From this configuration and its sheer facticity he in no way emancipates himself in order to isolate from out of the concatenation of accidentals clustering around it its essential abstractive form. Everything in the total chance-conglomerate offered to his perception to him seems relevant and goes into the making of the conception of justice he frames.

On the one hand this conception, for all its concreteness, must be said to embody a *concept* of justice and to be using rudimentary symbols to exhibit it. But the symbols are nothing apart from the raw materials of fact, that is to say, the actual objects of contention. The horses are not merely the poet's ruling *Dingsymbole* — this has been convincingly shown by B. von Wiese — they are very rudimentary object-symbols for Kohlhaas, too, and they are invested with an all but magic power. We are repeatedly told that his concern is not a materialistic one with his horses *qua* horses. Told, after the first decision of the tribunal at Dresden, on which occasion the narrator explicitly states: 'Kohlhaas, dem es nicht um die Pferde zu tun war — er hätte gleichen Schmerz empfunden, wenn es ein Paar Hunde gegolten hätte — Kohlhaas schäumte vor Wut'[a]. We are repeatedly shown what we have thus been told: a little later, having forced one of Tronka's servants to save the beasts from the burning stable, Kohlhaas fails to reply to the question as to what should be done with them and walks off; much later still, having identified the half-dead brutes in the market at Dresden, he leaves them there, to be looked after by the police. Thus we must conclude that the horses, together with the other articles of contention on which Kohlhaas bases his strikingly moderate claim and of which he will most generously dispose, to him are symbols at once concretely embodying *and* representing the wrong that has been done to him[4].

---

[a] 'Kohlhaas, who did not mind about the horses — he would have felt no less pained had a couple of hounds been at issue — Kohlhaas foamed with rage.'

On the other hand, they are exceedingly primitive symbols, in no way weaned from the factual conglomeration they are meant to make transparent, and in their sheer opacity incapable of exhibiting the concept behind his conception of justice in a fashion that is communicable and public. This flaw in his position is shrewdly utilised in the first sentence of the Brandenburg tribunal — significantly framed without the elector's knowledge — in which Kohlhaas is stigmatised as 'ein unnützer Querulant': that is to say, as a quarrelsome nuisance who unreasonably and obdurately insists on the actual repair of trivial objects which circumstances have rendered irreparable.

Up to now, Kohlhaas has been pressing his claim in a patient and level-headed manner which exculpates him from the charge, as frequently raised as it has been denied, that he is a congenital fanatic. His investigation of Herse, the narrator's comparison of his sense of justice with a *Goldwaage* — goldsmith's scales — (Jupiter's word for Alkmene) and his insistence that Kohlhaas is familiar 'mit der gebrechlichen Einrichtung der Welt' — 'with the world, that frail institution' — all these together testify to his moderation. His 'wohlerzogene Seele' — 'his well-bred soul' — has been operating within the mental framework of his limited conception of justice — the right of a tradesman to pursue his trade peaceably and equitably — and within the legal framework at his disposal as a citizen of his commonwealth. Now, at the point when the darkly sensed representative nature of his claim is denied, and denied at that by mediate functionaries rather than by the fountain-head of order, his country's sovereign, his quest takes on a character that is absolute. In a flash, the concept behind the conception becomes clear to him. He 'cannot remain in a country which fails to protect his rights'; and: '"Rather be a dog if I am to be kicked around, than a human being!"' and immediately frames his resolution to bring a claim he now feels to be absolute, before the absolute guarantor of justice in his realm, the elector himself, '"wenn es mir nur gelingt, durch die, die ihn umringen, bis an seine Person zu kommen"'[a]: a rider which, as we shall see, is all-important.

2.

We might say that Kohlhaas is now embarking on the second, abstractive, phase of his venture[5]. Like Hermann, he immediately proceeds to clear out of his way all ties which might hamper his quest for the Absolute he is after, the thing-in-itself. Selling his properties, both in Brandenburg and Saxony, 'in Bausch und Bogen', and preparing to send his wife and children 'über die Grenze' — 'across the border' — he strips himself of the warm contextual reality in which his existence has hitherto been embedded, '"damit ich in den Schritten, die ich für meine Sache tun will, durch keine Rücksichten gestört werde"'; for: 'es könne Zwecke geben, im Vergleich mit welchen, seinem Hauswesen, als ein ordentlicher Vater, vorzustehen,

---

[a] '"If only I succeed in getting past those who surround him, to see him in person"'

untergeordnet und nichtswürdig sei; und kurz, seine Seele, müsse er ihm sagen, sei auf große Dinge gestellt'[a]. It is, in fact, set upon 'the thing-in-itself'.

The business of divesting himself of all attachments that might clutter up the mental configuration before him is made easier for him than for Hermann; but by that token it also remains a more extraneous act. Elisabeth, his faithful wife, is killed, a circumstance freely invented by Kleist who in this point deviates from his source, according to which she survived her husband by several years. Where Hermann in a concerted intellectual effort sets aside everything that he calls his own, *as though* he had already forfeited it, Kohlhaas at one bitter stroke finds himself *actually* bereaved, and cuts his losses *in toto* '. . . sold the house, despatched the children, packed into a carriage, across the border', retaining nothing but money, arms and his little band of men. Uprooted, like Hermann, he seems mobilised for an all-out assault upon the Absolute of Justice that is being withheld from him. He has sold his material assets and burnt his emotional bridges; and as Hermann jumps the guns of all intermediate contexts, proclaiming

> Allein muß ich in solchem Kriege stehn,
> Verknüpft mit niemand als nur meinem Gott . . .,[b]

so Kohlhaas declares himself a man '"subject to no king or country, and answerable to God alone"', waging a single-handed war against a society that has repudiated his concept.

But the difference is enormous. It is true Kohlhaas, like Hermann, seeks to penetrate through the corona which shrouds the sovereign's conception of his cause and vitiates his concept of it: he seeks to gain direct access to the Elector of Brandenburg who is encircled by many outsiders — his wife dies from a blow dealt to her 'von dem bloßen rohen Eifer einer Wache, die ihn umringte' — 'by the rash and brutal dutifulness of the bodyguard surrounding him' — as later on, in Dresden, he will seek a direct hearing with the Saxon Elector who is similarly encircled: we shall come back to this all-important and familiar motif. But for all these painful thrusts to meet justice incarnate face to face, his own concept of it becomes hazed over by its attendant corona almost as soon as he has glimpsed it. He 'dresses it up' in his original conception, time and again demanding that the Junker von Tronka come in person to restore his blacks to their original condition. The war for the world's justice degenerates into a private crusade against the *dürren* — 'scraggy' — Junker for his *dürre* — 'scraggy' — beasts, recurring epithets which betoken the wretched triviality of the symbols exhibiting his concept, the disastrous discrepancy between the material signs to which he is beholden and their spiritual significance. Identified as he is with his 'articles of

---

[a] '"so as not to be hampered by any considerations in the steps I intend to take for my cause"'; for: 'there might be other aims compared with which presiding over his home as a dutiful father was a subordinate and unworthy thing; in short, he would have to admit, his soul was set upon great things.'

[b] I must stand alone in such a war,/ Allied to no one save alone my God.

faith', his concept of justice after one short abstractive spurt becomes wholly hypostasized, as hypostasized, indeed, as were the young Kleist's own notions of spiritual *Eigentum*[6].

But even that intellectual strain, in a Kleistean figure as wedded to concretion as is Kohlhaas, proves to be excessive. In one of his rare evaluative statements the narrator stigmatises Kohlhaas' extravaganzas — *his* way of sighting the Absolute directly, abstractly — as being 'eine Schwärmerei krankhafter und mißgeschaffener Art' — 'an abnormal and misshapen hysteria'[7]. Where Hermann sustains and contains the stress of exposure to the Absolute, Kohlhaas becomes unhinged and deranged, hallucinating, in a 'Raserei der Gedanken' — 'in a brainstorm of his mind' — as Luther has it, that he is an emissary of the archangel Michael. Did Kleist know that the meaning of the Hebrew word for Michael is 'who is like God'? It is only luminous — and numinous — figures like Jupiter who can sustain the sight of essences *per se*: to an earthbound character even as delicately wrought as Alkmene, let alone to a Michael Kohlhaas, the encounter with their naked radiance holds the seeds of insanity.

How little Kohlhaas is able to see abstractively becomes evident in his conversation with Martin Luther. By a conscious or unconscious anachronism on the poet's part, Luther powerfully operates with the concept of 'the state' — *Staat, Staatsgewalt, Staatsverbindung* — a concept which in its modern sense did not in fact spread widely through Western Europe until the beginning of the seventeenth century[8]; and so do Kohlhaas' Saxonian adversaries, who freely use it together with derivatives like *Staatsbeschluß, Staatsrat, Staatsmänner, staatsbürgerlich, staatsklug, staatsgesetzlich* and so on. ' "Welch eine Raserei der Gedanken ergriff dich? Wer hätte dich aus der Gemeinschaft des Staats, in welchem du lebtest, verstoßen?" ' the reformer thunders at Kohlhaas, and: ' "Ja, wo ist, so lange Staaten bestehen, ein Fall, daß jemand, wer es auch sei, daraus verstoßen worden wäre?" '[a] We may here remind ourselves of the poet's personal quirk we referred to at the beginning of the preceding chapter: In *Über die allmähliche Verfertigung der Gedanken beim Reden* Kleist spoke of the stupefaction caused by the need to expatiate on such abstract concepts as *Staat* and *Eigentum*. Now it is striking that Kohlhaas himself at no point uses, takes up, or understands the legal implications of this highly abstractive concept. He speaks, and answers, in terms of primitive *Gemeinschaften* or *Gemeinheiten* — 'communities' — from which members are free to opt out when legal satisfaction has been denied them, a freedom not granted to the citizens of that highly organised community, a full-blown modern state. Whether Kleist's anachronism here is deliberate or not would be an interesting point to clarify: the answer, most probably, would be that he envisaged the historical situation in terms of Rousseau — a most meaningful figure to him

---

a ' "What brainstorm has seized your mind? Who is supposed to have expelled you from the community of the state in which you used to live? Indeed, where would you find a single case since states were instituted, of anyone whatever being expelled from one of them?" '

from his early days onward — and his theory of the *contract social*, a conception entirely alien to Luther. What is more immediately relevant and beyond all doubt, is the idiosyncratic restriction he has so patently placed on Kohlhaas' terminology. This suggests a deliberate ploy on the narrator's part devised to highlight the limitations of Kohlhaas' intellectual grasp, especially in contradistinction to his Machiavellian opponents, that is to say, his total inability to think in abstract terms.

As I see it, it is in this framework that Luther's refusal to give Kohlhaas the sacrament of the Eucharist demands to be seen. The overt reason Luther names for withholding this grace from Kohlhaas is the inability of the latter to forgive Wenzel von Tronka, his arch-enemy. '"Der Herr aber, dessen Leib du begehrst, vergab seinem Feind"', Luther reminds the horse trader: '"Willst du . . . dem Junker, der dich beleidigt hat, gleichfalls vergeben: nach der Tronkenburg gehen, dich auf deine Rappen setzen, und sie zur Dickfütterung nach Kohlhaasenbrück heimreiten?"'[a] Kohlhaas replies that the Lord did not forgive all his enemies. '"Laßt mich den Kurfürsten, meinen beiden Herren, dem Schloßvogt und Verwalter, den Herren Hinz und Kunz, und wer mich sonst in dieser Sache gekränkt haben mag, vergeben: den Junker aber, wenn es sein kann, nötigen, daß er mir die Rappen wieder dick füttere"'[b].

Luther does not, and can not, accede to this request. For Kohlhaas to forgive Tronka because the Lord forgave *his* enemies would be to understand his forgiveness here and now as an instance of a *kind* of act, an act *like* those of the Lord in which forgiveness is perfectly exemplified. But that is to say that it would be to understand his own act here and now abstractively, symbolically. And that the horse trader cannot do.

3.

And now Kohlhaas enters upon the third, and penultimate, phase of his quest. We may describe it as being a progressive strangulation of his vision. This phase significantly opens immediately after his encounter with Luther, and the narrator broaches it in the paragraph directly following Luther's dismissal of his guest. Luther advises the Elector of Saxony to grant Kohlhaas an amnesty, '. . . nach einem bitteren Seitenblick auf *die seine Person umgebenden Herren**[9] Hinz und Kunz, Kämmerer und Mundschenk von Tronka, welche die Klage, wie allgemein

---

[a] '"The Lord, however, whose body you crave, forgave his enemy"' '"Are you likewise willing to forgive the squire who has done you wrong: to go to the Tronka castle, mount your blacks and ride them home to Kohlhaasenbrück there to nurse them back into condition?"'

[b] '"Let me forgive the electors, my two sovereigns, the castellan and his stewards, the lords Hinz and Kunz, and whoever else may have wronged me in this matter: but constrain the squire, if that may be, to feed my blacks back to their former condition."'

* my italics.

bekannt war, unterschlagen hatten . . .'[a]. We have already touched on the metaphor of being surrounded, or encircled, earlier on in this chapter. 'Der Herr selbst, weiß ich, ist gerecht', Kohlhaas has assured his wife, after his first claim has been diverted and quashed; 'und wenn es mir nur gelingt, durch die, die ihn umringen, bis an seine Person zu kommen, so zweifle ich nicht, ich verschaffe mir Recht . . .'[b]. In these words, and in this image, he has given expression to his resolve to penetrate through the 'corona' of misconception surrounding the sovereign to the source of justice, the sovereign himself, and to be understood by him as directly and immediately as he understands his own just cause. His plucky wife, we remember, has fallen victim to this desire of his to come face to face with justice incarnate. She has been kicked to death by the elector's guard 'die ihn umringten' — 'who encircled him'.

In this third phase of Kohlhaas' history what has been an ominous image progressively turns into reality, in four different ways: the inaccessibility of the sovereign is directly enacted in and through sentence structures; it is made palpable through the web of intrigue and counter-intrigue woven around his person; it is borne in on poor Kohlhaas as the noose in which he is treacherously caught becomes ever more tightened; and it becomes a visible scenic reality.

For the first, the enactment in the structure of sentences, we do not have far to seek. The very opening sentence following upon Luther's letter to the Saxon Elector runs as follows:

Der Kurfürst erhielt diesen Brief *eben**, als der Prinz Christiern von Meißen, Generalissimus des Reichs, Oheim des bei Mühlheim geschlagenen und an seinen Wunden noch daniederliegenden Prinzen Friedrich von Meißen; der Großkanzler des Tribunals, Graf Wrede; Graf Kallheim, Präsident der Staatskanzlei; und die beiden Herren Hinz und Kunz von Tronka, dieser Kämmerer, jener Mundschenk, die Jugendfreunde und Vertrauten des Herrn, in dem Schlosse *gegenwärtig** waren.[c]

Here is what I have called the intervening context become language. What here crowds in between the *eben* — 'at the very moment' — and the *gegenwärtig* — 'present' — and vehemently assails the sovereign's attention, his possible intents and his feelings, is more than enough to blot out Luther's distant missive and his plea on behalf of his client; and the densest layer around his sensibility is woven by 'die Herren Hinz und Kunz von Tronka', cousins of the evil-doer Wenzel, the

---

a 'After a bitter allusion to Hinz and Kunz of Tronka, chamberlain and cupbearer *surrounding his highness* who, as was generally known, had suppressed Kohlhaas' complaint . . .'

b The Sovereign himself is just, that I know' . . . ' and if only I succeed in getting past all those that surround him, to see him in person, I have no doubt but that I shall obtain justice.'

c 'The elector received this epistle *at the very moment* when Prince Christiern of Meißen, Commander-in-Chief of the realm, uncle of Prince Friedrich von Meißen who had been routed at Mühlheim and was still bedridden licking his wounds, the Grand Chancellor of the Courts of State, Count Wrede; Count Kallheim, President of the Chancery of State; and the two lords Hinz and Kunz of Tronka, the latter chamberlain, the former cupbearer, both his highness' boyhood friends and confidants, *were present* at the castle.'

* my italics.

childhood friends and confidants of the prince. It is they, together with Graf Kallheim (is it the same who turns up here in Dresden, or another? It matters little; the bombardment eye and ear suffer from new names and old merely serves to thicken the muffling blanket of intrigue and ambiguity) who succeeded in side-tracking and quashing Kohlhaas' charge against Tronka in the first instance.

The second way in which the sovereign becomes sealed off from Michael Kohlhaas' sight is through the sheer interference of multitudes of semi-anonymous figures and through the intrigues and counter-intrigues they all conspire to weave around his person. Kunz, Wrede, Meißen, Kunz, Meißen, Kallheim, and finally Hinz – they all propose moves and counter-moves; and it is no more accidental that Kallheim, leading the whole game *ad absurdum,* says 'daß man auf diese Weise *aus dem Zauberkreise, in dem man befangen**, nicht herauskäme'[a], than that the bewildering round of arguments starts with Kunz and ends with Hinz, those all but nameless members of the proliferating Tronka clan who are resolved to destroy their arch-enemy Kohlhaas, and who between them draw together the noose in which he is caught.

Of the ring of imprisonment that tightens around the trusting Kohlhaas it is not necessary to say much. It is only too patent. Curiosity surrounds him when he first enters Dresden: 'Die Nachricht, daß der Würgengel da sei, . . . hatte ganz Dresden, Stadt und Vorstadt, auf die Beine gebracht; man mußte die Haustür vor dem Andrang des neugierigen Haufens verriegeln, und die Jungen kletterten an den Fenstern heran, um den Mordbrenner, der darin frühstückte, in Augenschein zu nehmen'[b]. The guard has to make way for Meißen, and it is in view of the crowd pressing all around the house that he suggests that Kohlhaas voluntarily and for his own protection should accept a guard. This later, treacherously, turns into an enforced captivity; men close in all around Kohlhaas' house and their teams are noiselessly relieved; so that Kohlhaas succeeds neither in going back to his Brandenburg home nor indeed even in lunching with his children with an old friend at Lockewitz. Finally, he is told outright that the promised amnesty has been broken, and while he is assured by an official, 'auf eine dem Roßhändler Ekel erregende Weise' – 'in a manner that nauseated the horse trader' – that this information must be a misunderstanding, 'verriegelten die Häscher, auf seinen Wink, alle Ausgänge der Wohnung die auf den Hof führten; wobei der Offiziant ihm versicherte, daß ihm der vordere Haupteingang nach wie vor, zu seinem beliebigen Gebrauch offen stehe'[c].

---

[a] 'that it was impossible, in this manner, to break through the magic circle in which they were trapped'

[b] 'The news of the presence of the avenging angel . . . had brought out the whole of Dresden, the city itself and the outlying districts; one had to bolt the door of the house to keep the inquisitive crowd at bay, and the boys climbed up to the windows to get a look at the incendiary, who was breakfasting inside.'

[c] 'the guards, at his intimation, bolted all exits of the lodging giving onto the yard; whilst the officer assured him that the front entrance was at his free disposal, as before.'

* my italics.

One of the last and most moving instances of Kohlhaas' solitary confinement occurs on his trip in a closed carriage, under the guard of a Baron von Malzahn and six horsemen, to Berlin. Kohlhaas has meanwhile bought back his house as an immediate response to the amnesty, and has sent for his children in whose company he appears whenever he attempts to break out of his enforced isolation: significant actions telling us that he has long since left his 'abstractive phase' behind and is seeking to retreat back to the homely and familiar conception of his cause from which he so disastrously ventured out in the first instance. The Elector of Saxony has run into the sorry column and frivolously, in disguise, visits Kohlhaas in a secluded dairy farm where the latter has broken his journey to tend one of his children who has fallen sick. As the elector enters, it so happens 'daß Kohlhaas eben mit dem Rücken gegen die Wand auf einem Bund Stroh saß, und sein, ihm in Herzberg erkranktes Kind mit Semmel und Milch fütterte . . .'ª. This is no longer the unhinged plenipotentiary of the archangel Michael who flaunted his very name like a challenge to the powers that be. It is anonymous humanity with its back to the wall, in the archetypal situation of neediness and constriction, the situation of the manger almost, going about its ancient business of mercy and compassion. Kohlhaas has learned to accept mediacy. Broken, his vision spent, he is all sad tenderness and concretion.

That eclipse of his proud and fiery vision has taken place long ago. Some say in that grotesque and Kafkaesque scene when he identifies his horses on the market place at Dresden, where the knacker has arrived with two half-dead mares in response to the Tronkas' enquiries[10]. I would accord this occurrence the function of a palpable scenic enactment of a process of strangulation and sealing off long since under way. The whole bawdy scene – the flayer by his cart, letting water, the tottering mares surrounded by a pool of stinking filth, Wenzel, Hinz, Kunz, Kohlhaas, the servant who baulks at touching the disgraced beasts and Meister Himboldt who kicks the chamberlain into the mire – the whole indecent scene is played out inside a ring formed by a laughing and unruly mob, a sort of living amphitheatre sealing off all participants in an impermeable circle of obscenity; and if Kohlhaas accepts the knacker's ruins as being his – he who has always insisted that these were not his horses – impassively, his will to fight broken, it is because his vision is blotted out. It has never been the horses that concerned him, except as a primitive symbol of his faith in a justice he fully expected to meet face to face. He has been tricked out of that sight for too long. Rings of misconception have been woven around the elector, rings of captivity have laid themselves around him, heavy and opaque as lead. His amnesty has been broken, he has not been able to penetrate to the fount of justice; its very waters have been fouled. It is that throttling of the vision that has upheld him which is visibly enacted inside the obscene arena into which the market place has been turned; that inner asphyxia-

---

ª 'that Kohlhaas, who was just then sitting on a bundle of straw with his back to the wall, was feeding one of his children who had fallen ill in Herzberg, with a bun and milk . . .'

tion which makes him impervious to be being or non-being of the objects that, to him, have *been* justice, his 'articles of faith'. In one huge mocking circle, his conception and the Tronkas' lie mingled, obscurely and unrecognisably confused and alike vilified. His vision has not got through to its guarantor. It has fallen by the wayside exhausted, there, in the cruel encirclement of the market place.

4.

And yet that same Kohlhaas has been granted a momentary access to the Numinous which so cruelly shrouds itself from his starved senses. Ironically, this comes to light in that chance encounter between the humbled man cowering with his back to the wall and an elector who comes to see him, not face to face and in truth, but cynically and irresponsibly, to satisfy a woman's whim. It is here that Kohlhaas reveals the strange incident with the gipsy woman at Jüterbock where the two electors met. There, standing way at the back of the 'Volk, das sie um-ringte' — of the 'crowd surrounding them' — and climbing on to a bench to get a glimpse of his two overlords, his solitary figure was singled out from amongst the crowd by an old gipsy woman and the knowledge craved by the two sovereigns was imparted of all people to him. This is the story as Kohlhaas tells it to the stupefied elector:

> Ich . . . konnte hinter allem Volk, am Eingang einer Kirche, wo ich stand, nicht ver-nehmen, was die wunderliche Frau den Herren sagte; dergestalt, daß, da die Leute lachend einander zuflüsterten, sie teile nicht jedermann ihre Wissenschaft mit, und sich des Schauspiels wegen das sich bereitete, sehr bedrängten, ich, weniger neugierig, in der Tat, als um den Neugierigen Platz zu machen, auf eine Bank stieg, die hinter mir im Kirchen-eingange ausgehauen war. Kaum hatte ich von diesem Standpunkt aus, mit völliger Freiheit der Aussicht, die Herrschaften und das Weib . . . erblickt: da steht sie plötzlich auf ihre Krücken gelehnt, indem sie sich im Volk umsieht, auf; faßt mich, der nie ein Wort mit ihr wechselte, . . . ins Auge; drängt sich durch den ganzen dichten Auflauf der Menschen zu mir heran und spricht: 'da! wenn es der Herr wissen will, so mag er dich danach fragen!'[a]

Now, as close to the lord of justice and yet as severed from the disguised figure as he might ever be, the knowledge comes flooding back to him how for a flash the Numinous opened its magic circle and drawn him into it.

---

[a] 'Standing behind the crowd, by the porch of a church, I could not hear what the strange woman was saying to the sovereigns; such that, since people amidst laughter whispered to one another that she was not giving away her secrets to anyone and surged forward because of the spectacle about to take place, I, less from curiosity than from the wish to make room for others who were curious, climbed onto a bench that had been hewn into the masonry of the church porch behind me. No sooner had I gained an unimpeded view of the sovereigns and the old woman . . . from my vantage-point: than she gets up, leaning upon her crutches, looking about amongst the crowd; sights me who had never so much as exchanged a single word with her . . .; squeezes through the dense throng of people, close to where I am standing, saying: "There! if the sovereign cares to know, let him ask *you*!"'

Need we speak of the final resolution, once more enacted in a grandiose scenic panorama, the third of its kind? The Elector of Brandenburg stands surrounded by his entourage, amongst them Heinrich von Geusau, Kohlhaas' faithful patron, to his left Kohlhaas' own lawyer, to the right the imperial lawyer, 'ein Herold in der Mitte des halboffenen Kreises, den das Volk schloß, mit einem Bündel Sachen, und den beiden, von Wohlsein glänzenden, die Erde mit ihren Hufen stampfenden Rappen'[a]. Into the sanctuary of this ring Kohlhaas is now admitted, and his wildest dreams are surpassed at the consuming vision he is vouchsafed. He gazes upon the concept that has been his guiding power, a concept at once childlike and numinous, standing there visibly embodied before him, in the paradox of its two natures: flesh of the flesh of his blacks, and Word of the words spoken to him by his true *Herr*. He sees *universalium in re* and, mysteriously and miraculously, *res in universalio*. Now he is ready to receive the holy sacraments. Now it is for his shabby adversary, the Elector of Saxony, to stand outside 'die Wache, die ihn umringte' – 'the guard surrounding him' – and not to reach through to the man who alone could give him back his peace of mind. As for Kohlhaas' parting vision, let St. John speak for that: 'That which was from the beginning, which we have heard, which we have seen with our eyes, which we have looked upon and touched with our hands, concerning the word of life – the life was made manifest, and we saw it . . .'[11].

---

[a] 'a herald in the centre of the semi-circle which was sealed off by the crowd, with some things bundled together by his side, and the two blacks stamping the ground with their hooves, their coats shining with health.'

VII   Word into Flesh: The Quest for the Symbol

Warum kann der lebendige Geist dem Geist nicht erscheinen?
Spricht die Seele, so spricht, ach! schon die *Seele* nicht mehr.

Schiller

Geht einmal euren Phrasen nach, bis zu dem Punkt, wo sie
verkörpert werden.

Büchner

13 Descent into Matter

1.

The essay *Über das Marionettentheater* apart, the most immediately relevant statements of Kleist on matters aesthetic are probably his three fictitious letters: *Brief eines Malers an seinen Sohn* − *Letter of a Painter to his Son,* which is almost contemporaneous with *Brief eines jungen Dichters an einen jungen Maler* − *Letter of a young Poet to a young Painter* − written one month later, in November 1810, and *Brief eines Dichters an einen Anderen* − *Letter of one Poet to Another* − composed two months after that, in January 1811.

In some respects, these three documents resemble each other closely; in the passionate dedication they express to the process of making art as well as in the urgency of the need to communicate. Yet the letters addressed to the young painters strike a note that is considerably more robust than that from poet to poet. When Kleist is speaking of artistic inspiration in terms of a medium not his own, the erotic overtones of his language are difficult to miss. In the second cited of these letters, that from a young poet to a young painter, the point at issue is the painters' time-honoured tradition of learning their trade by copying the old masters instead of plunging straightaway into the business of original invention. The poet is at a loss to understand such dilly-dallying. Impetuously he would clamour to jump in *medias res,* as impetuously as Graf Wetter vom Strahl desires to immerse himself 'in all the pristine charms' of Käthchen, now that she is his. And how physical and sensual is the passion he describes! Were one to forbid one like himself to paint his visions on canvas, why, he would offer his back to unending blows rather than tolerate such a constraint.

> Die Einbildungskraft würde sich, auf ganz unüberwindliche Weise, in unseren Brüsten geregt haben, und wir, unseren unmenschlichen Lehrern zu Trotz, gleich, sobald wir nur gewußt hätten, daß man mit dem Büschel, und nicht mit dem Stock am Pinsel malen müsse, heimlich zur Nachtzeit die Türen verschlossen haben, um uns in der Erfindung, diesem Spiel der Seligen, zu versuchen.[a]

'Spiel der Seligen' indeed: it is nothing less than an amorous exploit the poet is describing here.

Such erotic overtones become overt in the letter of a painter to his son. The young man is trying to paint a Madonna. But, he complains to his father, his feelings are 'so impure and bodily' that he feels he ought to take holy communion

---

[a] 'Our imaginations would have stirred in our breasts quite insuperably and, as soon as we'd have realised that one uses the brush and not the stick to paint with, we would, in defiance of our inhuman masters, have furtively bolted our doors at night-time to try our hands at invention, that pastime of the blessed spirits.'

each time before taking up his brush. The old man, in his reply, pooh-poohs such old-maidenish scruples, encouraged though they be by current romantic practices such as that of the painter Caspar David Friedrich who was wont to pray before putting brush to canvas. Make do, as the old masters did, 'mit der gemeinen, aber übrigens rechtschaffenen Lust an dem Spiel, deine Einbildungen auf die Leinewand zu bringen'[a], the father exhorts his pernickety son, reminding him of the fact that frequently in 'this strangely made world' of ours the most divine effects issue from the lowest and most humble of causes. *Niedrigsten* is the word the father uses. By way of illustration he cites the making of a child, assuredly no sacred action for all that man is a sublime creature. Let a man approach this task with the purest intention of construing the concept of so lofty a being in the physical world, and he will produce a creature that is puny and frail — *gebrechlich* is the father's expression. But let a heedless lad embrace a girl on a warm summer's night, and lo! he will bring forth a robust boy roving between heaven and earth and giving a headache to the philosophers.

We think we hear Goethe speaking. There is the identification so natural to that poet with the material medium of the visual arts, the easy traffic between artistic and biological begetting which puts its unmistakable stamp on the youthful group of *Künstlergedichte*[1]. We think we hear the expostulation in Goethe's famous letter to Herder: 'Dreingreifen, packen ist das Wesen ieder Meisterschafft. Ihr habt das der Bildhauerey vindizirt, und ich finde dass ieder Künstler so lang seine Hände nicht plastisch arbeiten nichts ist.'[b]

And yet this letter is not as lighthearted nor indeed as straightforward as it sounds at a first reading. Kleist was no visual artist like Goethe. Indeed he was conscious of precisely this difference being the watershed between himself and his great rival. Where the creative genius of the latter flows from his affinity with colour, he writes in the summer of 1811, his own is invariably fed by music and draws on the insights derived therefrom[2]. Indeed, so great is the ambivalence of the younger poet towards his elder that we may well suspect from the outset an aesthetic credo articulated in terms of the medium so expressly associated with the other. And as a matter of fact, the letter of the old painter to his offspring, on closer inspection, reveals sombre overtones which belie its cheerful stance. There is the barely disguised fear of abstraction in its barrenness, a mental process which is quintessential to humanity, and to no human being more so than to the artist. Abstracting his nascent vision from the personal context in which it may present itself at first, breaking it down and re-embodying its essential pattern in the terms, and forms, of the — entirely artificial — medium which is to exhibit it: this is the artist's constant business. And this is where the analogy with biological begetting breaks down.

---

[a] 'with the common but perfectly honourable fun of transmitting your fantasies onto canvas'
[b] 'To seize and grasp is the essence of any kind of mastery. You have vindicated this for sculpture, and I find that every artist whose hands do not plastically fashion, is as nought.'

What is more, if we listen carefully, we may hear a heartfelt lament tucked away between the lines: 'Die Welt ist eine wunderliche Einrichtung' — 'the world is a wondrous institution' — the old painter writes; for in it the purest inspiration will lead to the most *gebrechlichen* results. We know the resigned formulations about the 'gebrechliche Einrichtung der Welt' — 'that frail institution, the world' — from *Penthesilea, Die Marquise von O.* and *Michael Kohlhaas.* Everywhere it figures as a *cri de cœur* — *the* quintessentially Kleistean *cri de cœur* — at the tragic incongruity that exists between vision and reality, between spiritual significances and their, profoundly misbegotten, material signs. What do these same words recurring here express, if not the poet's awareness of a deep chasm between inspiration and medium, perhaps the painter's material medium only, perhaps his own as well? It is an awareness that is lightly played over and cavalierly dismissed: but it is there, beneath the surface of his robust make-believe, and it is sombre.

Indeed, how deep the poet's misgivings at his own cheerful message are, may be readily seen from the third and latest of these letters, the one entitled *Brief eines Dichters an einen Anderen* — *Letter of one Poet to Another.* In this letter we discern the poet's authentic voice. Gone is the fiction of exhorting the young with vigorous and heartening cracks of the whip, and with it, that other fiction of being able to articulate his own poetic credo in the terms of an alien art employing a physical medium. The anguished concern transmitted by this epistle that the poet should communicate his vision undistorted by the medium which is to carry it, even though it be the immaterial medium of words, is Kleist's innermost heart-ache, as we may infer from the chapter entitled 'Faulty Medium'; and by comparison with that desperate yearning the breezy message penned for the exhortation by and to painters seems positively gross. In relation to his own art-making, the rough and ready rule of thumb 'go and realise your dream as a lad makes a sturdy child, make do with the "lowest" which in this strange world of ours engenders the most sublime results', will simply not hold water.

The poet who had been so bothered, from *Die Familie Schroffenstein* via *Amphitryon* and *Penthesilea* to *Die Verlobung in St. Domingo*, at the defilement of vision through the medium in which it is conceived or received, was bound sooner or later to come up with an aesthetic in which the problem of medium as an encumbrance of unalloyed communication assumed vital proportions. For this was a problem which did not merely haunt him in his art; it dogged him quite as much in the personal sphere. By way of illustration we may cite a passage from a letter to his step-sister Ulrike written on February 5, 1801, that is to say just at the time when the Kant-crisis was about to break over his head. He wants to be reassured that Ulrike is interested in what is going on inside him, and he would dearly love to tell her 'everything, if only that were possible'.

Aber es ist nicht möglich, und wenn es auch kein weiteres Hindernis gäbe, als dieses, daß es uns an einem Mittel zur Mitteilung fehlt. Selbst das einzige, das wir besitzen, die Sprache taugt nicht dazu, sie kann die Seele nicht malen, und was sie uns gibt sind nur zerrissene Bruchstücke. Daher habe ich jedesmal eine Empfindung, wie ein Grauen, wenn ich jemandem mein Innerstes aufdecken soll; nicht eben weil es sich vor der Blöße scheut, aber weil ich ihm nicht *alles* zeigen kann, nicht *kann,* und daher fürchten muß, aus den Bruchstücken falsch verstanden zu werden.[a]

These are startling and sad words for a poet to write; but they are genuine enough as is patent from the fact that he was to call himself 'mich *unaussprechlichen* Menschen' − 'the *ineffable* person that's me' −[3] as a shorthand for his being, as it were.

It is precisely this radical distrust of the medium of language which informs the fictitious letter of one poet to another. The writer starts out with a frank confession as to how he would ideally communicate: 'Wenn ich beim Dichten in meinen Busen fassen, meinen Gedanken ergreifen, und mit Händen, ohne weitere Zutat, in den deinigen legen könnte: so wäre, die Wahrheit zu gestehn, die ganze innere Forderung meiner Seele erfüllt.'[b] The same thought is later on reiterated: 'Denn warum solltest du . . . dem Geist, den ich in die Schranken zu rufen bemüht war, nicht Rede stehen, und grade wie im Gespräch, ohne auf das Kleid meines Gedankens zu achten, ihm selbst, mit Deinem Geiste, entgegentreten?'[c] We know this need to commune directly − foreshadowed almost verbatim in a letter written years earlier: 'Ich wollte ich könnte mir das Herz aus dem Leibe reißen, in diesen Brief packen, und dir zuschicken!'[d] Kleist writes in the same letter in which he coined the phrase about himself as an '*unaussprechlichen* Menschen' − an '*ineffable* person': it is Jupiter's need, and Graf Wetter vom Strahl's, as indeed it is the need of the Count F.: the need to jump the guns of phenomenal experiencing altogether and to be in the unmediated rapport of pure essences.

And here, in this aesthetic context as in the poetic formulations of the predicament of phenomenality, as indeed in the letters, the reason behind this need is the repudiation of medium *per se.* It is a faulty agent, be it the medium of physical embodiment or of language. The writer reprimands his fellow-poet for bestowing praise on points of prosody or form, 'die ihren größten Wert dadurch bewiesen haben würden, daß Du sie gar nicht bemerkt hättest.'[e] It is with thought

---

a 'But it is not possible, if for no other reason than that we lack a medium of communication. The only one we possess, language, is not adequate for the job in that it cannot depict the soul but only gives us tattered fragments. Wherefore something like horror seizes me every time I want to bare my innermost self to someone; not because it shuns being bared, but because I cannot show *everything,* I simply *cannot* do so, so that I live in fear of my fragments being misunderstood.'

b 'If, when writing poetry, I could reach into my bosom, pluck a thought from it and place it with my hands, without anything added, into yours: truth be told, the inner longing of my soul would all at once be stilled.'

c 'For why should you not answer the spirit I endeavoured to summon into the ranks and, disregarding the garb of my thoughts, meet it with your own spirit, head-on, exactly as though we were conversing?'

d 'I wish I could pluck my heart from my bosom, pack it into this letter and send it to you!'

e 'which would have proven their greatest worth by the very fact that you would never have noticed them'.

as with those evanescent, elusive chemical substances, he explains: to become manifest, they have to be conjoined with something grosser, something that has body:

> nur darum bediene ich mich, wenn ich mich dir mitteilen will, . . . der Rede. Sprache, Rhythmus, Wohlklang usw., und so reizend diese Dinge auch, insofern sie den Geist einhüllen, sein mögen, so sind sie doch an und für sich, aus diesem höheren Gesichtspunkt betrachtet, nichts, als ein wahrer, obschon natürlicher und notwendiger Übelstand; und die Kunst kann, in bezug auf sie, auf nichts gehen, als sie möglichst *verschwinden* zu machen.[a]

In their radical dualism these words are quite staggering. Speech and language, that glory the poet commands, are here conceded as 'true and necessary evils': what a strangely self-flagellating position for a writer to adopt! Evils comparable, at best, to a garb in which to clothe − *einhüllen* − spirit and thought! It is as though Herder had never written the impassioned words which so indelibly impressed themselves upon the young Goethe:

> Gedanke und Ausdruck! Verhält er sich hier wie ein Kleid zu seinem Körper? Das beste Kleid ist bei einem schönen Körper bloß Hindernis. − Verhält er sich wie die Haut zum Körper? Auch noch nicht gnug; die Farbe und glatte Haut macht nie die Schönheit vollkommen aus. Wie eine Braut bei ihrem Geliebten . . .? Wie zwei zusammen Vermählte . . .? Ein Paar Zwillinge . . .? Diese Bilder sind bedeutend, aber, wie mich dünkt, noch nicht vollständig . . . Gedanke und Wort, Empfindung und Ausdruck [verhalten] sich zu einander . . . wie Platons Seele zum Körper.[b4]

It is as though Goethe himself had never woven the miraculous verbal weave of his *Werther*, or wrought the sensuously saturated form and idiom of his Homeric idyll, or indeed let his Tasso − in a work with which Kleist was intimately familiar − extol the power of 'Melodie und Rede, die tiefste Fülle meiner Not zu klagen'.[c]

Besides, we recall the negative connotation the imagery of clothing assumed for Kleist as early as *Die Familie Schroffenstein* where a large body of imagery was gathered up in the central formulation

> Und alles, auch das Schuldlos-Reine, zieht
> Fürs kranke Aug die Tracht der Hölle an . . .[d]   (I, 2),

---

a 'this being the sole reason why, when I want to communicate with you, I make use of . . . speech. Language, rhythm, euphony etc., and whatever the charm of these things may be in so far as they garb thought, seen by themselves, and from this higher vantage point, they are but a real, if natural and necessary, nuisance; and as far as they are concerned, art has no object save to make them *vanish* as far as is ever possible.'

b 'Thought and expression! Are they here conjoined as a body is to its garb? When a body is beautiful, the finest dress is but an impediment. − Does expression relate to thought as the skin does to the body? Still not enough; the complexion and smoothness of skin are not all there is to beauty. Like a bride with her beloved . . .? Like married spouses . . .? Like twins . . .? These similes are meaningful, but, if I see matters right, still not exhaustive. Thought and word, feeling and expression [relate] to one another as Plato's soul does to the body.'

c 'melody and speech, to sound the bounteous depths of my distress'.

d And all, even the innocently pure,/ To the diseasèd eye takes on the garb of Hell.

as well as the poet's strange insinuations about his fiancée's *Äußeres*, an offensive exterior to him rooted in some deep-down flaw.

Halfway through the fictitious letter, the author comes clean and formulates his basic position as follows: 'Denn das ist die Eigenschaft aller echten Form, daß der Geist augenblicklich und unmittelbar daraus hervortritt, während die mangelhafte ihn, wie ein schlechter Spiegel, gebunden hält, und uns an nichts erinnert, als sich selbst.'[a] The virtue of true form is its coming as close as is ever possible to not being there at all, to showing forth mental essence as instantaneously as Jupiter sheds a sensuous embodiment that to him has been nothing more than a phenomenal nuisance. What purism! And how incongruously the poet rescinds the joyous sensuality that has flavoured his utterances as long as he was not treating of his own, linguistic, medium but the physical one of the painter!

Here again we must look back to Kleist's letters, to the image of the mirror he used some ten years earlier, as the storm clouds of the Kant-crisis were gathering about his head. There, the 'warped and sullied mirror' squarely stood for the badness of an embodied self which he had repudiated lock, stock and barrel. Here, in this aesthetic context, the 'bad mirror' which detracts the attention from the spirit's message to its outer trappings makes its reappearance. The sensuous embodiment of thought in language is as vehemently rejected as the sensuous embodiment of the self was. In assessing the authenticity of the poet's stance as he expresses it, first in terms of an alien, physical medium and then in terms of his own, immaterial one, we must rely on such supportive evidence as we are offered by his significant use of language elsewhere. Here, embedded in the soil of his intimately personal experience of self, we detect the true aesthetic credo of the mature poet: *Prinz Friedrich von Homburg* is a few months in the coming, and Kleist's own life will end before the year is out. The only true form, according to that final and definitive statement from poet to poet, is the form which vanishes, disembodied, enabling us to meet the spirit face to face, in its naked glory[5].

2.

It is I think reasonably safe to say that never has a creative artist's credo misrepresented the true nature of his art more radically than Kleist's does here, in the aesthetic theory he construes. For the most outstanding thing about his poetry, be it in the narrative or in the dramatic vein, is surely the way in which his linguistic medium thrusts itself on the attention, enveloping thought, winding itself about it or tearing it apart as the case may be. The last thing one would say about it is that it is translucent. Passages where language flows limpidly are few and far between: perhaps the lovers' drinking together in Kleist's first tragedy, the

---

[a] For this is the hallmark of whatever may be called true form, that the spirit steps forth from it instantly and immediately, whereas a form that is defective holds it captive, like a flawed mirror, reminding us of nothing save itself.

close of *Das Erdbeben in Chili* and *Michael Kohlhaas*, Penthesilea's trance-like words after Achilles' murder and those magic exchanges with Stranz as Homburg goes to his execution; few beside[6]. For the most part it is its sheer opacity, the compact density of structure and idiom, which stands out in the mind. Whether we think of a tragedy like *Penthesilea* or short stories such as *Die Verlobung in St. Domingo* or *Das Erdbeben in Chili*, not to speak of *Das Bettelweib von Locarno*, we are kept breathless and on mental tiptoe by an inner tempo deriving from the strict functionality of parts subordinated to the *telos* of the whole, and by the ensuing remorselessness with which characters and events drive onward towards their appointed climax and conclusion. How could we but be supremely alive to the relentlessly tripartite form of works whose tranquil middle-section – the love-encounters in *Penthesilea* and *Die Verlobung*, the idyllic interlude in *Das Erdbeben* and the level-headed investigation of the numinous event in *Das Bettelweib* – is in every instance so clearly marked as an *adagio* on false pretences, a mistaken lull begotten by the law of contradiction, and by that same law bound to be a springboard for a renewed and final assault on catastrophe[7]? Those large forms evince the same startling and obtrusive rhythm as does the syntax of single sentence units, where the principal event, more often than not banished into subordinate clauses – consecutive, final or temporal as the case may be – turns out not to be a terminus and a resting place, but to be itself marking the opening phase of a new narrative move. One illustration, taken from *Michael Kohlhaas*, must do for many:

> Es traf sich daß der Kurfürst von Sachsen auf die Einladung des Landrosts, Grafen Aloysius von Kallheim, der damals an der Grenze von Sachsen beträchtliche Besitzungen hatte, in Gesellschaft des Kämmerers, Herrn Kunz, und seiner Gemahlin, der Dame Heloise, Tochter des Landrosts und Schwester des Präsidenten, andrer glänzenden Herren und Damen, Jagdjunker und Hofherren, die dabei waren, nicht zu erwähnen, zu einem großen Hirschjagen, das man, um sich zu erheitern, angestellt hatte, nach Dahme gereist war; dergestalt, daß unter dem Dach bewimpelter Zelte, die quer über die Straße auf einem Hügel erbaut waren, die ganze Gesellschaft vom Staub der Jagd noch bedeckt unter dem Schall einer heitern vom Stamm einer Eiche herschallenden Musik, von Pagen bedient und Edelknaben, an der Tafel saß, als der Roßhändler langsam mit seiner Reuterbedeckung die Straße von Dresden daher gezogen kam.[a]

---

[a] 'It so happened that the Elector of Saxony, at the invitation of the high bailiff, Count Aloysius von Kallheim, who at that time owned considerable properties near the Saxonian border, accompanied by the chamberlain, Herrn Kunz, and his wife, Dame Heloise, daughter of the high bailiff and sister of the president, as well as by other illustrious lords and ladies, hunting squires and courtiers whom we shall not mention here, had travelled to Dahme to attend a big stag hunt which had been arranged as a pleasurable pastime: such that, in the shelter of tents gaily adorned with pennants, which had been erected across the road on a hillock, the whole party, still covered with the dust of the hunt, to the strains of a cheerful band grouped around the trunk of an oak tree, and served by pages and noble youths, were seated at table, when the horse trader slowly approached under cover of his mounted escort on the highway from Dresden.'

There is no resting point in this sentence. The whole first part, starting from 'Es traf sich', is by way of preparation for what follows after the caesura; yet that statement, misleading by a certain epic breadth – like Penthesilea's face to face encounter with Achilles – is itself no more than a grace-note preceding the new chord that is struck, again in a subordinate clause relentlessly pointing forward: the fateful appearance of Kohlhaas[8].

To characterise the 'feel' of Kleist's linguistic medium, I can do no better than quote two passages, neither of which is overtly concerned with matters aesthetic but which have both to do with the impingement upon the self of the forces of reality and life. In *Die Familie Schroffenstein* Johannes, that helpless prey to violent and conflicting impulses, expresses his sense of encroachment thus:

> Es hat das Leben mich wie eine Schlange,
> Mit Gliedern, zahnlos, ekelhaft umwunden.[a]   (II, 3)

The second passage, closely similar, stems from a short prose piece entitled *Von der Überlegung. Eine Paradoxe – Of Reflection. A Paradox*. In it Kleist is concerned to argue the priority of doing over thinking, and compares our existential situation which demands instant action and reaction to impingements from the outside, with that of an athlete or, more precisely speaking, of a wrestler. He concludes his argument as follows: 'Wer das Leben nicht, wie ein solcher Ringer, umfaßt hält, und tausendgliedrig, nach allen Windungen des Kampfes, nach allen Widerständen, Drücken, Ausweichungen und Reaktionen, empfindet und spürt: der wird, was er will, in keinem Gespräch, durchsetzen; vielweniger in einer Schlacht.'[b]

It is not accidental after all that a reflection on thrust and counter-thrust in life should, by a twist of the tail, afford us an entry into the semantic sphere. Taking up Kleist's own cue, I propose to take a look at the poet's own statement as to how his sentences come into being, before investigating the shape into which he has wrought them, and before enquiring into the effect such a shape has upon the reader.

The essay *Über die allmähliche Verfertigung der Gedanken beim Reden* emphatically envisages the act of speech as a running battle between external stresses and the interior resistance set up by these[9]. The operative words of the essay are stressful – *angestrengt*, duress – *Not*, and necessity – *Notwendigkeit*. Communication is an act of sustaining, under duress, the inner pressure engendered by an opening gambit, a pressure which is countered as well as enhanced by external interference, to the point where the statement, once begun, is completed. It is snatched – the words *entreißen* and *an sich reißen* occur several

---

[a] In its embrace life clasps me like a snake/ With toothless limbs, and nauseatingly.

[b] 'He who does not hold life in his grip like such a wrestler, nor feels and registers it as though he had a thousand limbs in every torsion of the combat, in all its resistances, pressures, evasions and retaliations: such a one is not going to enforce his will in any conversation, much less on the battlefield.'

times — from the very teeth of hostile encroachment. The image of resistance stiffening in the degree in which the opponent steps up his charge recurs three times. Nothing, Kleist reports, is more fruitful in the pursuit of his nascent thought than an interruption on the part of his sister: 'denn mein ohnehin schon angestrengtes Gemüt wird durch diesen Versuch von außen, ihm die Rede, in deren Besitz es sich befindet, zu entreißen, nur noch mehr erregt, und in seiner Fähigkeit, wie ein großer General, wenn die Umstände drängen, noch um einen Grad höher gespannt.'[a] In the act of formulating his thought Mirabeau discovers 'was den ganzen Widerstand, zu welchem seine Seele gerüstet dasteht, ausdrückt' — 'that which expresses the whole resistance with which his soul has armed itself'. The faster speaker has an advantage over the diffident one 'because he leads more troops into battle, as it were, than the other'. The whole account of Mirabeau's lightning inspiration *vis-à-vis* the master of ceremonies, after what was to be the last session of the French monarchy, is not so much a description of the event: it is an enactment of it. And so is Kleist's opening illustration of speech snatched from his sister, which I shall quote. It is not that she tells him what he means to say or worms it out of him by astute questions:

> Aber weil ich doch irgend eine dunkle Vorstellung habe, die mit dem, was ich suche, von fern her in einiger Verbindung steht, so prägt, wenn ich nur dreist damit den Anfang mache, das Gemüt, während die Rede fortschreitet, in der Notwendigkeit, dem Anfang nun auch ein Ende zu finden, jene verworrene Vorstellung zur völligen Deutlichkeit aus, dergestalt, daß die Erkenntnis, zu meinem Erstaunen, mit der Periode fertig ist.[b][10]

How could the force of those thousandfold 'Widerständen, Drücken, Ausweichungen und Reaktionen' — 'resistances, pressures, evasions and retaliations' — to which the speaker's mind is exposed be more perfectly expressed than through the constant intrusions upon the principal clause by causal, conditional, temporal, infinitival and consecutive clauses? In the very act of creating pressure, these release a counter-pressure which victoriously sees the statement through to its final conclusion.

The speaker's resistance, so the essay tells us, grows in the measure in which increased pressure is brought to bear on him. But equally the obverse is true: in the measure in which his sense of self is enhanced by the resistance it encounters, he *causes* that resistance to stiffen yet further, to help him consolidate this primary consciousness.

---

a 'for my mind, already tensed up, is the more activated by the extraneous attempt to snatch the speech that is on the tip of its tongue, from it, and its potential, like that of a great general under pressure of events, is raised to a yet higher pitch.'

b But since I have, after all, some dark intimation which somehow hangs together from afar with what I am after, my mind, once I have made a brave start, as the conversation proceeds, and driven by the necessity to find an end to what it has begun, articulates that initial confused inkling into perfect clarity, such that, to my surprise, my own understanding is completed together with the period.'

We are here once again encountering a phenomenon we have had occasion to isolate earlier on in this study, notably in the chapter on Kleist's early letters and the Kant-crisis. This is the deep ontological insecurity of the poet's selfhood, which led to the curious hypostasization of the concept *Eigen-tum*, a word which, as we have repeatedly seen, dogs him in the present context, too. The whole essay with which we are now dealing is concerned to develop a strategy designed to boost a self which cannot 'feel' itself except in a condition of extreme stress. It is a *poet's* strategy designed to remedy through a semantic ploy what is essentially an existential predicament. The grammatical subject that has successfully sustained its impetus and, by working its way through a syntactical tangle, has succeeded in completing its utterance in a meaningful period is, in fact, the threatened self which maintains its identity and integrity in the face of encroachments so violent as to threaten to disrupt its unity[11]. The famous isolation of the grammatical subject from its predicate, brought about by the intervention of the most extreme syntactical torsions, represents, or rather enacts, the implosion into the consciousness of disruptive experiential elements, together with the extreme difficulty encountered by that consciousness in keeping a hold on its selfhood, or 'getting itself across' to another[12]. The risk of *logical* discontinuity inherent in a Kleistean sentence is directly expressive of the risk of *ontological* discontinuity on the part of the speaker's self; a risk, however, he surmounts the more triumphantly the greater it is. The *Selbstzufriedenheit* — 'self-contentment' — of Mirabeau on having transmitted his thoughts to the king's master of ceremonies is the precise equivalent of the 'große Selbstzufriedenheit' the Marquise von O. experiences as she finds, in the depths of her maternal self, the thread that keeps body and soul together; it corresponds to the incomparable 'Ruhe und Zufriedenheit' — 'tranquillity and contentment' — of Kohlhaas' last days when he is at one with his own self and has successfully communicated this singleness of mind to his sovereign.

Indeed, the *Verwicklungen* — an important word here, as indeed it is in the vocabulary and plot of the novellas or in the action of Kleist's dramas — the 'embroilments' of the Kleistean sentence fully enact the entanglement of his characters in that enveloping context which separates them from understanding themselves or from being understood by others in the concretion of their situation, 'in meiner Tat' — a predicament we have often enough discussed. That *enveloping* aura or 'corona' through which they perceive, which taints their view of themselves and blinds them to the, similarly obscured, situation of the other, is very properly syntactically represented by a host of *intervening* matter keeping the subject at arm's length from 'getting itself across' to itself or another, and from completing its communication. For what is psychologically experienced as an implosion from the *outside*, on the syntactic level is properly represented as *intruding* matter[13].

By way of illustration, let us consider two sentences; one that graphically enacts the difficulty of one self from communicating with another, a communication vital for both; the other to exemplify the threatened discontinuity within the speaker's own self. To illustrate the first, we may once again look back to the sentence from *Michael Kohlhaas* I have already cited a few pages above: the sentence describing Kohlhaas arriving in Dahme, at the precise point of time when the Saxon Elector is involved in a pleasure hunt. It is crucial for both, the elector and Kohlhaas, to meet. Their fates are entwined: Kohlhaas' with that of the elector, because he wants to transmit his conception of justice to the sovereign; the fate of the latter with that of Kohlhaas, because the horse trader holds the secret of his overlord's future. But how hopelessly the elector is entangled in the concrete context of *his* reality: how bombarded by impingements from the outside which, imploding as they do into this unresisting psyche, are very properly represented by so many syntactical incursions between the subject — 'der Kurfürst von Sachsen' — and its predicate — 'gereist war'. What intervenes are the names of the Tronka-clan — Kallheim, Kunz von Tronka and his wife, Kallheim's daughter — who together with their network of influential relations have successfully kept Kohlhaas' case from reaching either elector[14]. This inaccessibility, this being encircled, beleaguered and insulated by his *entourage,* has found beautiful expression in the cluttered opening sentence in which the subject — the elector — loses its own predicate all but out of sight. The colon concluding it accentuates the completeness of the elector's involvement, which is yet more enhanced by the consecutive clause introduced by 'dergestalt' in which the circus around him is envisaged in all its multifarious concretion. Set against this whirl the principal event, Kohlhaas' coming, reported in a slow-moving, short, subsidiary clause which trails along all but unrelated to the rest of this involved sentence, simply stands no chance of being truly registered. The horse trader and the elector presently meet, it is true; but this encounter takes place under false pretences on the part of the latter and neither 'gets through' to the other.

To illustrate the other possibility, the threatened disruption of the character's own sense of inner continuity, let us consider the following sentence, again from *Michael Kohlhaas*. It is taken from the episode in which Kohlhaas fruitlessly searches for Wenzel von Tronka in the convent of the villain's aunt, deaconess at Erlabrunn. The old lady has exhorted Kohlhaas to fear God and do no wrong — words which must set his mind thinking of his wife's dying plea — and Kohlhaas, about to set fire to the building, has been checked in his ferocity by a deafening thunderbolt landing in his immediate vicinity.

> Kohlhaas, indem er sein Pferd zu ihr zurückwandte, fragte sie: ob sie sein Mandat erhalten? und da die Dame mit schwacher, kaum hörbarer Stimme antwortete: eben jetzt! 'Wann?' — Zwei Stunden, so wahr mir Gott helfe, nach des Junkers, meines Vetters, bereits vollzogener Abreise! — — — und Waldmann, der Knecht, zu dem Kohlhaas sich, unter finsteren Blicken, umkehrte, stotternd diesen Umstand bestätigte, indem er sagte, daß die Gewässer der Mulde, vom Regen geschwellt, ihn verhindert hätten, früher, als eben jetzt, einzutreffen: so sammelte sich Kohlhaas; ein plötzlich furchtbarer Regenguß, der die Fackeln verlöschend, auf das Pflaster des Platzes niederrauschte, löste den Schmerz in seiner unglücklichen Brust; er wandte, indem er kurz den Hut vor der Dame rückte,

sein Pferd, drückte ihm mit den Worten: Folgt mir, meine Brüder; der Junker ist in Wittenberg! die Sporen ein, und verließ das Stift.[a]

Kohlhaas' vehement question − the previous sentence has described him as 'in die Hölle unbefriedigter Rache zurückgeschleudert' − 'hurled back into the hell of frustrated vengeance' − is rendered in a short yet disjointed main clause. The inner riot it has released in him is enacted in a tremendously involved subordinate clause punctuated by fierce exchanges rapped out in direct oration as well as by the eloquent dashes that follow, and 'swelled' by Waldmann's report of the swollen river, clearly a symbolical device externalising the rising pressures in Kohlhaas' tormented soul. It is after these interpolations, directly expressive of the impingements that throng into his unwilling mind, that he catches himself, but only just, in the short predicative clause 'so sammelte sich Kohlhaas', which is so far removed from the subject that this has to be unequivocally reiterated in lieu of the pronominal 'er'. The two main clauses that follow form the coda to the preceding statement: still disjointed, though increasingly calmer, they enact, through their jagged syntax as well as through their nature symbolism, the gradual subsiding of the tremors that have shaken him: an emotional earthquake the force of which may be directly gauged by the all but complete disruption of the period which has the crisis of his consciousness for its subject[15].

A curious parallel suggests itself here. The poet's characteristic way of structuring speech and thought in the face of heavy pressure − and this is, as we have seen, equally his way of structuring a threatened personality − calls to mind his favourite image of the arch which occurs in his letters, in *Penthesilea* and in *Das Erdbeben in Chili*. The arch does not collapse, Kleist writes, because every one of its stones wants to tumble down at one and the same time. It cannot fall, we may add, because the weight of, and on, the keystone is balanced by the upward components of the forces from the neighbouring stones and, ultimately, by the compressive force of the abutments[16]. We may compare the weight of, and on, the keystone − the weight of the air or any given superstructure it sustains − with the stresses that assault the self, wedge themselves in, *keilförmig*, as Kleist frequently has it, and threaten to disrupt it. Analogously, this onslaught is counter-balanced by the upward and compressive force of the foundations, that is to say, by the very buoyancy and rebound of a self that is thus weighed down and invaded. The arch stands poised, but only just;

---

[a] 'Kohlhaas, turning his horse to face her, asked her: whether she had received his manifesto? and when the lady, in a feeble voice that was scarcely audible, replied: Just now! 'When?' − Two hours, so God help me, after my nephew's, the squire's, departure! − − − and Waldmann, the farmhand, to whom Kohlhaas turned with black looks, stammered that this was indeed so, explaining that the waters of the river Mulde, swollen as they were by the rains, had prevented him from arriving until this moment: Kohlhaas collected himself; a sudden fearful cloudburst which, extinguishing the torches, clattered down upon the cobblestones of the courtyard, released the spasm in his unhappy heart; raising his cap briefly to the lady, he turned his horse, dug in his spurs, saying: follow me, my brothers, the squire is in Wittenberg! and forthwith left the convent.'

the self maintains continuity, but only just: a more precise symbol for the precarious cohesion of Kleist's prose-style it would be difficult to find.

The time has come to draw some preliminary conclusions from our findings in this section. Is Kleist's idiom in truth the transparent veil he would have us believe it to be? A prose more obsessively embodying thought and kinaesthetically enacting it would be hard to imagine. However neoplatonic his stance where he theorises, however evanescent and immaterial he supposes language enshrining pure thought to be: in his practice he was – and how could he fail to be? – the heir to Goethe's legacy and, through him, of Herder's. If Herder writes that even in the untutored idiom of ordinary speech thought 'cleaves' to expression – *kleben* is the word he actually uses – this insight goes for Kleist. If Herder calls poets aside and communes with them, saying:

> Nun, armer Dichter! und du sollst deine Empfindungen aufs Blatt malen, sie durch einen Kanal schwarzen Safts hinströmen; du sollst schreiben, daß man es fühlt, und sollst dem wahren Ausdrucke der Empfindung entsagen; du sollst nicht dein Papier mit Thränen benetzen, daß die Tinte zerfließt; du sollst deine ganze lebendige Seele in tote Buchstaben hinmalen und parlieren, statt auszudrücken . . . du mußt den ganzen Ton deiner Empfindung in dem Perioden, in der Lenkung und Bindung der Wörter ausdrücken . . . wie sehr klebt hier alles am Ausdrucke, nicht in einzelnen Worten, sondern in jedem Teile, im Fortgange derselben und im Ganzen! – :[a][17]

who would understand him better than that same Kleist who wanted, when writing poetry, 'to reach into my bosom, grasp my thought and place it into your bosom as it is, without anything added'? If anyone knew about the unnaturalness of the poet's medium, that wholly artificial body which, like that of a wrestler, must yet register and be responsive to all 'Widerständen, Drücken, Ausweichungen und Reaktionen' – 'resistances, pressures, evasions and retaliations' – of the mind, and must transmute them all and sundry into the twists and torsions of his periods, their 'Lenkung and Bindung', it was assuredly he. With his keen haptic sense he explored and exploited the bodiliness of language as few have done before or after him, quite unbothered by the fact that it was a wholly artificial body he was fashioning, and supremely untroubled by the recognition that he was bending it into more highly wrought and patently less 'organic' and flowing shapes than any German writer before or at his time. '. . . in der Kunst kommt es überall auf die Form an, und alles, was eine Gestalt hat, ist meine Sache'[b], Kleist once proudly wrote[18]; and in this workmanlike dictum he is truer to himself than in the

---

[a] Now then, poor poet! and you are supposed to paint your emotions onto a sheet of paper, to conduct their stream through a channel of black juice; you are to write in such a manner that it is felt, renouncing the natural expression of emotion; you are not to wet the paper with your tears, so that the ink blotches; you must paint the whole of your living soul in dead letters and hold discourse, rather than utter . . . you must express the whole tenor of your feeling in periods, in the way you steer and harness your words . . . how utterly everything cleaves to expression here, not as it inheres in the single words, but in every part, in their progression and in the whole!'

[b] '. . . in art everything depends on form, and all that has shape is my *métier*'

esoteric statements that creep into his theorising on matters aesthetic, which are a
transparent variant of what I have called the subjective fallacy. Indeed, to follow
him to the full into his most daring explorations of the soma of his linguistic
medium will be our business in the remainder of this chapter.

3.

In a letter written soon after his arrival in Paris Kleist praises the elegance and ease
of the French mind. By contrast, his own countrymen fare badly. 'Man nenne
einem Deutschen ein Wort, oder zeige ihm ein Ding,' he observes, 'darauf wird er
kleben bleiben, er wird es tausendmal mit seinem Geiste anfassen, drehen und
wenden, bis er es von allen Seiten kennt, und alles, was sich davon sagen läßt,
erschöpft hat.'[a][19] Whatever we may think of this characterisation of the German
mentality in general, it certainly rings a bell as far as Kleist himself is concerned;
and the mind is inevitably drawn to that most literal of all his figures, Frau Marthe
in *Der zerbrochene Krug*. She certainly 'cleaves' to her words and worries the life
out of them, as a dog will worry a dry bone. Her mind — if we can speak of her as
having a mind at all — literally handles words (Kleist characteristically uses the
word *anfassen*); she manhandles and dismantles them, until she has dismembered
them into their component parts and has lost their meaning. In a previous chapter
we watched Frau Marthe's reduction of the concepts *entscheiden*, *ersetzen* and
entschädigen to the connotation of their stem-components, a reduction *ad
absurdum* issuing in statements which are ludicrously inadequate to the legal
context in which they are being used.

Wer wird mir den geschiednen Krug entscheiden?[b] (6)

she indignantly asks, and:

Setz Er den Krug mal hin, versuch Ers mal,
Setz Er'n mal hin auf das Gesims! Ersetzen![c] (6)

As for indemnification, as far as she is concerned

Die könnten sonst was in den Krug mir tun,
Als ihn entschädigen. Entschädigen![d] (6)

It is of the essence of poetic metaphors to retrieve, and renew, the basic meaning
of words, to make them shine like pure ore. But Kleist is here going very far
towards dislocating the concepts he places onto Frau Marthe's lips, or rather, into
her hands. She dismembers and de-composes them, straining towards a meaning

---

a 'Name a German a word, or show him a thing, and he will get glued to it, handle it with
   his mind a thousand times, turn and twist it around, until he knows it from every angle,
   and has exhausted all that may be said of it.'
b Who then will impart justice to my parted jug?
c Go, place the pitcher, let him try it,/ Go, place it on that sill! Replace indeed!
d Into my pitcher they could pour I shan't say what,/ But not my pitcher mend. Amends,
   indeed!

that is material to the point of grotesqueness[20]. Needless to say, this is a deliberate ploy on the poet's part, as is patent from the fact that each time he places the word in its full and restored meaning side by side with her emasculated version of it. But then Frau Marthe is his creature, and we must watch out for similar tendencies on his part elsewhere, perhaps in weightier contexts.

The obvious work to which to turn is, surely, *Penthesilea*. Here is a figure of full tragic stature, about whom the poet wrote in bitter earnest, a vessel into which he poured the 'ganze Schmutz zugleich und Glanz' − ' all the filth and radiance' − of his soul[21]: yet she is also of the most primitive, and it is here that we may suspect him of having carried his explorations into the bodiliness of language to their extreme conclusion.

A great deal could be said about the imagery of that play, with its constant drift towards the physical, indeed the animal, realm. But our particular concern here is not so much with the *kind* of word or image Kleist uses as with the *way* in which he uses them: with the exploration of their somatic potential.

In this connection the passage in the twenty-fourth scene stands out in which Penthesilea, now remembering what she has done, tries to explain her murderous deed[22]. This helpless self-exculpation is tendered in three small speeches which are remarkable in that they are speeches about words and the act of speaking itself. From a Hermann such reflections would not surprise us. As we have seen, he is concerned with the nature of language and symbols. On the lips of a Penthesilea, they startle. For throughout the drama the inarticulacy of a mind which slips from understanding to seeing, from there to mis-taking and thence to actual eating has been borne in on us. She cannot internalise what she loves save by 'taking it in' in the most primitive manner imaginable. She bodily incorporates what she would mentally digest.

It is in fact with that characteristically Kleistean drift − Adam and Eve's − from wanting to know to perceiving, and from there to grasping − *greifen*, that Penthesilea's first speech is concerned. This is how it runs:

> So war es ein Versehen. Küsse, Bisse,
> Das reimt sich, und wer recht von Herzen liebt,
> Kann schon das eine für das andre greifen.[a]

Here is the extreme form of a theme that is thoroughly familiar to us.

> Was ich mit Händen greife, glaub ich gern . . .[b]

Ruprecht says; a formula echoed by Charis'

> Man nimmt ein falsches Kleid, ein Hausgerät,
> Doch einen Mann greift man im Finstern.[c]

---

a It was an oversight, no more. Love-rites and bites,/ They make a rhyme, and he who loves deep from the bottom of his heart,/ May well get hold of one and miss the other.
b What I may grasp with hands, I'd fain believe . . .
c You catch hold of a garb, an implement that's wrong;/ But your own man you grab at dead of night.

But there is more to Penthesilea's words. They are words about words. Her confusion is deep down on the physical level of language. *Küsse* rhymes with *Bisse*. The sound-shape of words signifying different meanings and even more incommensurable activities, is alike and becomes confused. In fact, under the umbrella of this one confusion there hide three distinct confusions which we must isolate one by one. In the first place, Penthesilea fails to distinguish between the physical signs of words and their significances. She goes by their physical signs — their sound-shape[23]. Secondly, she fails to distinguish between these significances themselves. Kissing means something different from biting. Thirdly, she confuses the material sign of a conceptual term with the physical act it denotes. She confuses speaking *about* biting with the *act* of biting, a slip which is tragically summed up in the word *greifen*.

Every one of these confusions signals that same straining from the conceptual plane into the physical domain within the semantic sphere which characterises her mode of responding on the level of overt behaviour.

Her second speech is at the feet of Achilles' mutilated corpse.

> Du Ärmster aller Menschen, du vergibst mir!

she exclaims, and continues thus:

> Ich habe mich, bei Diana, bloß versprochen,
> Weil ich der raschen Lippe Herr nicht bin;
> Doch jetzt sag ich dir deutlich, wie ichs meinte:
> Dies, du Geliebter, wars, und weiter nichts.
> *(Sie küßt ihn)*[a]

Again, the confusion between two radically opposed acts in both of which her 'hasty lips' are involved, is expressed in terms of a confusion on the physical plane of words: this time a slip-up in the physiological process of articulating sounds. Again we find ourselves *vis-à-vis* a reduction of the meaning of verbal symbols and the acts denoted by them to the somatic aspect of the sounded word.

Penthesilea's third speech offers the most generalised explanation of her deed. Having kissed the dead Achilles, she reflects:

> Wie manche, die am Hals des Freundes hängt,
> Sagt wohl das Wort: sie lieb ihn, o so sehr,
> Daß sie vor Liebe gleich ihn essen könnte;
> Und hinterher, das Wort beprüft, die Närrin!
> Gesättigt sein zum Ekel ist sie schon.
> Nun, du Geliebter, so verfuhr ich nicht.
> Sieh her: als *ich* an deinem Halse hing,
> Hab ichs wahrhaftig Wort für Wort getan;
> Ich war nicht so verrückt, als es wohl schien.[b]

---

[a] You poorest of all mortals will forgive me!/ By Diana, 'twas but a slip of tongue, no more,/ Because I cannot rule my all too hasty lip;/ But now I'll tell you plainly how 'twas meant: 'Twas this, my own belovèd, nothing else./ *(She kisses him)*

[b] How many a lass, her arms clasped round her boy,/ Will say the word: she loves him, oh, so much/ That she could eat him straightaway for very love!/ Then afterwards, pondering

Penthesilea here resorts to a figure of speech only to erode it. Metaphors do indeed draw on an overlap between two distinct spheres, yet they rely on the awareness of their distinctness to realise their essential figurative function[24]. In Penthesilea's words this distinction between the mental and the physical components of the metaphor she uses is slurred over: indeed, it is deliberately denied. It is the others, who use words figuratively, that are mad: not she. The statement 'hab ichs wahrhaftig Wort für Wort getan'[a] is a grisly euphemism for 'hab ichs wahrhaftig Biß für Biß getan'[b]. Penthesilea, in this speech, obliterates the force of metaphorical speech in that she confuses the figurative meaning with the act signalled by the physical component of the phrase; and this act she duly performs.

Thus we have traced Penthesilea's threefold drift into the physical domain of the semantic patterns she herself scrutinises. This fact is not merely significant in that it symbolises her over-all regression into physicality. It is important because it shows her inability to use, and to understand the nature of, verbal symbols *per se*. By slipping into the somatic zone of words — first, through being arrested by their sound-shape, second, through stumbling over the physiological processes involved in speech, and third, through acting out the physical component operative in metaphor — she testifies to her total unawareness of their conceptual status, that is to say of their capacity to function *qua* symbols.

Penthesilea's words about words that are acts are, as it were, her first gropings towards human language. They arise out of the intense silence of her miming which is an altogether pre-symbolic semantic[25]. In their turn, they usher in what is her first symbolic act. It is an act made of words, icy and acid words articulating her 'annihilating feeling'. Yet even this first symbol which is of her own forging — the metaphorical dagger — assumes a sheer physical force which is enough to kill.

This is the most extreme instance of Kleist's journeying into the physical regions of his medium. Can we adjudge this exploration of its lower somatic fringe in which it ceases to carry its full conceptual freight to have been a controlled poetic ploy? The answer must, I think, be in the negative. That the poet himself was heavily emotionally involved in the literalism of this his figure is attested by the regressiveness of his words about the tragic sequences he had penned: 'Sie hat ihn wirklich aufgegessen, den Achill, vor Liebe'[c][26], we read in a letter of the time; and the sheer facticity of this account together with the sob-like staccato bursts of this cadence tell their own tale. We have corroborating reports of similar remarks made with the tears streaming down his cheeks. The psychic distance between creator and creation must be judged to be nil.

---

her word, the fool!/ Finds she is sated and feels sick of him./ Now, my beloved, this was not my way./ Look: when *my* arms were clasped around your neck,/ I well and truly did it word by word;/ I was not as insane as I appeared.

a 'I well and truly did it word by word'
b 'I well and truly did it bite by bite'
c 'She has eaten him up, Achilles, really, for love',

Besides, is not this creation in line with that besetting literalness of mind which is the poet's hallmark everywhere? Is not his obsession here with the raw material of language paralleled by his characters' obsessive cleaving to the absolute raw matter of any given situation, to amputated fingers or sense organs, to horses, gloves or jugs? It is in this connection that the anecdote *Von einem Kinde, das kindlicher Weise ein anderes Kind umbringt* once again obtrudes itself upon the mind. This would seem to be the precise analogue, on the level of action, of Penthesilea's failure to grasp the symbolic status of words. With the exception of the narrator's 'sie ordneten . . . an' — 'they detailed' — which reads like a stage-direction, the whole anecdote is one extended piece of miming — save for one word Kleist introduces into the narrative as he found it: 'verabredetermaßen' — 'by arrangement'. This word places the story into a human orbit, but only just sufficiently for it to have any relevance whatever. The children do not enact roles, that is to say, envisage *kinds* of behaviour patterns of which they have formed a concept, however dim. Indeed to speak of any conceptualisation and 'dressing up' of such a concept in any conception, however primitive and crude, would be misleading. There is no *universalium* here, only brute *res*. The butcher does not enact the *kind* of person a butcher would be, nor is the action he performs the *kind* of action expected of a butcher, a kind of action moreover from which all reality features have been eliminated by a process of abstraction. He *is* the butcher as the sow *is* the sow as the knife *is* the knife as, indeed, the slaughter *is* the actual brute act of slaughtering. The abstractive symbolising power exhibited in this piece of acting out — which, save for the word 'verabredetermaßen' is prehuman — is absolutely nil. And that same deficiency becomes apparent in the test devised to establish the 'childlike' innocence of the culprit. The Rhenish florin held out to him *represents* a value that is *abstract* and *symbolic*. The child's instead choosing an apple with its pure reality-appeal demonstrates its incapacity to abstract from the immediate and edible good, even so much as to recognise the level of reality of the *token* held out to him. It is into such prehuman perspectives that we need to place Penthesilea's failure to apprehend the symbolic status of words which to her signal oral activity, and her consequent acting out of them in the literal incorporation of Achilles[27].

The same straining to the physical depths of language, the regression even towards regions which lie the other side of language altogether, is perceptible elsewhere, in Kleist's personal as well as his poetic utterances. To his fiancée he writes: 'Aber das Ganze ist ein Brief geworden, den ich Dir nicht anders als mit mir selbst und durch mich selbst mitteilen kann, denn, unter uns gesagt, es ist mein Herz. Du willst aber schwarz auf weiß sehen, und so will ich Dir denn mein Herz so gut ich kann auf dieses Papier malen'[a][28]; and in another letter, much

---

[a] 'But the whole thing has become a letter which I can but transmit to you together with and through myself, for, between you and me, it is my heart. However, you want to see something black on white, and so I shall try to paint this heart onto this sheet of paper as best I may . . .'

later: 'Wie soll ich es möglich machen, in einem Briefe etwas so Zartes, als ein Gedanke ist, auszuprägen? Ja, wenn man *Tränen* schreiben könnte – doch so – – –!'ᵃ²⁹ This is a strangely incongruent thought actually to come from a poet. And yet it has found its way into Kleist's creative writing. For we meet it again in *Das Käthchen von Heilbronn*. There it is echoed in Graf Wetter vom Strahl's first monologue, in which he desperately seeks utterance for his love. A patently 'poetic' speech by one unversed in this personal idiom, this strange mixture of lyricism and bombast culminates in the following meditation:

> Du Schönere, als ich singen kann, ich will eine eigene Kunst erfinden, und dich weinen. Alle Phiolen der Empfindung, himmlische und irdische, will ich eröffnen, und eine solche Mischung von Tränen, einen Erguß so eigentümlicher Art, so heilig zugleich und üppig, zusammenschütten, daß jeder Mensch gleich, an dessen Hals ich weine, sagen soll: sie fließen dem Käthchen von Heilbronn! – – – ³⁰ᵇ (II, 1)

This descent through the physical depths of language, past the very bounds of language, into sheer matter is a movement which links up, 'circularly' and paradoxically, with that disdain of even the immaterial medium of his art which the poet has confessed to his fellow poet: an ultimate touching of opposites no less strange than that of Teniers and Raphael, the bear and the god, or indeed the perplexing coalescence of the subjective and objective fallacies.

He could write like an angel – one thinks of the lovers' exchanges in his first drama or of the prince's words to Stranz in his last – and yet, in this creature of extremes, the involvement with the unleavened matter of his medium could be so heavy, so dragging the feet of its spirit, that one feels like crying with the Romans stuck in the German mud:

> Das Heer schleppt halb Cheruska an den Beinen,
> Und wird noch, wie ein bunter Specht,
> Zuletzt, mit Haut und Haar, dran kleben bleiben.ᶜ
>
> *(Die Hermannsschlacht, V, 1)*

We have travelled a long way with Kleist, and in the end the route has turned out to be circular. The poet, we have seen, formulates an aesthetic fully affirming the force of medium – the painter's material medium – only to deny it his ultimate allegiance. For his own part, an artist working in the evanescent substance of words, he entrenches himself in an idealistic neoplatonic position, repudiating the objective, material pole of his art-making as a necessary evil. In his

---

ᵃ 'How am I to make it possible to forge, in a letter, something so tender as is a thought? Of course, if one could write *tears* – but this way – – –!'

ᵇ 'You more lovely one than I can sing, I shall invent an art all of its own and weep you. I shall unlock all phials of emotion, heavenly and earthly ones, and brew such a potion of tears, an outpouring so singular, so sacred and at the same time so voluptuous, that everyone on whose shoulder I weep, shall say: they flow for Käthchen of Heilbronn! – – –'

ᶜ The troups drag half Cheruska by their feet/ And, like some gay-hued woodpecker, will end/ By getting stuck in it, skin, hair and all.

practice, however, the extreme opposite emerges – up to a point. Kleist works as obsessively in and through his words as van Gogh did through colour and brush. Indeed, in his ferocious exploration of the syntactical and kinaesthetic potential of his medium, he can scrape the bottom of the barrel, to the point where language is stripped down to the skeleton of a soma heavily bespeaking itself; and beyond that again to the point where, in yet another incongruous reversal, naked emotional matter takes over, ineffable in its subjectivity, and speech altogether ceases. The regressive movement of the four brothers in 'Die heilige Cäcilie' from language as an instrument of abstract thought to silence and thence to inarticulate noises is perhaps not quite so bizarre or unique an event in Kleist's mental universe as might at first sight appear.

A supreme fashioner of words yearning to invent a semantic of tears: here is the paradox this strangest of poets knew himself to be when he called himself 'mich *unaussprechlichen* Menschen' – 'the *ineffable* person that is me.'

14   The Scandal of Particularity

1.

'. . . die ganze Darstellung dringt sich mit gewaltsamer Gegenwart auf'[a], Goethe wrote of Kleist's *Zerbrochener Krug*[1]. And although it is generally maintained that he did not do full justice to that play, dividing it into acts – perhaps in the very endeavour to mitigate that *gewaltsame Gegenwart* – yet, as I see it, there is a great deal of truth in his statement, a truth more general in its application than to Kleist's comedy alone. For this poet's writings, his novellas and essays and anecdotes as much as his dramas or his letters, do obtrude themselves with the vehemence of their immediacy. I should like to follow Goethe's cue and expatiate on his judgment. To do so, however, I must go back to the beginning and try to elucidate the structure of Kleist's experiencing a little further than I have done hitherto.

In the chapter given over to the analysis of Kleist's letters we noted a marked tendency towards the reification of animate objects and the hypostasization of what is unsubstantial. This trend, we explained, sprang from the deep ontological insecurity of his self-hood – *Eigen-tum* – a trait we also noted in the essay *Über die allmähliche Verfertigung der Gedanken beim Reden*. There we observed the tremendous strain to which this self is exposed, indeed to which it needs to expose itself in order to feel itself at all and to assure itself of its cohesiveness. It is a trait we found amply confirmed in the poet's stylistic and in particular syntactical idiosyncrasies. We must now investigate in what manner this ontological insecurity determines the structure of Kleist's experience of the non-self and indeed stamps the strange topography of his mind.

In his *Seelenprobleme der Gegenwart* C. G. Jung apodeictically states that 'Bewußtsein ist . . . immer Ich-Bewußtsein. Um meiner selbst bewußt zu sein, muß ich mich von andern unterscheiden können. Nur wo diese Unterscheidung existiert, kann Beziehung stattfinden.' He then goes on to make a point that is important for Kleist: 'Obschon im allgemeinen unterschieden wird', he writes,

> so ist normalerweise die Unterscheidung stets lückenhaft, indem vielleicht sehr umfangreiche Gebiete des seelischen Lebens unbewußt sind. In Bezug auf unbewußte Inhalte findet keine Unterscheidung statt, und daher kann in ihrem Bereiche auch keine Beziehung hergestellt werden; in ihrem Bereich herrscht noch der ursprünglich unbewußte Zustand einer *primitiven Identität* des Ichs mit dem andern, also eine vollständige Beziehungslosigkeit[b][2].

---

[a]   '. . . the whole presentation obtrudes itself with a vehement presence'.

[b]   'Consciousness is . . . always consciousness of the self. To be conscious of myself, I must be able to distinguish myself from others. Relationships only exist where this distinction obtains.' 'Although one distinguishes in a general sort of way, such a distinction is

We need only look at Prinz Friedrich von Homburg to appreciate the relevance of these observations for Kleist. The sleepwalking prince − like Käthchen, like Penthesilea − is totally devoid of self-consciousness; and in this state, the one, we must remember, most highly prized by his creator, his primitive identity with what forms the unconscious content of his psyche − Natalie, honour, fame, love of country and sovereign − is tantamount to a total unrelatedness as becomes apparent when, rudely jolted into self-consciousness, this self cracks and its unconscious freight is unscruplingly jettisoned. To become truly related to what he now repudiates he must first establish a separate self, which is what the elector's person to person communication helps him to do.

More lately, R. Laing has taken up Jung's position and expatiated on the correlativity between separateness and the capacity for relationship. Starting out from the premiss, shared amongst others by Martin Buber, that man is set in an existential I-thou context − again a presupposition that is highly problematic in its application to Kleist − he argues as follows: 'Separateness and relatedness are mutually necessary postulates. Personal relatedness can exist only between beings who are separate but not isolates. We are not isolates and we are not parts of the same physical body'[3]. Further on in his study, Laing designates the psychic state which allows for separateness as well as relatedness. It is − as Jung has already shown − a sense of autonomy.

> If the individual does not feel himself to be autonomous this means that he can experience neither his separateness from, nor his relatedness to, the other in the usual way. A lack of sense of autonomy implies that one feels one's being bound up in the other, or that the other is bound up in oneself, in a sense that transgresses the actual possibilities within the structure of human relatedness'[4].

Again a host of Kleistean figures springs to mind, notably Käthchen von Heilbronn and Graf Wetter vom Strahl whose beings are inextricably entwined with one another. For all Strahl's unwillingness to admit it, they live in a kind of symbiosis allowing neither for separateness nor for true relatedness, and violently oscillate between a desire totally to merge and an abrupt and total withdrawal, on his part, into inaccessibility. A similar picture is presented by Penthesilea, a figure whose autonomy or sense of identity is swamped by unconscious collective allegiances, in her polarised relation to Achilles.

In the sequel to his argument, Laing pinpoints precisely these violent swings as the only remaining option to a developed sense of autonomy.

> Utter detachment and isolation are regarded as the only alternative to a clam- or vampire-like attachment in which the other person's life-blood is necessary for one's own

---

normally of an intermittent nature, in that quite likely there are sizeable tracts of psychic life which have remained unconscious. With respect to unconscious psychic contents no distinction takes place, and this is why within these areas no relationship can be established; within these areas the primordial unconscious state of a *primitive identity* between self and other obtains, which is tantamount to saying, a total lack of relatedness.'

survival, and yet is a threat for one's survival. Therefore, the polarity is between complete isolation or complete merging of identity rather than between separateness and relatedness.

We know this oscillation from Kleist's personal relationships with, say, Wilhelmine von Zenge or his half-sister Ulrike, where inordinate demands for intimacy and trust alternate with abrupt withdrawals into isolation. We meet it in greatly intensified form in the creatures of his artistic imagination. Penthesilea is 'unverwandt' or devouring, or both. And so are Strahl, Amphitryon-Jupiter or, indeed, Graf F. in *Die Marquise von O.*, unrelated stranger and rapist in one. I have throughout this study operated with the formulae of the subjective and the objective fallacies in an endeavour systematically to conceptualise these two deviants from the norm of separateness and relatedness. As we have seen, these two reaction patterns may appear distributed over different characters, or side by side in one person and even in one state. The clamouring for a direct communion of souls — the expression of an excessive desire to merge identities — alternates or even coalesces with the utmost detachment from the other — the expression of an all out refusal to enter into any mutually modifying relatedness whatever. Only in rare instances does Kleist transcend this polarisation and portray a separateness signifying neither isolation nor introjection but true relatedness: notably in Trota and Alkmene, in Natalie and Kottwitz, and in the prince, after his crisis.

As we have already seen, the lack of a sense of autonomy of the self, with the resultant threat of that self being engulfed, lies at the root of Kleist's encounter with Kant. Kant had recognised that to posit the ontologically self-sufficient status of the object world was to gainsay any intelligible explanation of what knowledge of this world we do possess. Objects existing independently of the knower, he had argued, cannot be cognised it any predictable fashion: they must be present in our senses to be known at all; and even so, *a posteriori*, a rational explanation of how such objects could conceivably have 'wandered over' into our mind there to leave their representations is not possible. Such a transmigration must be attributed to an inspiration, which is tantamount to saying it is not rationally intelligible at all.

To account for what *a priori* synthetic knowledge we do have of the sensible world, Kant had, as it were, robbed objects of their solid thing-character. He had explained them as part-constructs of the synthesising mind which provides the space-time continuum in which they appear and, through its categories, construes the given sensa into coherent experience of objects or — and this comes to the same thing — into coherent objects of experience.

This semi-mental status of the object world represented a psychologically unendurable threat to one as deeply devoid of a sense of autonomy and in danger of being engulfed by the 'other' as was Kleist. He *needed* ontologically independent objects — *Gegen-stände* — in all their undilute 'thingness' to demarcate, by means of a solid *vis-à-vis*, a self that was embryonic and but precariously established. Things to him were the indispensable frontiers of and, as we have seen, surrogates for, his problematic self-hood: they defined his *Eigen-tum*. Thus he turned his back upon the phenomenalistic account of the object world which is the price paid by the theory of Transcendental Idealism, and obdurately entrenched himself in a position of Naïve Realism.

I say 'obdurately' advisedly, because philosophically speaking this realist, having once been exposed to Kant's revolution of thought, was anything but naïve. He had formed a mental image of Kant's universe − a mind-imbued transparent phenomenal zone in a mental spatio-temporal continuum where knower and known interlace, bounded by the unknowable sphere of noumenal essences − and had repudiated it. The image of the world of experience he formed, in an opposition to Kant sprung from the deepest psychological need, was the exact reversal of Kant's own: he envisaged the self as set in an absolute temporal-spatial continuum peopled by ontologically independent, noumenal objects which, through the fact of being thus independent, are absolutely opaque to the knower and unrelated to him. Indeed, to speak of a knower is to be guilty of an overstatement, since the self has no access to the impenetrably mind-independent noumenal entities around it. Unrelated, self and non-self, like so many windowless monads, meet in a frontal collision[5]; an encounter which bears the features of a direct noumenal visitation from outer space, or − and here the after-effects of Kant's phenomenalistic teaching become patent − of an equally direct delusion or hallucination.

Two quotations from *Penthesilea* may serve to clarify the model of the experiential encounter as Kleist envisaged it in his regressive revulsion from Kant. They describe the meeting of two entities desirous of entering into a knowing relation with one another. The one runs as follows:

> Jetzt, eben jetzt, da ich dies sage, schmettern
> Sie, wie zwei Sterne, auf einander ein![a]   (7)

The other, perhaps even more telling:

> Achill und sie, mit vorgelegten Lanzen,
> Begegnen beide sich, zween Donnerkeile,
> Die aus Gewölken in einander fahren.[b]   (8)

In these two passages, all the features we have gleaned from our reconstruction of Kleist's mental universe in his rebound from that of Kant are patently present: the externality, indeed the numinous nature of space, the noumenal, and numinous, character of the object of experience − Penthesilea and Achilles are each selves, but impermeable objects for one another − the threatening unpredictability and violence of their approach, their total impenetrability to one another, and their consequent unrelatedness. We must hold fast to the fact that in Kleist's universe, what noumenal objects − *Erscheinungen* − appear to the self, by reason of being mind-independent and unknowable are *always* experienced either as vehement

---

[a] Now, even now, as I am saying this,/ They crash into each other like two stars!
[b] She and Achilles, with their lances couched,/ Meet one another, like twain thunderbolts,/ Roaring into each other from the clouds.

visitations or as equally vehement delusions. Never are they hailed as phenomena in Kant's and Goethe's senses, which, veiled manifestations of the truth though they be, nevertheless signal it, in Goethe's instance symbolise it, and in any case stand in some rationally comprehensible relation to it[6]. As against that, Kleist's noumenal and numinous objects are singular, discrete, outside any mental frame of reference, and alike devastating in the vehemence of their impact whether they are experienced as visitations from the yonder or as delusions in the here and now. And that annihilating concreteness of the experienced object, whether it remains unrelated or implodes into the other, or both, is at no point mitigated by the fact that it is experienced serially, in a mental order, as one of its kind: it remains particular, *sui generis*, and thus utterly overpowering[7].

2.

We are now in a position to appreciate Goethe's observation about the vehement immediacy with which Kleist's world obtrudes itself on the percipient; more crucially even, we may begin systematically to understand the ineluctable particularity which we have seen is attached to Kleist's work in its every aspect and its every phase.

This particularity of vision is perhaps most marked in Kleist's anecdotes. Everywhere it is the absolutely singular, opaque occurrence that arrests the poet's attention. The very titles tell their tale: *Mutwille des Himmels*; *Sonderbare Geschichte, die sich, zu meiner Zeit, in Italien zutrug*; *Geistererscheinung*; *Unwahrscheinliche Wahrhaftigkeiten*; *Geschichte eines merkwürdigen Zweikampfs*; *Beispiel einer unerhörten Mordbrennerei*; *Außerordentliches Beispiel von Mutterliebe bei einem wilden Tiere*; *Merkwürdige Prophezeiung*; *Merkwürdiges über den General Westermann*[8]; and *Von einem Kinde, das kindlicher Weise ein anderes Kind umbringt.*[a] The anecdotes themselves keep the promise of their titles: they relate truly 'unheard of occurrences': there is the stroke of lightning that obliterates the epitaph on the tombstone of a niggardly woman in such a manner that the only remaining letters read *sie ist gerichtet* – she is judged; the dead man who, to satisfy a quirk of his mind, has to be buried half clean shaven, half soaped, and stark naked; the story of a man consulting a doctor and reporting the most bizarre accidents caused by doctors running him over, all of which he has survived; the brief encounter between a young man and a lady wearing a beauty spot at the right side of her mouth from which her partner emerges sporting a beauty spot on the left side of his mouth; the *unwahrscheinlichen Wahrhaftigkeiten* of a soldier with a bullet hole through chest and back who

---

[a] *Wilfulness of Heaven*; *Strange Story Which Took Place in Italy in My Time*; *A Ghostly Visitation*; *Improbable Veracities*; *Story of a Strange Ordeal*; *Example of an Unheard of Incendiarism*; *Extraordinary Instance of Maternal Love in a Wild Beast*; *Strange Prophecy*; *Memorable Facts about General Westermann*, *Of a Child that Kills Another Child in a Child-like Fashion*.

is practically unhurt since the bullet, deflected by his sternum, travelled skin-deep around his ribcage; of the boat which is bodily lifted by the blast caused by a falling rock from one bank of the river Elbe to the other; and of the flagbearer who is similarly transported through the force of an explosion from one bank of the river Schelde to the other, baggage, flag and all, unhurt.

Much of the opaque particularity of these anecdotes[9] has found its way into the plots of Kleist's narrative and dramatic art. We have discussed this aspect at length in a previous chapter of this study dealing with the structures of ambiguity this poet created; and it will be sufficient here to remind my readers of a few instances where the eccentric nature of the central occurrence is particularly marked: I would recall the earthquake in St. Jago and its paradoxical consequence of saving, indeed even engendering, life; the pregnancy of a woman conscious of having had no intercourse; the visitation of another by one identical to her husband who yet is not her husband; the visitation of Käthchen by a man who miles away lies in his bed mortally sick; the performance of an oratorio by one likewise bedridden and dying; and the sleepwalking performance by a high-ranking Prussian officer.

Such singularity on the level of the external action has its match in the famous *corpora delicti* which play such a notorious part in 'thickening the plot': the amputated fingers in *Die Familie Schroffenstein*, the broken pitcher in the drama of that name, the initialled diadem in *Amphitryon*, the birthmark on Käthchen's neck as well as Kunigunde's deed in its case, arrow and ring and indeed the physical consequences in *Der Zweikampf*, the pair of blacks in *Michael Kohlhaas* and the dead stag which, true to the gipsy's prophecy, arrives in the market place, the lock of hair in *Die Hermannsschlacht*, the glove in *Prinz Friedrich von Homburg* and, finally, the mysteriously changing body of the Marquise von O.

I have spoken of these 'articles of faith' as 'thickening the plot', and advisedly so. For these objects are experienced in precisely the fashion I have endeavoured to define in the foregoing section of this chapter. They are eminently envisaged as direct incursions from some outer orbit of the noumenal, indeed, the numinous sphere into the sense world, making it incomprehensible. This is patently so in the case of Amphitryon's diadem, the stag in *Kohlhaas*, Natalie's glove and the changing body of the marquise. Condensations of the noumenal realm, they directly impinge — for in Kleist's world the noumenal does directly impinge — upon the phenomenal scene, visitation or hallucination, who knows, and tantalising in their inscrutability. Of the intrusion of such iridescent objects into the action and their cruel implosion into the sensibilities of those affected Amphitryon and Hohenzollern give us a vivid impression: Amphitryon, when he finds the casket emptied in which the diadem has lain and exclaims:

> Ich habe sonst von Wundern schon gehört,
> Von unnatürlichen Erscheinungen, die sich
> Aus einer andern Welt hieher verlieren;

Doch heute knüpft der Faden sich von jenseits
An meine Ehre und erdrosselt sie . . .;[a] (II, 2)

Hohenzollern, when he describes the impact on the prince of finding a piece of his nocturnal vision in his very hands:

Dies Stück des Traums, das ihm verkörpert ward,
Zerstört zugleich und kräftigt seinen Glauben.[b]

Always these objects *par excellence* − for this is how Kleist envisages all objects as such − are 'articles of faith', that is to say, reified emanations of the Numinous, 'threats from the yonder'; and always such condensations of the Numinous impinge with the devastating immediacy of vision or delusion, and erode any possible certainty in the here and now they enter. The yonder, overcontiguous and thronged with noumenal, indeed numinous, entities, contracts into an alien object which points up the ultimate uncanniness and unknowability of the empirical world and paralyses the characters' inner freedom of movement *vis-à-vis* this world.

That this inner freedom of movement is severely restricted, we have repeatedly seen. Into a complex world, still further complicated by such signs signifying nothing, Kleist has placed a host of figures who are exceedingly simple in their mental make-up yet obdurately pledged to the Absolute. These figures cleave to the particular in a twofold fashion: by mistaking material signs for hidden spiritual significances and interpreting the situation in which they find themselves in terms of such perceptual pointers; and by insisting on understanding themselves and on being understood by others 'in meiner Tat', that is to say, within the highly specific context in which they happen to be placed. To Frau Marthe the broken pitcher *is* Eve's honour as for Kohlhaas his two blacks *are* justice. And they all − Eve and Kohlhaas and Alkmene and Littegarde and Penthesilea and Toni and the prince, to mention only some − want to understand themselves and be 'seen through' by others *in* the concretion of their singular predicament.

Besides, these characters cannot be said to develop in any usual sense of the word. Kohlhaas and Frau Marthe end as they begin, without any perceptible widening of their mental horizon: the one still lamenting her broken jug, the other gazing upon justice face to face, in the shape of his shining blacks. This literal cleaving to the particularity of their situation is more often than not the case. It mars the deaths of Gustav in *Die Verlobung in St. Domingo* and of Antonio Piachi in *Der Findling*, deaths shrouded in total fragmentation of vision, a fact made palpable by the narrator's emphasis on grisly anatomical details; whilst at the other end of the spectrum even the prince and, with him, Kottwitz and Natalie,

---

a Before this I have heard of miracles,/ Unnatural events whose trail, emitted/ In some other world, has lost itself in our own;/ But on this day the thread spun in the yonder,/ Entangled with my honour, strangles it . . .

b This piece of dream that put on flesh for him,/ Alike confounds his faith and lends support to it.

cling to their highly idiosyncratic and particular vision of law and state. It is the individual in its involuntary grace that triumphs in Kleist's last play.

And how ineffably difficult this poet's characters find it to rise to the truly symbolic utterance or action. That quintessentially human capacity to apprehend the general in the particular, the concept in the conception, refracted through this poet's prism becomes grotesquely distorted. The four brothers in *Die heilige Cäcilie* reach out for a symbolic interpretation of the sacrament of the Mass and end up raving mad, relapsing into the altogether presymbolic mode of mime. Penthesilea traverses a pitiful passage from a prehuman incorporation of the other *via* an extended mime to a first symbolic utterance so charged with violence that it kills. Hermann and Thusnelda rise to a symbolic act, he in exhibiting the concept of dismembered *Germania* in the dismemberment of human carrion, she in letting her own vengeance be represented by the she-bear tearing Ventidius into shreds. But how primitive these symbols are is only too patent. It takes a concerted mental effort to distinguish them at all from the entirely presymbolic 'acting out' with which the anecdote *Von einem Kinde, das kindlicher Weise ein anderes Kind umbringt* is concerned. It is only because the young culprit's piece of miming is altogether presymbolic — as is proven by his choice of the pretty apple in preference to the Rhenish florin *representing* a value — that he is exonerated. An exculpation of Hermann's or Thusnelda's symbolisms would, if anything, be a more problematic thing to attempt.

3.

So far we have spoken about the cleaving to particularity of the poet's creations, the plots of his devising and his characters. What about the creator himself? Quite late in his short life, in his last summer, Kleist makes an extraordinary confession to his cousin Marie: he cannot sustain the memory of people or his feelings about them. 'So geschäftig dem weißen Papier gegenüber meine Einbildung ist', he writes,

> und so bestimmt in Umriß und Farbe die Gestalten sind, die sie alsdann hervorbringt, so schwer, ja ordentlich schmerzhaft ist es mir, mir das, was wirklich ist, vorzu-stellen . . . der Gegenstand, fühle ich unaufhörlich, ist kein Gegenstand der Einbildung: mit meinen Sinnen in der wahrhaftigen lebendigen Gegenwart möchte ich ihn durch-dringen und begreifen. Jemand, der anders hierüber denkt, kömmt mir ganz unverständ-lich vor; er muß Erfahrungen angestellt haben, ganz abweichend von denen, die ich darüber gemacht habe. Das Leben, mit seinen zudringlichen, immer wiederkehrenden Ansprüchen, reißt zwei Gemüter schon in dem Augenblick der Berührung so vielfach aus einander, um wie viel mehr, wenn sie getrennt sind. An ein Näherrücken ist gar nicht zu denken . . . Müller, seitdem er weg ist, kömmt mir wie tot vor, und ich empfinde auch ganz denselben Gram um ihn, und wenn ich nicht wüßte, daß Sie wieder kommen, würde es mir mit Ihnen ebenso gehn [a][10].

---

[a] 'However industriously my imagination busies itself *vis-à-vis* a sheet of blank paper, and however defined the figures it produces are as regards contour and colour, to imagine what

Kleist is here putting his finger on what is now recognised to be a very early and deep-seated impairment: the inability to 'hold' an emotional situation, perhaps because of the very violence with which it implodes in him – *zudringlich* is the word he himself uses – and the consequent inability to experience symbolically what he cannot thus internalise in the absence of the actual object[11]. True, he opposes this human shortcoming to his ability as a poet: yet clearly he himself suspects a connection between the two spheres, for he writes: 'Wirklich, in einem so besondern Fall ist noch vielleicht kein Dichter gewesen'[a].

Could it be that the painful lack of holding power, of memory, of definition to which this 'unbegreiflich unseliger Mensch' is subject in his capacity as a human being, by way of compensation accounts for the over-consistency, the too-long memory, the over-determination which is the hallmark of his poetry? In short, for the obsessive and tortuous cleaving to the contingencies of the here and now, which marks his creations in their entirety?

In the preceding chapter we have at length spoken of Kleist's prose-style and observed his meticulous exploration of his linguistic medium, to the point where its sheer bodiliness – which is its most particularised aspect – obtrudes itself upon the attention *zudringlich* or, as Goethe would say, *mit gewaltsamer Gegenwart* – 'with a vehement presence' – strangulating, almost, its message. We have watched Penthesilea's pitiful first semantic steps and have seen her getting hopelessly embroiled in the soma of her vocabulary. That same drift towards the literal, the utterly particular, we have noted in the poet's letters. The reification of what is living and the hypostasization of what is unsubstantial – material riches for relatedness in love or for *Bildung* – are all part of that drift. In the *Katechismus der Deutschen* or the poem *Germania an ihre Kinder* we see the poet himself painfully practising the very steps towards abstraction and conceptualisation he lets his Hermann take, whilst in *Der Engel am Grabe des Herrn he* laboriously rehearses that victory of resurrection over the dead weight of matter which dogs the figures of Kleist's first and last plays.

That same straining towards the concrete and opaquely particular is the hallmark of Kleist's poetic imagery. As always, it stems from his envisagement of the world as made up of noumenal, mind-independent and mind-resistant entities with an aura of dense 'thingness' about them[12]. Most remarkable perhaps is his

---

is real for me is difficult, I might even say outright painful . . . the object, I incessantly feel, is no object for the imagination: I crave to penetrate and to grasp it with my very senses in the real and live present. Anyone who thinks differently in this matter, to me seems quite incomprehensible; his experiences must deviate utterly from those I myself have made in this respect. Life, obtruding itself with its ever-recurring claims, wrenches two minds apart a thousandfold even at the moment they meet, how much more so when they are at a distance from one another. Drawing closer is quite unthinkable . . . Since Müller has departed, he is as good as dead to me, and I mourn him in just the same manner as though he were in fact dead, and if I didn't know that you are going to come back, I would feel the same about you.'

a Truly, possibly no poet has as yet been in such a singular predicament.

nature imagery and the space-time continuum along which it is set. With few exceptions, the natural scenes he presents are violent, menacingly over-contiguous and charged with numinosity. One thinks of the two descriptions of Achilles against a thunderous background which I have quoted in another chapter, of the evocation of the cathedral at Aachen in *Die heilige Cäcilie* or, for that matter, of the encounter of Achilles and Penthesilea 'like twain thunderbolts roaring into each other from their clouds'. The thunderous overproximity of such imagery at its grandest is easy to understand so long as we remember that for Kleist what is non-self is always the noumenal, indeed, the numinous directly impinging upon the self with unmediated vehemence.

This structure of experiencing has found its most extraordinary precipitate in his envisagement of space and time. For Kant these were mental forms of our experiencing. For Kleist they are, as I have indicated, external entities, as mind-resistant and opaque as all other objects of experience; and it is with a curious density that he tends to represent them. In his letters we have three or more descriptions of a hilly landscape such as that embedding Würzburg, envisaged as an amphitheatre or even a theatre, with the sky as a vaulted ceiling, God looking on from a box, and the sun hanging from the centre like a chandelier! And in his poetry, too, the skies he depicts have some of the solidity of cast-iron. Yet for all this static quality, his evocations of landscapes, and particularly skyscapes, are also highly dynamic and thunderous; a curious mingling which is readily explained so long as one remembers that they are direct emanations from the numinous sphere, a numinosity, however, which is always experienced in reified form.

Even time is represented as though it were solid. The poet evokes it by setting side by side two sequential events, say Penthesilea's mind outpacing the horse she rides, or Achilles overtaking her by the length of three arrow shots. The slower moving of these sequences in its graphic presentation becomes as it were a visible yardstick against which the faster one can be read off spatially, like the mercury column of a thermometer against its scale. Such is the precipitate, on the poetic plane, of Kleist's 'Naïve Realism', that is to say, his literal interpretation of time and space, together with the rest of the object world, as ontologically self-sufficient entities enjoying the status of full 'thinghood'.

When we come to the imagery deployed to articulate events in the more specifically human sphere, the drift from the abstract to the concrete and from the general to the particular is seen to remain in full force. We are entitled to say that it is the *poet's* drift, over and above that of his characters: for it is manifest regardless of the respective characters' mental endowment and intellectual ken. Sosias and Jupiter, in this crucial respect, speak the same language. The one, hidebound, literal-minded and materialistic to a fault, may legitimately answer Mercury's enquiry as to his station:

> Von welchem *Stande**?
> Von einem auf zwei *Füßen**, wie ihr seht.[a]   (I, 2)

[a] Of what *standing*?/ Of one upon two *feet*, as you may see.

He may muse:

> Wenn ich fünf *Stunden** unterwegs nicht bin,
> Fünf Stunden nach der Sonnenuhr in Theben,
> Will ich *stückweise** sie vom Turme schießen.[a] (I, 2)

It is a different matter altogether when Jupiter, Kleist's most intellectually sophisticated figure by far, speaks in almost the same strains, lapsing from the abstract into the concrete in a metaphor such as this:

> Den *Eid**, kraft angeborner Macht, *zerbrech** ich,
> Und seine *Stücken** werf ich in die Lüfte.[b] (II, 5)

Again, it is one thing for Johannes, in *Die Familie Schroffenstein*, to protest that he has found the right corpse, saying:

> Wär ich *blind**,
> Ich könnt es *riechen**, denn die Leiche *stinkt** schon.
> Wir wollen uns dran niedersetzen, komm,
> Wie Geier ums *Aas**.[c] (V, 1)

This language is perfectly apposite. Johannes is a sensualist and a materialist, and the degeneration of his perceptual imagery from the visual to the olfactory plane, together with the fact that his perception actually misguides him, is exactly what we would expect in Kleist's poetic world. It is an altogether different and stylistically more problematic matter if Jeronimus, an eminently rational and clear-sighted man, expresses himself in much the same idiom, lapsing from the abstract and differentiated into the use of savagely primitive and particularised hyperbole. Accused of courting Sylvester's daughter Agnes, he replies:

> Du meinest, weil ein seltner Fisch sich zeigt,
> Der doch zum Unglück bloß vom Aas sich nährt,
> So schlüg ich meine *Ritterehre** tot
> Und hing die Leich an meiner *Lüste Angel**
> Als *Köder** auf −[d] (I, 1)

Again, it is one thing for Penthesilea to identify a mental function − feeling − with the physical parts in which it is commonly thought to be lodged; such as when she asks:

> Wo ist der *Sitz** mir, der kein *Busen** ward,
> Auch des *Gefühls**, das mich zu Boden wirft?[e] (5)

---

* my italics throughout.

[a] If 'tis not five *hours* since I started out,/ Five hours by the sun dial in Thebes,/ I'll shoot them from the tower *piece by piece*.

[b] The *oath* I break by dint of inborn power/ And toss its *pieces* high into the air.

[c] 'If I were *blind*,/ I could *smell* it, for the corpse has begun to *stink*./ Come, let us sit down by it,/ As vultures will by carrion.'

[d] You deem because a rare fish has appeared,/ Which feeds on nought but carrion by bad luck,/ My *knightly honour* I would beat to death/ To trail its corpse as *bait* from my *desire's hook*?

[e] Where would the *seat* be, mine, the *bosom*less,/ Of such a *love* as hurls me to the ground?

or, later on, apostrophises her 'heart', i. e. her burgeoning love, as follows, in somewhat blatant physiological detail:

> Hinweg jetzt, o mein *Herz**, mit diesem Blute,
> Das aufgehäuft, wie seiner Ankunft harrend,
> In beiden *Kammern dieser Brüste** liegt.
> Ihr Boten, ihr geflügelten, der Lust,
> Ihr *Säfte** meiner Jugend, macht euch auf,
> Durch meine Adern fleucht, ihr jauchzenden,
> Und laßt es einer *roten Fahne** gleich,
> Von allen *Reichen** dieser Wangen wehn:
> Der junge Nereïdensohn ist mein!ᵃ   (14)

Thus to slip into deepest physicality in endeavouring to give utterance to an event of spiritual and emotional significance is in order for one as tragically primitive as Penthesilea. But it is an entirely different matter for Diomedes, an astute Greek rationalist, similarly to drift from the abstract to the concrete, from the mental functions of reason and will to their imagined locus in the body. This is how he sums up the worried discussion of the Greek generals about the Amazons' strategy and Achilles' inane pursuit of their queen:

> Laßt uns vereint, ihr Könige, noch einmal
> *Vernunft* keilförmig**, mit Gelassenheit,
> Auf seine rasende Entschließung *setzen**.
> Du wirst, erfindungsreicher Larissäer
> Den *Riß** schon, den er beut, zu finden wissen.ᵇ   (2)

Fourth and last: it is one thing for Kottwitz, with his glorious simplicity, to say to the elector:

> "Als mich ein *Eid** an deine Krone band,
> Mit *Haut und Haar**, nahm ich den *Kopf** nicht aus,
> Und nichts dir gäb ich, was nicht dein gehörte!"...;ᶜ   (V, 5)

quite another for the elector himself, with his superior mind, similarly to lapse from the abstract to the concrete and from the envisagement of a general situation

---

a Away, my *heart*, with all this mass of blood,/ Which lies, as though awaiting his advent,/ Congested in both *chambers of these breasts*./ Winged heralds of desire,/ Ye *juices* of my youth, come on, come on,/ Fly through my veins, delirious with joy,/ And hoist the message, like a *scarlet flag*,/ In all the *kingdoms* of these rosy cheeks:/ The Nereid's young son, Achilles, he is mine!

b Let us together once again, ye kings,/ With cool collectedness *place reason*, like a *wedge*,/ Upon the raving madness of his choice./ You will, Larissian, with wonted ingenuity,/ Detect the *crack* that he is offering you.

c When, by an *oath*, I pledged me to your crown,/ *Hair, skin* and all, I did not save my *head*,/ And give you nought that is not yours by rights . . .

* my italics throughout.

to one almost absurdly particularised: hearing of Kottwitz's unscheduled arrival in Fehrbellin, the elector muses:

> Seltsam! – Wenn ich der Dei von Tunis wäre,
> Schlüg ich bei so zweideutgem Vorfall Lärm;
> . . .
> Doch weils Hans Kottwitz aus der Priegnitz ist,
> Der sich mir naht, willkürlich, eigenmächtig,
> So will ich mich *auf märksche Weise fassen**:
> Von den drei Locken, die man silberglänzig,
> An seinem Schädel sieht, *faß** ich die eine,
> Und *führ** ihn still, mit seinen zwölf Schwadronen,
> Nach Arnstein, in sein Hauptquartier, zurück.
> Wozu die Stadt aus ihrem Schlafe wecken?[a]   (V, 2)

Needless to say, the prince's previous play on the words *Fassung* and *sich fassen* in the prison scene adds considerable force to the elector's slip into the sphere of concrete particularity and unabashed physicality here.

This linguistic tendency has its counterpart in the often noted tendency of the action to drift from metaphor into literal reality. Adam *becomes* the devil limping away on his clubfoot. Penthesilea, so heavily associated with animal-imagery from the start, *becomes* a bitch amongst her hounds, sinking her teeth into the man she loves, and the somnambulist prince *becomes* all the things he was dreaming of in the beginning: an immortal victor and a bridegroom. To which we may add that the foundling Nicolo who idly cracks nuts between his teeth when we first encounter him, is himself cracked open like a nut between his father's bare hands, at the end.

More immediately relevant to our theme is the return, at the end of a story or play, to the particularity of its beginning. It is not only a Frau Marthe or a Kohlhaas who show an unleavened concern with the objects that have exercised them at the start: it is the dramatist and the narrator as well. It is the dramatist who has appended the anticlimactic last scene figuring a disgruntled Frau Marthe after the illuminations between the lovers in the preceding one, which is given still incomparably greater weight and depth in the *Variant*. It is the narrator who lets the curtain drop over a dying Kohlhaas utterly contented at the sight of his well fed blacks. No new perspectives are opened up by the endings of *Die Familie Schroffenstein, Die Verlobung in St. Domingo* or *Der Findling*, whilst *Das Käthchen von Heilbronn*, like *Der zerbrochene Krug*, ends on a decidedly anticlimactic note, returning to the peripheral intrigues of Kunigunde. Even where new insights are gained, these are barely articulated, the closed form creating a

---

[a] Odd! – If I perchance were the Tunisian's Dey,/ I'd beat alarm at this ambiguous event./ . . ./ But as it is Hans Kottwitz from the Priegnitz,/ Who comes uncalled, anarchic and self-willed,/ I'll *take myself in hand* the native way:/ Of the three strands of silvery hair/ You see upon his skull, I shall *take* one/ And *lead* him back with his twelve squadrons/ to Arnstein quietly, where his quarters are./ Why rouse the town from its nocturnal sleep?

* my italics throughout.

dominant impression of stationary circularity. Alkmene's final 'Ach!' echoes her first one at the departure of Jupiter; the angel-devil imagery at the conclusion of *Die Marquise von O.* similarly gathers up verbal strands which lead back to the beginning; Hermann's concluding speech draws on the image of the *Raubnest* which has been richly deployed in the opening sequences; and the identity of setting and mime at beginning and end of *Prinz Friedrich von Homburg* apart, Kottwitz's affirmation in answer to the prince's question: 'Ein Traum, was sonst?' — 'a dream, what else?' — transports us back to the nocturnal scene at the start; after which the final 'In Staub mit allen Feinden Brandenburgs!' — 'back into dust with all the foes of Brandenburg!' — to any one not intimately familiar with the ramified meaning of the word *Staub* in this play[13] — the dust to which the first couple are condemned to cleave — is once again decidedly anticlimactic.

Apart from *Das Erdbeben in Chili* which is unique in Kleist's œuvre, perhaps the only ending that is outright meditative is that of *Penthesilea.* Yet there, too, the metaphor of the oak tree has had a good run throughout the play, so that formally the end is closed off. As for the quality of the pronouncement, it is problematic. Kleist here uses a much rehearsed metaphor, employed previously in *Die Familie Schroffenstein* and in a letter. And its general message that he who is vital is vulnerable does not intimately tie in with, let alone transcend, the immensely rich and complex thematic texture of that play as I read it. It is something of a *tour de force* which only just escapes being a cliché[14].

The question of Kleist's endings deserves close attention, because these are manifestly the poet's own. Our review has shown their tendency to convolute, turning in upon themselves and reverting to the particularity of their beginnings. In this important respect Kleist's dramas — to concentrate on these for a moment — differ radically from those of the Greeks and of Shakespeare; a comparison which is particularly relevant since Kleist, in his *Robert Guiscard,* sought to rival Aeschylus, Sophocles and the British playwright. In the three Theban tragedies Sophocles dismisses us from the carnage and agony to which he has subjected us, ending on a note of generalised reflection on the human condition, the most famed being the last lines of the most gruesome of these plays, *Oedipus King of Thebes* itself:

> Then learn that mortal man must always look to his ending,
> And none can be called happy until that day when he carries
> His happiness down to the grave in peace.

This manner of dismissal is already prefigured in Aeschylus' *Choëphoroe* and *Euminides,* and utilised to the full by Euripides in his *Iphigenia in Tauris, Electra* and *Hippolytus.*

As for Shakespeare, he has taken much care not to dismiss us *in mediis rebus,* but to return us from the strained concentration upon a particular destiny played out in a particular action to a tranquilly meditative frame of mind. He has achieved this end — to which German classical aesthetics would heartily subscribe — by a variety of means: by songs and epilogues, prolonged farewells from the victims of the action which sum up their being — Othello holds up an image of his own being in an epilogue spoken by himself — by reviews of the total situation and the opening up of new perspectives for the future. Neither are generalising reflections on the human condition missing. We need only think of Caesar's closing words in *Antony and Cleopatra* —

> High events as these
> Strike those that make them; and their story is
> No less in pity than his glory which
> Brought them to be lamented. . . .

or, more memorably still, of Albany's at the end of *King Lear:*

> The weight of this sad time we must obey;
> Speak what we feel, not what we ought to say.
> The oldest hath borne most; we that are young
> Shall never see so much, nor live so long.

As against such examples of great tragedy carrying an enormous emotional freight and treading the tightrope of a psychical distance which is at vanishing point whilst yet restoring some equilibrium, Kleist's endings make one thoughtful. As often as not he has exposed his spectators to an all but unendurable emotional brunt; yet save for the consolation of the closed form he does not dismiss us gently from the vice of his dramatic embrace. He remains as riveted upon that particular destiny forged in that particular chain of events as do his characters. And the question arises whether Kleist, the creator of such profoundly literal figures as Frau Marthe or Kohlhaas or Amphitryon or indeed Penthesilea, is himself capable of rising to a symbolic perspective. Were we to adjudicate this question by reference to the characters alone with which he has peopled his poetic world, the answer would have to be no. But that would be an illicit or at least an inadequate criterion. However, we have in addition scrutinised the poet's own linguistic idiosyncrasies both in and out of his works, and *his* presentation of his material, both narrative and dramatic, especially with regard to any possible widening of mental horizons towards the end: and our answer remains the same. He cleaves to the particular as do his characters. Like them, he consolidates his poetic statement at the end, but he does not transcend it and its matter by the deployment of altogether different mental and linguistic resources.

To explain my meaning, I should like for a moment to consider the closing lines of *Faust II* :

> Alles Vergängliche
> Ist nur ein Gleichnis;
> Das Unzulängliche,
> Hier wird's Ereignis;
> Das Unbeschreibliche,
> Hier ist's getan;
> Das Ewig-Weibliche
> Zieht uns hinan.[a]

---

[a] All that is transient/ Is but reflected;/ What was deficient/ Here is enacted;/ What there we could not say/ Here it is done;/ The Ever-Womanly/ Beckons us on.

These verses poetically articulate the theme of *Faust,* which is the theme of Goethe's life and work in its entirety: the symbolic character of the phenomenal and, therewith, its essential meaningfulness. On the one hand, they are a poetic symbol of a world itself envisaged symbolically; on the other, they offer us a conceptual distillation of that awareness in that, in them, the nature of symbolism itself becomes the overt theme of discourse. Goethe's language here is fully adequate to discharge this doubled function. It is, one might say, poetry plus. Intensely musical — a beguiling lyricism of texture achieved through the all-pervasiveness of the rhyme scheme — it offers, as it were, a presentational symbol of the poem's total import. Through the beauty of its sound-shape richly embodying its meaning it enacts the statement the drama makes as a whole, namely, that the phenomenal is an adequate vehicle of spiritual significances. But over and above that, Goethe's language here also conceptualises this total statement. For however mellifluous and light, it also represents its meaning discursively. Abstract words — *Vergängliche, Gleichnis, Unzulängliche, Ereignis, Unbeschreibliche, Ewig-Weibliche* — are deployed to articulate a highly esoteric import, explicated in three promissory statements about the relation between the phenomenal and the noumenal, and a fourth one in which the nature of the passage from the one to the other is disclosed.

At the risk of sounding paradoxical, I would contend that it is the very length and weightiness of those abstract adjectival nouns which engender the unearthly lightness and floating grace of these verses taken as a whole. For these words, charged with meaning, pensively gathering in the mental harvest of a lifetime and the shared experience of a whole culture, gently release us from our bondage to their carrying-medium, however sweet such a bondage may be, and affirm the more outward-bound universal fellowship of our common *humanitas.* That is why these lines breathe, liberate and suggest unending spaces. The very re-introduction of 'representational' discursive elements into a richly presentational weave signifies that ultimate transcendence, in love, which is made good in the last word of the tragedy — *hinan.*

It is this esoteric extra-dimension of language, the poetic-discursive which lies at the far side of the poetic-presentational, which in Kleist is missing, in especial measure in his endings which lack the authority of the truly representative utterance. He no more transcends the bodiliness of his linguistic medium than the particularism of his own, or his characters', vision. He cleaves to his thematic matter and to the soma of his language as the Romans cleave to the muddy soil of Germany in which they get stuck. There is little or no leavening, floating or opening out of character, language or theme; for this, paradoxically, takes the deployment of conceptual language, 'der Gedanken muntres Heer', capable 'auf meinem Flug mir munter nachzuschwingen'[a]: it takes language soaring aloft in its abstractive universality, because a distilled weight that is shared becomes light[15].

---

[a] 'The army of lively thoughts that merrily accompany my flight'

But then, how could a Kleist rise to a symbolic leavening of his own poetic matter, let alone celebrate the transparency of the phenomenal and garner the symbol of the symbol? He who lived in a cast-iron space peopled by noumenal entities, mind-independent, utterly opaque and as impenetrably particular and alien as meteoric splinters? To such a one the fraternity of self and non-self, the brotherhood of all things phenomenal as true if mediate reflectors of the One Divine was beyond grasp. Unrelated, or in turn struck down by the vehement implosion of the singular visitation or delusion, he could never rise to the sustained wisdom of the large symbolic utterance. In that essential respect, he was the 'unbegreiflich unseliger Mensch' − 'the incomprehensibly doomed person' − he knew himself to be: devoid of memory to hold experience and thus incapable of the symbolic mode − for memory is the nurturing soil of the symbol: a unique predicament for a poet to be in, as he himself realised.

4.

Yet poet he was, and a great one at that. What is it he achieved, and why does he compel us now, heirs of two wars and denizens of the atomic age?

To answer this question, I should like to return once again to the metaphor of the arch which is rightly considered to be one of the key images affording us an entry into that poet's mind.

The ancestry of the image goes back to a letter written to his fiancée soon after his decisive trip to Würzburg. He felt downhearted and depressed, he recollects, as he walked through the town. 'Als die Sonne herabsank war es mir als ob mein Glück unterginge.' Then he passed through 'das gewölbte Tor' − 'the arched gate'. 'Warum, dachte ich, sinkt wohl das Gewölbe nicht ein, da es doch *keine* Stütze hat? Es steht, antwortete ich, *weil alle Steine auf einmal einstürzen wollen* − und ich zog aus diesem Gedanken einen unbeschreiblich erquickenden Trost, . . . daß auch ich mich halten würde, wenn alles mich sinken läßt.'[a][16] This analogy has received its final formulation in *Penthesilea*, here, too, at the point when the figure addressed is at her lowest ebb.

> Sinke nicht,
> Und wenn der ganze Orkus auf dich drückte!
> Steh, stehe fest, wie das Gewölbe steht,
> Weil seiner Blöcke jeder stürzen will!
> Beut deine Scheitel, einem Schlußstein gleich,
> Der Götter Blitzen dar und rufe, trefft!
> Und laß dich bis zum Fuß herab zerspalten,
> Nicht aber wanke in dir selber mehr,

---

a 'When the sun set I felt as though my lucky star were going down.' 'Why, thought I, does the arch not collapse, seeing that it has *no* support? It stands, I replied, *because all its blocks want to tumble down at once* − and from this thought I derived the ineffably quickening comfort, . . . that I too would stand up, even if everything else were to let me down.'

> Solang ein Atem Mörtel und Gestein,
> In dieser jungen Brust, zusammenhält.[a]   (9)

Kleist's physics are entirely correct. The arch is stable because the weight of and on the keystone is counter-balanced by the upward component of the forces from the neighbouring stones and by the compressive force of the abutments. In the preceding chapter I have already contended that this model is paradigmatic for Kleist's syntax. I would now go further and contend that it is paradigmatic for the total form of Kleist's works of art and for the psychic structure of the poet who has given us these works.

As we have observed, everything in Kleist's dramas and novellas tends downward, towards the sheer facticity of the material domain. Take the plots first. What is metaphorical becomes real. What tended towards generality, reverts to the opacity and heterogeneity of the particular. A circle is closed and sealed off formally. The characters analogously descend into progressive literalness. Whatever vision they may initially possess becomes atomised in a perceptual approach which degenerates into ever cruder modes. At the lowest ebb, language ceases and presymbolic mime takes over: witness Halli's silent collapse and death, the mute ritual enacted by the four brothers, Robert Guiscard sitting down on the kettledrum, Amphitryon crushing the plume on his helmet, and, most important, Penthesilea's silent ablution after her murder of Achilles. We observed an analogous tendency on the part of the poet's language to strain towards literalism and particularism in his handling of metaphor, and towards an excessive exploration of the somatic potential of his medium in his prose syntax.

Further, we noted the unleavened denseness of actions cluttered up with ambiguity and made more enigmatic still by the invasion of *corpora delicti* – such as fingers or diadems or gloves – condensations and reifications of the Numinous, part vision, part illusion, which trick Kleist's characters, naïvely realistic yet intensely religious as they are, like so many will o' wisps in the impenetrable jungle of their here and now.

All these gravitational stresses combine to produce that deep entanglement in the sheer matter of existence in which the Kleistean character no longer perceives the truth of his situation or his relationship in and through the cluster of appearances surrounding him. The dead weight of accumulated heterogeneous matter chokes the truth, material signs bury immaterial significances. At the nadir of the action, vision suffers a total eclipse *vis-à-vis* a phenomenal world experienced in its terrible concretion. The onslaught of sense-data upon the mind – so precisely enacted in a syntax where the subject is utterly separated from its predicate – is felt to be crushing. By the seamless wedging of all these

---

[a] Pray do not fall,/ E'en if all of Orcus pressed on you!/ Stand, and stand fast, as yonder arch does stand,/ Because each of its blocks would tumble down!/ Offer your brow, that keystone of your arch,/ To lightning hurled by gods and cry out, smite!/ And let yourself be rent from tip to toe,/ But do not waver any longer in yourself,/ So long as but one single breath conjoins/ Stonework and mortar in this youthful breast.

multifarious pulls towards materiality the utmost density and opacity of the inner as well as the outer situation is accomplished. Concrete particulars such as make up the here and now of the respective situation remorselessly interlock, and a maximum of discrete, uninterpreted and impenetrable matter effectively serves to blanket from sight any thing *per se*. The mind is shrouded in sheer heterogeneity tantalisingly shot through with the Numinous.

Such pressure corresponds to the colossal weight besetting the keystone of the arch, a weight tending towards the collapse of a total structure made up, paradoxically, of discrete particular blocks. (No cement is required to hold the separate segments of a properly constructed arch in place.) Julietta 'whose senses threatened to tear' and Littegarde whose senses do in fact tear are subject to this pressure. So is Kohlhaas when his vision goes into eclipse, shrouded by a web of impenetrable appearances; so is Homburg when he faces extinction in a world that has become incomprehensible; and so is Gustav when he wakes up to find himself bound hand and foot.

At this point of maximal pressure and impermeable density a counter-force is released from the inside as it were. The dead weight upon the keystone is neutralised by the upward thrust of its neighbours pressing against it and the compressive force exerted by the foundations.

We have seen that counter-force at work in the essay *Über die allmähliche Verfertigung der Gedanken beim Reden*. The tensions engendered by the dialogue situation in general, and by the intrusions of the partner in particular, through the operation of the law of contradiction generate an enhanced resilience and resistance on the part of the speaker. The statement once begun must be ended, and all the hurdles encountered on the way stiffen his resolution to 'see it through'. This we have found to be the law of Kleist's syntax. As the web of interpolated concrete matter gets denser, as the mass of imploding particulars threatens the collapse of the whole period, the force of cohesion becomes stronger and the subject, resisting the invasion of the here and now, wins a hard-fought battle and completes its utterance.

It is the same with the characters and, indeed, the dramatist or narrator who manipulates them. The maximal pressure releases the maximal cohesive and compressive force, releases even a buoyancy generated by the very stress. The Marquise von O. experiences this lift when she withstands the pressure which is brought to bear upon her to give up her children:

> Durch diese schöne Anstrengung mit sich selbst bekannt gemacht, hob sie sich plötzlich, wie an ihrer eigenen Hand, aus der ganzen Tiefe, in welche das Schicksal sie herabgestürzt hatte, empor. Der Aufruhr, der ihre Brust zerriß, legte sich, . . . und mit großer Selbst-zufriedenheit gedachte sie, welch einen Sieg sie, durch die Kraft ihres schuldfreien Bewußtseins, . . . davon getragen hatte. Ihr Verstand, stark genug, in ihrer sonderbaren Lage nicht zu reißen, gab sich ganz unter der großen, heiligen und unerklärlichen Ein-richtung der Welt gefangen.[a]
>
> [a] 'Acquainted with herself by this glorious effort, she suddenly arose, as though drawn

We could quote a closely similar passage from *Der Zweikampf*; but it is this one here, in *Die Marquise von O.*, that most transparently translates the mechanical law by which the arch stands – the cohesiveness and buoyancy released by pressure upon what is basically a fragmented structure of discrete constituents – into terms of fiction and art. The marquise's 'große Selbstzufriedenheit', we said, echoes not only Mirabeau's on completing his speech: it also echoes the serenity of Kohlhaas and Homburg and Penthesilea when, under deadly stress and at a great price, they see their quest through and complete the statement their lives were intended to make. It is the satisfaction and rebound of beings profoundly threatened in their selfhood, near-fragmented, assailed by what is unredeemed in its particularity and in its violence from within and without, who yet affirm that self as a cohesive force and preserve its vision, all violent impingements notwithstanding. It is the satisfaction of deeply religious beings who preserve their integrity and their allegiance to the Absolute in an unintelligible world to whose enigma they are fully exposed.

But in the last resort that 'große Selbstzufriedenheit' which reverberates through Kleist's endings for all the hell his characters have endured, mirrors yet another contentment, an artistic one. It reflects the deep satisfaction of a poet who has salvaged the spontaneity of his genius from the deadly pressures of self-consciousness. To trace this ultimate import, we must pursue the image of the arch and its ramifications yet a little further.

The analogy of the arch first appears in Kleist's letters, in close association with speculations about ways and means of making limited resources go a long way. The poet ponders Galileo's and Pilâtre's ingenuity in discovering antigravitational forces wrested from gravity itself. Galileo's pendulum is kept in motion by the inertia of its own weight; and Pilâtre established the principles of aeronautics by observing that the weight of smoke can carry a freight such as a balloon, and make it airborne[17].

Clearly these reflections bear on Kleist's thoughts about the arch. For here too gravity is surmounted from the inside, as it were. The weight of the stones has an upward component; and this, together with the compressive force exerted by the abutments, keeps it standing. Similar thoughts occupy the poet in the essay *Über das Marionettentheater* and yet again in a crucial pronouncement about music; and we must follow Kleist in both these directions. In the essay, it is the economy of the puppet-master's movements in relation to those of the puppets that arrests his attention. The lively and complicated movements of the dolls and their pendula are caused by a simple ellipse effortlessly and organically executed by the

---

up by her own hand, from the abysmal depth into which fortune had flung her. The commotion which rent her bosom, subsided . . . and with every self-satisfaction she pondered what a triumph she had scored by virtue of her spotless conscience. Her mind, strong enough not to give in her extraordinary situation, surrendered itself wholly to the great, sacred and inexplicable ordinance of the world.'

puppet-master's wrists; and Kleist compares the ratio between exertion and effect with that obtaining between numbers and their logarithms. A similar *aperçu* underlies his much discussed assertion that music is, as it were, the algebraic formula of all the other arts, and that the thoroughbass in particular contains the secret of poetry[18].

Clearly, it is the notion of an economy of effort and a reliable calculus that is the common denominator underlying these various observations[19]. The keystone of the arch utilises the upward component from the forces of the neighbouring blocks. The balloon utilises the upward component of gas or smoke, themselves objects of some weight. The pendulum utilises the momentum maintained by its weight. All these antigravitational forces are calculable as, indeed, are the puppet-master's movements which effortlessly obey the natural structure of his wrist. But how does the figured bass fit into this train of observations?

The figured bass, too, represents an economy, not merely of notation, but of creation. The bare figure below the staves indicates a variety of ways in which the harmonisations of the melody can be realised. What is more, it can be used as a key for extemporising melodies, again in a variety of ways, but within certain limits. (We may note in parenthesis that both types of extemporisation were described in great detail in Carl Philip Emanuel Bach's music manual which was universally used around the turn of the century. Whether Kleist received musical tuition along these or indeed any lines is a matter of uncertainty. What is certain is that he was *au fait* with the music of Handel, the greatest master of the figured bass, who was very much in vogue at that time and enjoyed an intensive renaissance in Vienna, Berlin and elsewhere[20].)

What is of particular relevance to us here is that Kleist's speculation about the figured bass intimately ties in with his reflections about puppets, arches, aeronautics, pendula and logarithms. The common element in all these is his fascination with what we might call a creative economy capable of being rationalised in a calculus. Such a fascination need not surprise us in a man who always looked for safety devices, ever dogged as he was by the threat to his genius of self-conciousness[21], a man, moreover, who could no more rely on his creative memory than on the continuance of those concerts he spontaneously heard in his mind's ear, unconscious compositions which would vanish at the merest soupçon of reflection. A built-in, self-regulating economy of his resources and a calculus to store them was precisely what he needed[22]. May we not infer that it was as a secret key to his creativity that the figured bass commended itself to him, and that analogously it was the translation of gravitational into antigravitational, of depressive into creational forces which fascinated him in the instances from the sphere of physics, notably the arch?

In the last resort I would suggest that it was for the hard-won cohesiveness and stability of his poetic genius that the arch and the figured bass served as a shorthand, and that it was to this precarious cohesiveness that Kleist gave *sotto voce* utterance in the hard-won satisfaction experienced by the creatures of his imagination. The loss of spontaneity, 'die Verwirrung des Gefühls', and the terrible threat of implosion suffered by his characters were dangers he knew only too well from the inside of his experience as an artist. That the arch stands poised because all its stones want to collapse at once, this unstable and accident-prone genius knew.

5.

Kleist fails us so long as we look to him for large solutions, surmounting the bewildering plurality of opaque particulars by soaring symbolisms. He satisfies us, deeply, in that he patiently and unflinchingly exposed himself to the gravitational stresses of the absolutely real, the inscrutably concrete, without yet ultimately forfeiting coherent structures of integrity and meaningful experience[23]. But such integrity and cohesiveness of experience were bought at prohibitive cost. Never was a poet less sparing in his existential engagement or, dare we say it, more deeply incarnate than was Kleist. With his figures he dwelt in a dark outer space threatening to obliterate him with the blinding onslaught of its visitations, tasting the bitter fruits of his literalmindedness, facing the danger of splintering as artist and man[24], and transcending it through the strength of his loyalty to an impaired yet glorious self and its vision.

So steep was his descent into the sheer stuff of life, into the very body of his medium, that sometimes we feel like crying:

> O! that this too too solid flesh would melt,
> Thaw and dissolve into a dew;

more often we are grateful that through him the word became flesh, voicing its brave *Gloria in Excelsis* from the deeps of the human predicament.

Notes

Notes to Chapter 1

1 Cf. Chapter 14, section 4 and note.

2 This, according to Paul Böckmann, is the hallmark of Kleist's characters. 'Sofern sie sich nicht zieren können,' he observes, 'fehlt ihnen jenes Menschliche, das Goethes Gestalten Lebensnähe und subjektive Wahrheit gibt.' As an illustration Böckmann cites Gretchen's reaction to Faust in front of the church where he first addresses her. ('Kleists Aufsatz "Über das Marionettentheater"' in: *Kleists Aufsatz über das Marionettentheater. Studien und Interpretationen*, ed. W. Müller-Seidel, Berlin, 1967, p. 42.

3 In: *Geist und Buchstabe der Dichtung*, Frankfurt am Main, 1962, p. 297. Cf. also Paul Böckmann, 'Heinrich von Kleist 1777–1811' in: *Genius der Deutschen*, ed. H. Heimpel, Th. Heuss and R. Reifenberg, Berlin, 1966, p. 309 and Hans Heinz Holz: *Macht und Ohnmacht der Sprache. Untersuchungen zum Sprachverständnis und Stil Heinrichs von Kleist*, Frankfurt am Main und Bonn, 1962, both of whom place Kleist's 'Sprachnot' into the centre of their studies, the latter in relation to the dramatic mode.

4 Cf. Donald W. Winnicott, *Collected Papers. Through Paediatrics to Psycho-Analysis*, London, 1958, pp. 145 ff. and 229 ff.; by the same author, *The Maturational Processes and the Facilitating Environment. Studies in the Theory of Emotional Development*, London, 1965, pp. 37 ff.

5 Cf. Susanne K. Langer, *Philosophy in a New Key*, New York, 1948 (Third Printing 1951), p. 101 f. and p. 108. Also E. Cassirer, *An Essay on Man*, New Haven and London, 1944, p. 132.

6 In this connection, cf. D. W. Winnicott, *Playing and Reality*, London, 1971, esp. the chapters on 'The Location of cultural Experience' (pp. 95 ff.) and 'The Place where we live' (pp. 104 ff.).

7 Cf. Chapter 4, p. 72 f.

8 Some critics have interpreted the role of the puppet-master negatively, in the light of such pessimistic allusions to the metaphor as are to be found in Kleist's letters, especially to Ulrike von Kleist, Frankfurt an der Oder, Mai, 1799 (Sembdner No 5) and to Wilhelmine von Zenge, Berlin, 9. April, 1801 (Sembdner No 41). E. L. Stahl (in: *Heinrich von Kleist's Dramas*, Oxford, 1960 (second ed.) p. 36 f.) and R. E. Helbling (in: *The Major Works of Heinrich von Kleist*, New York, 1975, pp. 36 ff.) read the metaphor much as I do, as symbolising a divine motive-force that is benign.

9 This incongruity has, to the best of my knowledge, escaped critics' attention hitherto.

10 Berlin, 5 February, 1801 (Sembdner No 36).

11 [Königsberg], 31. [August 1806] (Sembdner No 97).

12 J. Kunz attributes grace to the youth because and as long as he lived 'im unbewußten Einverständnis mit seinem Spiegelbild'. ('Kleists Gespräch "Über das Marionettentheater"', in: *Kleists Aufsatz über das Marionettentheater*, ed. cit. p. 79). This, on my reading, is an untenable position to adopt.

13 Cf. Chapter 10, section 1.

14 Cf. Chapter 10, section 2.

15 Cf. Chapter 10, section 2.

16 Cf. my *Kant – Goethe – Kleist. Of Knowing and Relating*. An Inaugural Lecture delivered at University of London King's College on 17th February 1976.

[17] Cf. Chapter 6.
[18] Cf. Chapter 4, section 4.
[19] Cf. Chapter 13.
[20] This possibility has not yet been critically explored. The only scholar who has touched on it, in relation to *Prinz Friedrich von Homburg*, is Franz Hafner, in his sensitive study *Heinrich von Kleists 'Prinz Friedrich von Homburg'* (Zürich, 1952, p. 73 f.). W. Müller-Seidel's analysis stops short at this vital point (*Versehen und Erkennen*, Köln/Graz, 1961), and J. Kunz, in an article excitingly entitled 'Das Phänomen der tragischen Blindheit im Werke Kleists' (*GRM, Neue Folge*, XIII, 1963) disappointingly fails to make any real contribution to the subject.

Notes to Chapter 2

[1] H. Meyer-Benfey, *Das Drama H. von Kleists* (Göttingen, 1911), pp. 448, 483.
[2] E. g., Curt Hohoff, in: *Komik und Humor bei Heinrich von Kleist* (Berlin, 1937), p. 44. Cf. also Friedrich Gundolf, *Heinrich von Kleist* (Berlin, 1924), pp. 69 f.
[3] Letter to Fouqué, [Berlin] 25 April, 1811 (Sembdner No 199).
[4] Cf. especially Meyer-Benfey (*op. cit.*). For a predominantly negative attitude, cf. Friedrich Gundolf (*op. cit.*, p. 44); Roger Ayrault, *Heinrich von Kleist* (Paris, 1934), pp. 502 ff.; Julius Forssmann, *Rationalismus und Intuition in H. von Kleists Seelenhaltung und Dichtung* (Riga, 1928), p. 20. Significantly, such studies in depth as Gerhard Fricke, *Gefühl und Schicksal bei Heinrich von Kleist* (Berlin, 1929), and Hanna Hellmann, *Heinrich von Kleist, das Problem seines Lebens und seiner Dichtung* (Heidelberg, 1910), do not discuss the comedy. For more positive views, cf. Walter Muschg, *Kleist* (Zürich, 1923); J. C. Blankenagel, *The Dramas of Heinrich von Kleist: A Biographical and Critical Study* (Chapel Hill, 1931); Friedrich Braig, *Heinrich von Kleist* (München, 1925); E. L. Stahl, *Heinrich von Kleist's Dramas, op. cit.*
[5] The pitcher in the novel is adorned with a scene from the Garden of Eden, and its breakage gives rise to lamentations about the Fall from grace, while Gessner's jug represents the adventures of the gods and goddesses of a prehuman mythological age.
[6] Cf. Meyer-Benfey, *op. cit.*, p. 488. Karl Siegen, *Heinrich von Kleist und Der Zerbrochene Krug* (Sondershausen, 1879), notes the connection between Zschokke's short story and Kleist's nomenclature, but does not pursue the matter any further.
[7] It is curious that critics have time and again taken this grotesque description at its face value, hailing or condemning it, without discerning the underlying point of its absurdity. Meyer-Benfey condemns the passage on the grounds that it is 'eine starke Zumutung an unsere Phantasie, uns auf der Wölbung eines Kruges eine so ausgedehnte, figurenreiche Darstellung auszumalen, die den großen Marktplatz mit Häusern und Kirchenpforten und darauf das Gewimmel so zahlreicher, einzeln erkennbarer Gestalten umfaßt' (*op. cit.*, p. 483). We are not asked to identify ourselves with what Frau Marthe describes, but to note the characteristics of her mode of perception. The representation on the jug itself is by no means impossibly detailed; it is no more crowded than many a mediaeval painting or Renaissance bas-relief. It is Frau Marthe's account of this representation which distorts the perspective and creates the effect of an impossible crowding. This effect is achieved by the reduction of the vast historical reality that is represented to the scale of the material representation with which it is identified. It is an entirely deliberate effect, created to provoke us into an awareness of Frau Marthe's characteristic response. Similarly, Blankenagel misses the point when he praises Frau Marthe's description as 'a masterpiece . . . The figures fairly seem to step forth from their background, endowed with life and colourful individuality' (*op. cit.*, p. 119). Blankenagel does not see that this description far exceeds the limits of what can legitimately be addressed as a realistic account, and that

its whole function lies, not in giving us a vivid impression of the pitcher or the picture on it, but in characterising Frau Marthe's mode of perception.

8 Adam's humour, too, springs from his failure to acknowledge a spiritual reality beyond the palpable reality of material things. But, contrary to Frau Marthe, his failure is caused, not by an inability to recognise spiritual values, but by his unwillingness to submit to their discipline. His is an out and out materialism and opportunism. An exhaustive study of the comic in Kleist's play would necessitate a separate examination of Adam. A study of its thematic structure can dispense with this. The prime mover of the outer action, Adam remains on the fringe of a poetic theme which is concerned with the failure of faith rather than with its deliberate denial.

9 Yet the poet has made it clear that Ruprecht has not solved his problem once and for all. For in the new confusion that arises between Eve and Walter, he mistakes Walter's intentions as readily as he mistook Eve's and with undiminished obtuseness clings to the outward facts.

10 Other instances of signs that are senseless are Adam's wig, token of justice; his faked letter containing the alleged instructions which, significantly enough, Eve cannot read; and the faked certificate of ill health, appropriately called 'der Schein'. All this confusion, it is true, is instigated by Adam. But he has not caused the complexity of this world; he merely exploits it. The bewildering world itself is the ultimate poetic metaphor of every one of Kleist's dramatic works.

11 The various falls are related four times over, at great length, once by Frau Marthe, twice by Ruprecht, and once more by Eve. Such emphasis, far in excess of the requirements of the plot, indicates the thematic importance the poet attaches to the event.

12 [Königsberg], 31. [August 1806] (Sembdner No 97).

Notes to Chapter 3

1 Notably by G. Blöcker who writes: 'Es ist bezeichnend für Kleist, daß er ebenso ungestüm fordert, daß man ihm vertraut, wie er selber ungestüm mißtraut.' (*Heinrich von Kleist oder Das Absolute Ich*, Berlin, 1960, p. 52). For similar observations, cf. also Heinz Ide, *Der junge Kleist . . . in dieser wandelbaren Zeit . . .*, Würzburg, 1961, p. 140.

2 Blöcker aptly calls the drama 'die tragische Groteske des Erkenntnisbankrotts'. (*Op. cit.*, p. 21 f.)

3 Berlin, 22 March, 1801. (Sembdner No 37).

4 Cf. E. Cassirer's classic 'Heinrich von Kleist und die Kantische Philosophie' in: *Idee und Gestalt*, Berlin, 1924, pp. 170 ff.

5 E. g. by H. J. Paton in: *Kant's Metaphysics of Experience. A Commentary on the First Half of the 'Kritik der Reinen Vernunft'* (2 vols.), London and New York, Second Impression, 1951. Vol. I, pp. 166 ff. and p. 183; and by S. Körner in: *Kant*, Pelican, Harmondsworth, 1955, p. 37.

6 B. v. Wiese quotes Eustache's protestation as a *bona fide* expression of the poet's reliance, in that play, on the immediate knowledge of love. (In: *Die deutsche Tragödie von Lessing bis Hebbel* (2 vols.), Hamburg, 1948, Vol. 2, p. 47.) In his most illuminating study entitled: *Die dichterische Entwicklung Heinrich von Kleists*, in: *Philologische Studien und Quellen*, ed. W. Binder, H. Moser, K. Stackmann, Heft 41, Berlin, 1968, H. J. Kreutzer pertinently observes: 'Dies Gefühl wird aber schon in den nächsten Versen durch ihre eigenen Worte widerlegt.' (p. 102). In an impeccably documented campaign against Gerhard Fricke and his followers, Kreutzer demonstrates that ' "Gefühl" kommt nur in einem *Ausschnitt* des Kleistschen Werkes vor und dort nur selten in zentraler Position' and concludes: 'Die Kategorie des Gefühls ist daher kaum geeignet, ein ganzes Werk völlig

aufzuschließen' (p. 104). My own basic position in this book is agreeably confirmed by Kreutzer's findings which came to my attention only after completing my manuscript.

[7] The hard realities behind a person's name are pointed up by Ottokar's airy-fairy manner of bestowing a name of his own choosing upon Agnes, early in the play. Naming, in the stark reality of the lovers here, signifies nothing less than the decisive move in the direction of relatedness and, therewith, identity. Cf. Chapter 1. F. Hafner has good observations to make on the incantatory, almost magical intensity with which Kleist's characters name one another, precisely to bridge the gulf that separates them. (*Op. cit.*, p. 8).

[8] In Stahl's view no character in the play save Ottokar uses his rational powers (*op. cit.*, p. 55). This view, on which his pessimistic reading of the play hinges, I hope to have disproved.

[9] A fact noted by Gundolf (*op. cit.*, p. 32) in an otherwise unfavourable reading of the play, as also by Helbling (*op. cit.*, p. 98).

[10] P. Witkop has pointed out the paradox that in this tragedy it is the blind alone that see. But neither he nor anyone else has, to my knowledge, perceived the universality with which that paradox holds good in Kleist's poetic world, nor indeed recognised that such blindness constitutes a specifically religious organ of knowledge. (*Heinrich von Kleist*, Leipzig, 1921, pp. 61 and 68). Cf. Chapter 8, section 5 and Chapter 10, section 5.

Notes to Chapter 4

[1] The only reference I have found to Kleist's predilection for money and associated imagery – which I consider to be of basic importance and on which much of my argument in this chapter is based – occurs in E. Fischer, 'Heinrich von Kleist', in: *Heinrich von Kleist. Aufsätze und Essays*, ed. W. Müller-Seidel, *Wege der Forschung*, Band CXLVII, Darmstadt, 1967. Fischer notes the recurrent money imagery but considers it to be extraneous and regards Kleist as standing above it (p. 474). Fricke shows some awareness of the importance of Kleist's idiosyncrasy when he cites the poet's use of the word *Erwerb* in relation to truth as an illustration of his profoundly realistic approach to what to him is a religious Absolute; but that is where he leaves the matter (*Op. cit.*, p. 10). It is precisely Kleist's systematic hypostasization of immaterial goods which leads me to challenge Fricke's reading of him as a metaphysical mind, a reading echoed by H. Hellmann who states 'Kleist war Metaphysiker, wie es nur je ein Dichter war' ('Über das Marionettentheater' in: *Kleists Aufsatz über das Marionettentheater. Studien und Interpretationen*, ed. cit., p. 24), as indeed I would reject Blöcker's and Korff's coinage of him as being a 'metaphysischer Realist'. (Blöcker, *op. cit.*, p. 190; H. A. Korff, *Geist der Goethezeit. Versuch einer ideellen Entwicklung der klassisch-romantischen Literaturgeschichte*, 2nd printing of the second revised edition. Vol. IV, *Hochromantik*, Leipzig, 1958, p. 52.)

[2] Stahl rightly stresses the streak of cruel and sadistic teasing in Kleist's make-up (*op. cit.*, p. 31), as indeed Gundolf has emphatically done before him (*op. cit.*, pp. 52, 73, 145).

[3] B. v. Wiese notes 'etwas Unentwickeltes, Infantiles' in Kleist's character (*op. cit.*, p. 25). F. Koch stresses his 'Ichungewißheit' (in: *Heinrich von Kleist. Bewußtsein und Wirklichkeit*, Stuttgart, 1958, p. 53). E. von Reussner comes closest to the position maintained here in arguing, with an almost obsessive monotony which detracts from the value of what purports to be a structural study, that 'das Ich nicht etwas [ist], das für sich ist, sondern das ist, insofern es bezogen ist.' (In: *Satz. Gestalt. Schicksal. Untersuchungen über die Struktur in der Dichtung Kleists*, Berlin, 1961). For psychological studies which, among others, have helped me formulate the view developed here, cf. Chapter 1, notes 4 and 6; also R. D. Laing, *The Divided Self. A Study of Sanity and Madness*, London, 1960, R. D. Laing, *The Self and Others. Further Studies in Sanity and Madness*, London, 1961

and Melanie Klein, Paula Heimann, Susan Isaacs and Joan Riviere, *Developments in Psycho-Analysis*, ed. Joan Riviere, London, 1952.

4 As R. Gray emphasises in relation to Penthesilea, in: '"Jenseits von Sinn und Unsinn" Kleist's *Penthesilea* and its critics', *PEGS New Series*, Vol. XXXVII, 1966–67. In the eyes of Penthesilea, Gray argues, Achilles is 'an object to be commented upon' (p. 63) or 'a possession to be played with' (p. 68), neither of which attitudes adds up to loving.

5 Commenting on this passage, Blöcker seems strangely off the mark. He writes: 'Das ist der Ekel vor der Nacktheit des Erkennens, eines Erkennens, das allerdings nichts mehr mit barer wissenschaftlicher Bemühung zu tun hat, sondern das der Wahrheitsblick des Genies ist.' (*Op. cit.*, p. 60).

6 Blöcker is emphatic on the possibility of an artistic realisation of a creative potential that has not otherwise been lived. His book excels in that he continually stresses the erotic energies involved in the process of art-making which make an artist's life a *lived* life, and sees the necessity of the artist's erotic potential being deployed in this and no other way. His aesthetic position approximates closely to the one I consistently maintain in my two studies on Goethe: *Goethe and Lessing. The Wellsprings of Creation*, London, 1973, and *Goethe: Portrait of the Artist*, Berlin and New York, 1977. Blöcker writes: 'Dichten war für Kleist ein hocherotischer Vorgang, keine Ersatzleistung, sondern effektiver Vollzug.' (*Op. cit.*, p. 40). Again: 'Wenn gesagt worden ist, Kleist sei das Leben mißraten, so muß man die Frage stellen, in welcher Sphäre es für einen Dichter ein Gelingen geben kann, wenn nicht in der des Werkes'. (p. 122).

7 The two most important contributors to this problem – E. Cassirer in his *Heinrich von Kleist und die Kantische Philosophie* (*op. cit.*) and L. Muth in: *Kleist und Kant. Versuch einer neuen Interpretation* (Köln, 1954) – are agreed on the fact that between September 1800 when Kleist was an ardent adherent to Kant's religion of reason and March 1801 when he announced the collapse of all his most sacred convictions through his encounter with Kant's critical philosophy, it must be assumed that Kleist read a philosophical work which showed him Kant's Transcendental Idealism in an entirely novel light. Cassirer assumes that this work was Fichte's *Bestimmung des Menschen*. As against this, Muth advances the thesis that it was the second – teleological – part of Kant's own *Kritik der Urteilskraft*. It is not necessary for me to discuss the merits or demerits of either hypothesis here, because I believe – and have argued – that it did not take the confrontation from the outside, as it were, with any philosophical work for Kleist's development to take the course it did in fact take. As I have tried to show, especially through my analysis of the poet's use of the mirror-image (which has to date received no critical attention), this is a continuous and internal process for which no extraneous catalyst needs to be stipulated. I would in fact maintain that it was Kant's first Critique, in its epistemological sections, the recollection of which might at a given point have triggered off Kleist's devastated reaction, a thesis put forward, on different grounds, by Norbert Thomé in: *Kantkrisis oder Kleistkrisis?* (Philosophical Dissertation, Bonn, 1923). In fact I would think it quite possible – and shall argue it – that the famous sentence from the second introduction 'I had to deny knowledge to make room for faith' was 'the point of the thought' which wounded Kleist's heart 'in seinem heiligsten Innersten'. (Letter to Wilhelmine von Zenge, Berlin, 22 March, 1801).

8 In this connection, see my Inaugural Lecture: *Kant – Goethe – Kleist. Of Knowing and Relating*. (*Op. cit.*).

9 Cf. chapters 5 and 6 of this book.

Notes to Chapter 5

[1] Müller-Seidel stresses the undue 'Sinnengläubigkeit' of Amphitryon and concludes: 'In dem derart übersteigerten Vertrauen in die Verläßlichkeit der Sinne wird Amphitryon zur komischen Figur'. (*Op. cit.*, p. 55). Blöcker, in a section called 'Die Welt im Verhör', argues that Kleist's characters have two possible guides: 'die Offenbarungen des Inneren und der detektivische Verstand. Wo jene ausbleiben, da tritt dieser in Funktion. (*Op. cit.*, p. 141). H. W. Nordmeyer who gives a balanced portrait of Amphitryon, emphasising both the fact that there is after all some qualitative affinity between him and Jupiter who represents his highest potential, and that he undergoes a significant development during the play, pithily writes: 'An seinem Eheproblem nagt er mit allen Zähnen des Verstandes.' (In: 'Kleists "Amphitryon". Zur Deutung der Komödie.' *Monatshefte* Vol. XXXVIII, 1, 2, 3, 4, 1946 and Vol. XXXIX, 2, 1947. Vol. XXXVIII, 3, p. 354.

[2] New York, 1897, p. 23 f.

[3] Th. Mann strangely indicates that Amphitryon's obtuseness is due to lack of reason and intelligence. To him, Amphitryon is the simple, mindless soldier. Altogether in his beautiful essay the degeneration of a complex emotional and spiritual response into a simplistically perceptual one has little part – with one exception: in his opening paragraph, the distinction between *Liebe* and *Treue*, with its emphasis on the inevitable cessation of living memory in time, though ostensibly a personal comment on the author's relation to his subject, anticipates and enshrines the problem of Amphitryon to a nicety: an artist's critical triumph! (In: 'Kleists Amphitryon. Eine Wiedereroberung.' In: *Adel des Geistes, Stockholmer Gesamtausgabe der Werke von Thomas Mann*, Stockholm, 1955, p. 64 and p. 47). For an interpretation closer to my own, cf. Nordmeyer, XXXVIII, 4, pp. 356 and 359.

[4] '. . . the existence of a God . . . could not be intellectually more evident without becoming morally less effective; without counteracting its own end by sacrificing the life of faith to the dead mechanism of a worthless because compulsory assent.' Coleridge, *Biographia Literaria*.

[5] In seeing *Amphitryon* as a precipitate of Kleist's Kant-Crisis, I find myself in agreement with Stahl (*op. cit.*, p. 40).

[6] For a very illuminating discussion of the figure of Jupiter, cf. Fricke (*op. cit.*, pp. 77 ff.), and Nordmeyer (XXXVIII, 1 and 2).

[7] For similar readings, cf. Mann (*op. cit.*, p. 67) and Korff (*op. cit.*, p. 64).

[8] Mann stresses Alkmene's capacity for relatedness as the primary factor of her identity (*op. cit., p. 65) and Nordmeyer goes so far as to equate her 'Du-Gefühl' with her religiosity, a position I would wholeheartedly endorse (XXXIX, 2, especially p. 118). On the other hand, Helbling comments, à propos of Homburg but clearly with a more general application: 'Kleist seems to be expressing the existential insight that the acceptance of the other as an autonomous person is possible only after one has been able to accept oneself.' (*Op. cit.*, p. 239), whilst H. P. Herrmann brilliantly but, to me, not convincingly argues the case, for the novellas, that the '"Ich existiert gar nicht vor der Begegnung mit der zufallsbestimmten Wirklichkeit, sondern wird durch den Zusammenstoß mit ihr überhaupt erst geschaffen; es ist in seinem Wesen reaktiv.' ('Zufall und Ich. Zum Begriff der Situation in den Novellen Heinrich von Kleists'. In: *Heinrich von Kleist. Aufsätze und Essays*, ed. cit., p. 382). Cf. Chapter 1 of this book (p. 15) and notes 4 and 6 to that chapter.

[9] Müller-Seidel and Helbling take exception to Alkmene's identification of the man with the god. Alkmene, to Müller-Seidel, is a confused victim of a Kleistean 'Versehen'; 'auch ihr obliegt das schwierige Geschäft der Unterscheidung' (*op. cit.*, p. 132). Helbling juxtaposes Kleist's own 'Kierkegaardian leap into the uncertainty and loneliness of his personal and existential search' to Alkmene's 'Pascalian fear and trembling before the Infinite' (*op. cit.*, p. 136) and deplores 'the metaphysical shortcomings of her love' (p. 135). As against this, Korff (*op. cit.*, p. 63 f.), Blöcker (*op. cit.*, p. 169) and especially Nordmeyer

(XXXIX, 2) regard this inability to distinguish in an entirely favourable light. Cf. also Staiger's interpretation of Alkmene as a 'vollkommene Mensch'. In: 'Heinrich von Kleist', in: *Heinrich von Kleist. Vier Reden zu seinem Gedächtnis*, ed. W. Müller-Seidel, Berlin 1962, p. 54.

10 Cf. my book *Goethe: Portrait of the Artist*, (*op. cit.*) Chapter 2.

11 B. v. Wiese writes that Jupiter is 'Gegenspieler der Alkmene, der das Göttliche aus ihr erst herausfragt' (*op. cit.*, p. 51). Similarly, M. Kommerell comments beautifully: 'Wie die Folter aus einem Menschen die schlimme Wahrheit hervornötigt, so foltert das Kleistische Schicksal eine Seele, bis sie ihre Wahrheit preisgibt; aber diese Wahrheit heißt: daß die Seele schöner ist, als sie sich selbst gedacht hat.' In: *Geist und Buchstabe der Dichtung*, p. 260.

Notes to Chapter 6

1 This is a point noted by M. Hamburger, in his chapter on Kleist, in: *Reason and Energy*, London, 1957, p. 133.

2 Cf. Hamburger who writes: 'Graf F. is one of those very Kleistean characters who leap before they look; hence his courage, his ardour and his devotion; and hence the impetuosity with which he satisfies his desire for the Marquise.' (*Op. cit.*, p. 133).

3 In a reading which is at pains to stress the marquise's unconscious collusion in the 'unerhörte Begebenheit', Dorrit Cohn points out the wide spectrum of meaning attaching to the word 'wissen' in this story and refers the 'unwissentliche Empfängnis' here to Luther's rendering of Mary's conception of Christ. The marquise's use of that term here would 'seem to indicate that the midwife had not misunderstood her, that the marquise had indeed reached for a miraculous explanation, hoping against hope that immaculate conception occurs not only in the Bible, but also "im Reiche der Natur".' ('Kleist's Marquise von O . . . The Problem of Knowledge', in: *Monatshefte*, Vol. 67, No 2, 1975, p. 136.)

4 Helbing terms what in this study I call 'articles of faith' the 'eloquent object'. Of it he writes: 'When human reason and speech fail to attain clarity, inanimate objects, in an almost surrealistic inversion of function, speak all the more eloquently — for better or for worse.' (*Op. cit.*, p. 68). This would seem to be an appropriate description of the 'Dingsymbole' in, say, Goethe's *Wahlverwandtschaften*; here it will hardly serve. For Kleist's *Indizien* are not born, primarily, of *Sprechnot* — which is the context in which Helbling's statement occurs: they are born of an epistemological confusion which in its turn is set in motion by a deep ontological insecurity. Cf. Chapter 4 of this book.

5 I am using this term in the signification given to it by M. Masud R. Khan in: *The Privacy of the Self*, London, 1974, pp. 219ff., following Winnicott.

6 In: *Meisterwerke deutscher Sprache*, Zürich, 1957.

7 I am unable to agree with the reading of Müller-Seidel who, following Fricke (*op. cit.*, p. 179 and 181) interprets Hohenzollern's 'sich träumend' as signifying the prince's own 'Reflexivität' in his dream state, as the manifestation 'eines von Reflexion gestörten Gefühls', and regards the whole passage as evincing the closest proximity to the anecdote of the Narcissus-like youth in the essay *Über das Marionettentheater*. 'Kleist. Prinz von Homburg' in: *Das Deutsche Drama vom Barock bis zur Gegenwart*, ed. B. v. Wiese, Düsseldorf, 1958, (pp. 389ff. and 400). Cf. also Müller-Seidel's *Versehen und Erkennen*, *op. cit.*, p. 135.

8 Cf. Fricke's 'Kleists "Prinz Friedrich von Homburg"' in which, contrary to the critical interpretation accorded to the prince's somnambulist state in *Gefühl und Schicksal bei Heinrich von Kleist*, a wholly positive one is emphatically advanced which comes much closer to my own reading here and in Chapter 10 of this book. (In: *Studien und Interpretationen*, Frankfurt am Main, 1956, pp. 239, 243f. and 263).

9 Cf. Fricke: 'Es ist der Punkt, da der Prinz, wie fast alle Menschen Kleists, durch die unleugbare und unwiderlegbare Beweiskraft des Wirklichen notwendig und unvermeidlich

in eine ihr ganzes Dasein gefährdende Täuschung und Verwirrung verstrickt wird.' (In: 'Kleists "Prinz Friedrich von Homburg"', *loc. cit.*, p. 243).

10 Müller-Seidel remarks on the sequence of verbs in this apostrophe as being expressive of transience. Of course they are; but it seems to me that their strong kinaesthetic component is of greater importance. In: 'Kleist. Prinz Friedrich von Homburg'. (In: *Das Deutsche Drama vom Barock bis zur Gegenwart, ed. cit.*, p. 391.)

11 Such imagery, which goes back to the Kant-crisis, evokes the subjective aura in which the experience of the individual is inevitably embedded. Kleist has not only time and again articulated this 'intervening context' in imagery of this type: he has enacted it through syntactical devices and in direct scenic presentation. Cf. Chapters 3, 12 and 13 of this study.

12 Cf. Fricke who writes: 'Der reinen Subjektivität entrissen, sieht er sich der reinen Objektivität preisgegeben.' (In: 'Kleists "Prinz von Homburg"', *loc. cit.*, p. 253).

13 In a study which emphasises the prince's artistic temperament placing him into close proximity to Goethe's Tasso, W. Wittkowski stresses the fact that in his confrontation with death he is saved by the interpolation of an image. 'Der Prinz betrachtet und gestaltet [sein Entsetzen]'. (In: 'Absolutes Gefühl und Absolute Kunst in Kleists "Prinz Friedrich von Homburg"'. *DU* 13/2, June 1961.) I would argue that the devastating feature of the *Todesfurchtszene* is precisely the lack of any such mediacy – 'Den schaun die Röhren an der Schützen Schultern/ So gräßlich an . . ./ – a point in fact made by Max Kommerell (*op. cit.*, p. 280) and Arthur Henkel. ('Traum und Gesetz im Prinzen von Homburg', in: *Heinrich von Kleist. Aufsätze und Essays, ed. cit.*, p. 591f.)

14 Cf. Chapter 10 of this book.   15 Cf. Chapter 14, section 1 of this book.

16 It is precisely because of the intervention of a fall – the biblical Fall – that I cannot agree with Lugowski's and Böckmann's reading of Penthesilea as being comparable to a dancing, unconscious puppet in her *Unmittelbarkeit* (Lugowski) or *Unbedingtheit* (Böckmann). The 'fallen' Penthesilea is going through 'the second chapter in the history of the world.' (C. Lugowski in: *Wirklichkeit und Dichtung. Untersuchungen zur Wirklichkeitsauffassung Heinrich von Kleists*, Frankfurt am Main, 1936, p. 177f.; and P. Böckmann in 'Kleists Aufsatz "Über das Marionettentheater"' in: *Kleists Aufsatz über das Marionettentheater. Studien und Interpretationen, ed. cit.*, p. 43). Cf. also Böckmann, 'Heinrich von Kleist. 1777–1811.' *Ed. cit.*, p. 160. For a contrary view, closer to my own, cf. v. Wiese who writes: Penthesilea is *'nicht nur Marionette, sondern tragische Existenz*, die zwischen die Unschuld der Bewußtlosigkeit und die Ursünde des Bewußtseins gestellt ist und deren Seele sich an diesen beiden entgegengesetzten Polen todwund schlägt.' (In: *Die deutsche Tragödie von Lessing bis Hebbel, op. cit.*, p. 59).

17 E. Fischer speaks of 'das verzweifelte Greifen nach dem Unmöglichen' (in: 'Heinrich von Kleist', in *Heinrich von Kleist. Aufsätze und Essays, ed. cit.*, p. 509). Korff speaks of the Kleistean realism which 'in einem Endlichen, wie Penthesilea in Achill, das Absolute zu ergreifen [glaubt] und darum sich umsetzt in jene absolute Leidenschaft zu dem Einem.' He calls this realism metaphysical in that 'die Tiefe und Unbewußtheit dieser Leidenschaft *nicht mehr im Endlichen zu erfüllen ist* und darum das höhere Schicksal in sich trägt . . .' (*op. cit.*, p. 71f.). Explicitly Korff states: in Penthesilea 'wird die Realität durch das Metaphysische gesprengt.' (*Op. cit.*, p. 72). Cf. my Introduction. Interestingly enough, Korff adduces much the same arguments I outline there, in relation, and only in relation, to *Die Hermannsschlacht*. There he judges 'daß eine solche Verabsolutierung des Gefühls keineswegs in Ordnung ist . . . Immerzu verbeißen sich Kleist und seine Helden in irgendein endliches Gefühl, ohne dessen Endlichkeit, d.h. seine immer nur relative Berechtigung zu begreifen. Immerzu wird alles von ihm absolut gesetzt.' (*Op. cit.*, p. 285). Such a rethinking of his basic categories after the Nazi-era does not surprise in relation to *Die Hermannsschlacht*. It should, however, be extended to Kleist's poetic œuvre in its entirety.

¹⁸ Hamburger considers, rightly in my view, that Kleist's characters are habitually beset by a 'confusion of all the faculties'. (*Op. cit.*, p. 135).

¹⁹ Böckmann (in: 'Heinrich von Kleist. 1777–1811', *ed. cit.*, p. 165), v. Wiese (in: *Die deutsche Tragödie* etc., *op. cit.*, p. 63) and Helbling (*op. cit.*, p. 60) all stress the conventional and anonymous modes of thought that are current in the Amazon-state.

²⁰ Cf. Chapter 14, section 3 of this book.

²¹ Cf. Chapter 4, note 4.

²² Cf. K. Jaspers' formulation of Kleist being an 'Absolutist des Konkreten' (In: *Psychologie der Weltanschauungen*, Berlin, 1923, 3. Aufl., p. 400). In contradistinction to the many formulae essayed by critics that tie in Kleist's supposed metaphysical bent with his realism, I consider this to be an eminently acceptable description.

²³ Cf. Chapter 4, section 4, and Chapter 14, section 1.

²⁴ This has of course been variously noted. Cf. e.g. Müller-Seidel (*op. cit.*, p. 221) and Hamburger (*op. cit.*, p. 134).

²⁵ The significance of the mutilated breast is pointed out by B. Blume ('Kleist und Goethe' in: *Heinrich von Kleist, Aufsätze und Essays, ed. cit.*, p. 168) and by C. David (*ibid.*, p. 225). David writes: 'Diese verkehrte, pervertierte Welt wählte Kleist als Symbol der Liebe.'

²⁶ Kommerell writes: 'Das Zwieschlächtige der Leidenschaft, zu verzehren und verzehrt zu werden, hat Kleist zu Ende gedacht nach Maß seiner eigenen Wildheit.' (*Op. cit.*, p. 271). v. Reussner comments: 'Penthesilea sein heißt, sie ist in der Beziehung zu Achill, aber so (indem sie ihn nicht fühlt, als bloßes Ich), daß sie ihn töten muß.' (*Op. cit.*, p. 53). Staiger speaks of the inevitability of disaster in a world 'wo mit den alten Vokabeln der Liebe, der Rede von "Du in mir und ich in Dir" konkretester Ernst gemacht wird.' ('Heinrich von Kleist' in: *Heinrich von Kleist. Vier Reden zu seinem Gedächtnis, ed. cit.*, p. 52).

Notes to Chapter 7

¹ [Berlin], 10 November, 1811.

² Cf. R. Laing, *The Divided Self, op. cit.*, pp. 47 ff.

³ Cf. Chapter 6, note 25.

⁴ Cf. Chapter 6, note 19.

⁵ Critics' views on Achilles are predominantly negative. Cf. Kommerell (*op. cit.*, pp. 274 ff.), v. Wiese (*op. cit.*, p. 62), I. Kohrs (*Das Wesen des Tragischen im Drama Heinrich von Kleists. Dargestellt an Interpretationen von 'Penthesilea' und 'Prinz Friedrich von Homburg'.* Marburg/Lahn, 1951, p. 58 f.), Braig (*op. cit.*, p. 236), Fischer (*ed. cit.*, p. 510) and v. Wiese (*op. cit.*, p. 62). Only Korff characterises him as being 'zart' (*op. cit.*, p. 68 f.), a description with which I would concur whilst stressing his Goethean receptivity and ready submission to the other's law. (Cf. my *Kant – Goethe – Kleist. Of Knowing and Relating, op. cit.*, p. 28).

⁶ Kommerell speaks of Penthesilea's *Amazonentum* as being her 'Denkkategorie'. (*Op. cit.*, p. 250 f.) 'Dieser Begriff (Schablone, Kodex, Einrichtung, Sitte)', he writes, 'wirkt manchmal in ihr nach; sie ist gewohnt, sich nach ihm selbst auszulegen, und beginnt also sich mit sich selbst zu entzweien. Also beeinträchtigt dieser Begriff das Verstehen dessen, der sich ihr nähert.' (*Op. cit.*, p. 257 f.).

⁷ Cf. Blöcker (*op. cit.*, p. 183).

⁸ This point is stressed by Böckmann ('*Heinrich von Kleist. 1777–1811*', *ed. cit.*, pp. 306 ff.), who operates with the conception of a 'Sprachnot' in a paradoxical world that is intractable to language which is governed by the law of contradiction. For a reading along similar lines, cf. Holz (*op. cit.*, pp. 25 and 65 f.).

⁹ To Wilhelmine von Zenge, Berlin, 22 March, 1801.

¹⁰ Cf. D. W. Winnicott, 'String: A Technique of Communication' in: *The Maturational Processes and the Facilitating Environment, op. cit.*, pp. 153 ff.

Notes to Chapter 8

¹ Cf. Blöcker who writes: '. . . seine Menschen [suchen] in tragischer Souveränität und unter Überspringung der geschichtlichen und gesellschaftlichen Kategorien die Pforte zur Wahrheit aufzureißen und unmittelbar mit dem Universum in Kontakt zu treten . . . Ein Mensch, der, herausgehoben aus dem Menschenbürgerlichen und doch ins Menschenbürgerliche gebannt, ebenso erschreckend ist in seiner Nacktheit und selbstzerstörerischen Glut wie bezaubernd in seiner lächelnden Unschuld . . .' (*op. cit.*, p. 16).

² Helbling comments: 'It is as though they wanted to force others to accept unquestioningly their inner vision of truth and goodness on a frantic attempt to overcome their inner isolation.' (*Op. cit.*, p. 53 f.).

³ Böckmann notes the paradoxial quality of Hermann's quest (*ed. cit.*, p. 167).

⁴ This has been frequently noted, first by Kommerell who argues that the fountain-head of Kleist's drama is 'Charakter als Rätsel' (*op. cit.*, p. 245 f.), and asks: 'Hat Kleist je etwas anderes geschaffen als unaussprechliche Menschen?' (*Op. cit.*, p. 244). Cf. also Müller-Seidel (*op. cit.*, p. 99) and Helbling (*op. cit.*, p. 48).

⁵ Cf. Helbling who writes: 'The backdrop to the existential experience of his [i. e. Kleist's] heroes is the *deus absconditus*, the hidden, mysterious but nevertheless omnipotent God of Protestant theology.' (*Op. cit.*, p. 49). For a similar assessment of *Der Zweikampf*, cf. Müller-Seidel who comments: 'Die neue "Theologie" in der Optik der Erzählung meint den deus absconditus.' (*Op. cit.*, p. 95).

⁶ Helbling speaks of 'Man's "alienation" from a reality that has become impenetrable and chaotic' (*op. cit.*, p. 50).

⁷ Blöcker writes: 'Ein Unbedingter vom Schlage Kleists korrigiert seine Bewußtseinswelt nicht, um sich vor dem Scheitern zu bewahren; er verwirklicht sie im Werk, und sei es um den Preis des Lebens.' (*Op. cit.*, p. 122).

⁸ In this context Müller-Seidel's rubrics of the 'Fraglichkeit der typischen Denkweise' and 'Der Einbruch in die vermeintliche geordnete Welt' are illuminating (*op. cit.*, pp. 43 ff. and 80 ff.).

⁹ Böckmann quotes the 'Satz vom Widerspruch' in this connection and comments: 'Das Rätselhafte wirkt bedrängend, weil es der in der Sprache angelegten Logik widerstreitet.' (*Ed. cit.*, p. 163).

¹⁰ Lugowski adduces the illustration of *Amphitryon*, where the diadem is the incontrovertible piece of objective evidence and contradictoriness is pursued to the point 'wo der Wahnsinn beginnt'. (*Op. cit.*, p. 145). He rightly stresses '. . . die ganze Gegnerschaft des beweisbaren Wirklichen gegen den allein gelassenen Menschen'. (*Op. cit.*, p. 145 f.) Cf. also Koch, *op. cit.*, p. 38.

¹¹ Müller-Seidel emphasises the Romantics' love of the paradox and maintains, correctly in my view, that this is a Christian legacy (*op. cit.*, p. 121).

¹² Lugowski writes: 'Kleist zwingt ihn [den kämpfenden Menschen] . . . mit den furchtbarsten Mitteln, in seinem Kampf ganz und gar und überhaupt auf allen Halt objektiver Erkenntnis zu verzichten' (*op. cit.*, p. 157).

¹³ Blöcker (*op. cit.*, p. 178) maintains as I do that the marquise is in an unconscious collusion with the count, a thesis Helbling (*op. cit.*, p. 149) rejects.

¹⁴ This point is made by Müller-Seidel (*op. cit.*, p. 111).

¹⁵ A point made by Müller-Seidel (*op. cit.*, p. 132 and 202) and grossly overstated by Helbling (*op. cit.*, p. 135 f.).

16 A number of critics, amongst them Fricke (*op. cit.*, p. 146), Müller-Seidel (*op. cit.*, p. 85), Herrmann (*loc. cit.*, p. 400f.) and Helbling (*op. cit.*, p. 48) maintain that here as elsewhere Kleist moves in a religious dimension, the link with Christianity being variously assessed. Lugowski emphatically rejects any religious reading. He argues that all Kleist was concerned to do through the introduction of the divine ordeal was to construct a case resting on incontrovertible evidence challenging the inner sureness of his characters (*op. cit.*, p. 162).

17 A number of critics maintain, as I do, that in the feeling-experience of faith an organ of cognition is disclosed. The link with blindness here and elsewhere has been noted. (But cf. note 28 to chpt. 10.) Cf. my Introduction and Chapter 10, sections 2 and 5. F. Röbbeling writes: 'Das Gefühl ist gleichsam die Seele der Seele. Es ist ein höheres *Wahrnehmungsvermögen* und zugleich ein intuitives *Erkenntnisvermögen*, denn es dringt aus dem Sinnenschein zum Wesen vor und schlägt den Verstand aus dem Felde.' (In: *Kleists Käthchen von Homburg*, Halle, 1913, p. 57). Similarly, F. Hafner maintains: 'Es [das Gefühl] ist das einzige Organ, das die Welt in ihrem Wesen zu erkennen vermag.' (In: *Heinrich von Kleists 'Prinz Friedrich von Homburg'*, Zürich, 1952, p. 9). Blöcker comments: 'Fühlen . . . wird zu einem Mittel der Wahrnehmung . . . das Gefühl [tritt] aus der Sphäre bloßer Empfindsamkeit in die einer emotionalen Geistigkeit über'. It is 'ein Instrument der Erkenntnis'. (*Op. cit.*, p. 163). Kreutzer points out that the conception of feeling as an organ of cognition dates back to before Kleist and cannot be regarded as his 'discovery'. (*Op. cit.*, p. 86).

18 J. Ellis is much concerned to stress the ambiguity of the teleological evaluations in the story ('Kleist's *Das Erdbeben in Chili*', *PEGS*, N.S., Vol. XXXIII, 1962–63), a thesis echoed by Helbling (*op. cit.*, pp. 110ff.).

Notes to Chapter 9

1 Cf. Kleist's letter to H. J. von Collin, Dresden, 8 December, 1808. (Sembdner No 141.)

2 The paradoxial nature of the *Gewölbe*-image familiar from *Penthesilea* is well brought out in Blöcker's formulation: 'Das ist das Bild der positiven Katastrophe: die Summe unserer Hinfälligkeiten läßt uns aufrecht stehen'. (*Op. cit.*, p. 58).

3 By Walter Silz ('Das Erdbeben in Chili', in *Heinrich von Kleist, Aufsätze und Essays*, *ed. cit.*, p. 354).

4 W. Kayser regards this episode as being a 'glatter Stilbruch' (in: *Die Vortragsreise*, Bern, 1958, p. 175), a judgment rightly repudiated by Ellis (*loc. cit.*, p. 27). Ellis states that the idyll 'makes us uneasy' and goes on to ask: 'is it not all too good to be true?' (*ibid.*) In my own view, this kind of *ritardando* in the middle-section of a Kleistean novella or drama is entirely characteristic of him. Cf. chapter 13, p. 233.

5 Both Kayser (*op. cit.*, p. 234f.) and Ellis (*loc. cit.*, p. 40f.) point out that a series of teleological judgments which are mutually incompatible is made, and that the narrator himself is 'interpreting the story as he goes along' (Ellis, p. 41), groping for understanding from stage to stage.

6 The narrator's 'Als-Ob' constructions have been variously noted and critically utilised. Müller-Seidel, in an excellent analysis of the story, argues that the lovers 'versehen sich im Als-Ob Charakter der Welt' (*op. cit.*, p. 139). Ellis maintains that the interpretation of the various 'Als-Ob' teleological judgments advanced or implied by the narrator constitutes the very theme of the story which dismisses us 'sceptical even of scepticism as a reaction to the world'. (*Loc. cit.*, p. 54). W. Wittkowski maintains that the teleological 'Als-Ob' attitude of the narrator is matched, and transcended, by the 'Noblesse' of characters who consistently act 'as though' the moral maxims which govern their behaviour were binding. He writes: '. . . im *Erdbeben* wie sonst . . . verbindet

Kleist das Dekorativ-Zeremonielle, das Anmutige aristokratischer Gesellschaftsformen mit den Tugenden der Noblesse zu einem innerlich wie äußerlich schönen Verhalten von unbestrittener ethischer Verbindlichkeit . . . Sie allein bleibt siegreich übrig, nachdem die metaphysische Frage als verfehlt abgetan wurde. Nicht ein religiöser Glaube, sondern allein das praktische moralische Verhalten macht die wahrhaft existentielle Dimension aus und die Qualität solchen Verhaltens den eigentlichen Wert des Menschen. Das ist die "Botschaft" dieser Dichtung.' ('Skepsis, Noblesse, Ironie. Formen des Als-Ob in Kleists *Erdbeben*', in: *Euph.* 63, 1969, p. 254).

[7] Ellis stresses the self-centredness of this judgment. 'Their arrogance is disturbing, and their confidence even more so', he writes (*loc. cit.*, p. 27). Wittkowski repudiates Ellis' judgment, arguing that the lovers use causal but not teleological categories, a position which in view of the final 'damit' to me seems untenable. (*Loc. cit.*, p. 251).

[8] By reason of the formal link between the flower simile and the description of the deeds performed — both are similarly 'ungrounded' and transcend the nexus of mechanical causation — I would adjudge this passage to be the central one of the story. It is a metaphor of the — equally ungrounded — faith in which it culminates. Cf. below, p. 167.

[9] This is the second time that an affirmative teleological judgment issues in a reference to the lovers' self-centred plan of rescue. The two seem geared to one another. The poet seems to be driving home the fact that, for pure faith to flower, all cognitive supports and all provisos to total self-giving need to be withdrawn. Thus I would tend to disagree with both Ellis' and Wittkowski's judgment that the story dismisses us into a metaphysical void. Most certainly it does not dismiss us into a religious one.

[10] This would seem to be Wittkowski's, Helbling's (*op. cit.*, p. 108) and, with certain provisos, Ellis' final verdict which I am unable to accept.

Notes to Chapter 10

[1] This question needs to be asked in all seriousness, in view of the regressive formulation Kleist himself uses at the end of *Über das Marionettentheater*.

[2] To Wilhelmine von Zenge, Berlin, 16 (and 18) November, 1800. (Sembdner No 28.)

[3] Blöcker reads the faints as '. . . Erneuerung aus den Elementarbeständen des Seins.' 'Alle Höhepunkte Kleists sind ein Versinken.' (*Op. cit.*, p. 86). Koch writes, in a more negative vein: 'Die endgültige, unabwendbare Zerstörung der Bewußtseinswelt findet ihren Ausdruck in der Ohnmacht.' (*Op. cit.*, p. 42. Cf. also p. 196).

[4] To Wilhelmine von Zenge, Würzburg, 19(−23) September, 1800. (Sembdner No 23.)

[5] Cf. my *Goethe: Portrait of the Artist* (*op. cit.*, Chapter 10).

[6] Cf. Blöcker, *op. cit.*, pp. 197 ff.

[7] For a different view, cf. W. Müller-Seidel, 'Die Struktur des Widerspruchs in Kleists "Marquise von O. . ."'. (In: *Kleist. Reden und Aufsätze*, ed. cit., p. 259.)

[8] Blöcker formulates: 'Das absolute Ich tritt seine Herrschaft an, unbeeinträchtigt vom Bewußtsein des Endlichen, sicher beheimatet in der Ewigkeit des Seins und ausgestattet mit der Anmut der Unschuld und der Unfehlbarkeit des Spontanen.' (*Op. cit.*, p. 196).

[9] *Etwas über die erste Menschengesellschaft nach dem Leitfaden der mosaischen Urkunde.* (1790)

[10] This circularity has been noted, and variously interpreted, by M. Garland, (*Kleist's Prinz Friedrich von Homburg. An Interpretation through Word Patterns*, The Hague, Paris, 1968, p. 40), M. Ellis (*Kleist's 'Prinz Friedrich von Homburg'. A Critical Study*. Berkeley, Los Angeles, London, 1970, pp. 58 ff.), and Helbling (*op. cit.*, pp. 237 ff.) whose reading follows that of Ellis which in my view overinterprets the text.

[11] Kommerell, *op. cit.*, p. 311.

[12] W. Wittkowski in 'Absolutes Gefühl und Absolute Kunst in Kleists "Prinz Friedrich von Homburg"' (*loc. cit.*, p. 62).

[13] By Wittkowski who writes: 'Tatsächlich rückt Kleist seine Figuren . . . auch dem Kind, dem Tier, dem Gliedermann [nahe]' (*loc. cit.*, p. 68). This formulation implicitly raises the question whether the transcendence of consciousness for Kleist means progress or regress. Cf. also A. Henkel's perceptive remark '. . . es ist, als schaue er [Kleist] mit geheimem Neid auf das sichere, unbewußte Tier'. ('Traum und Gesetz in Kleists "Prinz von Homburg". Ein Vortrag', in: *Heinrich von Kleist. Aufsätze und Essays*, ed. *cit.*, p. 580.)

[14] Both Hafner (*op. cit.*, p. 49) and Ellis (*op. cit.*, pp. 64ff.) explore this episode and its imagery, however in relation to the elector, and come to diametrically opposed conclusions. Whilst Hafner stresses the elector's self-control and willingness to give up his horse, Ellis, in a study intent on tracing the Oedipal rivalry between the older and the younger man, emphasises the elector's competitiveness and impetuosity. In its entirety, Ellis' study raises the problem of the fruitfulness of depth-psychology as a tool of literary criticism. His observations are often convincing in detail; yet they leave one with a picture of the drama as a whole which seems altogether too far removed from the poet's intent to compel one's full assent.

[15] Hafner comments: 'Wie der Reiter von seinem Pferd getragen wird, so lassen sich die Kleistischen Helden von ihren Trieben davontragen.' (*Op. cit.*, p. 34).

[16] Stahl remarks that like Natalie, Kottwitz 'defends a principle of anarchy'. (*Op. cit.*, p. 108).

[17] Among others, by S. Burckhardt who devotes a chapter to a comparison of the two dramas (in: *The Drama of Language. Essays on Goethe and Kleist*, Baltimore and London, 1970, pp. 94ff.), K. Mommsen, (*Kleists Kampf mit Goethe*, Heidelberg, 1974, pp. 164ff.) and B. Blume, 'Kleist und Goethe', (in: *Heinrich von Kleist, Aufsätze und Essays*, ed. *cit.*, p. 176f.). Blume perceptively adduces the sleep-walking motif in both dramas as the effective link between them.

[18] A trend especially predominant in Fricke (*op. cit.*, pp. 179ff.) but rescinded, without overt mention, in his later interpretation 'Kleists "Prinz von Homburg"', (in: *Studien und Interpretationen*, Frankfurt am Main, 1956). For a predominantly negative interpretation, cf. also Müller-Seidel (*op. cit.*, p. 135) and in 'Kleist. Prinz Friedrich von Homburg', in: *Das Deutsche Drama vom Barock bis zur Gegenwart* (ed. *cit.*, pp. 389ff.), and Helbling (*op. cit.*, pp. 217ff.).

[19] Of the glove incident Fricke writes: 'Es ist der Punkt, da der Prinz, wie fast alle Menschen Kleists, durch die unleugbare und unwiderlegliche Beweiskraft des Wirklichen notwendig und unvermeidlich in eine ihr ganzes Dasein gefährdende Täuschung und Verwirrung verstrickt wird.' (In: Kleists 'Prinz von Homburg', in: *Studien und Interpretationen*, *op. cit.*, p. 243).

[20] This is the position held by Kommerell (*op. cit.*, p. 288).

[21] P. Ernst, *Der Zusammenbruch des Deutschen Idealismus*, München, 1918, p. 306.

[22] Korff, *op. cit.*, p. 302f.

[23] Aussee, 13. IX, [1912].

[24] A number of critics have recognised the religious and, more specifically, Christian overtones of this act of forgiveness. Cf. Fricke, *Gefühl und Schicksal bei Heinrich von Kleist*, who writes: 'Wahrhaft und völlig vergeben kann nur Gott' and argues that a genuine analogy can be seen to exist between the prince's spiritual transformation and the 'christlichen, realpersonhaften Begriff der Wiedergeburt' (p. 193). Similarly Koch maintains that 'das Verhältnis von Kurfürst und Prinz . . . steht in Parallele zu dem Verhältnis von Gott und Mensch im Neuen Testament' (*op. cit.*, p. 245). Koch sees in this relationship a reflection of the parable of the prodigal son (*op. cit.*, p. 246f.). Cf. also Braig (*op. cit.*, p. 406) and Müller-Seidel (*op. cit.*, p. 186 and *loc. cit.*, p. 403).

25 Koch writes: 'Im Evangelium redet Gott nicht mittelbar (wie im Gesetz . . .), sondern unmittelbar personhaft zum Menschen, ebenso wie der Kurfürst in seinem Brief den Prinzen personhaft anredet.' (*Op. cit.*, p. 256).

26 To Marie von Kleist, [Berlin, 19 November 1811]. (Sembdner No 233.) Hafner has noted this link (*op. cit.*, p. 74 f.).

27 For widely divergent readings of this end, cf. Wittkowski (*loc. cit.*, pp. 62 ff.) and Ellis (*op. cit.*, p. 95 f.). Wittkowski maintains that there is no resolution of the dichotomy between the individual and the law save 'musikalisch, zeichenhaft, "absolut" . . . als *trügerischer Schein* . . .' (*loc. cit.*, p. 64), whilst Ellis argues that there is no real reconciliation between the rival figures of the elector and the prince (*op. cit.*, p. 96). In his most sensitive reading of the drama, Henkel, too, casts doubt on the permanence of the solution that has been achieved ('Traum und Gesetz in Kleists "Prinz von Homburg"' in: *Heinrich von Kleist. Aufsätze und Essays*, ed. *cit.*, p. 604).

28 Hafner and Garland are amongst the few that have noted the dialectic of seeing and blindness here. Hafner writes: 'Er, der so lange mit offenen Augen blind war, ist bei geschlossenen sehend geworden.' (*Op. cit.*, p. 73 f.) Garland speaks of 'the triumph of insight and recognition over sight' and remarks on Kleist's masterly exploitation of the 'ambivalence of the words of vision.' (*Op. cit.*, p. 67).

29 Henkel writes beautifully: 'Es gibt für Kleist – auch vor dem Tod – keine Entweltlichung, die das Seiende abwertet. Selbst in der zarten Geste der Zerstreutheit nimmt der Prinz . . . noch die Essenzen der schönen Welt wahr.' ('Traum und Gesetz in Kleists "Prinz von Homburg"', in: *Heinrich von Kleist, Aufsätze und Essays, ed. cit.*, p. 602).

30 To Marie von Kleist [Berlin, 19 November, 1811]. (Sembdner No 223.)

Notes to Chapter 11

1 Cf. e.g. Lugowski who writes, in connection with the Kant-crisis: '. . . indem sie [die Ethik] sich an den Menschen überhaupt wendet, sind ihre Antworten zunächst außerwirklich und müssen von dem jeweils Handelnden erst in Wirkliches umgesetzt werden. Dazu war Kleist unfähig, und zwar deshalb, weil es für ihn eine unvollziehbare Vorstellung war, seine geschichtliche Wirklichkeit hier und jetzt auf dem Umweg über eine Idee wiederzugewinnen. An dieser Unfähigkeit zur Abstraktion brach Kleist letzthin zusammen.' (*Op. cit.*, p. 221). Similarly, Blöcker speaks of 'Kleists völlige Unfähigkeit zu abstrahieren' (*op. cit.*, p. 62) and emphasises his 'Mangel an Abstraktionsvermögen, das Un- und Antispirituelle seiner Natur' (p. 161). More cautiously, Burckhardt remarks on Kleist's singularly keen awareness of 'the opposed pulls of concreteness and abstractness' (*op. cit.*, p. 134).

2 Frankfurt an der Oder, 12 November, 1799. (Sembdner No 6.)

3 Cf. Chapter 4, section 1.

4 Cf. G. Ritter who writes: 'We . . . find consolation in the sacrament, not merely in a meal of remembrance, "not in the bread and wine, nor in the body and blood of Christ, but in the Word, which in the sacrament offers, presents, and gives to me the body and blood of Christ which was given and shed for me", a formulation . . . whose religious intention is clear, but which makes the sacramental process for the first time really enigmatic.' ('The Founder of the Evangelical Churches', in: *Luther. A Profile*, ed. H. G. Koenigsberger, London, 1973, p. 84 f.).

5 I am grateful to Professor James Cargill Thompson, of King's College, London, for clarifying this point in personal conversation.

6 In: *Die Kirche des Herrn. Meditationen über Wesen und Auftrag der Kirche*, Herder-Bücherei Bd. 307, Würzburg, 1965, p. 35.

that of H. P. Herrmann who observes, in a brilliant article, 'Kleists Menschen schauen immer "hinaus".' ('Zufall und Ich. Zum Begriff der Situation in den Novellen Heinrich von Kleists', in: *Heinrich von Kleist, Aufsätze und Essays, ed. cit.*, p. 391).

[2] Müller-Seidel stresses the fact that, through his relation to his sovereign, Kohlhaas' 'Rechtsgefühl' takes on a peculiarly personal complexion (*op. cit.*, p. 108 f.).

[3] Kohlhaas' innate sense of justice and moderation is denied by S. Zweig who condemns him as a fanatic (in: *Der Kampf mit dem Dämon. Hölderlin, Kleist, Nietzsche.* Leipzig, 1925, p. 175). It is stressed by v. Wiese ('Michael Kohlhaas', in: *Die Deutsche Novelle von Goethe bis Kafka. Interpretationen*, Düsseldorf, 1956) and heavily emphasised by Fricke who writes: 'So hat der Dichter alles nur Mögliche getan, um seinen Helden als das Gegenteil eines Rechtsfanatikers, Absolutisten oder radikalen Weltverbesserers zu erweisen' (in: 'Michael Kohlhaas'. *Studien und Interpretationen, op. cit.*, p. 218). Helbling adopts a middle of the road course, arguing that Kohlhaas develops from 'his megalomaniac pretence to restore justice to the world' to the subtle awareness 'that he was really defending his dignity as a person' (*op. cit.*, p. 208).

[4] Wiese similarly argues that for Kohlhaas his horses have 'eine nicht nur reale, sondern zugleich auch eine stellvertretende Bedeutung' (*loc. cit.*, p. 53).

[5] Fricke identifies this phase by distinguishing between Kohlhaas' 'reines Gefühl' and a faulty 'zeitliches Bewußtsein' which overlays and corrupts it for a while. I consider this latter, his favourite category, to be suspect: it smuggles in through a backdoor Kant's distinction between the empirical and the pure, transcendental self which he has taken such pains to throw out.

[6] Cf. Chapter 4, section 1.

[7] In his more recent analysis, Fricke exonerates Kohlhaas from such negative evaluations, maintaining, wrongly in my view, that they are expressive of contemporary opinion such as that of the chronicler (*loc. cit.*, p. 228).

[8] For a scholarly discussion of the emergence of the concept of the state, cf. J. H. Hexter, '*Il Principe* and *lo Stato*', in: *Studies in the Renaissance*, Vol. IV, 1957. Hexter writes: '. . . at the beginning of the fifteenth century the term [the state] was not used in its modern political sense in any western European language and . . . by the seventeenth century it was frequently so used in all of them.' (p. 115.)

[9] B. v. Wiese (*loc. cit.*, p. 48), Herrmann (*loc. cit.*, p. 373) and Helbling (*op. cit.*, p. 200) all stress what Hermann calls the 'Gestrüpp undurchdringlicher Verwandtschaftsverhältnisse und Instanzenzüge' in which Kohlhaas' cause is lost.

[10] B. v. Wiese (*loc. cit.*, p. 55 f.).

[11] First Epistle of St. John the Apostle, Chapter I.

Notes to Chapter 13

[1] Cf. my *Goethe and Lessing: The Wellsprings of Creation* (London, 1973), Chapter 5.

[2] To Marie von Kleist [Berlin, Sommer 1811]. (Sembdner No 212.)

[3] Cf. Kleist's letter to Ulrike von Kleist, Leipzig, 13 (and 14) March, 1803. (Sembdner No 72.) Kommerell comments: 'Hat sich je ein Dichter sonst so unmittelbar als einen unaussprechlichen Menschen bezeichnet? Hat Kleist je etwas anderes geschaffen als unaussprechliche Menschen?' (*Op. cit.*, p. 244).

[4] *Über die neuere deutsche Literatur*, dritte Sammlung von Fragmenten (*Werke*, ed. Th. Matthias, Bibliographisches Institut, Leipzig und Wien, no date, vol. I, p. 168 f.).

[5] Stahl maintains that Kleist 'only rejected form . . . which is imposed upon any material, regardless of its quality.' (*Op. cit.*, p. 29 f.) There is support for this statement in Kleist's letters; it is certainly not true of this, his culminating essay.

6 F. Beissner elevates the oscillating rhythm of 'stauenden, stockenden, schachtelnden Passagen und andern, gelösteren, befreiten, ebenmäßigen' into the ruling principle of Kleist's style: surely this is overstating the case for Kleist's 'released' passages. ('Unvorgreifliche Gedanken über den Sprachrhythmus', in: *Festschrift Paul Kluckhohn und Hermann Schneider gewidmet zu ihrem 60. Geburtstag*, Tübingen, 1848, p. 143.)

7 The tripartite form, notably of *Penthesilea* and *Das Erdbeben*, has of course often been commented upon. In the latter it has given rise to Kayser's charge of a 'Stilbruch' on the part of the poet. (Cf. Chapter 9, note 4.)

8 Cf. Herrmann's excellent analysis of sentences of the type 'es traf sich . . .; dergestalt, daß . . .', which permit Kleist 'in seiner von Zufällen regierten Welt immer wieder Zusammenhang zu stiften, ohne den Ereignissen etwas von ihrer gewaltsamen Unmittelbarkeit zu nehmen.' ('Zufall und Ich', *loc. cit.*, p. 375 f.)

9 Beissner rejects Kommerell's thesis of the 'Mühe des Sprechens', a thesis adopted by Böckmann (*loc. cit.*, p. 163) and Holz (*op. cit.*, p. 25 ff.). Beissner maintains: 'Immer ist es das Ich, dem ein Widerstand sein Ziel verstellen will, und der gestaltende Dichter kommt ihm zu Hilfe, indem er es eifervoll aufstutzt oder es andrerseits dem an seinem Widerstand wachsen läßt.' (*Loc. cit.*, p. 439); cf. also Hafner (*op. cit.*, p. 20 f.).

10 A very good analysis of this sentence and the whole Mirabeau passage is given by Holz (*op. cit.*, pp. 27 ff.).

11 Herrmann writes: '. . . erst, wenn ein Mensch durch besondere Ereignisse gezwungen wird festzustellen, was er weiß, ohne den Widerspruch abweisen zu können, der sich ihm ebenfalls aufdrängt, erst bei solcher Bedrohung der Sinneinheit der Welt kommt sein Ich, als gefährdetes Vertrauen, zu sich selbst. Die Gefährdung des Ich durch die Gefährdung der Einheit der Welt durchzieht als Grundproblematik, offen oder verdeckt, alle Novellen Kleists'. (*Loc. cit.*, p. 397 f.) I would wholeheartedly agree with this statement, and with Herrmann's demonstration of it on the level of Kleist's syntax, but for one – admittedly all-important – reversal of emphasis: where Herrmann regards the Ich as a 'Funktion der Wirklichkeit' (p. 397), I would regard the ambiguous reality as a function of the cognitively simplistic I. Cf. also Helbling's interesting observation that 'Kleist seems to be striving desperately to see "order" . . . in apparent disorder. Thus the syntax would have the function of interpretative commentary' (*op. cit.*, p. 68 f.), and Burckhardt's magnificent *aperçu*: 'If there is one thing that characterizes Kleist . . . it is his obsessive need and will to create orders which leave the particularity of things intact. His typical prose sentence is the syntactic analogue of his mature stories: a bitterly fought, hard-won battle between the multifarious "incidental" elements of experience that demand recognition and the periodic syntax that must shape them into an intelligible, orderly whole.' (*Op. cit.*, p. 134).

12 Kleist's isolation of the grammatical subject has received various interpretations. Staiger sees it as expressive of Kleist's tendency towards drama, in that the isolated subject is analogous to the name 'der sprechenden Person im Dialog.' ('Das Bettelweib von Locarno', *loc. cit.*, p. 106). He comes closer to my own position at the end of the essay when he speaks of the dramatist's claim to make sense of the world and his 'Probe, ob die Einigung mit dem, was gegenübersteht, gelingt. Die Isolierung des Subjekts am Anfang des Satzes ist dafür der adäquate grammatische Ausdruck (p. 116). Herrmann argues that the isolation of the subject is nothing but the 'ganz formale "Vertrauen"' of the speaker that he will be able to fit impingements from the outside into the nascent unity of his period. 'Sich durchzusprechen von einem Einzelnen, dem Unerwartetes zustößt, über die Ereignisse, die ihm begegnen, zum umgreifenden Allgemeinen, das im Bauplan des Satzes verheißen ist, aber erst im Konkreten eingelöst wird: das ist der Ablauf des Kleistschen Satzes, wie es der Ablauf etwa der Kohlhaas-Novelle, der "Marquise von O." und des "Zweikampf" ist . . .' ('Zufall und Ich', *loc. cit.*,

p. 406 f.). Cf. the previous note for the similarity of this position to that adopted by Burckhardt.

13 Helbling tentatively adopts a similar position when he states: '. . . the many interpolations could serve the purpose of rendering immediately the onrush of a welter of perceptions in mosaic-like fashion' (*op. cit.*, p. 68 f.).

14 Cf. Chapter 12, note 9.

15 Cf. Staiger's interesting comments on this passage. 'Heinrich von Kleist', in: *Heinrich von Kleist. Vier Reden zu seinem Gedächtnis*, ed. *cit.*, p. 51 f.

16 I am grateful to Professor Heinz Post of Chelsea Polytechnic for explaining to me, in personal conversation, the physics of the arch.

17 *Über die neuere deutsche Literatur*, dritte Sammlung von Fragmenten, ed. *cit.*, p. 166 f.

18 To Heinrich Joseph von Collins, Dresden, 14 February, 1808. (Sembdner No 130.)

19 To Luise von Zenge, Paris, 16 August, 1801. (Sembdner No 52.)

20 Fischer speaks of a process of 'Sprachzertrümmerung'. 'Die Metapher nimmt sich selbst beim Wort.' ('Heinrich von Kleist' in: *Heinrich von Kleist. Aufsätze und Essays*, ed. *cit.*, p. 496 f.).

21 To Marie von Kleist [Dresden, late autumn, 1807]. (Sembdner No 118.)

22 Cf. the − by now famous − controversy between F. Sengle ('Vom Absoluten in der Tragödie' *D. VjS.* XX, Heft 3, 1942) and W. Rasch ('Tragik und Tragödie. Bemerkungen zur Gestaltung des Tragischen bei Kleist und Schiller', in: *D. VjS.* XXI, Heft 3, 1943) which pivots on the interpretation of these speeches.

23 Gray takes particular exception to this speech because 'Penthesilea means the similarity of sound . . . to be taken seriously.' He also critically notes the 'slip of the tongue' in the following passage. ('"Jenseits von Sinn und Unsinn" Kleist's *Penthesilea* and its critics', *loc. cit.*, p. 72.)

24 S. Ullmann writes: 'It is an essential feature of a metaphor that there must be a certain distance between tenor and vehicle. Their similarity must be accompanied by a feeling of disparity; they must belong to different spheres of thought. If they are too close to one another, they cannot produce the perspective of 'double vision' peculiar to metaphor.' (In: *Style in the French Novel*, Cambridge, 1957, p. 214).

25 Burckhardt's judgment that 'Thusnelda is made to re-enact man's rise from the beginning' would be more appropriate to Penthesilea. (*Op. cit.*, p. 157.)

26 To Marie von Kleist [Dresden, late autumn, 1807]. (Sembdner No 116.)

27 Cf. E. Cassirer's valuable distinction, in relation to the development of linguistic forms, between the three subsequent phases 'des mimischen, analogischen und des symbolischen Ausdrucks'. In: *Philosophie der symbolischen Formen*, 2nd edition, Oxford, 1954, Vol. 2, p. 284.

28 Pasewalk, 20 August, 1800. (Sembdner No 13.)

29 To Karl Freiherrn von Stein zum Altenstein, Königsberg, 4 August [1806]. (Sembdner No 96.)

30 Kommerell deliciously comments: 'Vielleicht soll dies viele Geräusch mit Worten die angemessene Rede eines Menschen sein, . . . der sich selbst noch nach ritterlicher Schablone denkt.' (*Op. cit.*, p. 302).

Notes to Chapter 14

1 To Adam Heinrich Müller, Karlsbad, 28 August, 1807.

2 *Seelenprobleme der Gegenwart*, Zürich, 1946, p. 276.

3 *The Divided Self, op. cit.*, p. 25.

4 *Ibid.*, p. 55.

5 'Ich und Welt stehen sich in einem tödlichen Gegensatz gegenüber', Koch observes (*op. cit.*, p. 54). Similarly, v. Wiese speaks of the 'aufeinanderprallen' of two riddles,

'das Rätsel der Welt und das Rätsel des Ich'. ('Heinrich von Kleist − Tragik und Utopie', in: *Heinrich von Kleist. Vier Reden zu seinem Gedächtnis, ed. cit.*, p. 67.)

6 This is the conclusion of Blöcker and Blume. Blöcker writes that Goethe's wise renunciation 'den Sinn in den Phänomenen selbst zu sehen' was not given to Kleist (*op. cit.*, p. 129). Similarly, Blume contends that Goethe grasped the Absolute ' "am farbigen Abglanz": . . . Bei Kleist aber ist das Verborgene undurchdringlich, in der Natur und im Menschen'. ('Kleist und Goethe', in: *Heinrich von Kleist, Aufsätze und Essays, ed. cit.*, p. 157.)

7 Emrich argues, in my view, correctly, that Kleist ushered in 'eine dem klassischen Denken unvorstellbare oder zum mindesten unerträgliche Destruktion der in und durch die Kunst dargestellten Weltwirklichkeit, oder genauer, . . . die Aufhebung aller außerpersonalen, objektiven Eigengesetzlichkeiten, die in Natur, Geschichte und menschlicher Gesellschaft walten.' ('Kleist und die moderne Literatur', in: *Heinrich von Kleist. Vier Reden zu seinem Gedächtnis, ed. cit.*, p. 19). Similarly, Herrmann divines behind his language a poet 'der Ordnungen nur noch in ihrem konkreten Vollzug, gebunden an die Zeit, nicht mehr als sicheren Besitz, festen Bestand und fortdauernde Bewahrung erlebt.' ('Zufall und Ich', in: *Heinrich von Kleist, Aufsätze und Essays, ed. cit.*, p. 406 f.) Cf. also Ide (*op. cit.*), p. 292.

8 This anecdote is not printed by Sembdner.

9 Cf. Gundolf's comment, equally applicable to Kleist's critics as to the poet himself: 'Die Verherrlichung Kleists als des größten Individualisierers setzt bereits eine Wertordnung voraus: die Vergötterung des Besonderen an sich.' (*Op. cit.*, p. 31).

10 To Marie von Kleist [Berlin, Summer 1811]. (Sembdner No 210.)

11 In this connection, cf. Winnicott's *Playing and Reality* (*op. cit.*), especially Chapters 1, 7 and 8.

12 Cf. P. Ritzler's excellent article 'Zur Bedeutung des bildlichen Ausdrucks im Werke Heinrich von Kleists'. (*Trivium*, Jg. 2, 1944). Ritzler convincingly shows the link between the Kant experience and Kleist's loss of 'das Gegenüber . . ., das Du' (*loc. cit.*, p. 178). In this framework, she discusses Kleist's predilection for simile and allegory rather than the metaphor which is expressive of the 'Ineinander von Ich und Welt' (*loc. cit.*, p. 179), and demonstrates, through linguistic analyses, 'Kleists Ausgeschlossenheit aus der Wirklichkeit' (*loc. cit.*, p. 191). Ritzler writes: 'In der Allegorie, der gewaltsamen Vereinigung von Ich und Welt, tötet Kleist die Welt, so wie Penthesilea Achilles tötet in jener gewaltsamen Vereinigung, wo Küsse Bisse werden.' (*Loc. cit.*, p. 184). Cf. also Hafner who comments: 'Der symbolische Ausdruck, in welchem Innen und Außen, Gefühl und Bild untrennbar eins geworden sind, ist ihm fast gänzlich verwehrt.' (*Op. cit.*, p. 15). H. Ide comes to the conclusion that it is mistaken to use the term 'Symbol' in relation to Kleist, and opts for 'metaphorisches Bild' instead. (*Op. cit.*, p. 11 f.)

13 Garland remarks on 'Staub' being an 'image of dissolution' (*op. cit.*, p. 44), but misses the biblical allusion which is ever-present. Ellis reads this line as a 'super-cliché', a patriotic cry focusing attention 'on what the play has been concerned to question' (*op. cit.*, p. 99).

14 A point neatly taken by Gray who argues that healthy trees in fact have tougher roots and that in any case Penthesilea is strong rather than healthy. (*Loc. cit.*, p. 73.)

15 On this point there is a large critical consensus. Hafner comments: 'Kleist bleibt in seinen Überlegungen wie kein anderer an das Reale gebunden. Er kann nicht so leicht von der äußeren Wirklichkeit abstrahieren' (*op. cit.*, p. 81). Korff deplores his lack of 'geistige Distanz' (*op. cit.*, p. 286); similarly Koch speaks of his 'eigentümlichen, distanzlosen Konkretheit' (*op. cit.*, p. 216). Blöcker repeatedly remarks on Kleist's 'völlige Unfähigkeit zu abstrahieren' (*op. cit.*, pp. 62 and 161). 'An dieser Unfähigkeit zur Abstraktion brach er letzthin zusammen' writes Lugowski (*op. cit.*, p. 221). By way of a final

evaluative judgment Lugowski argues that Kleist represents a breakthrough to a primal
Germanic structure of experiencing, '. . . einen Durchbruch, den man allerdings
ebensogut als einen Rückfall in eine vorabendländische Seinsstufe bezeichnen könnte',
somewhat incongruously adding: 'Eine so anachronistische oder atavistische Auffassung
Kleists läßt sich im Grunde nicht halten'. (*Op. cit.*, p. 583.) Hoffmeister maintains:
'. . . er vermochte es . . . nicht, sich dem Unendlichen zu öffnen und von ihm durch-
walten und tragen zu lassen' (*loc. cit.*, p. 182). Herrmann admirably sums up his
argument by saying that Kleist is incapable 'Erfahrungen aufzubewahren, Gesetzmäßig-
keiten zu entwickeln, einen menschlichen Charakter als Entelechie zu entwickeln. Deu-
tungen zu geben, fehlt ihm die nötige Distanz . . . Die Unmittelbarkeit und Reinheit,
mit der die Sprache die Gebärden und Intentionen der Menschen und den Verlauf des
Geschehens aufbewahrt, wird erkauft mit einer Leibverhaftetheit, die die geistige Trans-
parenz der Erscheinungen gefährdet.' (*Loc. cit.*, p. 403 f.) Finally, Gundolf comments:
'Wir suchen in der Kunst ewige Lebensgeist-gesetze, die sinnliche Darstellung der Weltvernunft . . . und die Weltvernunft, als deren Offenbarer wir Goethe und Shakespeare
ehren, ist bei Kleist stumm und taub.' (*Op. cit.*, p. 108).

[16] Letter to Wilhelmine von Zenge, Berlin, 16 (and 18) November, 1800. (Sembdner
No 28.)

[17] *Ibid.*

[18] This statement has received unduly generalised interpretations by, e.g., Gundolf (*op. cit.*,
p. 25), Wittkowski ('Absolutes Gefühl und Absolute Kunst etc.', *loc. cit.*, p. 29) and
Hamburger (*op. cit.*, p. 111). For its most workmanlike discussion, cf. Hinton Thomas,
'Kleist and the Thorough Bass', *PEGS, New Series*, Vol. XXXII, 1961–62. Thomas who
links Kleist's musical statement with the essay on the puppet-show and his reflections
on balloons, stresses 'the technical nature of the reference' (p. 80 f.) which he considers
to be 'a serious and understanding reference to an essential and specific feature of Baroque
music' (p. 82 f.). In Baroque music, he argues, 'the upper voice or voices [acquired] a new
freedom, typified in freely moving figuration and extended convolutions of melody. But
it was a freedom on the foundation of a strictly ordered musical structure, which both
encouraged and controlled it.' (p. 85). Thomas considers this controlled freedom to be
analogous to Kleist's use of language, but does not pursue the matter in my direction.

[19] This is a view repeatedly advanced. Beissner suggests that what Kleist means is 'die
handwerkliche Gesetzmäßigkeit, das, was Hölderlin in seinen Sophokles Anmerkungen
die μηχανη [mechane] nennt oder das kalkulable Gesetz. Der neuern Poesie sei, meint
Hölderlin, das verloren gegangen, was die griechischen auszeichnet: die Zuverlässigkeit'
as well as the 'gesetzlichen Kalkul und sonstige Verfahrungsart, wodurch das Schöne
hervorgebracht wird.' ('Unvorgreifliche Gedanken etc.', *loc. cit.*, p. 429). Similarly,
Staiger considers that Kleist intimates by his reference to the 'Generalbaß', 'daß er sich
um ein rechnerisches Verfahren, um eine absolute, dem Zufall und dem Belieben ent-
rückte Gesetzlichkeit des poetischen Schaffens bemühт.' ('Heinrich von Kleist', in:
Heinrich von Kleist. Vier Reden zu seinem Gedächtnis, ed. cit., p. 49.) Kreutzer,
whilst asserting that '"Generalbaß" damals einfach so viel wie Harmonielehre oder
harmonische Gesetzlichkeit überhaupt bedeutete' (*op. cit.*, p. 29), tallies with Beissner's,
Staiger's and my own emphasis on the 'rationale Kalkül des Dichters.' (*Ibid.*)

[20] I am grateful to Professor B. L. Trowell of the Music Faculty, King's College, London,
for initiating me into musical and historical aspects of the thoroughbass to the point
where I could form my own view *vis-à-vis* Kleist and his critics.

[21] Gundolf perceptively writes: 'die schwerste Aufgabe der neueren Menschen und zumal
des Künstlers überhaupt: mit dem Bewußtsein belastet die Schöpfer-Sicherheit zu
retten . . .' (*op. cit.*, p. 171 f.).

[22] The preoccupation with a poetic calculus is clearly evident from two statements of
Kleist's: 'Ich kann ein Differentiale erfinden, und einen Vers machen; sind das nicht die

beiden Enden der menschlichen Fähigkeit?' (To Ernst von Pfuel, Berlin, 7 January, 1805.) (Sembdner No 86); and: 'Man könnte die Menschen in zwei Klassen abteilen; in solche, die sich auf eine Metapher und 2) in solche, die sich auf eine Formel verstehen. Derer, die sich auf beide verstehen, sind zu wenige; sie machen keine Klasse aus.' (*Berliner Abendblätter*, 10. December, 1810, Sembdner II, p. 338.)

23 Herrmann movingly writes of Kleist's capacity 'eine Zeit lang gleichsam ins Leere hinein leben [zu] können' ('Zufall und Ich', *loc. cit.*, p. 392), and states: 'Die neue Ordnung erreicht ihn, weil er bis hierher aushielt: das ist seine Leistung.' (p. 395). Ide writes: 'Kleist ist der erste, der dem modernen Problem des Nihilismus konfrontiert ist, und zugleich der letzte, der es in und nach einem lebenslangen Ringen noch einmal überzeugend meisterte.' (*Op. cit.*, p. 129 f.)

24 Burckhardt speaks obliquely yet unmistakably of the dangers confronting Kleist in the passage quoted in note 11 to Chapter 13.

Index

I Kleist's Works

II Names

Names of characters from Kleist's works are indexed under the title of the work in which they appear. Only names appearing in the text are listed.

III Themes, Concepts, Images and Key Words

7 I am saying this on the authority of Professor James Cargill Thompson.

8 Cf. Chapter 13, section 3.

9 Cf. Chapter 14, section 1.

10 Cf. the letter to Marie von Kleist [Berlin, Sommer 1811]. (Sembdner No 211.)

11 Letter to Adolfine von Werdeck, Paris, 28 (and 29) July, 1801. (Sembdner No 50.) Cf. also the letter to Wilhelmine von Zenge, Würzburg, 19(−23) September, 1800. (Sembdner No 23.)

12 Letter to Rühle von Lilienstern [Königsberg], 31 [August 1806]. (Sembdner No 97.)

13 Cf. Kleist's letter to Ulrike von Kleist, Coblenz bei Pasewalk, 21 August, 1800, in which he announces the coming of the book, saying: '. . . sein Inhalt muß nicht gelesen, sondern gelernt werden'. (Sembdner No 14.) The late echo is to be found in Kohlhaas' conversation with Luther, when the latter asks the horse trader whether he would not have done better to have forgiven Tronka, his enemy, and to have taken his horses home. Kohlhaas' reply: 'Kann sein! . . . kann sein, auch nicht!' etc. is a literal echo of Wallenstein's speech to Gordon (*Tod*, V, 5, 11. 3657−3663), a fact which to my knowledge has not been noted.

14 A paradox noted by Böckmann, 'Heinrich von Kleist. 1777−1811', ed. *cit.*, p. 167.

15 *Op. cit.*, p. 58.

16 *Op. cit.*, p. 58 f.

17 Hermann's demagogism is defended by Fricke (*op. cit.*, p. 168) and by Helbling (*op. cit.*, p. 188).

18 A point made by Gundolf (*op. cit.*, p. 132 f.) and Fricke (*op. cit.*, p. 168).

19 Although he may be correct in absolute terms, Burckhardt in my view misses Kleist's intention when he adjudges Thusnelda's deed as being 'a descent, unredeemed and unrevoked, into bestiality' (*op. cit.*, p. 129) and argues that '. . . she does not just return to Hermann's level; she plunges below it.' (*Op. cit.*, p. 157). For all his astute observations on the dialectic, in Kleist, between abstractness and concreteness, he is in my view diametrically wrong in labelling Thusnelda's aberration as being 'a total immersion in the *unredeemed physicality of man's origins*.' (*Op. cit.*, p. 160). (My italics.) Stahl is nearer the mark when he compares Thusnelda's 'horrible deed of *premeditated* and perverted hatred' to Penthesilea's 'deed of perverted love' (*op. cit.*, p. 101). (My italic.) The peculiar perversion of Thusnelda's action lies, precisely, in her capacity to think abstractively, an ability indicated by Stahl's 'premeditated'. Whether this makes things better or worse is another matter.

20 Curiously, this fact has escaped Burckhardt who bases his analysis of the play on the lock-and-key metaphor.

21 Helbling considers the Halli episode to be a 'chilling parody of the grandiose type of patriotism' (*op. cit.*, p. 189 f.), a judgement with which I disagree, but has interesting things to say about contemporary usage of the term 'grotesque' (*op. cit.*, p. 190).

22 Cf. note 12 of this chapter.

Notes to Chapter 12

1 Needles to say, this concrete turn of mind has been variously stressed by critics. Fricke writes that Kohlhaas is 'unbedingt nicht in der abstrakten Idee, sondern in der absolut-subjektiven, konkreten, realen Existenz *dieses* Menschen' (*op. cit.*, p. 127 f.). Similarly, Lugowski emphasises the 'gänzliche Abwesenheit eines Sinnes für das Grundsätzliche und Allgemeine' (*op. cit.*, p. 196). More recently, Blöcker maintains that 'Das Absolute wird in das Endliche aufgenommen' (*op. cit.*, p. 120) and evocatively comments: 'Wo immer dieser Mann [Kleist] flieht, da ist es eine Flucht nach vorn − in die Dinge hinein, nicht von ihnen weg' (*op. cit.*, p. 127) − a formulation no doubt influenced by

And the Word became flesh . . .

St. John

O! that this too too solid flesh would melt . . .

Shakespeare